100 COUNTRIES 5000 IDEAS

100
COUNTRIES
5000
IDEAS

WHERE TO GO · WHEN TO GO · WHAT TO SEE · WHAT TO DO

FOREWORD BY RUDY MAXA,
HOST OF *RUDY MAXA'S WORLD* ON PUBLIC TELEVISION AND RADIO

NATIONAL GEOGRAPHIC

WASHINGTON, D.C.

Contents

Foreword

The Internet is a boon to travelers, who can research exotic (and not-so-exotic) destinations online. With a few clicks, we can buy a ticket to an opera in Verona, read restaurant reviews of and book a table at a Hong Kong restaurant, or look at webcam pictures of beaches in Australia.

Today, the challenge isn't so much finding information as it is *making sense* of the massive amount available.

As a consumer travel writer and broadcaster, I'm constantly asked questions like this: "My family and I are going to Europe. We're going to Italy, France, and Spain. What should we be sure to see?"

The question is so enormous, I don't know how to begin to answer. "Don't miss Paris"? "You'll love Barcelona"? Entire guidebooks, after all, are written about *cities and regions* in each of those countries.

But I know what those folks want. They want a trusted source, a friend who's been there, someone who can advise them on what not to miss in the limited amount of time they have for a visit. And they don't have the time to read a half dozen guidebooks or visit 60 websites that may or may not be reliable.

And that's where this book comes in. It is an entertaining stroll through the top hits of 100 countries, with a side of helpful information on climate, travel resources, and handy maps that let you know the relative distance between, say, Rome and Venice or Naples. It's a terrific starting point that a traveler may use to go the next step—if pubs are of interest to you when visiting London, *100 Countries, 5,000 Ideas* lists the best

neighborhoods; you can take it from there with a quick Internet search that will deliver you names, addresses, and reviews of specific pubs.

Writer and traveler Paul Theroux once suggested that the trips one remembers the most are the ones where something goes wrong. He's mostly right. But when life on the road costs hard-earned money, as it does for most of us, and when it must be accomplished in a limited amount of time, as it must be for most of us, an overall understanding of a destination and basic information are helpful starting points for any traveler.

I have my own system for getting to know a city that's new to me if I arrive without benefit of much preparation. I identify (but don't necessarily stay at) the fanciest hotel in town. It's often in the center of the best neighborhoods; taxi drivers know how to find it in case I get lost and don't know the language; and there are usually two important attributes of that hotel: clean restrooms and a concierge desk with helpful staff who, if approached with a smile and a tip, may be willing to help with directions and recommendations. (When it comes to restaurants, I always ask, "Don't tell me where you send tourists—tell me where *you* eat or where you take your spouse for an anniversary dinner.")

You're welcome to borrow my technique when you land in a new destination. But before you go, this book is your trusted source, your friend who's been there. Use it to plan a richer experience.

—Rudy Maxa

How to Use This Book

If you dream of roaming the world, *100 Countries, 5,000 Ideas* is the right guide for you. As you plan your trip, let us help you decide *where to go, when to go, what to see, what to do*.

The first choice made by any traveler is the most obvious and the most difficult: *where to go*. You may want to start by reading the first of the book's three sections, which outlines different types of thematic travel—for example, spa vacations, all-inclusive trips, adventure treks, and eco-friendly resorts. If you find that you have a certain travel style, use that to shape your ultimate choice of destination. Otherwise, you can begin with charts in the final section of the book to answer a series of questions: What is my budget? Do I prefer to travel in a certain season? Who will be coming with me?

Your answers should help you build a list of countries to consider, so flip to the main body of the book—100 countries, A to Z. Decide *what to see* and *what to do* as you read comprehensive descriptions of each country's main attractions, organized by geographical region. Begin to prioritize: Are you interested in history or hiking? Secluded beaches, mountain hamlets, or bustling cities? Ancient monuments or modern art museums? The world is your oyster. Don't forget to check the Traveler's Notebook for each country—this chart provides a host of details and essential background information on travel documents, languages, currency, population, safety issues, and more to help fill out the picture for each country. In addition, our Advice sidebar gives you some honest feedback on the pros and cons of travel for each country, as well as special tips that give you bonus ideas on what to see and do…and how best to approach your visit.

Next consult the detailed maps for each country to help you figure out how much time to allow for side trips to neighboring regions or countries for sites and activities that you just can't miss.

You picked a country, found the perfect region, and planned to allow time for some worthwhile excursions. All that remains is the question of *when to go*. Read the description of climate and geography for your country and check the When to Go charts within each country listing to help you select the seasons with the weather best suited to your plans.

Pages 2–3: A nighttime visit to Petra's rock-hewn "Treasury" in Jordan

Page 4: On every traveler's wish list: to see the Eiffel Tower in Paris

Page 6: Venetian masks are readied for Carnival season.

LOCATOR MAP

A small world map lets you quickly locate each country on the globe.

FLAG

Each country's flag appears with the introductory text.

WHAT TO SEE AND DO

A sidebar gives a quick overview of a country's highlights, typical activities, landscapes, cities, and cultural heritage.

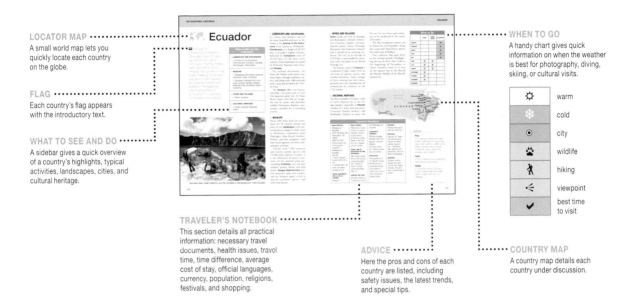

TRAVELER'S NOTEBOOK

This section details all practical information: necessary travel documents, health issues, travel time, time difference, average cost of stay, official languages, currency, population, religions, festivals, and shopping.

ADVICE

Here the pros and cons of each country are listed, including safety issues, the latest trends, and special tips.

WHEN TO GO

A handy chart gives quick information on when the weather is best for photography, diving, skiing, or cultural visits.

☼	warm
❄	cold
◉	city
🐾	wildlife
🚶	hiking
◁	viewpoint
✔	best time to visit

COUNTRY MAP

A country map details each country under discussion.

CHARTS

A number of charts in the front and back of the book are designed to help you choose the right trip for your interests and lifestyle, allowing you to find the right time of year to travel, compare cost and length of stay, and prepare you with essential health and passport information.

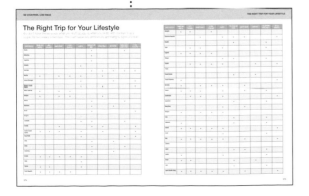

Map Key

▪	Beach / Seabed / Diving zone / Notable water feature
⊛	National capital
◉	Other capital
●	City
∴	Monument / Archaeological site
▪	Park / Reserve
▫	Point of interest
527₊	Peak elevation in meters (1 meter = 3.28 feet)
🔆	View / Remarkable landscape / Hiking site
▨	Dry salt lake

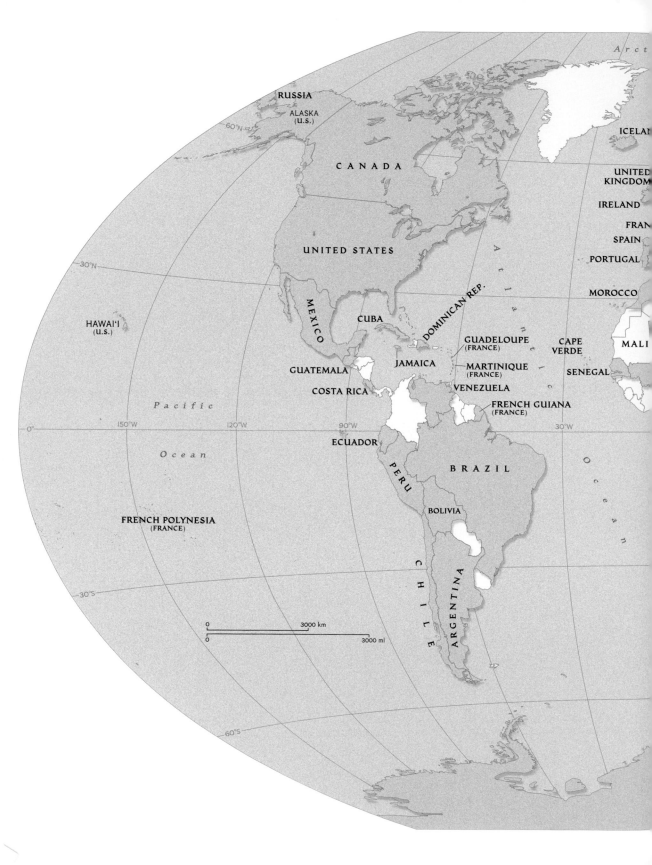

Themed Destinations

The following section presents a variety of ideas for themed travel. Whether you're interested in planning an adventure, organizing a trip with children, cruising the tropics, or seeking out rich cultural sites, these pages provide a wealth of choices, with best times to travel and useful contacts.

Exploring Desert Landscapes

Silent, the desert has a special pull on many travelers.

The character of desert travel has changed. Even in the past century, travel in unexplored desert regions was a dangerous, carefully planned expedition, but today such excursions are relatively routine, although still fascinating. There must be a thousand good reasons why the desert has such a magical pull on people: to search for a lost paradise, to unwind from stress, to find oneself—almost every traveler has a particular reason for a desert trek.

Indeed, the desert offers rare experiences. In the morning, awakened by the rising sun and feeling its warming rays after a cold night, the great silence that surrounds you is magical. In the evening, when you lie down and look at the clear, star-filled sky, you are awed by the incredible visibility compared with the light-polluted night sky back home.

It's to be hoped that the increasing popularity of arranged desert travel does not negatively affect the quality of guides and camel drivers, and that safety can be guaranteed even in the most remote zones. For desert travel in the future, it's imperative that strict environmental and tourist policies are in place to keep desert ecology in balance.

Desert Destinations

COUNTRY	DESTINATIONS	COMMENTS	BEST TIME TO GO	AVERAGE COST
Chile	Atacama Desert	The driest place on Earth, marvelous colors, best visited together with the Uyuni Salt Flats of Bolivia.	October to March	$3,810/£2,475 for 20 days
Egypt	Western Desert (White Desert and Siwa Oasis), Sinai Desert	The Sinai Desert is well known, but the bizarre White Desert on the other side of the Nile is still a secret.	Mid-October to end of April	$1,015/£660 for the week, $1,900/£1,240 for 15 days
Israel	Judean Desert, Negev	Israel's deserts are not often visited but can be combined easily with Jerusalem and Eilat for a one-week trip.	End of October to end of April	$1,650/£1,070 for 8 days
Jordan	Wadi Rum	The world of Lawrence of Arabia is one of the most colorful deserts in a barren landscape.	October to mid-May	$1,650/£1,070 for 9 days
Mongolia	Gobi	A bactrian camel trek through the pebbly Gobi makes for a legendary but expensive trip.	June to August	$3,175/£2,060 for 15 days
Morocco	The Great South	Although it is still only the sub-Sahara, the sand dunes (ergs) in the Great South are impressive.	Beginning of October to end of April	$1,015/£660 for the week
Niger	Aïr Massif, Blue Mountains, Arakao, east of Ténéré	The sand dunes of the Arakao "crab claw" are simply a miracle for some, and it would be a pity to miss out on the Ténéré.	Beginning of November to end of March	$1,270/£825 for the week
Oman	Wahiba Desert	One of the last deserts to open up to tourism, with numerous wadis and jebels.	Mid-October to mid-April	$1,525/£990–$1,650/£1,070 for the week
Tunisia	Great Eastern Erg	Similar to the sub-Sahara in Morocco	Beginning of October to end of April	$1,015/£660 for the week
United States	Mojave Desert	Death Valley in the Mojave Desert is the driest, lowest, and hottest place In North America. Wildflowers are in bloom from February to early May.	November through mid-May	$1,778/£1,155 for 12 days

Cruising the Caribbean or Mediterranean

A behemoth of a modern cruise ship

The building boom in the cruise ship industry is producing ever larger vessels. Even Europe now uses ships holding up to 3,000 passengers. These giants are advertised as "swimming hotels," "fun ships," and "megaships." They are up to 1,000 feet long and 230 feet high, with 1,500 cabins on ten decks. The cabin choices range from multibedroom luxury apartments with private pools and butlers to more spartan, much less expensive interior cabins.

Today's passengers don't want to simply sit on deck with a good book; they take advantage of a myriad of amenities offered on board: swimming pools, whirlpools, rock-climbing walls, tennis courts, jogging paths, health clubs, basketball courts, and even miniature golf courses and ice skating rinks.

There are often performances of plays, musicals, opera, or dance, sometimes with well-known professionals. Up to a dozen restaurants offer a wide range of delicacies, as do the numerous bars with long lists of drinks. Video games and Internet cafés are available, and of course the full gamut of spa services.

▶ WHERE TO GO

Cruises to the Caribbean usually depart from the Miami area and may include the Bahamas, Jamaica, the Cayman Islands, or Mexico, with countless variations. Many West Coast cruises leave from Los Angeles for Alaska, Hawaii, and the Pacific coast of Mexico. Mediterranean cruises typically depart from ports in Spain, France, or Italy for any number of destinations between Morocco and Turkey. Other options include Baltic cruises and more itineraries around the world.

▶ BEST TIME TO GO

For the Caribbean, it's best to travel between January and June, before hurricane season. The Mediterranean is fine all year long, but preferred times are April to October. West Coast cruises to Hawaii are ideal when winter weather moves into the continental U.S., from December through March.

▶ COST

A one-week cruise through the Caribbean can start as low as $600/£390 (per person, based on double occupancy). A week in the Mediterranean begins around $1,000/£650. Look for special deals, which may include round-trip flights. Cruise lines typically offer discounts for "early bird" reservations, and sometimes there are special last-minute deals. A child under age 18 can often travel in the cabin with parents for free.

▶ TYPES OF SHIPS

There are numerous options in choosing a ship: medium, large, and enormous cruise ships; large sailing vessels and small yachts; small coastal cruisers such as the Norwegian packet boats; river craft like the feluccas of Egypt; or historic ships such as the *Bou-el-Mogdad* on the Senegal River.

▶ "TRENDY" DESTINATIONS

From May to September: eastern and western Mediterranean (Greece, Turkey, North Africa), Indian Ocean (Kenya to Réunion), the fjords of Norway or Alaska, the Baltic Sea. From October to April: South America (from Brazil to Tierra del Fuego), Antarctica, Mediterranean.

Traveling With Children

Foreign travel with children was relatively rare until recently. Many parents worried about the strain of travel on the children and insufficient medical care in foreign countries. But no more. Travel options have increased for family vacations—for example, with resort hotels in Mexico and around the Mediterranean. Glossy travel brochures show photos of children sliding down sand dunes in the Sahara or watching wildlife on a safari. Medical care abroad has improved as well. And reliable travel agencies can guarantee rapid transport home in case of an accident or a serious illness.

Parents have to consider the different needs and interests of their children. The little ones are quickly bored, but tour operators have leaped into the breach with a variety of special children's programs.

Family vacations are costly, but special rates may be available: A child age 12 or under sleeping in the parents' room usually costs only 50 percent, and larger families can have the youngest child stay free of charge.

Travel With Children

COUNTRY	WHAT TO SEE	WHEN TO GO	COST
Australia	Animals (kangaroos, koalas), beaches	Spring and fall	$3,175/£2,060
Canada	Animals (caribou, bears, whales)	June to August	$1,650/£1,070
Costa Rica	Rain forest, animals	December to April	$2,160/£1,400
Egypt	History, Nile cruises, beaches on the Red Sea coast	March to June and September to December	$950/£620
Kenya	Wildlife reserves, meeting Maasai	June to October	$2,030/£1,320
Morocco	Excursions into the desert, camels	October to March	$1,140/£740
Senegal	Birds, settlements	October to June	$1,900/£1,230
South Africa	Wildlife reserves	May to October	$1,900/£1,230
Thailand	Elephants, tropical flora	November to February	$1,525/£1,000
United States	National parks	July to September	$1,900/£1,230

In Search of Marine Wildlife

Travelers never tire of watching dolphins' antics.

Dolphins and whales are the stars of the world's oceans. Observing these lovely creatures has become a major industry for companies offering whale-watching cruises. The International Fund for Animal Welfare (IFAW) considers whale-watching the 21st-century alternative to whale hunting.

But all this interest is not without problems. These large mammals, which grow to as much as 100 feet in length and weigh up to 150 tons, are endangered by high-speed boats and close encounters.

Nearly every country with a coastline offers whale-watching cruises during the seasons when they can be spotted. The peaceful baleen whales are the clear favorites. Typically, these cruises take tourists out for a few hours to watch the whales swim, feed, play, and with luck, breach—soaring partway out of the water—as the boats stay a respectful distance away. In some places, tour operators take passengers closer to the whales by Zodiac, although this is usually discouraged by authorities as being too distressing for the whales.

Dolphins are as popular to watch as their larger cousins, at least since the 1960s television series *Flipper*. These intelligent creatures can be found in all the oceans and may accompany a lucky swimmer during a dive.

Where and When You Can See Whales and Dolphins

COUNTRY	PLACE	SPECIES	DATES
Antarctica	Coasts	Humpback whales	January to March
Argentina	Valdés Peninsula	Right whales	May to November
Azores (Portugal)	Faial and Pico Islands	Blue whales, sperm whales, dolphins	April to September
Canada	Gulf of St. Lawrence, Tadoussac Hudson Bay and Nunavut Vancouver Island	Fin whales, blue whales Beluga whales Gray whales	April to December July to August Spring
Croatia	Along the Dalmatian Coast	Bottlenose dolphins	June to September
Dominican Republic	Samaná Bay	Humpback whales and their calves	January to April
France	Atlantic and Mediterranean coasts	Dolphins, porpoises	All year round
French Polynesia	Austral Islands	Humpback whales	July to October
Greece	Coasts	Bottlenose dolphins	June to September
Iceland	Grindavik and Sandgerdi, near Keflavik on the southwest side of the island	Mostly white-beaked dolphins and small fin whales, humpback whales (sometimes), Bryde's whales, blue whales (seldom)	April to October
Ireland	West coast	Pilot whales, dolphins, porpoises	End of summer, beginning of fall
Italy	Along the Ligurian coast and Sardinia	Several species of dolphins	Summer
Mexico	Baja California (Ensenada, Cabo San Lucas, Ojo de Liebre Lagoon, and San Ignacio)	Humpback whales, gray whales	January to April
New Zealand	Kaikoura (east coast of South Island)	Whales, sperm whales, dolphins	All year round
Spain	Atlantic coast and south coast near Algeciras Canary Islands	Several species of dolphins Dolphins and fin whales	June to September Summer
United Kingdom	Along Cornwall Scotland (north coast) Wales (west coast)	Bottlenose dolphins Porpoises Several dolphin species	Summer
United States	Alaska (Skagway, Sitka) Hawaii (Lahaina)	Gray whales Gray whales	Summer December to April

Cultural Travel

Can culture be marketed? For tour operators, culture has become as much a "product" as any other travel attraction. People want to know all about a country they are visiting, its history, and its culture.

Special tours advertised as cultural visits to a historic city or a summer music festival have advantages and disadvantages. Flights are often overbooked and the hotels mediocre; on the other hand, the travel agent takes care of all the details such as ticket reservations for exhibits or performances, so travelers avoid standing in line.

Cultural cruises are also fashionable. They are carefully organized for travelers with special interests and a high level of sophistication.

Although there is plenty of competition, cultural travel is on the increase. And perhaps because culture is often related to higher aspirations, the prices are also elevated.

In many cases, the higher prices are justified, because these trips are usually accompanied by a well-known lecturer, or maybe led by a professor of ancient history, astronomy, or the arts, and lodging is in the luxury category. An organized cultural trip is generally more expensive than something travelers could plan on their own, but participants can be sure of not missing anything important.

▶ WHERE
Some preferred cultural destinations are Europe's capitals, including London, Paris, Vienna, or Madrid, where museums feature major exhibitions by famous artists. Specialized travel agents also offer themed destinations to countries with a strong cultural tradition, such as Egypt, or newly emerging countries, such as Armenia.

▶ WHEN
At any time of year, but especially in spring. Preferred (long) weekends are between Easter and May/June.

▶ COST
For a cultural weekend of three days and two nights in western Europe, budget a minimum of $525/£340 per person, all-inclusive, with meals, lodging (shared double room), transport from one major European city to another by plane or train, and museum entrance fee. A two-week themed trip to a faraway country such as Brazil or China will cost about $3,000/£1,950.

Vienna is one of the great cultural centers of Europe.

Adventure at Any Price

Great adventures such as those experienced by the early explorers, or by writers and world travelers like Joseph Conrad, simply aren't possible anymore. But "adventure travel" can still provide unforgettable experiences off the beaten path, such as long endurance hikes in regions where few foreigners travel. That, after all, is the adventure.

A conventional Vietnam tour, for example, traveling along the coast through the cities and main attractions, may be too tame for some people. These travelers might prefer to participate in an organized trekking tour through the mountains of the far northern region where hill tribes such as the Hmong, Nung, and Dao live.

Such a tour involves a daily hike of five to six hours through rough terrain in hot and humid weather with simple meals and spartan lodging. In places where the local peoples still live traditionally and travelers have a chance to participate in daily life, this sort of tour can turn into a unique adventure. Reputable tour operators limit the number of participants and make sure that the locals are treated with respect.

This is the new adventure travel.

Besides organized adventures, travelers can book their own flights and find their way through a country using public transportation. Before departing on such a trip, it's important to get all necessary safety information from the State Department, embassies, or consulates to assess any possible risk.

If sudden money problems crop up, it's good to remember that Western Union can help out with a quick transfer of funds via most post offices around the world.

Connect with locals, but try not to change them.

Tour Operators Specializing in Adventure Travel

- **Adventure Travel**
  800-763-4840
  www.adventuretravel.com

- **Austin Lehman**
  800-575-1540
  www.austinlehman.com

- **Canadian Mountain Holidays**
  800-661-0252
  www.canadianmountain holidays.com

- **Deeper Africa**
  888-658-7102
  www.deeperafrica.com

- **International Expeditions**
  800-234-9620
  www.international expeditions.com

- **Off the Beaten Path**
  800-445-2995
  www.offthebeatenpath.com

- **Pure Adventures**
  800-960-3221
  pure-adventures.com

- **REI Adventures**
  800-622-2236
  www.rei.com/adventures

- **Uncharted Outposts**
  888-995-0909
  www.unchartedoutposts .com

- **Wilderness Travel**
  800-368-2794
  www.wildernesstravel.com

- **Zegrahm Expeditions**
  800-628-8747
  zegrahmexpeditions.com

In addition, the Adventure Travel Trade Association (ATTA) maintains a database of more than 250 recommended adventure tour operators worldwide at *www.adventure.travel*.

Travel With a Conscience

Many tourists are interested in fair-minded and sustainable travel, as much for ecological reasons as for egalitarian ideals. The ecology of many regions has been severely affected by mass tourism and can hardly withstand much more. Tourism has also changed the way of life of many people, and yet the locals have rarely profited from the outsiders. Many travelers feel it's time to distribute spending more equitably.

The travel industry has coined several categories to distinguish different approaches. "Fair tourism," as in "fair trade," is concerned with supporting local efforts and letting locals rather than corporations gain from tourism.

Take a village in South America or Africa with the means and interest of initiating a project for the local economy via a nongovernmental organization (NGO). This could be done through fair trade or with the help of tourism. A Western NGO can support a project by helping villagers build simple but comfortable lodging, appropriate for travelers who are interested in the local traditions and crafts. The villagers are in charge of the new accommodations and may decide to share in the profits or perhaps to reinvest them in a new school. In the meantime, the NGO ensures that the project is continued.

These kinds of projects must be organized with great integrity, being careful not to be paternalistic toward the local population. A number of tour operators participate in such projects, and fair tourism is on the rise, with an estimated 5 percent participation worldwide.

▶ WHICH COUNTRIES?

Fair tourism is developing worldwide. It is catching on especially in Burkina Faso, Benin, and Mali in Africa, and in Bolivia, Brazil, Ecuador, and Peru in South America, and this list is far from being exhaustive.

▶ EXPLANATION OF TERMS

Fair Trade in Tourism

The local population participates in welcoming tourists and finding lodging for them, without interference from middlemen, so that a reasonable profit is distributed locally.

Some Useful Addresses

- **Center for Responsible Travel**
  1333 H Street, NW
  Suite 300 East Tower
  Washington, DC 20005
  (202) 347-9203
  www.responsibletravel.org

- **Green Globe**
  703 Pier Avenue
  Suite B286
  Hermosa Beach, CA 90254
  (310) 337-3000

- **National Geographic Center for Sustainable Destinations**
  1145 17th Street, NW
  Washington, DC 20036
  (202) 828-8045
  sustourism@ngs.org

- **Sustainable Travel International**
  835 SW William Drive
  White Salmon, WA 98672-5500
  (800) 276-7764

Responsible Tourism

Local populations are responsible for considering the ecological impact of new tourism projects.

Solidarity Tourism

Tourists demonstrate solidarity with the locals through the money they spend and invest there and through committed involvement. The investment may be used for important projects such as building a school or clinic.

Sustainable Tourism

Tourism that focuses on respecting the ecology and the people of an area. It involves not only the tourists but also the locals. As the name indicates, sustainable tourism is concerned with long-range plans and the sustainability of the infrastructure.

Tourism in support of local traditions and trade is possible, as seen here in Mali.

All-Inclusive Vacations

An all-inclusive vacation covers everything for one price and gives travelers a certain sense of security. The concept usually means four-night to one-week vacations in a resort with a pool by the ocean on one of the Caribbean islands, in Mexico or Central America, or elsewhere in the world.

Everything is included in the price—the flight, transfers from airport to hotel, lodging, insurance, and for "full room and board," three meals a day (breakfast, lunch, and dinner); "half board" or "half pension" means lodging with breakfast and either lunch or dinner. Some packages may even include drinks. Thus, the all-inclusive traveler doesn't have to worry about unplanned expenses driving the price of a vacation out of range.

However, it is important to note that the all-inclusive package almost never covers airline taxes or other airline fees, which can easily add 10 percent to the total price—although by booking early, some of these fees can be avoided. Also, the hotels usually offer various additional-cost excursions; if these tours have not been booked in advance, they can add significantly to the total cost, so it's wise to compare offers.

What is the difference between an all-inclusive vacation and travel organized for an individual by a travel agent? A travel agent will sit down with a potential traveler and suggest an itinerary according to the client's wishes: domestic or international flights, lodging in a hotel or with a local, rental car (and if so, hotels along the route), excursions or not, restaurants, and so forth.

Cancún, Mexico, and its welcoming beaches

Some Examples
(Prices per person, double occupancy)

- **Cyprus** About $1,900/£1,235 for 7 nights, all-inclusive, in a three-star hotel near Paphos, from London

- **Dominican Republic** About $800/£520 for 4 nights, all-inclusive, in a four-star hotel in Punta Cana, from New York

- **Egypt** About $1,800/£1,170 a week, all-inclusive, during peak season in Hurghada; double that amount during New Year's week in a four-star hotel in Sharm al-Sheikh, from London

- **Kenya** About $2,300/£1,500 for a week at half-pension in a three-star hotel on a beach south of Mombasa, from London

- **Mexico** About $750/£485 for 4 nights, all-inclusive, in a four-star hotel in Cancún; about $900 for a similar vacation in Cabo San Lucas, from New York

- **Morocco** About $1,300/£850 in a simple three-star hotel in Marrakech; the same in a *riad,* including flight but without meals, from London

- **Spain (Canary Islands)** About $2,000/£1,300 for a week, all-inclusive, in a four-star hotel on the south coast of Tenerife, from London

- **Tunisia** About $1,300/£850 for a week in a three-star hotel in low season at Hammamet on the Jasmine Coast, from London

Spa Vacations

Water: In a spa, everything begins and ends with water.

A photo of a young woman relaxing on a mat, water reflecting the arch of an ancient structure above her, perhaps a *hammam,* or Turkish bath: This is how some travel brochures promise exotic vacations. Spa vacations are on the increase as a distinct complement to travel. "Spa" usually means a luxurious wellness treatment center that may be decorated like a Moorish palace in North Africa, a temple garden in Vietnam, or a maharajah's palace in India. Treatments generally revolve around water, both fresh and salt water, in various applications.

The promise of relaxation and rejuvenation is addressed to a mature, affluent clientele, but tour operators also hope to attract a younger, less well-off crowd. Travel ads abound that extol the virtues of the perfect vacation—which can be complete only in a hotel with luxurious spa services.

Most spas offer thalassotherapy, massage, aromatherapy, and various other treatments guaranteed to produce complete bliss.

Traditionally, spas developed at the site of hot springs or mineral springs, but today any number of resorts offer a full menu of spa services. Savvy travelers to exotic locations demand treatments with time-honored local ingredients.

Some Spa Destinations

- **Austria** The elegant hotels and thermal springs in the Tyrol can boast years of experience.

- **India** Some former maharajah's palaces are being turned into luxurious wellness temples.

- **Mexico** Luxurious spa resorts have sprung up around Mexico's hot thermal springs, such as Río Caliente.

- **Morocco** The towns of Agadir and Essaouira are opening new spas, but will be in serious competition with Marrakech and its many spa options. Treatments with Moroccan argan oil as well as Sahara sand rubs are in fashion.

- **Thailand** Modern Bangkok is ever more inventive in providing some of the most luxurious spa resorts worldwide.

- **Tunisia** The land of jasmine is one of the preferred spa vacations for Europeans. People travel to Tunisia specifically to visit a spa with therapies that compete with the best in Europe. Hammamet on the Jasmine Coast is one of the famous spa centers, but Djerba Island also has much to offer, along with time in the desert.

- **Turkey** Turkey is appealing because of its beautiful coast on the Aegean, its antiquities on the south coast, and the thermal spas of Pamukkale.

Unforgettable Nights

A once-in-a-lifetime experience: spending a night in an igloo

The time when travelers paid little attention to the ambiance of their hotel room beyond wanting to sleep well is gone. Nowadays, the quality and originality of lodging play an ever greater role for tour planners. Original and unusual types of lodging in far off places can be costly, but many exotic accommodations guarantee—besides the cultural and sociological aspects—an unforgettable experience by themselves.

The following is a survey of the latest novelties in lodging worldwide. Besides the options listed, there is a vast range of other possibilities—from spending a night in various converted palaces, pagodas, and monasteries to staying in buildings of the Salvation Army, missions, or youth hostels. The last few are not only inexpensive but sometimes attractive alternatives.

For extravagance, the ice hotels of Canada and Finland take first place, as much for location as price. These hotels are an evanescent luxury; they have to be rebuilt year after year. To provide 50 rooms, the builders need 20,000 tons of snow and 3,000 tons of ice. The design of these hotels is unique in that everything, from floor to ceiling, including the beds, is made of ice. Of necessity, the temperature inside seldom reaches

Lodging

KIND OF LODGING	WHERE	DESCRIPTION
Jungle lodge	French Guiana	Open lodge that serves as shelter and camp
Hacienda	Mexico	Former country estates that have been converted into guest houses or hotels
Igloo	Canada	Despite competition from ice hotels, igloos are still enjoyed in the Great White North.
Motu	French Polynesia	A small private island with bungalows, restaurants, and all kinds of water sports and diving activities
Parador	Spain	Old castles or abbeys turned into hotels—beautiful, expensive, and almost always booked, so reserve ahead.
Pousada	Portugal	Small hotels, administered by the state. They have competition from the quintas (estates) in the Douro Valley and on Madeira.
Riad	Morocco	Traditional home in Morocco, especially in Marrakech, with interior courtyard, central fountain, and glazed tiles
Ryokan	Japan	Typical Japanese inn, preferred by families, with tatami-matted rooms
Yurt	Central Asia	Movable wood and felt tent of the nomads of Central Asia and Mongolia

Moroccan riads can be trendy lodges.

even 32°F. On average, travelers should budget for $400/£260 a night.

Other interesting nighttime refuges are caves. This kind of lodging has been popular for some time. In some regions—for instance, in Matmata, Tunisia, and Cappadocia, Turkey—they are a kind of trademark. Less well known are the cave lodges in western France. The caves are often cool and damp, but have a wonderful atmosphere and can be fairly reasonable at about $500/£325 per week.

COUNTRIES FROM
A TO Z

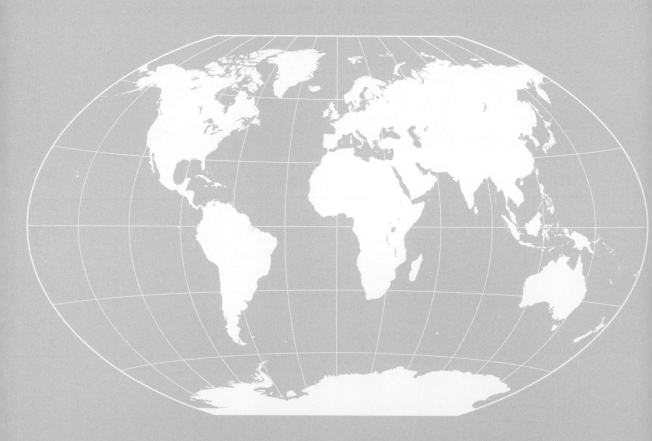

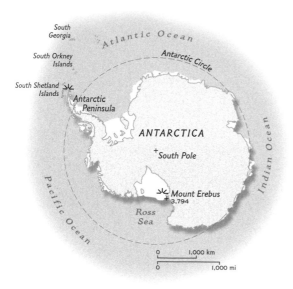

Antarctica is slowly becoming a popular travel destination, but the impact of tourism may adversely affect the environment. Ecologists fear that too many cruise ships will pollute and disturb the pristine nature of the continent. These concerns aside, let's think about this exceptional experience.

What to See and Do in Antarctica

▶ **LANDSCAPE**

• Cruises along the Antarctic Peninsula: ice cliffs, ice shelves, mountains, icebergs

• The South Shetland Islands, the South Orkney Islands, the Antarctic Peninsula, South Georgia

▶ **WILDLIFE**

• Penguins, petrels, elephant seals, whales, leopard seals, orcas

Antarctica

▶ **LANDSCAPE**
The Continent and Islands
Most cruise ships leave from Punta Arenas in Chile or Ushuaia in Argentina for the **South Shetland Islands** and sail along the **Antarctic Peninsula,** with several stops at research stations. Some 30 countries maintain permanent research stations throughout Antarctica and make up a cooperative international research zone, but no one lives there permanently. On this incomparable voyage, you will see towering

Traveler's Notebook

MAIN CONTACTS No embassies in Antarctica www.iaato.org **TRAVEL DOCUMENTS FOR U.S. & U.K. CITIZENS** Passport	**HEALTH ISSUES** It's vital to have proper clothing that will protect against severe wind and cold. **TRAVEL TIME TO DESTINATION & TIME DIFFERENCE** 10 days to 3 weeks	by sea from Ushuaia, Argentina; all 24 time zones exist **AVERAGE TRIP COST** $5,800/£3,700 for a 10-day cruise **LANGUAGE & CURRENCY** Languages:	primarily English and Spanish Currency: Argentine peso, Chilean peso, U.S. dollar **POPULATION** No permanent population, but steadily shifting personnel at the research stations

A tour group from Cape Horn in Chile reaches the Antarctic Peninsula on the world's most remote continent.

icebergs, steep cliffs, ice shelves, and spectacular mountains and have opportunities to step ashore for hikes onto ice fields and close-ups with penguins and seals that are unafraid of people.

The cruise ships stop at surrounding islands or follow in the footsteps of Ernest Shackleton to the island of **South Georgia,** where he managed to find help to rescue his stranded crew and where he died and was buried in 1922 on the way to another expedition.

▶ WILDLIFE

Right from the beginning of the cruise you can spot elephant seals, humpback whales, earless seals, leopard seals, orcas, and baleen whales. The penguin colonies are impressive by their number and organization, and their antics are

a pleasure to behold. Most difficult to spot are the emperor penguins. Petrels, albatrosses, skuas, and the imperial shag—a black-and-white

When to Go		
	CRUISES	CLIMATE
JANUARY	⬅	☀
FEBRUARY	⬅	☀
MARCH		☀
APRIL		
MAY		
JUNE		
JULY		
AUGUST		
SEPTEMBER		
OCTOBER		
NOVEMBER		
DECEMBER	⬅	☀

cormorant—complete the bird population here. The sight of Antarctic wildlife in its natural element is a not-to-be-missed spectacle and the main reason for traveling into the heart of this "white paradise."

Advice

■ **Pros**
• A unique experience, with a varying choice of cruises, often enhanced by specialized lecturers. Impressive and rare wildlife.

■ **Cons**
• Ice and weather determine the itinerary.

■ **Special Tip**
• Some Antarctic cruises include the Falkland Islands.

On the border of Argentina and Brazil, Iguazú Falls are celebrated as some of the most beautiful in the world.

Argentina

What to See and Do in Argentina

▶ **LANDSCAPE**

- Iguazú Falls, the Andes
- Pampas, Patagonia, Glaciers National Park, Tierra del Fuego, Mount Aconcagua, Mount Fitz Roy

▶ **MONUMENTS AND CITIES**

- Buenos Aires, Ushuaia
- Spanish colonial architecture, Jesuit missions

▶ **MARINE WILDLIFE AND THE COAST**

- Wildlife of the Valdés Peninsula and the Ushuaia region
- Mar del Plata

Argentina has become a prime destination for tourists from around the world thanks to its varied landscapes, its marine wildlife along the Valdés Peninsula, its elaborate colonial architecture, and, of course, the tango.

▶ **LANDSCAPE**

In Argentina's northeast corner, on the border with Brazil, the **Iguazú Falls**—combining 275 falls across nearly two miles and spurting 269 feet down—are counted among the most spectacular falls in the world. Equally amazing is the **Andes** mountain range, marking the country's western border from north to south.

In the northwest, the high plateaus are cut by narrow mountain valleys, such as the **Quebrada de Humahuaca.** The small town of Purmamarca, with its astonishing Cerro de los Siete Colores (Hill of Seven Colors), and Los Cardones National Park, established to protect *el cardón,* the giant cactus, are obligatory stops on the road to Cachí.

Ischigualasto National Park, or Valley of the Moon, so called for its strange geological formations, holds dinosaur (rhynchosaur) fossils

Traveler's Notebook

MAIN CONTACTS

Embassy of Argentina
1600 New Hampshire Avenue, NW
Washington, DC 20009
(202) 238-6400
www.embassyof
argentina.us
www.turismo.gov.ar/
eng/menu.htm
www.en.argentina.ar/
_en/tourism/
Embassy of Argentina
65 Brook Street
London W1K 4AH, UK
+ 44 (0) 20 7318 1300
www.argentine-

embassy-uk.org
www.turismo.gov.ar

TRAVEL DOCUMENTS FOR U.S. & U.K. CITIZENS
Passport

HEALTH ISSUES
Vaccinations are not necessary. Malaria prophylaxis is recommended in some areas near the borders of Bolivia and Paraguay.

TRAVEL TIME TO DESTINATION & TIME DIFFERENCE
New York to Buenos

Aires: 10 hours 30 minutes nonstop flight; EST +1. London to Buenos Aires: 15 hours 40 minutes connecting flight; GMT -3

AVERAGE TRIP COST
$2,200/£1,800 for 12 days of excursions

LANGUAGE & CURRENCY
Official language: Spanish; other languages: Guarani and other Indian dialects
Currency: Argentine peso

POPULATION
Of the 40,303,000

inhabitants, 86 percent are of European descent, largely Spanish or Italian. The remainder are Creoles (12 percent) or Indians (2 percent). Capital: Buenos Aires (metropolitan area population, 12 million)

RELIGION
Nine out of ten Argentineans are Catholic.

FESTIVALS
January: International folklore festival in Cosquín (Córdoba

province); before Lent: Carnival, with parades accompanied by *murgas* (popular musical theater); August: snow festival in San Carlos de Bariloche

SHOPPING
Handwoven fabrics from the Andes, sweaters of guanaco wool, ponchos, silver jewelry, and leather goods

and tracks. To the west of Córdoba, salt mines, volcanoes, multicolored cliffs, and old Indian villages give the region a special distinction.

Aconcagua, the highest mountain in the Andes at 22,841 feet, is arid, subject to strong winds, bathed in a blinding light, and yet a favorite of mountain climbers. Not far from there, the **Puente del Inca,** a natural bridge 160 feet long, crosses the Vacas River. **San Carlos de Bariloche** on Lake Nahuel Huapi is prized as a mountain resort.

Farther south in the **Pampas,** gauchos welcome ever more tourists, especially during the holidays. In the far southwest, in **Patagonia,** the deep blue of Lake Argentino is the gateway to **Glaciers National Park** with its many glaciers, the best known and largest of which is Perito Moreno. From there, it's not far to **Mount Fitz Roy** on the Chilean border, the "ultimate" for experienced mountaineers.

The journey ends on the lakes of the national park of Tierra del Fuego and Ushuaia, the southernmost city in the world and staging point for excursions into the bay and Beagle Channel.

▶ MONUMENTS AND CITIES

The colonial period has left its imprint on such cities as **Humahuaca, San Salvador de Jujuy,** and **Salta** (cathedral) and on the ruins of Quilmes, once home to pre-Hispanic indigenous people, not far from Cachí. Other remnants can be seen in the 17th- and 18th-century Jesuit missions of the Guaranis (San Ignacio Mini, Santa Ana, and San Francisco in Mendoza).

Buenos Aires has numerous museums and churches, the pink government house known as Casa Rosada, Recoleta cemetery where

Evita Perón is buried, and varied neighborhoods (Palermo and its "new tango"; San Telmo, hotbed of tango argentino and artists' haunts) in an altogether modern city. **Ushuaia** at the southernmost

point perpetuates its myth with a Museum of the End of the World and a maritime museum.

▶ MARINE WILDLIFE AND THE COAST

The Golfo Nuevo near Puerto Pirámides **(Valdés Peninsula)** harbors a multitude of marine wildlife: sea lions, elephant seals, southern right whales (between May and December), pink flamingos, and the largest colony of emperor penguins in the world. Only the southernmost point (Beagle Channel and the Ushuaia region) can rival this display.

The beaches near Buenos Aires, especially **Mar del Plata,** have their share of beachcombers.

When to Go

	NORTHEAST AND BUENOS AIRES	TIERRA DEL FUEGO	IGUAZÚ VALDÉS
JANUARY		☼	
FEBRUARY		☼	⋵
MARCH		☼	⋵
APRIL			⋵
MAY	☼		⋵
JUNE	☼		
JULY	☼		
AUGUST			
SEPTEMBER			⋵
OCTOBER	☼		⋵
NOVEMBER	☼		
DECEMBER			

Advice

▪ Pros

• The natural wonders, from north to south, and cultural heritage. The revitalization of the tango.

▪ Cons

• The cost of an extensive visit. For some, the reversed seasons (winter is in July and August).

▪ Safety

• Only the poor or touristy quarters—which are sometimes the same ones, such as La Boca in Buenos Aires—require vigilance. There are few problems elsewhere.

▪ Special Tip

• Unless you are a dance prodigy, you cannot learn the tango in two days and three steps in one of the establishments in San Telmo in Buenos Aires. But you can take dancing lessons there or simply admire the grace of the dancers.
• Another option is climbing Aconcagua, the highest mountain in the Americas. There you have to have strong legs of a different sort and be sure of your physical stamina.

What to See and Do in Armenia

▸ **MONUMENTS**

- Churches (Echmiadzin), monasteries (Geghard, Noravank), ancient cemeteries (Noraduz)
- Greco-Roman temple (Garni)

▸ **CAPITAL**

- Yerevan

▸ **LANDSCAPE**

- Transcaucasia

Armenia, with its mountainous countryside and ancient religious history, has much to offer. The country's cultural heritage of fourth- and sixth-century village churches and monasteries and the capital Yerevan, founded in the eighth century, will delight any art historian.

Armenia

▸ MONUMENTS

The country's religious buildings are among the most ancient in all of Christianity. The most famous is the cathedral of **Echmiadzin,** a fourth-century vaulted basilica, flanked by a museum filled with relics. The fourth-century **Geghard** monastery has chapels carved into the rock of a mountain. The Noravank monastery and its two churches are nestled in a narrow gorge. Rising near Mount Ararat, the Khor Virap monastery is one of the holy places of the Armenian Apostolic Church. Other monasteries include Hayravank, overlooking Lake Sevan, and Sanahin, one of the most important

Traveler's Notebook

MAIN CONTACTS
Embassy of the Republic of Armenia
2225 R Street, NW Washington, DC 20008
(202) 319-1976
www.armenia emb.org
www.armenia info.am
www.armenia .travel/
Embassy of the Republic of Armenia
25a Cheniston Gardens
London W8 6GT, UK
+ 44 (0) 20 7938 5435
www.armenian embassy.org.uk

TRAVEL DOCUMENTS FOR U.S. & U.K. CITIZENS
Passport and visa

TRAVEL TIME TO DESTINATION & TIME DIFFERENCE
New York to Yerevan: 16 hours 35 minutes connecting flight; EST +9. London to Yerevan: 5 hours nonstop; GMT -4

AVERAGE TRIP COST
$2,000/£1,000 for 12 days of culture and excursions

LANGUAGE & CURRENCY
Official language: Armenian (99 percent of the population speaks it); other

languages: Azerbaijani and Russian
Currency: dram

POPULATION
2,972,000 inhabitants, one-third of whom live in the capital, Yerevan. During the war years, many Armenians chose exile, largely in the United States and France.

RELIGION
The Armenian Orthodox Church has kept to its traditions and represents the interests and unity of the Armenian people.

FESTIVALS
April 24: Medz Yeghern (commemoration of the World War I genocide); May 28: Hanrabedoutian (Day of the First Republic); July 19: Vardavar (Transfiguration Day); September: Moussa Ler (Independence Day), celebrated on a hill near Yerevan; October: traditional music festival in honor of the founding of Yerevan

SHOPPING
Something unusual: Armenian paper that serves as a room-freshener

Majestic Mount Ararat, just over the Turkish border, backs Khor Virap monastery, an iconic image of a country just opening up to tourism.

holds some 2,000 ancient Armenian manuscripts. The most prized is the Echmiadzin Gospel, enhanced with illuminations from the sixth, seventh, and tenth centuries. Other sights include the fortress of Erebuni, Yerevan's mosque and market, and the city's theaters and museums (Parajanov Museum, medieval paintings).

▶ LANDSCAPE

Armenia lies mainly in **Transcaucasia,** a panorama of severe beauty because of its rough terrain. The country is becoming a popular destination for hikers for its combination of trails and cultural features.

High plateaus, volcanic landscapes, and depressions such as **Lake Sevan,** which the Armenians call "blue-eyed beauty," follow in quick succession, while the snowy flanks of Mount Ararat loom on the horizon.

Christian centers from the 10th to the 13th centuries.

The cemetery of Noraduz and its field of a thousand *kachkars* (cross-bearing tombstones) is a treasure. So, too, are the small churches—often crowned by a two-level cupola—dating to the seventh century, among them the churches of St. Hripsime and St. Gayane in Echmiadzin, Karmravor in Ashtarak, and St. Zoravor in Yerevan.

In the village of **Garni,** a first-century B.C. Greco-Roman temple built by King Tiridates I perches on the edge of a cliff.

▶ CAPITAL

Yerevan, not far from Mount Ararat, is one of the oldest cities in the world. The capital is famous for its national library, the Matenadaran, which

When to Go		
	CLIMATE	NATURE
JANUARY		
FEBRUARY		
MARCH		
APRIL	☼	🐾
MAY	☼	🐾
JUNE	☼	🐾
JULY	☼	
AUGUST	☼	
SEPTEMBER	☼	
OCTOBER	☼	
NOVEMBER		
DECEMBER		

Australia

Australia is called "the lucky country" for its abundance of raw materials, sunshine, and natural wonders. Although too young to offer major historical treasures, it has begun to celebrate the Aboriginal culture, including its rock art, while still clinging to its image as a country of settlers. The wide horizons of the interior rival the vistas at the coasts and the Great Barrier Reef.

▶ LANDSCAPE
The Center

The destination that is foremost on many visitors' minds is the outback, the wide-open spaces of the interior of semiarid brushland and red earth, rocks, and dry trees. This is where many Aborigines live, where huge sheep stations spread out, where seemingly endless trucks—the so-called road trains—roll by, where kangaroos jump and wild dromedaries graze.

From this middle ground spreads the Simpson Desert, known as the Red Center for its long red dunes sprinkled with brush. The walls of **Kings Canyon** and the desert city of **Alice Springs** rise alone above

---

What to See and Do in Australia

▶ LANDSCAPE

- The center: the Red Center (Kings Canyon, Uluru, Kata Tjuta), Lake Eyre, the Flinders Ranges, Coober Pedy
- The east: the Blue Mountains, Hunter Valley (vineyards)
- The north: Arnhem Land, Aboriginal rock art in Kakadu National Park, Kimberley, Bungle Bungle, rain forests of Queensland
- The west: Karijini National Park, the Kalgoorlie-Boulder gold mines
- The south: Tasmania

▶ COASTS

- East coast: rivers and islands of the Great Barrier Reef
- North coast: Melville Island, Bathurst Island
- West coast: Broome, Perth
- South coast: Byron Bay, Sydney, state of Victoria
- Tasmania and Norfolk Island: Wineglass Bay

▶ WILDLIFE

- Wallabies, koalas, kangaroos, emus, dolphins, whale sharks, manta rays, sea turtles, seals, opossums

▶ CITIES

- Sydney, Alice Springs, Melbourne, Adelaide, Perth

Melville Island

Bathurst Island

Darwin • ✹ ARNHEM
Kakadu ▢ LAND
National Park

Cape York
Peninsula

Lake Argyle
KIMBERLEY ✹

Broome • Bungle Bungle Range

NORTHERN TERRITORY

Tanami Desert

Cairns

Pacific Ocean

Karijini National Park ▢

Exmouth

A U S T R A L I A

Kings Canyon ●

Alice Springs ●

Simpson Desert

QUEENSLAND

WESTERN AUSTRALIA

Kata Tjuta + + Uluru
(Mt. Olga) (Ayers Rock)
1,069   863

Coober Pedy ●

Lake Eyre

SOUTH AUSTRALIA

Lamington National Park ●   Brisbane ▢
                                   ● Byron Bay

Shark Bay

Indian Ocean

Kalgoorlie ✹

Perth ●

Adelaide ●

Kangaroo Island

Flinders Ranges

Darling

NEW SOUTH WALES

Murray

CANBERRA ⊛

VICTORIA

Warrnambool ●
Port Campbell National Park ▢ ● Lorne
Otway National Park

Wilsons Promontory

Hunter Valley Vineyard ✹

Sydney ●
Blue ● Bondi Beach
Mountains
Nat. Park

Melbourne ●

TASMANIA

Cradle Mt.-Lake St. Clair National Park

Freycinet National Park
Hobart

Tasmanian Sea

Great Barrier Reef

G R E A T   D I V I D I N G   R A N G E

0   400 km
0   400 mi

The bizarrely shaped rocks on the coast of Port Campbell, called the Twelve Apostles, edge the Great Ocean Road.

Koalas in Featherdale Wildlife Park pose for a visitor.

The East

Not far from Sydney you'll find the **Blue Mountains,** where eucalyptus forests cover the slopes and sandstone forms vertical canyon walls (Grose, Gowett, Cox) dotted with waterfalls (Katoomba and especially Govett's Leap) and limestone caves (Jenolan). Highlights are Aboriginal rock art sites and Featherdale Wildlife Park, where koalas seem to be waiting for the tourists.

North of Sydney, **Hunter Valley** invites wine connoisseurs. From here, a vast tropical forest spreads north toward Cairns.

The North

The "Top End," **Arnhem Land,** is bordered by the Katherine River Gorge and the large **Kakadu National Park,** where the movie *Crocodile Dundee* was filmed. You can explore Aboriginal art at Ubirr and Nourlangie Rock (thousand-year-old cave paintings).

In the northwest, the **Kimberley** region sheltered the first Aborigines some 40,000 years ago. The gorges and rock towers of the **Bungle Bungle** region, as well as the Tanami

the plain. **Uluru** (Ayers Rock), a sandstone monolith nearly six miles in circumference, is the sacred mountain of the Aborigines, who have decorated its rock caves with paintings and engravings. You can scale the 1,142-foot-high rock (though the Aborigines would prefer you didn't) or walk around it (a three-hour hike). Or simply stay to watch the sunset, when the light seems to change the rock from red to orange; a similar display can be seen on the 36 domes of **Kata** **Tjuta** (Mount Olga) 12 miles farther west.

On the way south to Adelaide, you come to **Lake Eyre,** a mixture of salt, mud, and brackish water, until you find yourself in the **Flinders Ranges** and a greener landscape around Wilpena Pound that is great for hiking. Not far from there, you come to the town of **Coober Pedy,** the "opal capital" of the world, with its elaborate underground homes, shops, and opal mines.

Traveler's Notebook

MAIN CONTACTS

Embassy of Australia
1601 Massachusetts
Avenue, NW
Washington, DC 20036
(202) 797-3000
www.usa.embassy.gov.au
www.australia.com
Australian High Commission
Australia House
The Strand
London WC2B 4LA, UK
+ 44 (0) 20 7379 4334
www.uk.embassy.gov.au

TRAVEL DOCUMENTS
For U.S. Citizens:

Passport and visa
For U.K. Citizens: Passport (and visa for stays of more than 90 days)

TRAVEL TIME TO DESTINATION & TIME DIFFERENCE
New York to Sydney: 22 hours 30 minutes connecting flight; EST +16.
London to Sydney: 21 hours 30 minutes connecting flight; GMT +10

AVERAGE TRIP COST
$2,540–$3,175/
£1,640–£2,010 for 15 days of excursions

LANGUAGE & CURRENCY
Official language: English; other languages: some Aboriginal dialects
Currency: Australian dollar

POPULATION
Because the country was settled only fairly recently, the population of 20,434,000 (6 million in the Sydney metropolitan area alone) is relatively low compared to area, with a population density of one person per square mile. Most people are of British descent,

followed by those of Central European, Italian, and Greek origin, and 140,000 Aborigines. Capital: Canberra

RELIGION
Catholics and Anglicans each make up about 26 percent of the population, followed by Unitarians, Presbyterians, Eastern Orthodox, Baptists, and others.

FESTIVALS
January 26: National Day; March: Festival of Melbourne (Moomba), Mardi

Gras for Gays and Lesbians in Sydney; second Monday in June: Queen's Birthday; December 26: Boxing Day

SHOPPING
Besides the boomerang and didgeridoo, a traditional Aboriginal musical instrument, other typical crafts include wood carvings and paintings. For gemstones, Australia's opals are renowned.

Australia inspires individual exploration, as here in the Bungle Bungle region in the country's north.

Desert with its huge Wolfe Creek Crater, also merit a visit.

The northeast, at the Cape York Peninsula, the tip of **Queensland,** is a large, unspoiled wilderness area of tropical rain forests that includes Iron Range National Park.

The West

Leaving Exmouth and traveling toward the interior, you cross the **Karijini National Park** with its red-tinted gorges, waterfalls, and natural pools.

In the southwest, the town of **Kalgoorlie-Boulder,** between Perth and Adelaide, lies at the heart of a region that had its gold rush at the end of the 19th century. The Museum of Goldfields and the Hannans North mine remain as principal reminders.

The South

The island of **Tasmania** has many national parks, forests, lakes, and waterfalls. The area in the southwest attracts hikers (Mount Field Park), and the island's west, where the 50 miles of the Overland Track across Cradle Mountain-Lake St. Clair National Park constitute the most famous bush walk, is enlivened by tree ferns, fog, marsupials, and wallabies. Some 60 miles away in the town of Hobart thrill seekers can visit the former penal station of Port Arthur during a

When to Go						
	CENTER	GREAT BARRIER REEF	SYDNEY	NORTH	SOUTH	WEST
JANUARY					☼	☼
FEBRUARY					☼	☼
MARCH			◉		☼	☼
APRIL	☼		◉		☼	☼
MAY	☼			☼		
JUNE	☼		◉	☼		
JULY	☼	⋜	◉	☼		
AUGUST	☼	⋜	◉	☼		
SEPTEMBER	☼	⋜	◉	☼		
OCTOBER		⋜		☼		☼
NOVEMBER		⋜				☼
DECEMBER		⋜				☼

short sea crossing to the Island of the Dead.

▶ COASTS

East Coast

The eighth wonder of the world, according to Australians, is the **Great Barrier Reef**—about 1,600 miles long, comprising 2,900 individual reefs, 900 islands, and 350 different kinds of coral (tourists are implored not to take or damage them)—which alone justifies a trip to Australia. It's on this reef that a dream vacation becomes reality. Dunk Island, for example, east of Cairns, has ideal beaches and access to the reef. Heron, Lizard, and Fraser Islands offer water sports, wildlife-watching, and plenty of coral to see from glass-bottom boats or while snorkeling.

North Coast

Tourism here is sparse, so you can enjoy **Melville Island** (where you will encounter Aboriginal people, the Tiwi) and **Bathurst Island** almost by yourself.

West Coast

The western beaches are seldom visited by international tourists, but include **Broome** (with its long, white Cable Beach) and **Perth,** ideal for surfers. The Australian coasts are famous for having some of the best waves and surfers in the world. (Surfers frolic not only around Perth but also on the southern and eastern coasts between Brisbane and Melbourne.)

South Coast

Traveling far to the southeast, you will reach **Byron Bay,** where vacationers flee the large crowds. Close to **Sydney,** beach resorts are sprinkled all around. The most renowned is Bondi Beach, where people indulge in "beach culture," displaying their perfect tans and surfing skills.

The beaches of the south coast around Adelaide, the Murray River, the Great Ocean Road, and the highlights of the state of **Victoria** (Wilsons Promontory and Port Campbell National Parks; Otway National Park, with one of the last temperate rain forests in the world; the salt lakes of the Desert Wilderness) all make a trip to southern Australia worthwhile. Southern right whales can be watched off the coast between Warrnambool and Cape Otway from June to September, and platypuses gambol off the beaches of Lorne. The nearby

With thousands of reefs and hundreds of types of coral, the Great Barrier Reef is as fabulous as its ecosystem is fragile.

Sydney's Circular Quay epitomizes this dynamic and innovative city.

township of Torquay is one of the surfing capitals of the world.

Tasmania and Norfolk Island

The coast of Tasmania is rather cool but beautiful, especially **Wineglass Bay** east of the Freycinet Peninsula.

Isolated **Norfolk Island,** between Australia and New Zealand, is inhabited by descendants of the H.M.S. *Bounty* mutineers.

▶ WILDLIFE

Australia has several unique marsupials, including the wombat, the koala (which lives mostly in the forests of Queensland), and of course, the kangaroo, which can be found around Adelaide as well as in the parks of Kakadu and the Blue Mountains. Kangaroo Island also gives shelter to koalas, opossums, and whales. Other unusual species are the platypus with its webbed feet, which frequents the rivers and lakes; the emu; and some 60 species of parakeets.

Tasmania, where the fauna and flora (rain forests of eucalyptus and redwoods) have been able to survive more easily than on the mainland, teems with many more species.

Western Australia delights divers with its plentiful marine wildlife: dolphins in Shark Bay and large groups of hammerhead sharks around Ningaloo Reef near Exmouth from April to June.

Besides viewing the Aboriginal cave paintings in Kakadu, visitors can also go on photo safaris to see giant crocodiles and termite mounds.

Along the Great Barrier Reef, sea turtles lay their eggs between September and March and a great variety of birds hang out near manta rays and multicolored fish.

▶ CITIES

Sydney is special, and not only because of the modern architecture of the Opera House. Indeed, since the harbor has been modernized and its cargo and wooden docks have been replaced little by little by entertainment complexes (theaters, restaurants, boutiques, and the aquarium of Darling Harbour) the city has become a great tourist magnet. The city's green spaces (Royal Botanic Garden, Hyde Park), "old" quarter (The Rocks), and port (Sydney Harbour Bridge), along with its outrageousness (Gay Mardi Gras) and cultural attractions (Aboriginal and Asian heritage at the Art Gallery of New South Wales), complete its renown as the most interesting city of the country.

Alice Springs (for its location in the heart of the desert), **Melbourne** (for its urbanism and botanic gardens), **Adelaide** (for Tandanya National Aboriginal Cultural Institute and its location at the foot of Mount Lofty), and **Perth** (for its splendid isolation, its marina, its maritime museum, and Fremantle port) are all worth a visit.

What to See and Do in Austria

▸ **LANDSCAPE, HIKING TOURS, AND SKIING**

- Tirol, Wildschönau, Vorarlberg, Carinthia, Neusiedler Lake, Hohe Tauern
- Winter sports (downhill and cross-country skiing)
- Summer tourism (hiking)

▸ **CITIES**

- Vienna, Salzburg, Innsbruck, Graz, Linz, Bad Ischl, Mayerling, Melk, Bregenz

▸ **CULTURAL HERITAGE**

- Music festivals, Christmas markets

Salzburg, Mozart's city, features medieval and baroque architecture.

Whether you're a skier, hiker, music fan, gourmet, or nature lover, Austria has something for everyone. The country unfolds with stunning Alpine scenery and traditional villages of chalets with flower-bedecked balconies. Above all, its romantic capital, Vienna, draws visitors from around the world.

Austria

▸ **LANDSCAPE, HIKING TOURS, AND SKIING**

Austria's tourism industry relies mainly on its snow. For downhill skiing, there are hundreds of villages that prize their reliable snow, such as Igls near Innsbruck and the famous resorts of **Kitzbühel,** Saalbach, Zell am See, and Sankt Anton. Cross-country skiing also has its place here, although three-quarters of the country is mountainous, culminating in the Dachstein and Grossglockner peaks.

In the **Tirol,** canyoneering, hiking, and mountain biking—as a

Traveler's Notebook

MAIN CONTACTS	TRAVEL DOCUMENTS FOR U.S. & U.K. CITIZENS	AVERAGE TRIP COST	RELIGION	
Embassy of Austria 3524 International Court, NW Washington, DC 20008 (202) 895-6700 www.austria.org www.austria.info/us *Embassy of Austria* 18 Belgrave Mews West London SW1X 8HU, UK + 44 (0) 20 7344 3250 www.bmeia.gv.at/en/embassy/london.html	Passport **TRAVEL TIME TO DESTINATION & TIME DIFFERENCE** New York to Vienna: 8 hours 45 minutes non-stop flight; EST +6. London to Vienna: 2 hours 15 minutes nonstop; GMT +1	$900/£600 for a week of hiking **LANGUAGE & CURRENCY** Official language: German Currency: euro **POPULATION** 820,000 inhabitants, with a very low immigration rate. Capital: Vienna	Primarily Catholic (85 percent). The largest minority is Lutheran. **FESTIVALS** New Year's Eve: Emperor's Ball in Vienna; New Year's Day: concert of the Vienna Philharmonic; mid-January to mid-February: Vienna Ball season; June: Schubertiades in Feldkirch and Styriarte in Graz; July: Lake	Constance concerts in Bregenz; August: Salzburg Festival; September: festival for the end of grazing season in Schwarzenberg, Tyrol; December: Christmas markets in Innsbruck, Linz, Salzburg, and Vienna

sport or pursued more leisurely— are the norm, as in the **Wildschönau Valley,** Fiss, or Alpbach. The villages still have their traditional look, with wooden chalets and balconies brimming over with geraniums. **Vorarlberg** offers similar pleasures with its wildflower valleys, forests, varied flora (spruce, larch, pine), and mountain lakes.

In the south, **Carinthia** has several national parks perfect for long hikes, as in the Lesach Valley or along numerous lakes such as Lake Millstatt. On the border with Hungary, **Neusiedler Lake** is surrounded by marsh reeds, which serve as a habitat for wildlife, especially migratory birds.

▶ CITIES

Vienna is worth a visit for many reasons: its location on the Danube allowing for minicruises; its retro charm; the baroque facades; the imperial palace, the Hofburg, where the famous Emperor's Ball is held every New Year's Eve; the famous opera house (Staatsoper); the churches (Gothic cathedral of St. Stephen); the former homes of Beethoven and Freud; the main thoroughfare (Graben); the concert house (Musikverein) and classic music festivals (spring and summer); the coffeehouses (Café Central, Café Bräunerhof); the pastries; and the grand balls (300 balls between the beginning of January and mid-February).

The capital looms large on the country's cultural scene: The city was already well endowed with 55 museums, among them the Kunsthistorische Museum

(Hieronymus Bosch, Rembrandt, Rubens) and collections in the Belvedere Palace (Klimt), but a new museum quarter was built in 2001, followed in 2008 by the reopening of the graphics collection of the Albertina.

On the outskirts, the famous **Schönbrunn Palace** is a major attraction; it's the Austrian Versailles, the imperial summer residence, meant to magnify the importance of the Habsburgs with some 200 rooms, 40 of which are open to the public.

Salzburg can easily compete with Vienna, with the ambiance of the old city and its baroque architecture, the museums, the white

When to Go			
	VIENNA	HIKING	WINTER SPORTS
JANUARY			❄
FEBRUARY			❄
MARCH			❄
APRIL			
MAY	☼	🚶	
JUNE	☼	🚶	
JULY	☼	🚶	
AUGUST		🚶	
SEPTEMBER	☼	🚶	
OCTOBER			
NOVEMBER			
DECEMBER			❄

Hohensalzburg, and the honor of being Mozart's birthplace. **Innsbruck** shows off with its landmark Golden Dachl—the copper-roofed balcony—the Hofkirche church, and the regional Tyrol museum. The old section of **Graz** is dominated by the Renaissance steeples of the city hall and the clock tower of the Schlossberg. **Linz** beckons with baroque facades and St. Martin, the oldest church in Austria.

Other towns of historic significance include **Bad Ischl, Mayerling, Melk** (famous abbey), and **Bregenz** (annual festival).

▶ CULTURAL HERITAGE

Austria is the birthplace of Mozart, Johann Strauss, and Schubert, a trio of major composers whose music festivals draw the crowds; the Salzburg Festival in August is the most prestigious. In Vienna, festival concerts are held in the Palffy Palace, the opera house, and the Musikverein.

Christmas markets are another tradition. The most famous ones are held in Linz, Salzburg, and Innsbruck, with Tirolean pastry specialties in abundance.

Baltic States

The three sister countries on the Baltic Sea do not currently rank high as world tourist destinations; nevertheless, more and more travelers are discovering their special charms. The Latvian and Estonian capital cities of Riga and Tallinn are the star attractions, with their welcoming spirit and abundant forests and lakes.

What to See and Do in Latvia

▶ **CITIES AND MONUMENTS**
- Riga, Cesis
- Castles and manor houses

▶ **LANDSCAPE**
- Lakes and forests (Gauja National Park, Daugavpils)

▶ **COAST**
- Jurmala

Latvia

▶ **CITIES AND MONUMENTS**

Riga, a former member of the Hanseatic League situated on the Daugava River, is steadily earning a reputation as one of Europe's hot new tourist destinations. In its favor are the many package deals encouraging weekend trips.

The baroque style permeates the city's old town districts. Art nouveau with a Latvian twist is evident in the many facades embellished with flowers, plants, escutcheons, and masks—the best examples of which can be seen on Alberta Street.

Many other architectural styles in the town center have contributed to Riga's recognition as a UNESCO World Heritage site. The Town Hall and the Blackheads Guild Hall, which were destroyed by bombs in World War II, have been completely reconstructed.

When to Go		
	CLIMATE	FESTIVALS
JANUARY		
FEBRUARY		
MARCH		
APRIL		✔
MAY		
JUNE	☼	✔
JULY	☼	✔
AUGUST	☼	
SEPTEMBER		
OCTOBER		
NOVEMBER		
DECEMBER		

Latvia's beaches and dunes near Jurmala, on the Baltic Sea, have an undeniable charm.

Other landmarks—such as the Great Guild Hall, Cat's House, St. Mary Magdalene's and St. Peter's churches, and especially the 13th-century cathedral—were left unscathed by the war.

Riga is famous for a host of museums (State Museum of Art, Museum of the History of Riga and Navigation, and the poignant Museum of the Occupation of Latvia) and for preserving the nation's music and dance heritage (notably with its summer festival).

Other interesting architectural sites include the imposing Rundale Palace (near Bauska), designed by

Traveler's Notebook

MAIN CONTACTS
Embassy of Latvia
2306 Massachusetts Avenue, NW
Washington, DC 20008
202-328-2840
www.latvia-usa.org
Embassy of Latvia
45 Nottingham Place
London W1U 5LY
+ 44 (0) 20 7312 0040
www.latvia
.embassyhome
page.com

TRAVEL DOCUMENTS FOR U.S. & U.K. CITIZENS
Passport

TRAVEL TIME TO DESTINATION & TIME DIFFERENCE
New York to Riga: 11 hours connecting flight; EST +7. London to Riga: 3 hours nonstop flight; GMT -2

AVERAGE TRIP COST
$350/£225 for a four-day weekend in Riga

LANGUAGES & CURRENCY
Official language: Latvian (or Lettish); other languages: Russian (40 percent of the population), German, English
Currency: lat

POPULATION
2,260,000 inhabitants, one-third of Russian origin. Capital: Riga

RELIGION
Lutheran majority, plus Catholic and

Russian Orthodox minorities

FESTIVALS
April: International Baltic Ballet Festival in Riga; June 23–24: Feast of St. John (Midsummer Night); July: Folklore Festival in Riga, and Beer Festival in Cesis

SHOPPING
Baltic amber necklaces and jewelry, knitwear, ceramics, and basketry

In Latvia, the Gauja River flows through Gauja National Park, where cliffs, caves, and medieval castles dot the landscape.

The Blackheads Guild Hall in Riga is an example of the city's rich architecture.

the architect of the Winter Palace in St. Petersburg, Russia; **Cesis,** a 13th-century town, whose castle is now a museum of Latvian history; and the Jelgava region, noted for its numerous castles and manors. Also worth visiting are the 13th-century castle ruins at Krimulda and Sigulda.

▶ LANDSCAPE

Three thousand lakes and mostly evergreen forests cover nearly half of the country. Particularly beautiful sites include **Gauja National Park** (hills, caves) and the southeastern region of **Daugavpils,** known as Latvia's "Little Switzerland."

▶ COAST

The seaside town of **Jurmala** boasts some six miles of beaches, dunes, *izbas* (fishermen's houses), and pine forests. The ever changing colors of the Baltic Sea and myriad vacation houses are evidence of a gentle climate, which can reach 70°F in the summer.

Lithuania

▶ CITIES

Vilnius has a well-deserved reputation as a top tourist destination. Its highlights include a medieval

---

What to See and Do in Lithuania

▶ **CITIES**
• Vilnius, Kaunas, Trakai

▶ **COAST**
• Dunes, Palanga, Neringa Peninsula

▶ **LANDSCAPE**
• Lakes, forests, Neman River Basin

---

castle, traditional wooden houses, baroque churches (SS. Peter and Paul Church; Church of St. John the Baptist and St. John the Evangelist, with its pink facades and gilded crown), the cathedral, a cloister (St. Basil), numerous museums (Museum of Traditional Arts), and unique architecture where brick and stucco facades blend with baroque style. The city's oldest buildings are well preserved, and the old town has been designated a World Heritage site. Vilnius is in the process of reviving the old Jewish quarter, where Yiddish was spoken before the neighborhood was destroyed in 1943.

Not far from Vilnius, another somewhat controversial tourist attraction is Grutas Park and Museum, which is a collection of monuments to the 1917 Revolution and the Soviet era, including dismantled statues of Lenin—intriguing to some visitors; questionable to others.

North of Vilnius is Europas Parkas, a European sculpture park symbolizing the geographical center of Continental Europe.

A quaint fisherman's house on the Neringa Peninsula, Lithuania

Kaunas, the second major city in Lithuania, is noted for its cultural traditions, 13th-century monuments, and museums. The town of **Trakai,** former capital of the Grand Duchy of Lithuania, features a 14th-century castle and several museums.

▶ COAST

Dunes enhance the beauty of the Baltic coastline. The seaside town of **Palanga** is a resort destination of note—something rather unusual in this region. On the narrow **Neringa Peninsula,** dubbed the "Lithuanian Sahara," numerous seaside towns promote their spa treatments (Druskininkai, Neringa, Palanga, Birstonas).

▶ LANDSCAPE

Five national parks are scattered throughout Lithuania. Thanks to its four thousand lakes, its rivers and forests, and the **Neman River Basin,** the Lithuanian landscape is the most diverse of the three Baltic countries.

Traveler's Notebook

MAIN CONTACTS

Embassy of the Republic of Lithuania
2622 16th Street, NW Washington, DC 20009
(202) 234-5860
www.ltembassyus.org

Embassy of the Republic of Lithuania
84 Gloucester Place London W1U 6AU, UK
+ 44 (0) 20 7486 6401
www.lithuanian

embassy.co.uk

TRAVEL DOCUMENTS FOR U.S. & U.K. CITIZENS
Passport

TRAVEL TIME TO DESTINATION & TIME DIFFERENCE
New York to Vilnius: 11 hours connecting flight; EST +7. London to Vilnius: 3 hours nonstop flight; GMT -2

AVERAGE TRIP COST
Similar to Tallinn and Riga, about $350/

£225 for a four-day weekend in Vilnius

LANGUAGE & CURRENCY
Official language: Lithuanian (an ancient language similar to Polish and Russian); other languages: German, English, Russian
Currency: lita

POPULATION
3,575,000 inhabitants; four out of five inhabitants

are Lithuanian. Capital: Vilnius.

FESTIVALS
June 23–24: Feast of St. John (Midsummer Night); July: Sea Festival in Klaipeda; September: Vilnius International Festival (theater, dance, music)

SHOPPING
Amber necklaces and jewelry, icons

From the overlook at Toompea Hill, Tallinn reveals its red-tile roofs and baroque flourishes.

▬ Estonia

▶ LANDSCAPE

East of Tallinn and bordering the Baltic, **Lahemaa National Park** is considered one of the most beautiful sites in the country for its forests and wildlife (bears, elk, lynx, wolves). The region is also known for the manor homes of former barons.

Estonia boasts over a thousand lakes (primarily in the south), which are the country's premier tourist attractions, yet still relatively undiscovered. The southeastern region is popular for cross-country skiing, for example, in **Otepää** and **Võru.**

Saaremaa Island, with its lush and pristine landscape, is especially pleasant in the summer. It also features a meteorite crater in Kaali.

▶ CITIES

The capital, **Tallinn,** is a city of contrasts. Approaching the city

Traveler's Notebook

MAIN CONTACTS
Estonian Embassy
2131 Massachu-
setts Avenue, NW
Washington, DC
20008
202-588-0101
www.estemb.org
Estonian Embassy
16 Hyde Park Gate
London SW7 5DG
+ 44 (0) 20 7589
3428
www.estonia.gov.uk

**TRAVEL DOCUMENTS
FOR U.S. & U.K.
CITIZENS**
Passport

**TRAVEL TIME TO
DESTINATION & TIME
DIFFERENCE**
New York to Tal-
linn: 11 hours con-
necting flight; EST
+7. London to Tal-
linn: 2 hours 45 min-
utes nonstop flight;
GMT -2

AVERAGE TRIP COST
$350/£225 for a
four-day weekend in
Tallinn

**LANGUAGE &
CURRENCY**
Official language:
Estonian (a Finno-
Ugric language);
one-third of the
population speaks
Russian
Currency: kroon

POPULATION
1,316,000 inhabit-
ants; two-thirds of
Estonian descent,
one-third Russians.
Capital: Tallinn

RELIGION
The majority of
the population is
Lutheran; Catho-
lics and Russian
Orthodox are the
most prominent
minorities.

FESTIVALS
June 23–24:
Feast of St. John
(Midsummer Night);
July: popular music
festival in Pir-
ita (part of Tallinn),
and Beer Summer
in Tallinn; August:
White Lady Days in
Haapsalu

SHOPPING
A variety of hand-
icrafts, including
jewelry, especially
Baltic amber;
wooden toys; pup-
pets; and blown-
glass objects

from the south, there are long stretches of nondescript neighborhoods; closer in, modern towers rise from the cityscape. In the historic city center, a fortress—with its distinctive red-tile roof, ramparts, and towers—keeps watch over the bay and the cities' two districts: Upper Town, located on Toompea or Cathedral Hill, and Lower Town.

A walk through Toompea offers many attractions, such as Alexander Nevsky Cathedral; the baroque castle with its pink facade; the Cathedral of St. Mary the Virgin, also known as the Dome Church; St. Olaf's Church; and houses topped with red-tile roofs. A tour of Lower Town begins in the Town Hall Square, the former commercial center for the Hanseatic League cities on the Baltic. Medieval houses from the 13th and 14th centuries abound, especially along Lai and Pikk Streets.

Two very interesting, yet decidedly different, sites are located on the outskirts of Tallinn: A couple miles to the east is Kadriorg Palace, built by Peter the Great for his wife, Catherine, and nearby the famous cottage where he once took refuge. In the northwest lies the beach resort of Pirita, whose claim to fame is the Tallinn Sound Stage, venue of the prestigious Festival of Song, held annually.

Another important city is **Tartu**—a former trading center of the Hanseatic League, home of the Estonian National Museum, and, every four years, host of the Festival of Song, with singers dressed in the traditional costumes of each village.

Not to be missed are two cities renowned for their medieval castles: **Narva** (Hermann Castle) and **Kuressaare** (episcopal castle).

On the coast, the resort city of **Pärnu** boasts wooden houses dating back to the early 20th century. **Haapsalu,** the "Venice of the Baltic," is also worth a trip.

Advice

■ Pros
• Riga and Tallinn are increasingly popular with Europeans for weekend getaways, thanks to bargain tour companies. Tourism to all three countries is on the rise, especially since they have become members of the European Union.

■ Cons
• The Baltic States' tourist image needs refining, particularly as the three countries are often confused with one another. Even in summer, the weather is often chilly.

In Brussels, the guildhalls together with the city hall form an attractive group around the Grand Place.

Belgium

■ *The cool North Sea and gray skies seem to be drawbacks for planning a trip, but Belgium's architecture and medieval cities outweigh any such concerns. The forests of the Ardennes and the High Fens–Eifel Mountains belie the idea that Belgium is entirely flat.*

▶ CITIES

Brugge lies between two romantic canals, earning it the moniker "Venice of the North." The medieval architecture of its historic center is well preserved with gabled houses, the Belfry's carillon, the Béguinage (a nunnery of an earlier time with expert lacemakers), and museums (early Flemish art in the municipal museum).

In **Brussels,** the fountain with the statue of the little boy, the Manneken-Pis, is a favorite tourist meeting point; even the Grand Place, with its Gothic town hall and guildhalls, can hardly rival it. Other important sites include the art nouveau houses (with the Horta Museum a point of pride), the Cathedral of St. Michel, Cinquantenaire park, Louise Avenue, Erasmus

Traveler's Notebook

MAIN CONTACTS
Embassy of Belgium
3330 Garfield Street, NW
Washington, DC 20008
(202) 333-6900
www.diplobel.us
www.visitbelgium.com
www.belgium
theplaceto.be
www.belgique-
tourisme.net
Embassy of Belgium
17 Grosvenor Crescent
London SW1X 7EE, UK
+ 44 (0) 20 7470 3700

www.diplomatie.be/
london

TRAVEL DOCUMENTS FOR U.S. & U.K. CITIZENS
Passport

TRAVEL TIME TO DESTINATION & TIME DIFFERENCE
New York to Brussels: 8 hours 30 minutes nonstop flight; EST +6. London to Brussels: 1 hour nonstop flight; GMT +1

AVERAGE TRIP COST
$200–$250/£125–£165 for 3 days/2 nights

LANGUAGE & CURRENCY
Official languages: French, Flemish, German
Currency: euro

POPULATION
With 10,392,000 inhabitants, the country is densely populated, distributed over ten provinces but mostly concentrated in the

cities, and divided into a Flemish majority and the French-speaking Walloons (80 percent of Brussels's population is Walloon). Capital: Brussels

RELIGION
96 percent Catholic

FESTIVALS
February or March: Carnival in Binche, Aalst, eastern districts, and Malmédy; March: Dead

Rat Ball in Oostende; spring: Zinneke parade in Brussels; Ascension Day: procession of the Holy Blood in Brugge; Pentecost: Maritime Festival in Oostende

SHOPPING
Three things are essential: handmade lace from Brugge; chocolates; and beer.

What to See and Do in Belgium

▶ **CITIES**

• Brugge, Brussels, Antwerp, Ghent, Liège, Leuven, Dinant, Mons, Tournai, Namur, Bouillon, Beloeil, Arlon

▶ **COAST**

• North Sea coast

▶ **FESTIVALS**

• Mardi Gras, *kermes*

▶ **LANDSCAPE**

• Dikes and canals around Damme

• Ardennes, High Fens-Eifel Nature Park

Advice

■ **Pros**

• The great cultural richness and architecture of the towns. The pleasant forest of the Ardennes Mountains.

■ **Cons**

• A climate that isn't often sunny.

■ **Special Tip**

• It's not as well known as mussels and french fries or the list of Belgian beers, but the biannual Zinneke parade (in even years) in Brussels comes close. The parade, which takes its name from the local word for mutts and celebrates Brussels's multiculturalism, brings people together from all walks of life, marching in colorful costumes to music and merriment.

House, the flea market at Marolles, the church of Notre Dame de Sablon, the Royal Art Museum, and the Museum of Modern Art.

Antwerp is notable for Notre Dame Cathedral (Brabantine Gothic, works by Rubens), the Grand Place (city hall, guildhalls), the charming lanes, the port, 17th- and 18th-century facades, Rubens House, the Plantin-Moretus Museum of book printing, and the Royal Museum of Fine Arts, filled with early Flemish art (Van der Weyden, Van Eyck).

Ghent rates highly for its medieval guildhalls along the quays of the Graslei and the Korenlei, Gravensteen Castle, its museums (SMAK, Design Museum, Museum of Fine Arts), and St. Bavo Cathedral with Van Eyck's altar masterpiece, "The Adoration of the Mystic Lamb."

Other cities worth a visit are **Liège,** with its pleasant museums and churches around the Palace of the Prince-Bishops; **Leuven,** where

Gothic architecture (city hall, St. Peter's Church) vies with baroque (Church of St. Michael, guildhalls); **Dinant,** situated between rocks and the Meuse River with its landmark Gothic church of Notre Dame and fortified citadel; **Mons** and its collegiate Church of St. Waltrude and baroque belfry; **Tournai,** with 17th- and 18th-century Notre Dame Cathedral, belfry, and the cloth hall; **Namur** (citadel, St. Aubin Cathedral); **Bouillon** (medieval castle); **Beloeil** (17th-century castle of the princes of Ligne and gardens); and **Arlon** (archaeological museum).

When to Go		
	CENTER AND COAST	ARDENNES REGION
JANUARY		
FEBRUARY		
MARCH		
APRIL		
MAY	☼	
JUNE	☼	☼
JULY	☼	☼
AUGUST	☼	☼
SEPTEMBER	☼	☼
OCTOBER		
NOVEMBER		
DECEMBER		

▶ **COAST**

The **North Sea** is not blue and not often sunny, but it offers great opportunities for water sports. Of the long sandy beaches, the best of all is Knokke-le-Zoute; the rest of the 45 miles of beachfront is more low key.

▶ **FESTIVALS**

The small town of **Binche** is famous for its Carnival days leading up to Mardi Gras, featuring *Gilles,* local men dressed as a sort of court jester, a symbol of the country's sense of humor. Other celebrations include the *kermes,* the holiday fair in each village for the blessing of the church on its anniversary.

▶ **LANDSCAPE**

Belgium's landscape is fairly flat, crossed by tree-lined canals and dikes, such as those surrounding the small town of **Damme.** In the east, the **Ardennes Mountains** are covered by thick forests, and farther north the **High Fens-Eifel** uplands reach far into Germany.

Lake Titicaca is the highest navigable lake in the world—a point of pride in Bolivia.

What to See and Do in Bolivia

▶ **LANDSCAPE**

- Altiplano, Lake Titicaca, Cordillera Real
- The Oriente (Amazon boat excursions)

▶ **CITIES AND VILLAGES**

- Potosí, Sucre, La Paz, Santa Cruz, Cochabamba
- Indian markets, Jesuit missions

▶ **MONUMENTS**

- Colonial architecture, pre-Columbian sites (Tiahuanaco)

▶ **FESTIVALS**

- Indian music, Oruro Carnival

Bolivia lives in the shadow of its neighbor Peru with fewer archaeological sites, but the country bears the stamp of the high plateau, the Altiplano, and of the Andes mountain range and has a well-preserved identity in the indigenous population.

Bolivia

▶ **LANDSCAPE**

Around La Paz and in the southwest, the **Altiplano** defines the rugged landscape at an altitude of 14,000 feet, including the strange salt flats of Uyuni, volcanoes, lakes (the emerald Laguna Verde), geysers, and canyons, as well as the rocky **Valle de la Luna** (Valley of the Moon), with its fairy chimneys. Not far from Sucre, the national park of **Torotoro** is known for its canyons and cave paintings.

Traveler's Notebook

MAIN CONTACTS

Embassy of Bolivia
3014 Massachusetts Avenue, NW
Washington, DC 20008
(202) 483-4410
www.bolivia-usa.org
Embassy of Bolivia
106 Eaton Square
London SW1W 9AD, UK
+ 44 (0) 20 7235 4248

TRAVEL DOCUMENTS

For U.S. Citizens: Passport and visa
For U.K. Citizens: Passport (and visa for stays of more than 90 days)

HEALTH ISSUES

Altitude sickness is a real problem because of a lack of oxygen at high elevations. Limit activities for at least the first 24 hours after arrival. Malaria prophylaxis is essential for the lower elevations, and yellow fever immunization is recommended for elevations below 5,000 feet.

TRAVEL TIME TO DESTINATION & TIME DIFFERENCE

New York to La Paz: 12 hours connecting flight; EST. London to La Paz:

21 hours 15 minutes connecting flight; GMT +5

AVERAGE TRIP COST

$2,500–$3,000/£1,650–£2,000 for three weeks of excursions in connection with Peru

LANGUAGE & CURRENCY

Official languages: Spanish, Quechua, Aymara
Currency: boliviano

POPULATION

Of the 9,119,000 inhabitants, 60 percent are Indians. The Indians of Aymara and the

Quechuas live on the Altiplano. Sucre is the constitutional capital, but La Paz is the seat of government.

RELIGION

Nine out of ten people are Catholic.

FESTIVALS

End of January: Alasitas Fair in La Paz; February 10: Miners Festival in Potosí; Saturday before Ash Wednesday: Carnival in Oruro; February or March: Carnival in La Paz, Santa Cruz, and

Tarabuco (Pujillay); June 21: Winter solstice festival in Tiahuanaco; August 6: National Day; November 2: All Saints' Day

SHOPPING

Handwoven fabrics, alpaca wool sweaters, and souvenirs such as figurines of Pacha Mama (a kind of Mother Earth) are popular items. You can find practically all handicrafts on Calle Sagarnaga in La Paz.

Lake Titicaca is the highest navigable lake on Earth. Legend has it that the "children of the sun" emerged from the lake to found the Inca Empire. Of greatest interest are the Isla del Sol (Island of the Sun) and the Pilkokaina Inca Palace.

East of the lake, the Cordillera Real splits into two massifs, the **Illampu,** 20,892 feet high, and the **Illimani**—at 21,122 feet the second highest mountain in Bolivia—whose three peaks dominate the valley of La Paz.

The country's east, the **Oriente,** is part of the green wilderness of the Amazon Basin. Here you can take boat trips through the jungle or visit pristine Mercado National Park.

▶ CITIES AND VILLAGES

Bolivia is one of the countries in South America where the life and customs of the indigenous population are well preserved. They are especially visible on the high plateaus during festivals and market days, for example, at Tarabuco.

Spain has left deep imprints on the villages and towns, as well, as in **Potosí,** classified as a World Heritage site, whose silver mountain made it the world's richest city in the 16th century and unleashed

endless greed. **Sucre,** a town built entirely of white stone, is dominated by the cathedral and other churches, convents, and the governor's palace.

La Paz is the seat of government and the highest capital city in the world, known for its old town center, craft stalls in Sagarnaga Street, the 16th-century baroque Church of San Francisco, and a rich national museum of art. The city's location in a basin, surrounded by the high Andean peaks, is extraordinarily scenic.

Other cities worth a detour include **Santa Cruz** on the Chaco Plain (cathedral, colonial buildings, Jesuit missions), **Cochabamba** (Santa Teresa church, Capuchin convent), and **Copacabana** on Lake Titicaca.

▶ MONUMENTS

Each colonial city has its churches, its cathedral, and buildings from the time of the Spanish conquest. But a pre-Columbian site, **Tiahuanaco,** the ceremonial center of the Tiwanaku, precursors of the Inca (semisubterranean temple, Gateway of the Sun), is a must for a detour. Two other cities, **Inkallatja,** close to Cochabamba, and **Samaipata,** near Santa Cruz, are Inca sites.

In the east around San Ignacio, you will find a number of old Jesuit missions that are now also classified as World Heritage sites.

▶ FESTIVALS

Bolivians love a celebration. In the evenings, they go to listen to the melancholic folkloric music played on the pan flutes and the *charango* (a kind of mandolin). During Carnival, they have a traditional "devil dance," followed by a colorful parade that may be "well lubricated." **Oruro** is known for the most

famous Carnival in Bolivia. Other celebrations are held in Tarabuco (Pujillay), La Paz, and Santa Cruz.

When to Go		
	ANDES (WEST)	PLAINS AND AMAZON REGION (EAST)
JANUARY	☼	
FEBRUARY		
MARCH		
APRIL		
MAY	☼	
JUNE	☼	⚹
JULY	☼	⚹
AUGUST	☼	⚹
SEPTEMBER	☼	⚹
OCTOBER	☼	⚹
NOVEMBER		⚹
DECEMBER		

Botswana

This country in southern Africa would not be such a tourist favorite if it were not for the Okavango Delta, a unique inland wetland. The game reserves here represent a last Eden in Africa.

▶ LANDSCAPE

As it crosses the Kalahari, the **Okavango River** weakens and spreads to form an interior delta of 23,000 square miles, which is one of the last unspoiled wildlife areas on Earth and thus a major tourist attraction. Hundreds of islands (seasonally home to lions and elephants), canals, and lagoons edged with papyrus and water lilies, offer opportunities for wildlife- and bird-watching (African fish eagles) by dugout canoe. The orange-tinted **Kalahari Desert,** home of the San (also known as Bushmen), is a dry and hostile environment. Traveling the 600 miles of the Trans-Kalahari Highway should only be undertaken with careful planning and guidance by a local San.

▶ NATIONAL PARKS AND WILDLIFE

Botswana's wildlife is among the most diverse and plentiful in Africa. **Chobe National Park** alone harbors some 30,000 elephants, the most of any one park, as well as lions, giraffes, antelopes (springbok), hyenas, and nearly 500 species of birds.

To the east of the park, the marshlands and plains of the **Moremi Game Reserve** along the Okavango

are rich in buffalo, elephants, zebras, giraffes, and kudus. Giraffes, buffalo, lions, and wildebeest can also be found near the Linyanti River and the Savute Channel.

To the south of Chobe at the edge of the sands of the Kalahari, the

What to See and Do in Botswana

▶ **LANDSCAPE**
- Okavango Delta, Kalahari Desert

▶ **NATIONAL PARKS AND WILDLIFE**
- Chobe National Park, Moremi Game Reserve, Kalahari Gemsbok National Park, Makgadikgadi and Nxai salt pans, Mabuasehube and Mashatu Game Reserves
- Elephants, lions, giraffes, antelopes, buffalo, wildebeest, kudus, zebras, springbok, cheetahs, hyenas, leopards, pink flamingos, and other birds

African elephants seek out a water hole at the end of the dry season.

Traveler's Notebook

MAIN CONTACTS
Embassy of the Republic of Botswana
1531–1533 New Hampshire Avenue, NW Washington, DC 20036
(202) 244-4990
www.botswanaembassy.org
www.botswanatourism.co.bw
Botswana High Commission
6 Stratford Place London W1C 1AY, UK
+ 44 (0) 20 7499 0031

TRAVEL DOCUMENTS FOR U.S. & U.K. CITIZENS
Passport

HEALTH ISSUES
Malaria prophylaxis is important, especially from November to June for the following regions: Boteti, Chobe, Ngamiland, Okavango, Tutume.

TRAVEL TIME TO DESTINATION & TIME DIFFERENCE
New York to Gaborone: 18 hours 45 minutes connecting flight; EST +7.

London to Gaborone: 13 hours 20 minutes connecting flight; GMT +2

AVERAGE TRIP COST
$3,000/£2,000 for 12 days on safari

LANGUAGE & CURRENCY
Official language: English; national language: Setswana
Currency: pula

POPULATION
A population of 1,816,000, spread across numerous tribes, including 6,000 Caucasians,

makes for the least densely populated country in the world. Capital: Gaborone

RELIGION
80 percent Christian, followed by animists and a small minority of Muslims

FESTIVALS
July 1: Sir Seretse Khama festival; September 30: National Day

SHOPPING
Baskets, textiles

white salt flats of **Makgadikgadi** and **Nxai** form a unique landscape, supporting giraffes and pink flamingos.

In the country's southwest, in the dunes of the **Kalahari Gemsbok National Park** and the **Mabuasehube Game Reserve,** you can look for antelopes, cheetahs, hyenas, lions, and nearly 200 species of birds.

Along the Limpopo River, the forests and rivers of **Tuli Block Farms** lead to the **Mashatu Game Reserve,** where elephants, lions, and leopards thrive.

Advice

▪ Pros
• African safari, enchanting landscape, rich game reserves, indigenous population. Still rather new, eco-friendly tourism.

▪ Cons
• Rather high cost of travel.

▪ Safety
• Botswana is known as a safe travel destination. The only problem could be a badly planned photo safari.

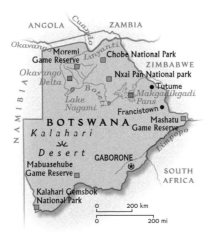

When to Go		
	CLIMATE	NATIONAL PARKS
JANUARY		
FEBRUARY		
MARCH		
APRIL		☻
MAY	☼	☻
JUNE	☼	
JULY	☼	
AUGUST	☼	☻
SEPTEMBER	☼	☻
OCTOBER	☼	☻
NOVEMBER		
DECEMBER		

Brazil

 Carnival in Rio and the beaches of Copacabana are the postcard views of Brazil, masking its multiple other attractions. This lively country also has unparalleled natural treasures to show off (the Amazon region, Iguaçu Falls, the Pantanal), as well as tropical beaches and towns where colonial architecture is well preserved. Brazil's varied forms of tourism, combined with entertainment and folkloric music and dance, make it a preferred destination even for the experienced traveler.

▶ LANDSCAPE

If humankind stops the deforestation of the **Amazon region** in time, it will remain one of the greatest biologically diverse zones on Earth, a riverine labyrinth covering some 50,000 square miles. A journey through the rain forest's "green hell" on the mighty Amazon usually begins at Manaus and winds its way down to the mouth near Belém, where the river becomes a vast estuary and ends in the thousand islands of the **Marajó Island** before it meets the Atlantic. The islands around Marajó attract bird-watchers from around the world and are the latest ecotourism centers.

What to See and Do in Brazil

▶ **LANDSCAPE**

• Amazon region (Amazon River, Marajó Island, Rio Negro)

• Rain forest, Iguaçu Falls, canyons, Pantanal wetlands

▶ **CITIES AND MONUMENTS**

• Rio de Janeiro, Congonhas, Ouro Preto, Parati, Salvador de Bahia, Brasília, Manaus, Belém, Recife, Olinda, São Luís

▶ **COAST**

• Beaches of Copacabana and Ipanema in Rio

• Beaches of the Bay Todos Santos and Itaparica Island near Salvador de Bahia, Angra dos Reis, Ilha Grande

• Northeast (Aracaju, Maceió), the seabed and corals of Fernando de Noronha Archipelago

▶ **CULTURAL HERITAGE**

• Carnival (Rio de Janeiro, Salvador de Bahia, Recife), musical folklore (samba, *forró*)

Rio de Janeiro, its bay, Sugarloaf Mountain, and the statue of Christ the Redeemer combine into one splendid view.

After the rains, the wetlands of the Pantanal sprout giant water lilies.

Traveler's Notebook

MAIN CONTACTS

Embassy of Brazil
3006 Massachu-
setts Avenue, NW
Washington, DC
20008
(202) 238-2805
www.brasilemb.org
www.embratur
.gov.br
Embassy of Brazil
32 Green Street
London W1K 7AT,
UK
+ 44 (0) 20 7399 9000
www.brazil.org.uk

TRAVEL DOCUMENTS

U.S. Citizens: Pass-
port and visa
U.K. Citizens: Pass-
port (and visa for
stays of more than
90 days)

HEALTH ISSUES

Yellow fever immu-
nization is highly
recommended
for travel in rural
areas in the west
of the country, as
well as malaria
prophylaxis.

**TRAVEL TIME TO
DESTINATION & TIME
DIFFERENCE**

New York to Rio de
Janeiro: 10 hours
15 minutes nonstop
flight; EST +1. Lon-
don to Rio: 13 hours
connecting flight;
GMT -4

AVERAGE TRIP COST

$2,000/£1,200
for 12 days of
excursions

**LANGUAGE &
CURRENCY**

Official language:
Portuguese
Currency: real

POPULATION

Of the 190,011,000
inhabitants, 55 per-
cent are Cauca-
sian, 39 percent
of mixed race, and
6 percent black.
Important urban
centers are São
Paulo (16 million)
and Rio de Janeiro
(10 million). Capital:
Brasília

RELIGION

The majority of the
population is Cath-
olic, but an impor-
tant minority follows
macumba rites, orig-
inally from Africa.

FESTIVALS

February or March:
Carnival in Rio,
Salvador de Bahia,
Recife, Olinda;
March or April:
Holy Week; June:
Festa Junina in the
northeast

SHOPPING

A Brazilian ham-
mock makes an
original souvenir.
Other items of inter-
est are baskets,
wooden sculptures,
leather goods, pot-
tery, tagua nut "veg-
etable ivory" jewelry,
musical instruments,
and coconut shell
carvings.

The **Rio Negro** also allows for boating excursions into the jungle starting at Manaus.

At the borders of Argentina and Paraguay, Iguaçu (Iguazú) Falls forms a double curtain of 275 falls across two miles and dwarfs Niagara Falls.

Elsewhere, canyons (chasm and caves of Rio Ribeira, Chapada dos Guimarães National Park), tropical grass plains, and mountains (Cerro do Cipo, Pico de Itabirito in Minas Gerais) offer an ever changing landscape. In the southwest, the marshland of the **Pantanal** constitutes the largest tropical wetlands in the world. In April after the rainy season, it becomes a huge recreation area. More than 600 species of birds (including toucans and jabiru storks) and 250 species of fish, as well as caimans, jaguars, pumas, lynx, and tapirs, make their home there.

▶ CITIES AND MONUMENTS

One of the most famous postcard views in the world is the bay of **Rio de Janeiro,** showing Sugarloaf, Corcovado with its statue of Christ the Redeemer, the beaches of Copacabana and Ipanema, and the skyscrapers in the distance. Rio is also a green city, thanks to its Tijuca National Park and botanical garden.

Vestiges of the different colonial periods can still be found in the towns and villages of the state of Minas Gerais, north of Rio de Janeiro. This state is known for two small towns that are famous for their baroque cityscapes, embellished by sculptor Aleijadinho: **Congonhas** (statues of the prophets, stations of the cross) and **Ouro Preto** (highly decorated 18th-century churches), both World Heritage sites. Baroque art reaches its pinnacle in **Parati,** a city of white houses, old churches, and famous religious festivals, and in **Salvador de Bahia,** the city of 365 churches dating from the 16th through 18th centuries (São Francisco, dos Aflitos, do Carmo, da Boa Viagem). Salvador de Bahia, the city of writer Jorge Amado and musician and politician Gilberto Gil, has a charm that is unrivaled in all of Latin America, thanks to its old town and Pelourinho, the queen of *capoeira,* an art form that combines martial arts moves, music, and dance.

The polar opposite of Salvador de Bahia's retro style is the capital, **Brasília,** with its futuristic cityscape by architect Oscar Niemeyer.

Many cities stand as nostalgic reminders of the wealth of the rubber plantation era (the end of the

The Pantanal Matogrossense National Park harbors thousands of animal and plant species, such as this toucan.

19th and beginning of the 20th centuries). In **Manaus,** for instance, the opera house is a small-scale replica of the Paris Opéra. The town has also an attractive city center and floating market. In **Belém,** the Theatro da Paz compares to La Scala in Milan, whereas the store in the Paris n' America building once dressed the locals in the latest French fashions, and the Ver-o-Peso produce market is unique.

In **Recife,** Brazil's Venice, the rococo-style churches stand out, as do those of the neighboring communities of Nazare and **Olinda.** Farther to the west, **São Luis,** capital of the state of Maranhao, is

When to Go			
	RIO	AMAZON REGION	SALVADOR DE BAHIA AND COAST
JANUARY			
FEBRUARY	☼		☼
MARCH			
APRIL			
MAY			
JUNE			
JULY	☼	☾	
AUGUST	☼	☾	
SEPTEMBER	☼	☾	☼
OCTOBER	☼	☾	☼
NOVEMBER		☾	☼
DECEMBER	☼		☼

Salvador de Bahia, the city with 365 churches

Advice

■ **Pros**
• A great destination that has something for every taste: nature, charming colonial villages, rich traditions, ecotourism. The low cost of travel into the northwest (charter flights to Salvador [Bahia], package tours).

■ **Cons**
• Security concerns in certain quarters of the large cities and in the *favelas,* as the shantytowns are called.

■ **Safety**
• There are always safety warnings about Rio de Janeiro and São Paulo: Don't show off valuable belongings, avoid the favelas, and be generally vigilant, especially in touristy places like Copacabana. These tips should be followed, but Brazil is a huge country, and in the interior, warnings are no more needed than for general travel anywhere.

■ **Special Tip**
• The beach resorts of the northeast, along the coast of Salvador (Bahia), with their modest prices, can rival resorts in Cuba and the Dominican Republic. But will lower prices in Brazil reduce this country to a destination for mass tourism? Many other options exist, for instance, an eco-tour in the wildlife paradise of the Pantanal.

filled with baroque art and boasts a 17th-century cathedral. Not far from there, Lençois Maranhenses National Park spreads out in a surprising succession of sand dunes and lakes.

▶ COAST

Brazil's beaches stretch for thousands of miles. If those of Rio de Janeiro—**Copacabana** and **Ipanema**—have reached celebrity status, those across from Salvador (Bahia), **Bay Todos Santos,** and **Itaparica Island,** bask equally in their tropical beauty and, in some places, their luxury status.

A dozen miles south of Rio, some other beaches have become popular, such as **Angra dos Reis** and those of the beautiful and mountainous **Ilha Grande,** covered by tropical forest.

The idea of a celebration takes on quite a different dimension in Rio during Carnival.

The northeast, Brazil's birthplace, has hundreds of long beaches, including those of **Aracaju** (in the state of Sergipe), **Maceió** (Alagoas), and Natal (Rio Grande do Norte). Like the coast of Salvador de Bahia, this region is upgrading its recreational areas, with luxury establishments along the Costa do Sauipe (four miles of beach).

Divers come to view the great quantity and variety of coral around the **Fernando de Noronha Archipelago,** about 200 miles from the northeast coast. Brazilian authorities recently decided to restrict development for tourism here to help preserve the biodiversity (dolphins, turtles) of these five islands.

▶ CULTURAL HERITAGE

Between the end of January and mid-February, Brazil celebrates Carnival (Carnaval). The famous Carnival in Rio is usually held 40 days before Easter along Avenue Marques de Sapucai, but suffers from tourist onslaught (the parades of the samba schools can be watched from the Sambadrome, but tickets must be reserved far in advance). Salvador de Bahia, Recife, Olinda, and other cities of the northwest challenge Rio with their own unique Carnival celebrations.

Brazilian folk music has been played for nearly five centuries and represents a mixture of native, Portuguese, and African cultures. Brazilians dance not only the samba but also the very sensuous forró from the northwest, accompanied by accordion music.

What to See and Do in Bulgaria

▶ **COAST**

• Beaches of the Black Sea around Varna in the north, the Sun Coast in the south

▶ **MOUNTAINS**

• Rhodope Mountains (Rila, Pririn), Balkan Range, Valley of the Roses (Kazanlak)

▶ **MONUMENTS**

• Orthodox monasteries and churches (Rila, Bachkovo, Troyan)

▶ **CITIES**

• Plovdiv, Sofia, Veliko Tarnovo, Koprivshtitsa, Nesebar, Kazanlak

Rila Monastery in the Rila Mountains exudes serenity in its harmonious lines.

Bulgaria

Although the Black Sea beaches seem to be the main tourist draw, they are far from the most interesting aspects of Bulgaria. The interior hides a seductive country of mountain landscapes and monasteries full of splendid icons and frescoes.

▶ **COAST**

The **Black Sea** coast was long the resort area for the Communist countries of Eastern Europe. But now Bulgaria is a member of the European Union, and if you want to avoid the beaches of the Mediterranean and plan a more affordable European beach vacation, there are hundreds of miles of coastline in Bulgaria with as much sunshine, white sand, warm waters, gentle depths, and spa treatments to rival the Mediterranean haunts.

Resort tourism is quickly developing along the north coast near **Varna,** and on the south coast (the **Sun Coast**).

▶ **MOUNTAINS**

The beautiful Bulgarian mountains have not yet been discovered

Traveler's Notebook

MAIN CONTACTS		TRAVEL TIME TO DESTINATION & TIME DIFFERENCE	POPULATION	FESTIVALS
Embassy of the Republic of Bulgaria 1621 22nd Street, NW Washington, DC 20008 (202) 387-0174 www.bulgaria-embassy.org www.bulgariatravel.org/eng/index.php *Embassy of the Republic of Bulgaria* 186–188 Queen's Gate London SW7 5HL, UK	+ 44 (0) 20 7584 9400 www.bulgarianembassy-london.org **TRAVEL DOCUMENTS FOR U.S. & U.K. CITIZENS** Passport **TRAVEL TIME TO DESTINATION & TIME DIFFERENCE** New York to Sofia:11 hours 25 minutes connecting flight; EST +7.	London to Sofia: 3 hours 5 minutes nonstop; GMT -2 **AVERAGE TRIP COST** $1,300/£800 for a week of excursions **LANGUAGE & CURRENCY** Official language: Bulgarian, written in the Cyrillic alphabet Currency: lev	7,323,000 inhabitants, which includes Turkish and Roma minorities. Capital: Sofia **RELIGION** A quarter of the population is Eastern Orthodox, and there are also Muslim, Catholic, and Protestant minorities.	March 1: Baba Marta (end of winter festival); spring: Orthodox Easter; May: Festival of the Roses in Kazanlak **SHOPPING** Two items are favorites: icons and lace tablecloths

by organized tourism. In the southwest, the **Rhodope Mountains,** and especially **Rila** and **Pirin Mountains** at an altitude of 10,000 feet, attract hikers with their scenic forests, emerald lakes, and limestone crests. In the center, more hiking trails wind through the Stara Planina and Sredna Gora ranges of the **Balkan Mountains** for 370 miles across the length of the country.

In winter, skiing takes over near the small town of **Bansko.**

Between May and June, the **Valley of the Roses,** near Kazanlak, is an endless field of blooms grown for the production of rose oil, which is celebrated each year with a lively festival.

▶ MONUMENTS

Of Bulgaria's famous monasteries, **Rila** is the most prestigious, with its large paved court, wooden tiered galleries, and church with amazing frescoes. Its great iconostasis—the partition, typical of Orthodox churches, of gilded wood and covered with icons, behind which the priests conduct the service—is the most inspiring symbol of Byzantine art.

Bachkovo Monastery, near Plovdiv, is less impressive, but its two churches with frescoes are more typical. **Troyan** Monastery, which

sheltered Vasil Levski, one of the heroes of the Bulgarian resistance against the Turks in the 19th century, is also rich with a beautiful iconostasis and frescoes.

The rock churches of Ivanovo and Boyana complete an architectural heritage of the first order.

▶ CITIES

On the Maritsa River, **Plovdiv's** ancient history goes back to Neolithic times. The city gained status as a Roman colony in the first century. Plovdiv's old quarter looks like an open-air museum, with several 19th-century churches, a museum of ethnology, mosques, a Roman amphitheater, and other Roman ruins.

Sofia, overshadowed by the popular Mount Vitosha, is not the most famous capital in eastern Europe, but it has its charms. The neo-Byzantine Alexander Nevsky Cathedral, with its onion domes, is Sofia's most famous site, but you will be surprised by the great variety

of architectural styles in the city, ranging from clumsy Soviet-style government buildings to beautiful 19th-century facades, seventh-century town walls, numerous churches (St. Nicholas), an impressive synagogue, and Western signage.

Veliko Tarnovo, the ancient Bulgarian capital, ranges over three hills with the old town and Samovodska market, the fortress, and medieval churches. The wooden houses of historic **Koprivshtitsa** merit a special detour. The small coastal town of **Nesebar** was named a World Heritage site thanks to its ruins from antiquity and the Byzantine period (churches, St. Sophia Basilica).

Kazanlak became famous in 1944 when the fourth-century tomb of a Thracian soldier was discovered.

When to Go			
	BLACK SEA	INTERIOR	SKIING IN THE PIRIN MOUNTAINS
JANUARY			❄
FEBRUARY			❄
MARCH			❄
APRIL			
MAY		☼	
JUNE	☼	☼	
JULY	☼	☼	
AUGUST	☼	☼	
SEPTEMBER	☼	☼	
OCTOBER		☼	
NOVEMBER			
DECEMBER			

What to See and Do in Cambodia

▶ **MONUMENTS**

• Temples of Angkor (Angkor Wat, Bayon at Angkor Thom, Ta Prohm, Preah Khan)

• Other Khmer ruins (Banteay Srei, Beng Mealea)

▶ **CAPITAL**

• Phnom Penh

▶ **LANDSCAPE AND COAST**

• Tonle Sap Lake, Ratanakiri, Sihanoukville

The Angkor Wat temple complex represents the best of ancient Khmer art.

Cambodia

With peace finally restored, Cambodia is embraced by growing crowds of tourists who want to visit the temples of Angkor, which have survived war and pillage and the ravages of time. Besides Angkor, travelers should not forget about other historic Khmer sites and the special ambiance of Phnom Penh, as well as the countryside.

Traveler's Notebook

MAIN CONTACTS
Royal Embassy of Cambodia
4530 16th Street, NW
Washington, DC 20011
(202) 726-7742
www.embassyof
cambodia.org
www.tourism
cambodia.com
Royal Embassy of Cambodia
64 Brondesbury Park
Willesden Green
London NW6 7AT, UK
+ 44 (0) 20 8451 7850
www.cambodian
embassy.org.uk

TRAVEL DOCUMENTS FOR U.S. & U.K. CITIZENS
Passport and visa

HEALTH ISSUES
Vaccinations are not necessary, but malaria prophylaxis is recommended.

TRAVEL TIME TO DESTINATION & TIME DIFFERENCE
New York to Phnom Penh: 20 hours 25 minutes connecting flight; EST +11. London to Phnom Penh: 14 hours 10 minutes connecting; GMT -6

AVERAGE TRIP COST
$2,540–$3,175/ £1,640–£2,010 for 15 days in combination with Vietnam

LANGUAGE & CURRENCY
Official language: Khmer
Currency: riel

POPULATION
The majority of the 13,996,000 inhabitants (90 percent are Khmer) live in rural areas. Capital: Phnom Penh

RELIGION
90 percent Buddhists

FESTIVALS
Beginning of April: Khmer New Year; November: Reversal of the Waters Festival on Tonle Sap Lake; November 9: National Day

SHOPPING
Locals wear traditional sarongs (long skirts) that can be attractive. There are also silk scarves, gems, silver jewelry, and baskets.

▶ MONUMENTS

The archaeological sites of **Angkor,** the ancient capital of the Khmer Empire, built between the 8th and 16th centuries, are some of the most visited tourist destinations in the world. The temples, a mixture of Hindu and Buddhist, are spread out in the jungle. The elegantly constructed royal temples, called "temple-mountains," are the most famous ones. **Angkor Wat,** with its five towers in a cross-in-square plan, its galleries, and its bas-reliefs, is the most representative example of Khmer architecture. Another extraordinary example is **Bayon** temple, which has sculptures of dozens of mysterious faces and numerous sanctuary towers and bas-reliefs. Bayon stands at the center of the ancient capital Angkor Thom, the city of the gods of the Buddhist cosmology, and rivals the earlier Paphoun temple there and the royal palace.

Other sights near Angkor include the jungle-covered **Ta Prohm, Preah Kahn,** the Ruluos group, and, away from the main group of temples, **Banteay Srei,** built on a smaller scale. A longer excursion includes **Beng Mealea,** the holy mountain of Phnom Kulen, with a causeway flanked by nagas. Each site has its distinctive character.

Although the Angkor temples would be the main focus of a trip, travelers should not forget such sites as Preah Vihear, which is accessible only from Thailand. The old capital Oudong, north of Phnom Penh, and the sanctuaries of Phnom Chisor and Phnom Da to the south are worth a visit, as well.

▶ CAPITAL

After long years of war and political strife, a period that has been

memorialized in the Killing Fields sanctuary, **Phnom Penh,** which at one time was known as the "Paris of the East," is being reborn on its site at the junction of the Mekong River and the Tonle Sap. Don't overlook the Vat Phnom sanctuary with the silver pagoda, the emerald and gold Buddhas in the royal palace, the colonial facades of the cityscape, the markets (central market, Russian market), and the National Museum of Fine Arts (Buddha collection, artifacts from Angkor).

▶ LANDSCAPE AND COAST

Tonle Sap Lake, south of Angkor, is unusual in that it begins to flood in June during monsoon season and changes the direction of its flow. Fishermen catch a bountiful harvest, and at the end of November, to celebrate the abundance, a great festival takes place with boat races and offerings made to the river.

The regions east of the lake, covered in bamboo forests, waterfalls, and red earth, were long inaccessible, but can now be visited, allowing for meetings with ethnic minorities, for example, at **Ratanakiri** near the Vietnamese border.

Tourists are beginning to discover the fishing villages on the coast of the Gulf of Thailand, where **Sihanoukville** and its laid-back beaches make for a popular area.

Advice

▪ Pros

• The temples of Angkor, one of the great archaeological sites in the world.
• A country that has become safe again, with a variety of tourist attractions.

▪ Cons

• The too-rapid development of tourism, which takes away some of Angkor's magic. The best season for travel is outside school vacations in the Western world. The continued presence of land mines in rural and isolated areas.

▪ Safety

• Adventurers must absolutely stay on the marked roads (there is a risk of land mines elsewhere). Follow advice from local travel agencies, and accept the presence of a guide to certain sites.

▪ Cultural Notes

• Southeast Asia has its unique rules: For example, take your shoes off at the entrance of a temple, and do not touch the head of a child. Play it cool. It's helpful to remember that Cambodians have undergone great traumas in recent history.
• Export of antiquities is forbidden, to discourage organized pillaging.

When to Go		
	ANGKOR	CLIMATE
JANUARY	‹	☼
FEBRUARY	‹	☼
MARCH	‹	☼
APRIL	‹	☼
MAY		
JUNE		
JULY		
AUGUST		
SEPTEMBER		
OCTOBER		
NOVEMBER	‹	☼
DECEMBER	‹	☼

Canada

 In Canada, nature is spelled with a capital N. Nature here is endless, mountainous, glacial, full of lakes, sometimes deserted (in the plains), sometimes crowded (around Niagara Falls). Canada's vastness can be explored in summer by all kinds of transportation, but in winter some places can be reached only by snowmobile or dogsled. Quebec, the French-speaking province, often seems like a slice of Europe.

What to See and Do in Western Canada

▶ LANDSCAPE

- Rocky Mountains (canyons, glacial lakes, waterfalls, Banff and Jasper National Parks), the Badlands
- Coasts: Vancouver Island (Douglas fir), fjords, archipelagos
- Glaciers, icebergs, boreal forests, lakes, canyons of the South Nahanni River, Mackenzie Delta
- Sites of the Klondike gold rush

▶ WILDLIFE

- Bears, bighorn sheep, elk, bison, gray whales, orcas, dolphins
- Dinosaur park

▶ CITIES

- Victoria, Vancouver, Edmonton

The West

British Columbia, Alberta, the Yukon, the Northwest Territories

▶ LANDSCAPE

One of the favorite ways to see the Canadian west is via the Trans-Canadian Railway, which connects Vancouver to Montreal across a region of ranchland dominated by the **Canadian Rockies** with striking vistas of Banff and Jasper National Parks. These parks are connected by a great ice field and glacier trail, which you can hike in summer and ski in winter.

Banff National Park owes its famed beauty mainly to Lakes Louise and Moraine. With luck, you may encounter brown bears, grizzlies, and wolves there. **Jasper National Park** is dominated by Mount Whistler and the Athabasca glacier (ice arches, crevasses, serac columns of icefalls), and Maligne and Medicine Lakes, where you will also find grizzlies, elk, caribou, and beavers.

Other sites include Fraser Canyon; Spectrum Range, with its brilliant colors; Hunlen Falls in Tweedsmuir South Provincial Park; and the many waterfalls of the Murtle River in Wells Gray Provincial Park.

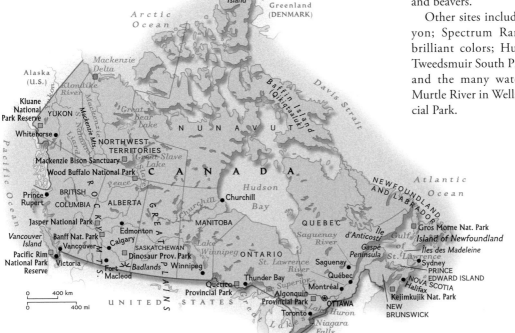

A typical scene in Canada's west: boreal forests, a lake, boats, and the ever present Rockies in the background

One curiosity in the **Badlands,** in the Red Deer River Valley southeast of Alberta, is the hoodoos, also called "fairy chimneys"—thin spires of rock shaped by the unceasing wind.

The islands and fjords of the Pacific coast are as famous as they are hard to reach. In Cathedral Grove on **Vancouver Island,** giant Douglas firs grow up to 230 feet high and are more than 700 years old. Glaciers, icebergs, boreal forests, large national parks (Wood Buffalo National Park in Alberta and the Northwest Territories with a thousand wild buffaloes; Kluane Park in the Yukon), and vast lakes (Great Bear Lake, Great Slave Lake) characterize this region, the largest and coldest of the country.

For a long time, the Northwest Territories did not see many tourists, but it is beginning to develop several attractions such as the "meeting of the trappers festival," ice-field hikes, wildlife tours (Mackenzie Bison Sanctuary), and fishing in the numerous rivers. The region also offers countless hiking trails and excursions by kayak and ski.

After having traveled down the slopes of Mount Mackenzie, the **South Nahanni River** forms three canyons to delight kayakers. Wildlife (grizzlies and other brown bears) is plentiful here, as are waterfalls (Virginia) and hot springs—the one at Rabbitkettle Lake has created tufa mounds similar to those of Pamukkale in Turkey. The South Nahanni River is a major tributary to the Liard River, which joins the **Mackenzie River** and flows north into the Arctic Ocean.

Thrill seekers can pan for gold in the Klondike River of the Yukon, where the famous gold rush took place at the turn of the 20th century in Dawson, Carcross, and Whitehorse.

▶ WILDLIFE

You may very well come face-to-face with brown bears, bighorn sheep, moose, and elk in the Canadian Rockies.

In Alberta, large herds of buffalo live in the national parks and reserves.

The latest attraction in Fort Macleod is the Museum of the North West Mounted Police.

Along the south coast of Vancouver Island, at Pacific Rim National Park Reserve, you can spot gray whales (in March and April), orcas, and dolphins.

Southeast of Calgary, Dinosaur Provincial Park, a UNESCO World Heritage site, exhibits fossils of some 40 dinosaur species.

▶ CITIES

The city of **Victoria,** capital of British Columbia, located on Vancouver Island, bears a very British imprint. By contrast, its Royal British Columbia Museum displays the history of the indigenous people of the west coast.

Cosmopolitan **Vancouver** is famous for its bay, its fjords, its long Seawall Promenade, and Stanley Park. An aquarium (orcas and beluga whales) and the Museum of Anthropology are city highlights.

Edmonton, with its large commercial center, boasts some 70 museums. The Native Culture Exhibit in the Royal Alberta Museum is among the leading destinations.

Calgary, located in the foothills of the Rockies, is a destination for winter sports and ecotourism.

Traveler's Notebook

MAIN CONTACTS
Embassy of Canada
501 Pennsylvania Avenue, NW
Washington, DC 20001
(202) 682-1740
www.canada international.gc.ca
www.canada.travel/
High Commission of Canada
Macdonald House
1 Grosvenor Square
London W1K 4AB, UK
+ 44 (0) 20 7258 6600
www.london.gc.ca

TRAVEL DOCUMENTS FOR U.S. & U.K. CITIZENS
Passport

HEALTH ISSUES
No problems, except protection against the cold in the north

TRAVEL TIME TO DESTINATION & TIME DIFFERENCE
New York to Montreal: 1 hour 30 minutes nonstop flight; EST; to Vancouver: 5 hours 50 minutes nonstop flight; EST –3. London to Montreal: 7 hours

nonstop flight; GMT –5. London to Vancouver: 9 hours 30 minutes nonstop flight; GMT -8

AVERAGE TRIP COST
$1,905/£1,230 for a week of multiple snow activities

LANGUAGE & CURRENCY
Official languages: English (62 percent), French (25 percent, spoken primarily in Quebec province, but also in Ontario and New Brunswick)
Currency: Canadian dollar

POPULATION
33,390,000 inhabitants, including 700,000 indigenous people (First Nations), a modest population density despite a long-sustained open-door policy for immigrants. Capital: Ottawa

RELIGION
Catholic: 46 percent; Protestant: 41 percent; almost all other religions represented

FESTIVALS
February: Carnival in

Quebec and Chicoutimi; July: Montreal Jazz Festival, and the Stampede in Calgary

SHOPPING
Most craft items are Indian-made: masks, fabrics, jewelry. And don't forget the maple syrup.

Besides its harbor, Vancouver is well known for its bay, its fjords, and Stanley Park.

The Prairies

Saskatchewan, Manitoba

▶ LANDSCAPE AND WILDLIFE

Two words describe this central region: wheat and wind. Wheat fields spread out endlessly on the horizon, and lacking obstacles along the way, the wind blows freely. The region features numerous rivers and waterfalls, as well as wildlife (beavers, moose) and **Lake Winnipeg** (fishing and canoeing). During the ten-day Festival du Voyageur in February, Winnipeg, the capital of Manitoba, celebrates with snow sculptures, dogsled races, and musical entertainment in the French quarter, St.-Boniface. The Manitoba Museum focuses on human and natural history.

Boreal forests stretch along the north-flowing rivers, such as the Churchill, which spreads out into lakes and falls until it reaches the township of Churchill on **Hudson Bay.** This town is famous for the many polar bears that make their way to the shore in autumn, waiting for the water to freeze so they can hunt for seals. How long will this spectacle repeat itself? Global warming has many people wondering.

What to See and Do in the Canadian Prairies

▶ LANDSCAPE AND WILDLIFE

- Great Plains, rivers, tundra, forests
- Lake Winnipeg, Hudson Bay
- Beluga whales, beavers, polar bears, Arctic foxes

When to Go			
	CLIMATE	WINTER SPORTS	MONTREAL AND QUEBEC
JANUARY		❄	
FEBRUARY		❄	
MARCH		❄	
APRIL			
MAY			
JUNE			
JULY			☼
AUGUST	☼		☼
SEPTEMBER	☼		☼
OCTOBER	☼		☼
NOVEMBER		❄	
DECEMBER		❄	

The Inuit have achieved independence for Nunavut as a federal territory of Canada.

The East

Nunavut, Ontario

▶ LANDSCAPE

Travelers in search of new horizons will find them in the tundra and frozen landscape of **Nunavut,** a federal territory of Canada since 1999. Comprising 750,000 square miles of land and 62,000 square miles of water, it is home to a population of about 25,000 Inuits. The people live between tradition and modern life—though the continuation of their traditional ways is in doubt as more and more ice melts in the Arctic.

Since becoming autonomous, Nunavut, host to caribou and polar bears, has seen a tourist miniboom of snowmobilers, dogsledders, cross-country skiers (especially on **Qikiqtaaluk,** formerly Baffin Island), and in summer, sea kayakers.

The best views of **Niagara Falls** lie on the Canadian side, 75 miles southeast of Toronto in Ontario; the falls have long been a favorite destination for honeymooners.

The region's parks are a point of pride and include **Algonquin Provincial Park,** near Whitney, and the large wilderness of **Quetico Provincial Park** in the **Great Lakes** region, adjacent to the Boundary Waters Canoe Area wilderness on the U.S. side. Lake Huron is renowned for its scenery and, besides beaches, shore excursions, and scuba diving (on the Bruce Peninsula), offers opportunities for hiking, climbing, and mountaineering. Large Manitoulin Island separates the North Channel and Georgian Bay from Lake Huron and is home to the Ojibwe Cultural Foundation, where powwows and other Native festivals are held in the summer. On the western arm of Lake Superior, west of Thunder Bay, Sibley Provincial Park and Kakabeka Falls are the most interesting sites in this part of Ontario.

▶ CITIES

The lively city of **Toronto** has great museums (Royal Ontario Museum, Air and Space Museum, Bata Shoe Museum) and modern architecture (1,815-foot-tall CN Tower) and represents Montreal's great rival.

What to See and Do in Eastern Canada

▶ **LANDSCAPE**

• Tundra and frozen landscapes of Nunavut

• Qikiqtaaluk (Nordic skiing)

• Niagara Falls

• Algonquin Provincial Park, Quetico Provincial Park, Great Lakes

▶ **CITIES**

• Toronto, Ottawa

By contrast, **Ottawa,** the national capital, makes few waves, despite its good museums (Museum of Fine Arts, Museum of Canadian Civilization); the Rideau Canal, which becomes the world's greatest skating rink in winter; and the biennial International Chamber Music Festival.

A female moose and her calf stride along the water's edge in Algonquin Provincial Park in Ontario.

Behind Montreal's modern skyline hide charming older neighborhoods.

Quebec

▶ LANDSCAPE AND WILDLIFE

French-speaking Quebec (Québec) is Canada's largest province. Much like elsewhere in Canada, nature here is still pristine, with the sugar maples a point of pride. When the leaves turn red in the fall, the magnificent Indian summer—although brief (end of September to the beginning of October)—takes over.

The valleys perpendicular to the St. Lawrence River are covered in pine trees and strewn with rivers, waterfalls, and lakes where nature lovers enjoy kayaking or exploring by canoe. In the spring, travelers can participate in collecting maple sap and boiling it—"sugaring off"—at a sugar shack, besides indulging in the many maple syrup festivals.

Favored destinations include the lakes (St.-Jean), the waterfalls (Montmorency, Ste.-Anne), steep cliffs (Malbaie River), and rivers (the **St. Lawrence,** economic lifeline of the province, and its tributary the **Saguenay,** which has carved a deep fjord). Between the city of Quebec and the Saguenay, the Charlevoix region has been designated an international biosphere reserve and is much like **Mont Tremblant National Park** northwest of Montreal—a concentration of all the best attributes of the province.

On the **Gaspé Peninsula,** Percé Rock with its natural arch, the last outcrop of the Appalachian

Mountains, is one of Quebec's famous vacation spots and, together with Gaspésie and Forillon National Parks, a hiker's paradise. In Gaspésie, you will find herds of white-tailed deer, caribou (migration in June is a great spectacle), and moose.

In the Gulf of St. Lawrence, the **Madeleine Islands** have been eroded by the winds, which keeps vegetation at a minimum, but that doesn't affect marine life (seals and their pups). Blue, fin, sperm, and beluga whales populate the St. Lawrence estuary, especially in Tadoussac Bay from April to October. Beavers and moose are common along the river in the spring.

Bonaventure Island is a migratory bird sanctuary, hosting flocks of gannets, cormorants, puffins, and gulls from April to November. A wealth of fossils exists in Miguasha National Park, including some 9,000 specimens of fossil fish and plants dating from 365 million years ago.

The forests and rivers of **Anticosti Island** at the outlet of the St. Lawrence River shelter white-tailed deer, moose, beavers, gannets, and Atlantic salmon.

▶ WINTER ACTIVITIES

Quebec has the rightful reputation as a recreational laboratory for winter sports (22,000 miles of groomed ski trails). Activities include tours by snowmobile (with overnight sheltering), dogsleds, snowshoe hikes, or a ride down a snowy slope by Zodiac.

Alpine skiing and cross-country skiing are practically birthrights at Mont-Ste.-Anne, Outaouais, Lac Beauport, and the Laurentians. Other sports include ice fishing (Lake St.-Pierre, Lake of Two Mountains, Saguenay Fjord).

▶ CITIES

Montreal (Montréal), wedged along the St. Lawrence River, is the second largest French-speaking city in the world. It is known for its redbrick Victorian cityscape—Jacques Cartier Bridge, the Old Port, and streets leading up to the Plateau Mont Royal neighborhood—the liveliness of the old quarter, its cultural offerings (Museum of Fine Arts, its important international jazz festival in July), its parks (Mont Royal Park, botanic gardens), its flair (recently named a UNESCO City of Design), and its churches and monasteries (Notre Dame and St.-Sulpice).

The lower town and historic Petit Champlain district of **Quebec** exude the most European style in North America, even if the general impressions are of the St. Lawrence River, the Château Frontenac, or the Plains of Abraham battlefield.

▶ FESTIVALS

At the end of January and beginning of February, the cities of Quebec and Chicoutimi celebrate Carnival with canoe races and ice sculpture competitions.

More ancient traditions bring other visitors to the north coast of Quebec and the borders of Ontario for meetings of the First Nations peoples.

Quebec has many cold-weather activities to offer, ranging from snowshoe hikes to snowmobile tours.

What to See and Do in the Atlantic Provinces

▶ **LANDSCAPE AND WILDLIFE**

• Coasts of New Brunswick, Prince Edward Island, Labrador

• National parks (Kejimkujik, Gros Morne), forests, Indian summer

• Whales, puffins, terns

▶ **CULTURAL HERITAGE**

• Acadians (Nova Scotia, New Brunswick, Prince Edward Island, Newfoundland)

Indian summer in the Atlantic provinces allows red maples to show off.

Atlantic Provinces

New Brunswick, Nova Scotia, Prince Edward Island, Newfoundland, Labrador

▶ LANDSCAPE AND WILDLIFE

The landscape of the Atlantic provinces practically seduces a visitor into roaming, stopping in little fishing ports where cod and lobster are plentiful.

Destinations include the national parks of Kouchibouguac and Fundy and the Fundy Trail Parkway in **New Brunswick.** In the Bay of Fundy, right whales, terns, and puffins can be sighted during the summer. In Nova Scotia, **Kejimkujik National Park** and the cities of Halifax and Sydney (17th-century fortress) give this region a special cachet. And **Prince Edward Island,**

The simple architecture and colors of the small port of Lunenburg in Nova Scotia are representative of the coastal towns.

setting of the children's book *Anne of Green Gables,* offers clean beaches and acres of lush farmland.

In New Brunswick and Nova Scotia, Indian summer goes full blast, as maple and red spruce mix their colors with those of balsam fir and yellow birch in the large forests along the St.-Jean River.

The northeast coast of **Labrador** is known for its fjords, cliffs, waterfalls, and marine wildlife. In the summer, cruise ships line up along its length.

Newfoundland's tundra, peat bogs, and **Gros Morne National Park** do not draw great crowds, but its fishing boats still go after cod and herring as they have ever since the first French settlers arrived here in the 16th century.

▶ CULTURAL HERITAGE

Some 350,000 French-speaking Acadians still live in Nova Scotia, parts of New Brunswick, Prince Edward Island, and Newfoundland, where their ancestors lived before they were driven out by the British in the 18th century.

Advice

■ **Pros**

• Like a breath of fresh air, the largely unspoiled Canadian countryside presents a nature lover's escape. A country that is frequently visited by tour groups but can easily be explored on one's own.

■ **Cons**

• The west and the Rockies are more expensive than Quebec.

■ **Recommendation**

• On the Indian reservations, don't confuse folklore with the realities of life.

■ **Special Tip**

• Train travel may be old hat to some people, but the Toronto-to-Vancouver train (the Canadian), traveling for three days and two nights to the west coast, lets you see the breadth of the country. Other routes are also worthwhile, such as Jasper to Prince Rupert in the Rockies or Winnipeg to Churchill, where with luck passengers can watch polar bears from the safety of the train.

Colorful houses line a street in the Cape Verde Islands, which once were ruled by Portugal.

This isolated archipelago in the Atlantic Ocean is seeing an increase in ecotourism on Santo Antão Island. Surfers and windsurfers will find the conditions just right.

Cape Verde

▶ LANDSCAPE

Santo Antão, the westernmost of the archipelago's ten islands, is also the most picturesque. *Ribeiras,* or small streams, and canyons cross the northern parts, where the land is terraced for agriculture. A system of coastal trails around Ribeira Grande (Ribeira do Paul and Figueiral), traditional sugarcane plantations, and diverse flora enhance a stunning landscape that may flourish under well-managed ecotourism.

On **Fogo Island,** the São Felipe Volcano is a highlight for backpackers. Elsewhere, the landscape changes from a rather dry land to luxuriant vegetation, for example, on **São Vicente Island,** home of the port city Mindelo with 96 percent of the island's population.

Trails for hiking or biking are becoming more and more accessible.

▶ COASTS

The idea of a paradise of seaside resorts, which could be expected from Cape Verde's location off the western coast of Africa, doesn't quite pan out. Santa Maria on **Sal Island** is the exception. Here, long, white, sandy beaches invite travelers to relax, whereas the others have mostly black volcanic sand. Even so, the trade winds encourage a variety of other recreational activities. Windsurfing takes precedence around Santa Maria, Boa Vista, **Santiago** (Praia), and São Vicente. And windsurfing by funboard is popular in the Bay of Sal Rei.

Traveler's Notebook

MAIN CONTACTS

Embassy of Cape Verde
3415 Massachusetts Avenue, NW
Washington, DC 20007
(202) 965-6820
www.virtualcape verde.net

Cape Verde Bureau
214 Smithdown Road
Watertree
Liverpool, L15 3JT, UK
+ 44 (0) 7935 091 509
www.capeverde bureau.com
Cape Verdean Ambassador to the United Kingdom
Avenue Jeanne 29
1050 Bruxelles
Belgium
+ 32 (0) 2 643 62 70

TRAVEL DOCUMENTS FOR U.S. & U.K. CITIZENS
Passport and visa

HEALTH ISSUES
Immunization against yellow fever is recommended; malaria prophylaxis for Santiago Island

TRAVEL TIME TO DESTINATION & TIME DIFFERENCE
New York to Sal Island: 21 hours 25 minutes connecting flight; EST +4. London to Sal Island: 7 hours 50 minutes connecting flight; GMT -1

AVERAGE TRIP COST
$1,651/£1,066 for a week of hiking

LANGUAGE & CURRENCY
Official language: Portuguese, but Cape Verdean Creole is becoming more prominent
Currency: escudo

POPULATION
Of the 423,600 inhabitants, 70 percent are of mixed race. A high percentage of the population has immigrated to Portugal, other European countries, Brazil, or the United States.
Capital: Praia

RELIGION
Catholic: 90 percent

FESTIVALS
February: Carnival in Mindelo (São Vicente); end of April: Flag Festival in Fogo; May 3-4: Abolition Festival; July 5: Independence Day; end of August: Music Festival in the Baia dos Gatos (São Vincente); September 12: National Day

SHOPPING
Textiles (embroidery) and objects made from shells. In Mindelo, take your time finding the best *morna* CDs.

Advice

■ Pros
• This group of islands is still in the early stages of tourism, but there is room for travelers to make their own discoveries. A perfect spot for surfers and windsurfers.

■ Cons
• Expensive flights and tours. The beaches are not suitable for family vacations because of the strong currents and few sandy beaches.

■ Safety
• At night, lone travelers should beware of muggers in places such as Praia or Mindelo. For swimmers and windsurfers, it's important not to venture too far from the coast, as the waves and currents are very strong at this latitude.

■ Special Tips
• Funboarding, windsurfing, and kitesurfing are the hot new sports in Cape Verde.
• For an evening of morna music, go to a nightclub in Mindelo.

From Sal, divers strike out to look for tuna, manta rays, hammerhead sharks, and multicolored fish above the coral reefs. Charters for deep-sea fishing (marlin, tuna) and hand-line fishing are starting up around Sao Nicolau.

No matter how experienced they are, fishers, divers, and swimmers must know that the Atlantic waters are strong and dangerous in these latitudes, especially when the trade winds blow.

▶ **CULTURAL HERITAGE**

When people hear of Cape Verde, some will immediately think of Cesaria Evora, "the barefoot diva" and an internationally known singer of *morna,* the distinctive Cape Verdean music and dance genre, expressing love and sadness, exile and poverty, and remembrance of past slavery.

The city of **Mindelo** in its pretty bay with gaily painted houses lets people forget all their cares during Carnival in February. On the other side of the island, the festival of the Baia das Gatas brings the major musicians of the country together in August.

Santo Antão
São Vicente
Mindelo
São Nicolau
Sal
Santa Maria
Atlantic Ocean
Sal Rei
Boa Vista
CAPE VERDE
Maio
Santiago
Sao Filipe
Fogo
⊕PRAIA

0 100 km
0 100 mi

When to Go		
	CLIMATE	SURFING AND WIND SURFING
JANUARY	☼	✔
FEBRUARY	☼	✔
MARCH	☼	
APRIL	☼	
MAY	☼	
JUNE		
JULY		
AUGUST		
SEPTEMBER		
OCTOBER	☼	
NOVEMBER	☼	
DECEMBER	☼	✔

Is there any desert more barren or drier than, and yet as colorful as, the Atacama?

Chile

 Chile's long, narrow extent is becoming a popular tourist destination for its scenery, architectural heritage, the Andes, its wildlife, and, far off the coast, the statues of Easter Island.

▶ LANDSCAPES AND EXCURSIONS

The Chilean landscape seems endless, stretching from north to south in a thin band that is bordered in the east by the **Andes.** Popular destinations include:

• The high-altitude **Chungara Lake,** which is ringed by several volcanoes, and **Lauca National Park**

Traveler's Notebook

MAIN CONTACTS

Embassy of Chile
1732 Massachusetts Avenue, NW
Washington, DC 20036
(202) 785-1746
www.chile-usa.org
Embassy of Chile
37–41 Old Queen Street
London SW1H 9JA, UK
+ 44 (0) 20 7222 2361
http://chileabroad.gov.cl/reino-unido/en

TRAVEL DOCUMENTS FOR U.S. & U.K. CITIZENS
Passport

HEALTH ISSUES
No problems, except for possible altitude sickness in the mountains

TRAVEL TIME TO DESTINATION & TIME DIFFERENCE
New York to Santiago: 10 hours 50 minutes

nonstop flight; EST +1. London to Santiago: 16 hours 15 minutes connecting flight; GMT -4

AVERAGE TRIP COST
$3,810/£2,460 for 15 days

LANGUAGE & CURRENCY
Official language: Spanish
Currency: Chilean peso

POPULATION
Of the 16,285,000 inhabitants, 52 percent are of European descent, 44 percent of mixed race. Capital: Santiago

RELIGION
Four out of five Chileans are Catholic.

FESTIVALS
May 21: Navy Day; first Monday in September:

National Unity Day; September 18: Independence Day; December: Fiesta Grande honoring the Virgin in Andacollo

SHOPPING
Textiles (ponchos, blankets, alpaca wool), silver jewelry, baskets

• The **Atacama Desert,** the driest place on Earth, with its portal at San Pedro de Atacama, followed in succession by salt flats (Salar de Atacama and Ramsar Site Salar de Surire), *lagunas* (Miscanti and Miniques), the Tatio geysers, and north of Calama, the open-pit copper mine Chuquicamata

• The vineyards and "wine route" in the central part of the country

• Osorno, Minchinmávida, and Corcovado volcanoes

• The blindingly blue **San Rafael glacier,** which calves into Laguna San Rafael

• **Torres del Paine National Park,** with its aquamarine lakes and towering granite walls

• **Tierra del Fuego** and the fjords of **Patagonia,** with nothing but wind, rain, sharp peaks, and a tumble of rocks, which together make for unforgettable scenery

Most of these sites lend themselves to numerous excursions, although some become rather challenging because of the altitude and are better left for experienced mountaineers.

▶ **FAUNA AND FLORA**

Chile protects its wildlife in some 30 national parks and as many reserves. Llamas and alpacas graze in Lauca National Park, as well as endangered species such as the wild vicuña and chinchilla. Pink flamingos are sheltered in the salt flats of the Atacama, guanacos and pumas in Torres del Paine, and condors and eagles in the Cordillera. Seals, penguins, and elephant seals play in the fjords of Laguna San Rafael.

The unique Araucania, southeast of Concepción, is a forest region with dense stands of South American trees, including the long-lived monkey puzzle tree (*Araucaria araucana*).

▶ **MONUMENTS AND CITIES**

On **Easter Island,** or Rapa Nui, giant statues carved from the tufa of the extinct Rano-Raraku volcano were erected by a Polynesian population some 1,500 years ago and still

When to Go			
	NORTH	CENTER	SOUTH
JANUARY	☼	☼	☼
FEBRUARY	☼	☼	☼
MARCH	☼	☼	
APRIL		☼	
MAY			
JUNE			
JULY			
AUGUST			
SEPTEMBER		☼	
OCTOBER		☼	☼
NOVEMBER		☼	☼
DECEMBER	☼	☼	☼

haven't revealed the secrets of their construction and purpose.

Chile has numerous old painted wood churches, for example, in San Pedro de Atacama and in **Chiloé,** where the houses are built on stilts.

In the port of **Valparaíso,** the colorful houses stretch higgledy-piggledy up the hills. In **Santiago,** the disheveled modern city presents only the historic La Moneda (the mint) along with the National Museum of Natural History, Fine Arts Museum, and Museum of Pre-Columbian Art as vestiges of an earlier time.

▶ **COAST**

There are only a few modest beaches around **Arica** in the north and at **Viña del Mar.** The black rock of **Cape Horn** marks the end of the South American continent and stands witness to heroic voyages of exploration both true and legendary.

China

In the majestic mountains along the Silk Road, shepherds of Xinjiang encounter the occasional backpacker and hiker.

When Chinese authorities decided to open their borders to travelers in the 1980s, they saw a crush of people avid to see the storied sites: the Forbidden City, the Great Wall, the remnants of the Silk Road, and Lhasa in Tibet. Today, tourists travel as casually to Beijing as they would to Paris, and the Middle Kingdom, as the country is officially called, has become a favorite destination. This large country can be explored by the individual traveler as well as by a group tour.

What to See in the North and Northwest of China

▶ **CITIES**

• Stops along the Silk Road: Xi'an, Binglingsi, Lanzhou, Dunhuang, Mogao, Urumqi, Turpan, Kashi

▶ **LANDSCAPE AND EXCURSIONS**

• Trekking in the deserts (Taklimakan, Dzungarian Basin), Tian Shan mountains

The North and Northwest

Gansu, Xinjiang

▶ CITIES AND SIGHTS

The **Silk Road,** the trade route from Orient to Occident, leading from the ancient capital of **Xi'an** to the Mediterranean, has achieved legendary status.

The first section, beginning at Xi'an, takes you past the Buddhist grottoes of **Binglingsi,** filled with sculptures and frescoes, followed by the industrial city of **Lanzhou,** capital of Gansu province, and **Dunhuang,** the most important crossroads of the Silk Road. Nearby are the 492 Caves of the Thousand Buddhas at **Mogao** with some of the finest examples of Buddhist art.

In the next section, **Urumqi,** the capital of Xinjiang, is a bastion of Chinese Islam, as its 20 mosques can attest. The **Turpan Depression,** an oasis west of the mountains of the Gobi desert, shelters the

Far from Beijing, the Uygurs of Xinjian let grapes dry in the sun.

ruins of the ancient imperial city of Gaoshang. **Kashi** in the foothills of the Pamir Mountains has the largest mosque in the country (Id Kah) and is the last station on the Chinese Silk Road.

▶ **LANDSCAPE AND EXCURSIONS**
Many writers have extolled the adventure of trekking across the **Taklimakan Desert;** it is arduous travel but the experience of a lifetime. The **Dzungarian Basin** stretches along the borders of Siberia and Mongolia.

Between these two deserts rise the **Tian Shan**, a range of mountains bordered by several oases, which were important stops for Silk Road traders.

Traveler's Notebook

MAIN CONTACTS
Embassy of the People's Republic of China
3505 International Place, NW
Washington, DC 20008
(202) 495-2266
www.china-embassy.org/eng/
www.tourismchina.org
Embassy of the People's Republic of China
49 Portland Place
London W1B 1JL, UK
+ 44 (0) 20 7299 4049
www.chinese-embassy.org.uk

TRAVEL DOCUMENTS FOR U.S. & U.K. CITIZENS
Passport and visa

HEALTH ISSUES
No immunizations are required, but malaria

prophylaxis is recommended for the provinces of Henan and Yunnan; a lesser malaria risk exists in the areas of Guangdong, Guizhou, Guangxi, Sichuan, and Fujian.

TRAVEL TIME TO DESTINATION & TIME DIFFERENCE
New York to Beijing: 13 hours 30 minutes nonstop flight; EST +12. London to Beijing: 10 hours 10 minutes nonstop flight; GMT -7

AVERAGE TRIP COST
$1,900/£1,230 for 10 days of a classic tour

LANGUAGE & CURRENCY
Official language: Mandarin, which is spoken by

70 percent of the population. In the west, seven million Muslims speak Turkic languages; in the southwest, Tibetan dialects rule.
Currency: renminbi. Exchanging dollars is no problem. Hong Kong dollars count as proper currency as well. Credit cards are accepted in hotels and stores of the larger cities.

POPULATION
With a population of 1,321,852,000, China holds one-fifth of the world's inhabitants. The Han are the majority group, comprising 95 percent of the population; 55 ethnic minority groups, such as Uygurs,

Manchurians, and Mongols, make up the rest.

RELIGION
Buddhism and Taoism are the two most important religions. Islam is practiced in the west, and Christianity is also represented.

FESTIVALS
The various calendars (lunar calendar, Tibetan calendar) may show different dates. January: Lantern Festival (15th day of the first month in the lunar calendar); February: Chinese New Year; April: Festival of Pure Brightness (14th to 16th day of the 5th month in the Tibetan calendar); June: Dragon

Boat Festival (5th day of the 7th month in the lunar calendar); July: Ghost Festival (15th day of the 7th month in the lunar calendar); October 1: National Day

SHOPPING
Beijing has become a shopper's paradise. Pearls, jade, silks, lacquerware, and traditional craft items are favorite souvenirs.
In Tibet, visitors shop for cashmere sweaters, paintings, and herbal medicines.

The Southwest

Tibet

▶ CITIES AND MONUMENTS

Lhasa, the holy city, is increasingly limited by the control of the central government, while still hoping for a return of the Dalai Lama.

The Potala Palace, former residence of the Dalai Lama; the Jokhang Temple, the oldest temple; Norbulingka, the summer residence of the Dalai Lama; and Drepung and Sera monasteries are the most important shrines of a religious center that has had difficulty maintaining its traditional ways.

In the eighth century, Guru Rinpoche, the Second Buddha, brought Buddhism from India to Tibet, meditating in 100 caves along the way.

Although the Tibetan uprising in 1959 has led to tragic repressions and destruction of most of Tibet's grand monasteries, the sanctuaries

A Tibetan monk combines prayer and music, the traditional means of preparing the mind for meditation.

When to Go					
	NORTHWEST	BEIJING AND NORTHEAST	CENTER	TIBET AND SOUTHWEST	SOUTH AND SOUTHEAST
JANUARY		☼			
FEBRUARY					
MARCH					☼
APRIL		☼	☼	☼	☼
MAY	☼	☼	☼	☼	
JUNE	☼	☼	☼	☼	
JULY	☼			☼	
AUGUST	☼			☼	
SEPTEMBER	☼	☼	☼	☼	
OCTOBER		☼	☼		☼
NOVEMBER					☼
DECEMBER					☼

The Potala Palace in Lhasa, Tibet, was the chief residence of the Dalai Lama, but it now holds a museum.

that remain represent a spiritual highlight for visitors.

Outside of Lhasa, on the route between Kathmandu and Lhasa, a stop at **Gyangzê** is mandatory for its large *stupas* (domed funerary or commemorative monuments) and at **Xigazê** for the Tashilumpo Monastery and its many Buddha statues. The other important sites are in the east: the city of **Kangding** with its Kham population and monasteries of the Gelupa school, and the small town of **Tagong** with its famous monastery.

▶ **LANDSCAPE AND EXCURSIONS**
Every traveler who longs for distant horizons has dreamed of going to Tibet one day. The "Roof of the World" offers excursions into one of the most exciting landscapes on Earth with its ocher-colored land and rocks, its craters and mountains where you can still see yaks grazing. The turquoise lakes (Yamdrok Tso, Mansarovar) are treasures to behold.

The Tibetan Buddhist monks' way of life has changed little over the centuries as they divide their time between prayers, monastic

rituals, and music. With the opening in July 2006 of the last leg of the rail line between Golmud and Lhasa, worldwide concern has arisen about China's possible tightening of political control over Tibet.

Visitors traveling westward via the Karakoram–Himalayan highway are awed as much by the beauty of the majestic peaks as by the treacherous route, arriving in Pakistan and the Karakoram Mountains at the Khunjerab Pass.

In the west, four sacred watercourses spring from **Mount Kailas:**

The Center

Anhui, Hubei, Jiangsu, Sichuan, Zhejiang

▶ CITIES

Shanghai, China's largest and most cosmopolitan city, spreads out along the Bund, the embankment of the Huangpu River, lined with historic buildings, and a towering modern skyline beyond. The Shanghai Museum's collections of ancient bronze works, porcelain, and jade are a must-see, as are the Yuyuan Garden and the Jade Buddha Temple.

Suzhou, on the lower Yangtze River, is known for its beautiful pagodas and well-designed gardens. Of the lakeside villages nearby, Zhouzhuang is often compared to Venice for its many canals and stone bridges. **Nanjing** in the Yangtze River Delta had its heyday during the Ming dynasty and still bears traces of that period, including the mausoleum of the first Ming emperor, Hongwu.

▶ LANDSCAPE

Lying east of the mountains of Tibet, the **Sichuan mountains** can boast of similar scenic beauty (gorges, peaks of more than 13,000 feet), including the **Jiuzhaigou Valley** with its lakes, waterfalls, and bamboo forests where the giant pandas live (Wolong Reserve).

In Hubei Province, the **Yangtze (Chang) River,** due to the hotly disputed Three Gorges Dam, has

Nanjing Road in Shanghai is the main shopping street.

the Ghaghara, Indus, Brahmaputra, and Sutlej Rivers. The holy mountain itself is said to be Shiva's throne, where Tibetans make pilgrimages to encircle *(khora)* the holy shrine. Tourists can join in on the trails at high altitude, side by side with sherpas and yaks. Not far from there is another important sanctuary, the hot springs of **Tirthapuri.**

At the border of Sichuan, the **Kham** region is also known for its monasteries and its nomadic people.

What to See and Do in Central China

▶ **CITIES**
• Shanghai, Suzhou, Nanjing

▶ **LANDSCAPE**
• Sichuan Mountains, Jiuzhaigou Valley, Yangtze River, Mount Huang, Mount Emei

▶ **MONUMENTS**
• Monasteries and temples of Sichuan, Caves of the Thousand Buddhas, Leshan Giant Buddha

lost some of the attraction of cruising between the cliffs (Qutang, Wu, and Xilin Gorge) to Yichang: With the higher water level, the gorges look less imposing. The river then passes ancient towns (Shashi and especially Jiangzhou) before it flows in the south between Wuhan and Shanghai, past the twisted pines and granite peaks of **Mount Huang.**

The last attraction in this region is **Mount Emei,** at 10,167 feet the highest of China's sacred Buddhist mountains.

▶ MONUMENTS

In the Mount Emei region, the **Leshan Giant Buddha** rises to 233 feet, sculpted from the rock. Other monuments near Nanjing include the **Caves of the Thousand Buddhas.**

What to See and Do in Northeastern China
▶ **CITIES**
• Beijing, Shenyang, Xi'an
▶ **MONUMENTS**
• The Great Wall, Ming dynasty tombs, Longmen Grottoes
▶ **LANDSCAPES**
• Yellow River, Shaanxi, Shanxi

The Northeast

Henan, Liaoning, Shaanxi, Shanxi

▶ CITIES

Most journeys to China include **Beijing.** The capital, with its famous monuments and 2008 Olympic stadium, has a pollution problem, and modernization has caused old quarters with traditional houses and courtyards, the *hutongs,* to be razed. But there is still plenty to see: the Forbidden City (ancient imperial palace filled with treasures), Tiananmen Square, the Monument to the People's Heroes, the Mausoleum of

The Giant Buddha in Leshan ranks as the world's largest stone Buddha.

The Great Wall, here in the mountains at Jinshanling, is listed as a World Heritage site.

Beijing moves rapidly these days, but the red roofs of the Forbidden City symbolize its ancient past.

Mao Zedong, the Temple of Heaven (with thousands of blue roof tiles, representing heaven), and the summer palace that was the residence of the last empress of China. An unforgettable experience is a visit to the Beijing Opera where performers dress in elaborate costumes.

Northeast of Beijing, the city of **Shenyang,** though not well known, is the largest city in the region, and its pagodas and Manchurian-style homes proclaim it as the gateway to Manchuria.

Xi'an, which was China's capital for 1,200 years and the departure point of the Silk Road, has much to offer as well: the Wild Goose Pagoda, the History Museum with its stele forest, a Neolithic village of the Yangshao culture, sculpted animals lining the way to Gen. Huo Qubing's tomb (first century B.C.), pagodas and other monuments of the Tang dynasty, a temple, mosques, the tumulus mound of Empress Wu Zetian, and the highlight, the 7,000 terra-cotta warriors and horses in the tomb of Emperor Qin Shihuangdi.

▶ MONUMENTS

Besides the monuments already mentioned, every tourist must see

not be missed. Carved between the 5th and 11th centuries, the more than 2,000 caves hold over 100,000 Buddha statues.

On the Shandong Peninsula, the massif of Tai Shan is one of the Five Great Mountains of China, its slopes studded with temples.

▶ LANDSCAPES

The **Yellow River** (Huan He) flows through the province of **Shaanxi,** which includes a loess plateau that is highly fertile but erosion prone. This yellow earth gives the landscape an unvarying sameness until ravines break up the terrain. The landscape looks quite similar in the neighboring province of **Shanxi.** The region is composed of a series of hills that culminate at Mount Wutai, another of the sacred mountains, where many of the most important monasteries and temples are located. The Yellow River forms the border between the two provinces, carving through earth and rock and creating waterfalls such as the Dragon Gate.

the **Great Wall.** Some 3,700 miles long, it was built starting in the third century B.C. to protect the country from intruders. The wall begins at the Bohai Sea and meanders to the Gobi desert.

Another famous site, not far from Beijing, is 13 **Ming dynasty tombs,** with sculpted animals along the Spirit Way to the tombs. In addition, the **Longmen Grottoes** should

In Xi'an, a terra-cotta army protects the mausoleum of Qin Shihuangdi.

The Zhuang ethnic minority lives in the autonomous region of Guangxi on the border with Vietnam.

The Southeast

Guangdong, Guangxi

▶ LANDSCAPE

The strange and mist-shrouded limestone formations and caves of **Guilin** offer visitors a scenic delight while cruising on the River Li between Guilin and Yangshuo.

Southeast of Guilin stretches Guangdong Province, where Baiyun Mountain, or White Cloud Mountain, is a point of pride and travelers can "walk in the clouds." The province is famous for its tea plantations and the high quality of its tea.

▶ CITIES

Guangzhou, China's third largest city and a hub of industry and commerce, still has plenty of historic sites to show off, such as the temple of the Six Banyan Trees, hundred-year-old bonsai trees at the Temple of the Chen Family, the Shishi Sacred Heart Cathedral, and the Huaisheng Mosque.

What to See and Do in Southeastern China
▶ LANDSCAPE
• Limestone formations of Guilin
▶ CITIES
• Guangzhou, Macau, Nanning

What to See and Do in Southern China

▶ **LANDSCAPE AND EXCURSIONS**

• Rice terraces, "stone forest," Red River Valley

▶ **CITIES AND MONUMENTS**

• Lijiang, Dali, Kunming, Shangri-La

The South

Yunnan

▶ LANDSCAPE AND EXCURSIONS

Along the borders with Vietnam and Laos, Yunnan Province is becoming a tourist destination for its scenic landscape of rice terraces and forests in the foothills of the Himalaya and its "stone forests" of limestone columns up to 100 feet high near the capital, Kunming.

In the south of the province, the **Red River Valley** is flanked by mountains and plateaus rising to the peaks of Mount Tianzi. This region is home to many minorities (Dai, Miao), who have preserved their ancient customs.

As long as the Chinese government leaves the current arrangement in place, **Macau** will continue to base its tourism on the lure of its casinos. Beyond gambling, visitors can wander through the narrow streets of the historic center, duck into some of the baroque churches, and tread in the footsteps of former Portuguese rulers.

The capital of Guangxi, **Nanning** prides itself on the Bronze Drum Exposition in the Provincial Museum. A memorial hall to Sun Yat-sen in Wuzhou celebrates the Chinese revolutionary leader.

▶ CITIES AND MONUMENTS

Another "Little Venice" can be found in the ancient city of **Lijiang,** featuring 350 bridges, many lakes, and canals, all located at 7,800 feet of altitude and overshadowed by the Jade Dragon Snow Mountain. Black Dragon Pool in Lijiang offers one of China's finest views, with the mountain reflected in its dark waters. Lijian's old town is on the World Heritage List.

The Tang dynasty pagodas of **Dali,** the Taoist temple of **Kunming,** the Tibetan monastery of **Shangri-La**—the legendary site in the heart of the Land of Sacredness and Peace—and its white pagodas all bear the Buddhist imprint of this region, which has seen a recent influx of tourists.

Advice

■ **Pros**

• One of the great tourist adventures. The possibility of traveling individually without risk.

■ **Cons**

• Little diversity in lodging. Difficulty with communication; there are few English speakers, even in Beijing. The oppressive situation in Tibet.

■ **Safety**

• For the solo traveler, caution is advised in Xinjiang, at the Chinese–Pakistani border, and in Inner Mongolia. Precautions should also be taken at some markets in certain regions during avian flu outbreaks. Otherwise, there are no problems. China is a safe country.

■ **Special Tip**

• The railway trip between Golmud and Lhasa in Tibet, open since July 2006, offers breathtaking scenery.

Arenal is one of the country's most active volcanoes, along with Poás and Irazú.

Costa Rica, the "Rich Coast," so named by Christopher Columbus, has become a favorite tourist destination in part because of the government's intelligent development of ecotourism in its nearly three dozen national parks.

Costa Rica

Traveler's Notebook

MAIN CONTACTS
Embassy of Costa Rica
2114 S Street, NW
Washington, DC
20008
(202) 234-2945
www.costarica-embassy.org
www.visitcosta rica.com
Embassy of Costa Rica
Flat 1
14 Lancaster Gate
London W2 3LH, UK
+ 44 (0) 20 7706 8844

TRAVEL DOCUMENTS FOR U.S. & U.K. CITIZENS
Passport

HEALTH ISSUES
No immunizations required; malaria prophylaxis is recommended for the lower altitudes

TRAVEL TIME TO DESTINATION & TIME DIFFERENCE
New York to San José: 5 hours 10 minutes nonstop flight; EST -1. London to San José: 13 hours 40 minutes connecting; GMT +6

AVERAGE TRIP COST
$1,900/£1,230 for 10 days

LANGUAGE & CURRENCY
Official language: Spanish; English widely spoken
Currency: colon

POPULATION
The majority (85 percent) of the 4,133,900 inhabitants are of European descent. Capital: San José

RELIGION
88 percent Catholic

FESTIVALS
April: Holy Week (processions); September 15: Independence Day; October: Carnival in Puerto Limón

SHOPPING
Woodcarvings, leather goods, baskets, hammocks, coffee

What to See and Do in Costa Rica

▶ **LANDSCAPES, HIKES, AND WILDLIFE**

• Flora (rain forests, observation in the tree canopy)

• Fauna (iguanas, caimans, quetzals, jaguars)

• Volcanoes (Arenal, Poás, Irazú)

• Excursions on foot or by raft

▶ **COASTS**

• Atlantic beaches (Tortuguero), Pacific beaches (Nicoya Peninsula)

• Diving (Cocos Island)

▶ LANDSCAPES, HIKES, AND WILDLIFE

In 33 national parks, visitors can explore the rain forest and discover the diversity of untouched fauna and flora that made Costa Rica the "laboratory" of, if not the precursor to, perfect ecotourism. One-quarter of the land is protected area, and the establishment of the National Biodiversity Institute of San José proves the government's serious concern for ecology.

Across the center of the country run a succession of rain forests (Monteverde Cloud Forest), tropical dry forests, and high-elevation forests (Guanacaste, Cordillera Central, Cordillera de Talamanca, and La Amistad National Park), which lend themselves to exploration on foot or on horseback. Iguanas, caimans, and thousands of birds (including the rare quetzal) populate the national park of **Santa Rosa** on the Pacific Coast, where leatherback turtles deposit their eggs. The quetzals also live in the Monteverde region. **Corcovado National Park** on the rough

Osa Peninsula plays host to hundreds of species of birds; alligators, anacondas, and other reptiles; and jaguars. Around **Tortuguero** and in the national park of the same name, a dense jungle protects crocodiles and howler monkeys. And there are yet more species to see: hummingbirds, parakeets, poison-dart frogs, and tapirs. Visitors can climb some of the active volcanoes including **Arenal, Poás,** and especially **Irazú,** where the ascent is easy and the view includes both the Atlantic and Pacific Oceans.

One unique experience is the train trip from Puerto Limón to Puntarenas, which passes from the Atlantic coast to the Pacific, crossing the jungle and the Cordillera Central. Or you can float down a river by raft, especially on the Corobicí, Pacuare, and Chirripó Rivers.

▶ COASTS

The **Atlantic** shores of Costa Rica are not ideal for beach life, although their proximity to the Caribbean would suggest this. These beaches

When to Go

	CENTRAL VALLEY	PACIFIC COAST	FLORA AND PHOTOGRAPHY
JANUARY	☼	☼	
FEBRUARY	☼	☼	
MARCH	☼	☼	
APRIL	☼	☼	
MAY			⋞
JUNE			⋞
JULY			⋞
AUGUST			⋞
SEPTEMBER			⋞
OCTOBER			⋞
NOVEMBER			⋞
DECEMBER	☼		

Advice

■ **Pros**

• The quality of the national parks in a country that is a leader in global ecotourism. A long peaceful history (there is no army in the country) and political stability, which is reassuring to any traveler.

■ **Cons**

• There are few alternatives to nature and beaches.

■ **Safety**

• Costa Rica is considered a safe country, though there is an occasional risk of car theft.

■ **Special Tip**

• Costa Rica is a destination dear to those who want responsible ecotourism or who want to share the country's wildlife with their children; a favorite spot are the suspension bridges in several parks that take you above the tropical forest canopy, close to the birds.

suffer from frequent rain, but the coconut palms, coral reefs, and strong surf attract tourists with other interests. The village of Tortuguero, for instance, which can only be accessed by boat or plane, may allow a rare glimpse at the protected nesting sites of green turtles in summer.

The **Pacific** coast attracts larger crowds. There are numerous beaches south of Puntarenas and around the Nicoya Peninsula (Tamarindo Beach), but the waves are often strong. The all-inclusive resorts of Papagayo offer golf, diving, fishing, and surfing.

Divers usually take a boat off the south coast to **Cocos Island** to see marlins, manta rays, whale sharks, and sea turtles, especially at the time of egg laying.

The pretty little town of Rovinj on Istria's west coast is one of Croatia's treasures.

Croatia has come back to the travel scene in a spectacular way after years of conflict. If suddenly beach tourism gets too crowded and boat rentals and cruises seem to multiply, then travelers might consider a visit to the coastal cities for their architecture and the splendor of the lakes of Plitvice National Park.

Croatia

▶ COAST

The thousand miles of coast on the peninsula of **Istria** (part of the 3,600 miles of the Croatian Riviera on the Adriatic Sea) are bordered by a rocky ridge, pine forests, creeks, and bays, with the Dinaric Alps in the background. The long littoral is severely cut up and flanked by 1,200 islands; fewer than a hundred are inhabited.

The Croatian coast offers endless boating choices, including bareboat or skippered yachts and fishing boats to rent, as well as trips by excursion boat.

The walled city of Dubrovnik was long the highlight of the **Dalmatian Coast** until "the troubles" of the 1990s, but tourists are now coming back in droves; the same is true for Makarska and other picturesque coastal towns. The beach resorts on

Traveler's Notebook

MAIN CONTACTS

Embassy of the Republic of Croatia
2343 Massachusetts Avenue, NW
Washington, DC 20008
(202) 588-5899
www.croatiaemb.org
www.croatia.hr

Embassy of the Republic of Croatia
21 Conway Street
London W1T 6BN, UK
+ 44 (0) 20 7387 1144
http://uk.mfa.hr

TRAVEL DOCUMENTS FOR U.S. & U.K. CITIZENS
Passport

HEALTH ISSUES
No problems

TRAVEL TIME TO DESTINATION & TIME DIFFERENCE
New York to Dubrovnik: 12 hours 40 minutes connecting flight; EST +6.
London to Dubrovnik: 4 hours 10 minutes connecting flight; GMT +1

AVERAGE TRIP COST
$1,300/£850 for a 10-day cruise

LANGUAGE & CURRENCY
Official language: Croatian
Currency: kuna

POPULATION
4,493,000 inhabitants. Serbians, who accounted for 12 percent of the population before the war in the 1990s, are now down to 150,000. Numerous Bosnian refugees. Capital: Zagreb

RELIGION
Around the year 1000, the Croatian Church decided to follow Latin rites rather than Eastern Orthodox ones, which reduced the Slavic influence. To this day, most Croats are Catholic.

FESTIVALS
February: Carnival in Rijeka; June: Vino Forum on the island of Krk (the second part of this festival takes place in September); July: Folkloric

Festival in Zagreb, and Summer Festival in Dubrovnik (classical music, theater); August 5: National Public Holiday

SHOPPING
Favorite items include embroidery, crystal, and fruit brandies.

What to See and Do in Croatia

▶ **COAST**

- Istria (Opatija, Porec, Pula, Rovinj, Umag)
- Dalmatia (Dubrovnik, the islands of Brac, Cres, Hvar, Korcula, Krk, Losinj, Mljet)

▶ **CITIES AND MONUMENTS**

- Dubrovnik, Pula, Sibenik, Split, Zadar, Trogir, Zagreb

▶ **LANDSCAPE**

- Dinaric Alps
- Plitvice Lakes

the islands of Brac, Cres, Hvar, Korcula, Krk, Losinj, and Mljet—a portion of which is a national park—are visited not only for the beaches but also for their architecture.

The west coast of Istria hides coastal villages that are somewhat overlooked by the beach crowds, including Porec, Rovinj, and Umag. By contrast, Opatija and the area around Pula, which became famous when Austro-Hungarian high society vacationed there in its heyday, never went out of style.

▶ **CITIES AND MONUMENTS**

With the help of UNESCO, **Dubrovnik** has been restored to its old self since the bombing of 1991, and the city is attracting tourists and holding its annual Summer Festival (theater, dance, classical music, jazz) again.

Besides its fortified walls, Dubrovnik owes its reputation to ancient history: Founded in the seventh century by refugees from Epidaurus, then named Ragusa, the city has been progressively graced by Roman, Gothic, Renaissance (St. Savior, Sponza Palace), and baroque architecture (galleries and

marble-paved Stradun Street, the Cathedral of the Assumption, St. Ignatius of Loyola Church).

The Romans left an amphitheater in **Pula.** Renaissance architecture enhances **Sibenik,** and the vast palace built by the Roman emperor Diocletian in **Split** in the fourth century is awe inspiring. The city of **Zadar's** pride is its medieval churches (St. Donat) and the remains of Roman and Venetian fortifications.

Trogir, with a Greek and Venetian past, has elegant sculptures in its churches, and other historic touches

When to Go	COAST AND ISLANDS	INTERIOR
JANUARY		
FEBRUARY		
MARCH		
APRIL		
MAY	☼	☼
JUNE	☼	☼
JULY	☼	☼
AUGUST	☼	☼
SEPTEMBER	☼	☼
OCTOBER	☼	
NOVEMBER		
DECEMBER		

can be found in all the small ports of Dalmatia and Istria. Dominated by its neo-Gothic cathedral, its Arts Pavilion, and baroque monuments, the capital, **Zagreb,** is also rich in art galleries and museums (Croatian Museum of Naïve Art, Archaeological Museum, Arts and Crafts Museum).

▶ **LANDSCAPE**

The *poljes,* flat-floored depressions of the **Dinaric Alps,** where the mountains and sparse vegetation enclose wide plains, make for an astonishing landscape. Even so, it is the lakes of Plitvice that leave travelers with the most lasting memories: Formed by runoff from the mountains, 16 lakes of shimmering water, grouped in an upper and lower cluster, are natural travertine dams over which dozens of waterfalls cascade, connecting the lake waters.

Cuba

It has been a few years since Cuba decided to promote tourism and make up for lost time. The country's attractions include hundreds of miles of coastline, mountains that invite hikers to explore, lively traditions like salsa music and dance, colonial architecture, and a warm reception by the people.

What to See and Do in Cuba

▶ **COASTS**
- Caribbean beaches (Varadero, Cayo Coco, Guardalavaca)
- Cruises

▶ **CITIES**
- Baroque churches, colonial cathedrals and houses (Trinidad, Havana, Santiago de Cuba, Cienfuegos, Sancti Spíritus, Baracoa), mausoleum of Che Guevara in Santa Clara

▶ **CULTURAL HERITAGE**
- Carnival, salsa, cigars

▶ **LANDSCAPE**
- Oriente (Sierra Maestra, Sierra del Escambray)
- Sierra de los Organos, Viñales Valley

▶ COASTS

Although they should not be the main reason for visiting Cuba, the beaches are by far its greatest physical asset. They are quintessential Caribbean beaches: long, with fine white sand and shallow shores, suitable for windsurfing, sailing, and diving. Edgy fashions prevail in the northern resorts and the Sabana-Camagüey Archipelago. The town of **Varadero** is situated on the Playa Azul, the long, sandy spit of land that stretches for ten miles northward. Along the coast unfold the *cayos,* or cays, Levisa, Las Brujas, Guillermo, and **Coco,** all the way to **Guardalavaca.** The northwestern cayos (Jutias) complete the group, all very beautiful with plenty of amenities.

The southern coast has fewer such sites, except in the southeast (Playa Las Coloradas, Playa Siboney). But the options include diving—for example, off the south coast of the Isle of Pines—and sailing and deepsea fishing. Cruise ships arrive and leave regularly from Havana. One classic cruise leaves from Grand Cayman and visits Jamaica before reaching the Cuban capital.

Baroque churches and colonial architecture make Trinidad one of Cuba's favorite destinations.

▶ CITIES

Havana encompasses several cities: the most classic and touristy is its historic heart. La Habana Vieja, Old Havana, around the Plaza de la Catedral, Plaza de Armas, and Plaza de San Francisco de Asís, is listed as a UNESCO World Heritage site. Its palace, balconied mansions, museums, and churches built in baroque and neoclassical style make a harmonious entity.

You have to leave the old town through Central Park and cross Centro Habana, the neighborhood that seems the most run-down, to see the most representative buildings, including the capitol and the Gran Teatro. On the beachfront promenade, the Malecón, people stroll past crumbling baroque buildings to get to modern Vedado, with the Paseo Central, Los Presidentes Avenue, and the immense Plaza de la Revolución, where people who heard Fidel Castro give one of his annual May Day addresses felt that they were witnessing a moment in history.

The only problem you may run into in Havana is getting pushed around a bit by the throng of tourists, who are already crowding the many restaurants and cafés in Old Havana, but their presence has also encouraged the opening of museums such as the National Museum of Fine Arts and the Anthropological Museum.

A few miles east of Havana is the Finca Vigía, where Ernest Hemingway lived and wrote; the small port of Cojimar, scene of his novel *The Old Man and the Sea;* and Las Terrazas, one of his favorite watering holes.

American cars from the 1950s are a common sight in the Cuban capital, Havana.

Traveler's Notebook

MAIN CONTACTS
Cuban Interests Section
2630 16th Street, NW
Washington, DC 20009
(202) 797-8609
http://embacu.cuba
minrex.cu
www.cubatravel.cu/otroe/
Embassy of Cuba
167 High Holborn
London WC1V 6PA, UK
+ 44 (0) 20 7240 2488
www.cubaldn.com

TRAVEL DOCUMENTS
For U.S. Citizens:
Check for up-to-date
travel information from the
U.S. State Department;
http://travel.state.gov/cis_
pa_tw/cis/cis_1097.html
For U.K. Citizens: Pass-
port and visa

**TRAVEL TIME TO
DESTINATION & TIME
DIFFERENCE**
London to Havana: 8
hours 30 minutes; GMT +5

AVERAGE TRIP COST
$1,300/£850 for a beach
week

LANGUAGE & CURRENCY
Official language:
Spanish
Currency: Cuban peso

POPULATION
Of the 11,394,000 inhab-
itants, more than 2
million live in the capi-
tal, Havana. Ethnicity
divides into 66 percent
Caucasian, 22 percent

mixed race, and 12
percent of African
descent.

RELIGION
Catholic: 40 percent.
There is also a Protes-
tant minority and many
members of Afro-Cuban
cults.

FESTIVALS
May: Folklore Festival in
Havana; July: Carnival
in Havana and Santiago;
December: Festival of

New Latin American Cin-
ema and Jazz Festival in
Havana

SHOPPING
Special purchases
include rum, cigars,
and wooden sculptures
(check for restrictions on
bringing goods back to
the U.S.).

Another Cultural Heritage site is **Trinidad,** one of the most interesting colonial cities in the Caribbean because of its baroque churches; low, pastel-colored houses; and balustraded courtyards.

Santiago de Cuba, the old capital, situated on a fine bay, has a fortified castle (Castillo de Morro), a cathedral, churches, and a passion for salsa to offer.

Cienfuegos, the pearl of the south and recently added to the World Heritage List, mixes its triple architectural past of French (wrought-iron balconies in the historic center), Spanish (Ferrer Palace), and Italian (Terry Theater, Palacio de Valle) styles. The botanic garden holds no fewer than two thousand plant species.

In the center of the country, **Sancti Spíritus** attracts visitors for the atmosphere in its old town. **Baracoa,** at the eastern tip of the island where Christopher Columbus is said to have landed, is called the first Spanish town in the New World. And the myth of revolutionary Che Guevara is well maintained in **Santa Clara** with a statue and the mausoleum where he is buried.

▶ CULTURAL HERITAGE

Cuba and Puerto Rico both claim to have originated salsa music, the Afro-Cuban rhythms of the late 1950s. It's the music you hear in the evening in the center of Havana or in the Vedado district, and everywhere on the main square of Trinidad. The music has had its effect on Cuban Carnival, which is best experienced in Santiago de Cuba in July.

You can visit cigar factories, where the famous smokes are handcrafted, especially in the Pinar del Río region.

Cuban bars feature largely traditional music.

▶ LANDSCAPE

Tourism infrastructure to explore the interior has been long neglected, but is under full development for hiking programs in the mountains, especially in the east (Oriente) where the **Sierra Maestra** overshadows Santiago de Cuba.

In the center of the country, a scenic road coming from Trinidad crosses the **Sierra del Escambray** with its cliffs, lakes, and coffee

When to Go		
	CLIMATE	FESTIVALS IN HAVANA
JANUARY	☼	
FEBRUARY	☼	
MARCH	☼	
APRIL	☼	
MAY		✔
JUNE		
JULY		✔
AUGUST		
SEPTEMBER		
OCTOBER		
NOVEMBER		✔
DECEMBER	☼	✔

plantations spreading all the way to Santa Clara. In the west, the **Sierra de los Organos,** between Havana and Pinar del Río, is not only considered to have the most beautiful valley **(Viñales)** but also continues on to the most important tobacco fields of the island (harvest from January to March).

What to See and Do in Cyprus

▶ **COASTS**

- Beaches (Limassol, Paphos, Ayia Napa, Polis)

▶ **LANDSCAPE AND EXCURSIONS**

- Troodos Mountains, Cedar Valley

▶ **TOWNS AND VILLAGES**

- Nicosia, Paphos, Larnaca

▶ **MONUMENTS**

- Byzantine churches, Greek Orthodox monasteries (Kykkos)
- Archaeological sites (Curium, Paphos, St. Hilarion Castle)

Beyond its port and fortress, Paphos's landmarks include ancient mosaics.

Cyprus

Proud of its 340 days of sunshine per year, Cyprus is one of those fortunate Mediterranean islands that can offer vacationers perfect beaches, scenic mountains, and Greco-Roman archaeological sites.

▶ **COASTS**

The beaches of Cyprus are largely pebble; sand is rare. Still, these beaches backed by sandstone cliffs aren't lacking anything, and sunbathers can enjoy them until November.

Mass tourism has invaded and spoiled the approaches to **Limassol.** Things are quieter around **Paphos** (Coral Bay) and **Ayia Napa.** The neighborhood of **Polis** in the northwest seems least affected. According to legend, Aphrodite, the Greek goddess of love, is supposed to have been born at serenely beautiful **Petra tou Romiou,** a rock on the road from Paphos to Limassol.

▶ **LANDSCAPE AND EXCURSIONS**

The **Troodos** mountain range, forested with pines, is dear to the Cypriots because in summer they

Traveler's Notebook

MAIN CONTACTS

Embassy of the Republic of Cyprus
2211 R Street, NW
Washington, DC
20008
(202) 462-5772
www.cyprusembassy.net
www.visitcyprus.com
High Commission of the Republic of Cyprus
13 St. James's Square
London SW1Y 4LB, UK
+ 44 (0) 20 7321 4100
www.mfa.gov.cy/mfa/high com/highcom_london

.nsf/DMLindex_en/ DMLindex_en

TRAVEL DOCUMENTS FOR U.S. & U.K. CITIZENS
Passport

TRAVEL TIME TO DESTINATION & TIME DIFFERENCE
New York to Larnaca:12 hours 45 minutes connecting; EST +7. London to Larnaca: 4 hours 35 minutes nonstop; GMT +2

AVERAGE TRIP COST
$775/£500 for a week in a beach resort

LANGUAGE & CURRENCY
Official languages: Greek, Turkish
Currency: in the north, the Turkish lira; in the south, the euro

POPULATION
About three-quarters of the 788,500 inhabitants live in the Greek Cypriot area. Capital: Nicosia

RELIGION
Eastern Orthodox: 77 percent; Muslim: 22 percent; small Maronite and Armenian minorities

FESTIVALS
March: Carnival in Limassol (50 days before Orthodox Easter, when parades wind through town); May: Anthestiria Flower Festival in Limassol and Paphos; Pentecost: Kataklysmos Festival in the coastal

villages; August 1: Day of Communal Resistance; September: wine festival; October 1: Independence Day

SHOPPING
You can find embroideries, leather goods, lace, baskets, and pottery.

0   30 km
0   30 mi

St. Hilarion
Kykkos   Castle   Kyrenia
Monastery   ● Bellapais Abbey
Polis   NICOSIA   ● Ammochostos
           (LEFKOSIA) ● Salamis (Famagusta)
      Cedar ⚲ Olympos   ● Ayia Napa
      Valley +1,951 Troodos Mts. Larnaca
Paphos ●   ● Choirokoitia
Petra tou ● ● Lemesos   **C Y P R U S** Sea
Romiou   (Limassol)
      Curium   Mediterranean

Advice

▪ Pros

• The best weather in the Mediterranean, warm and sunny. The shallow water makes it suitable for family vacations. The relaxing of the green line in Nicosia makes touring easier.

▪ Cons

• Organized tours often miss the famous sites of the interior. Few sandy beaches. Partitioned, even though the future looks more favorable.

▪ Safety

• There are few problems; don't expect the northern part to be inaccessible or dangerous. Since 2008, tourists can easily pass between north and south by simply showing their passports.

▪ Special Tip

• Leaving for a hike to Mount Olympus in the Troodos Range is simple and a pleasure, especially since most tourists stay on the beaches and forget the beautiful mountains of the interior.

like to wander up the easy hiking trails to Mount Olympus at 6,000 feet to cool off from the heat in the lowlands. In winter, it's sometimes possible to ski there.

Moving westward from the Troodos, hiking trails lead through pleasant **Cedar Valley.**

▶ TOWNS AND VILLAGES

The island was divided in 1974 into a Turkish northern third and a Greek Cypriot southern two-thirds, separated by a UN-controlled green line, but in 2008 the two communities opened the wall dividing the capital **Nicosia** for access to all. On the Greek side, the Old City has a Byzantine Museum with an exceptional collection of icons in the Archbishop's Palace, an archaeological museum, and a number of Byzantine churches. The Turkish side boasts St. Sophia Cathedral, which became a mosque, and the Lusignan Palace, seat of the Lusignan kings of the 12th to 15th centuries.

Paphos's landmarks include splendid third- to fifth-century mosaics, an Ottoman fortress, a pleasant port, and the vaults and

caves of the tombs of the kings. Besides an archaeological museum, **Larnaca** has a fort with a grand view over the city.

Villagers have kept to their own way of life, manifested in a number of traditional festivals, despite the onslaught of tourists.

▶ MONUMENTS

In the Troodos Mountains nestle a number of Byzantine churches with well-preserved frescoes, including Assinou, Ayios Nikolaos, and Panayia tou Araka, along with Greek Orthodox monasteries, the most famous one being the 11th-century **Kykkos** Monastery, lavished with gold, and a rich museum.

The archaeological sites of Choirokoitia (closed Neolithic village of round structures) and **Curium** (ancient Greco-Roman city), as well as **Paphos,** with mosaics in the Houses of Dionysos, Theseus, and Aion, are all well worth a visit.

In the Turkish zone are two imposing sites, both south of the port of Kyrenia: the castle of **St. Hilarion** (where the Byzantines protected themselves against Richard the Lionheart) and Bellapais Abbey (Norbertine).

To a lesser degree, Famagusta attracts visitors for its medieval quarter surrounded by ancient ramparts and Gothic monuments (St. Nicholas Cathedral, changed

to the Lala Mustafa Pasha Mosque) and Salamis, an ancient city-state destroyed in the seventh century.

When to Go		
	COASTS	INTERIOR
JANUARY		☼
FEBRUARY		☼
MARCH		
APRIL		☼
MAY	☼	☼
JUNE	☼	☼
JULY	☼	☼
AUGUST	☼	☼
SEPTEMBER	☼	☼
OCTOBER	☼	
NOVEMBER		
DECEMBER		

What to See and Do in the Czech Republic

▶ **CITIES**

- Prague, Brno, Plzen
- Karlovy Vary (Karlsbad), Marianske Lazne (Marienbad) (spas)

▶ **MONUMENTS**

- Cesky Krumlov, Karlstejn (castles)
- Cheb, Kutna Hora, Trebic, Olomouc, Austerlitz

▶ **LANDSCAPE AND ACTIVITIES**

- Giant Mountains, Prachov Rocks, Soos National Nature Reserve
- Cross-country and downhill skiing

Prague's picturesque Charles Bridge, flanked by statues, is one of Europe's landmarks.

Czech Republic

⚑ *Following Czechoslovakia's "Velvet Revolution" in 1989, tourists flocked to Prague in record numbers to rediscover one of the most beautiful cities in Europe.*

▶ **CITIES**

Situated on the banks of the Vltava River, **Prague**—the "City of One Hundred Thousand Rooftops," where Kafka and Mozart lived—is one of Europe's top tourist destinations. Perhaps Prague owes this distinction mostly to its beautiful vestiges of baroque architecture, which were miraculously spared the ravages of war.

The baroque religious statues of the Charles Bridge make it one of Europe's most famous and unusual bridges; a major restoration began in 2007 and will continue until 2020.

Traveler's Notebook

MAIN CONTACTS *Embassy of the Czech Republic* 3900 Spring of Freedom Street, NW Washington, DC 20008 (202) 274-9100 www.mzv.cz/washington www.czechtourism.com *Embassy of the Czech Republic* 26–30 Kensington Palace Gardens London W8 4QY, UK + 44 (0) 20 7243 1115 www.mzv.cz/london/	**TRAVEL DOCUMENTS FOR U.S. & U.K. CITIZENS** Passport **TRAVEL TIME TO DESTINATION & TIME DIFFERENCE** New York to Prague: 8 hours 40 minutes nonstop flight; EST +6. London to Prague: 1 hour 55 minutes nonstop flight; GMT +1 **AVERAGE TRIP COST** $450/£275 for a weekend (3 days and 2 nights) in Prague	**LANGUAGE & CURRENCY** Official language: Czech; other languages: German (frequently spoken), English, and French (less frequently). Currency: koruna **POPULATION** 10,229,000 inhabitants; mainly Czech, with German, Polish, and Russian minorities. Capital: Prague	**RELIGION** 66 percent Catholic; 4 percent Protestant **FESTIVALS** April 30: *Paleni Carodejnic* (The Burning of the Witches), a pre-Christian tradition, in Prague; September: Mozart Festival; November 17: Struggle for Freedom and Democracy Day	**SHOPPING** Bohemian crystal is available in abundance. Other artisanal products include wooden toys, puppets, pottery, and the famous pilsner beer from Plzen.

In Lesser Town (Mala Strana) is Malostranske Square, framed with Renaissance and baroque facades; in the neighboring Hradcany (castle) district are the palace, royal castle (collection of paintings by Rubens and Titian), and St. Vitus Cathedral. Across the Charles Bridge is Old Town (Stare Mesto), around Old Town Square, then New Town (Nove Mesto) and Wenceslas Square— once the heart of the Velvet Revolution, but now without a trace of its tumultuous past. The Jewish Quarter of Josefov, degraded to a ghetto well before World War II, has six synagogues (of which the Old-New Synagogue, built in 1270, is the oldest in Europe) and the Old Jewish Cemetery, with more than 12,000 haphazardly scattered tombstones.

Prague was once the cultural center of the Holy Roman Empire. Today, its ancient heritage is preserved in several of the city's museums, most notably the National Gallery.

The town of **Brno** does not share Prague's star status, but is well worth visiting. The city's highlights are Spilberk Castle and the old Cathedral of SS. Peter and Paul.

Plzen offers the attractions of St. Bartholomew's Cathedral, the Renaissance-style Town Hall, and gabled houses. However, the city is best known for its beer, which is still made using a 12th-century technique, commemorated in the Brewery Museum.

The country boasts two prestigious spa towns: **Karlovy Vary** (Karlsbad), known for its castle and famous visitors, including Goethe, Karl Marx, Beethoven, and Pushkin. Goethe also visited **Marianske Lazne** (Marienbad), with its

rococo-style palace, numerous parks, and beautiful fountains; it was also the former haunt of Mark Twain and Richard Wagner.

▶ MONUMENTS

Cesky Krumlov is a must-see for the diversity of its architecture—from an Italian Renaissance castle of the 13th century to medieval houses and local styles.

In **Karlstejn,** a tour of the 14th-century castle includes a portrait collection of 28 saints. Other important sites are: the Gothic and baroque houses in **Cheb;** the choir loft in St. Barbara's Cathedral and royal palace in **Kutna Hora;** the Jewish Quarter and St. Procopius

Basilica in **Trebic;** and the Holy Trinity Column and Chapel of St. John Sarkander (pilgrimage site) in **Olomouc.**

A more somber, yet very moving, site is the Peace Memorial in **Austerlitz** (Moravia), where Napoleon defeated the Russo-Austrian army in one of his greatest battles.

▶ LANDSCAPE AND HIKES

Near the Polish border, the **Giant Mountains** welcome hikers in summer (well-marked trails), and downhill skiers in winter. Northwest of the town of Jicin are the **Prachov Rocks** (Prachovské skaly), whose unusual shapes have inspired names such as The Monk, Leaning Tower, and Devil's Kitchen.

Another natural phenomenon can be seen at the **Soos National Nature Reserve,** where mofette, created from ancient volcanic activity, spew carbon dioxide gas.

Advice

■ **Pros**
• The attraction of Prague, one of the most beautiful cities in Europe. A wider variety of tourist attractions than one might imagine.

■ **Cons**
• Travel is expensive, and not only in Prague. High-season accommodations can be hard to find in the capital.

■ **Safety**
• Normal precautions are advised in tourist areas; otherwise, the Czech Republic has a relatively low crime rate.

■ **Special Tip**
• Spending a spa week in Marianske Lazne carries a bit of the romance of the old Europe. A week exploring Budapest, Prague, and Vienna would have a similar appeal.

When to Go		
	CLIMATE	PRAGUE
JANUARY		
FEBRUARY		
MARCH		
APRIL		
MAY	☼	✔
JUNE	☼	✔
JULY	☼	
AUGUST	☼	
SEPTEMBER	☼	✔
OCTOBER		
NOVEMBER		
DECEMBER		

Copenhagen's colorful houses in the port of Nyhavn, along with the statue of the Little Mermaid, draw crowds.

Denstick

 Despite its nearly 500 islands, Denmark sometimes gets overshadowed by its neighbors to the north. But the country is worth a visit on its own, not least for its beautiful cities, famous museums, and cliffs and dunes in a gentle natural environment.

Traveler's Notebook

MAIN CONTACTS
Embassy of Denmark
3200 Whitehaven Street, NW Washington, DC 20008 (202) 234-4300
www.amb washington.um.dk
www.visitdenmark .com
Embassy of Denmark
55 Sloane Street London SW1X 9SR
+ 44 (0) 20 7333 0200
www.amblondon .um.dk/en

TRAVEL DOCUMENTS FOR U.S. & U.K. CITIZENS
Passport

TRAVEL TIME TO DESTINATION & TIME DIFFERENCE
New York to Copenhagen: 8 hours 5 minutes nonstop flight; EST +6. London to Copenhagen: 1 hour 50 minutes nonstop flight; GMT +1

AVERAGE TRIP COST
$375/£250 for a weekend in Copenhagen

LANGUAGE & CURRENCY
Official language: Danish
Currency: Danish krone

POPULATION
Direct descendants of the Vikings, Danes number 5,468,000 today, giving Denmark a considerable population density. Capital: Copenhagen.

RELIGION
90 percent Lutheran

FESTIVALS
February or March: Fastelavn (Carnival, Monday before Lent); June 23–24: Sankt Hans Fest, the midsummer nights festival; December 13: St. Lucia Day

SHOPPING
Among the local products are amber from the Baltic Sea, porcelain, crystal, and Viking jewelry.

► CITIES AND MONUMENTS

If you are exploring **Copenhagen** on a sunny day, it may look to you like one of the youngest and most pleasant cities in Europe. The capital draws its visitors to the obligatory statue of the Little Mermaid and the colorful houses of Nyhavn, the old fishermen's neighborhood.

The Christiania neighborhood—a social experiment as a "free" town in the 1970s—seems to be looking for a history, and the central streets of the Latin Quarter near the university and the shopping area of Stroget are lively, as are the nearby Vesterbro district and Tivoli Gardens, the famous amusement park that has been in operation for 150 years.

Copenhagen has many canals in Christianshavn (a must-see by canal tour or waterbus), castles (Rosenborg Castle, Amalienborg Castle), and important museums (Glyptotek, Fine Arts Museum, National Museum, Ordrupgaard), as well as the new Dansk Design Center and the Carlsberg Visitor Center. About 20 miles north is the Louisiana, an important modern art museum.

In Århus, the old town, cathedral (1201), and prehistoric museum make a visit worthwhile. Farther north, Ålborg attracts tourists with its old quarter, the Fine Arts

Museum, and, a few miles outside town, an important Viking cemetery. **Odense** is known for the altarpiece and royal tombs of St. Canute Church as well as Hans Christian Andersen's house. In **Ribe,** one of the oldest towns in the country, you can admire the sculptures of the 12th-century Romanesque and Gothic church.

Most of the country's castles date to the 16th and 17th centuries. Best known are the castles of **Frederiksborg,** near Hillerød, and **Kronborg,** near Helsingør, the castle where Shakespeare set *Hamlet*'s Elsinore.

To the west of Copenhagen, **Roskilde,** the ancient capital, has a Romanesque and Gothic cathedral and a museum with Viking ships.

One of Denmark's most visited sites is the **Legoland** amusement park in Billund (Jutland) with a model village made of millions of Lego bricks.

► LANDSCAPE AND COASTS

Travelers will see wide-open skies and low terrain broken up with lakes and forests. The attractions of Jutland's coast, with its long shores along the Skagerrak strait, include a nature reserve and bird sanctuary at Tipperne; the town of Skagen at the

northernmost tip of the peninsula; the heath and sand dunes at Holmsland Klit; and the fjord at Hobro. For the island of Møn, the chalk cliffs of Møn Klint are the big draw.

The best beaches are on the islands in the east of the country: Funen Island, the south coast of Seeland, Lolland, and the small island of Bornholm south of the tip of Sweden.

Fishing is an important activity as much in freshwater as at sea.

When to Go		
	CLIMATE	LEGOLAND
JANUARY		
FEBRUARY		
MARCH		
APRIL	☼	
MAY	☼	✔
JUNE	☼	✔
JULY	☼	
AUGUST	☼	
SEPTEMBER	☼	✔
OCTOBER		
NOVEMBER		
DECEMBER		

Dominican Republic

🏁 *The Dominican Republic is one of the top choices for beach-going in the Caribbean. But its beaches are so captivating, they can prevent a visitor from getting to know the country's scenic interior. Here, surrounded by salt lakes and the green slopes of Pico Duarte, a visitor can suddenly feel alone in the world—except for the distant strains of bachata music floating on the breeze.*

▶ COASTS

The southeast coast (Costa de Coco) stretches for some 40 miles and is dotted with the main beach resorts (**Boca Chica, Punta Cana, La Romana**), and **Bayahibe** (fishing village turned beach and diving resort), across from the **Isla Saona.**

On the northeast coast, the **Samaná Peninsula** is part beach resort, part hippie enclave, and one of the prettiest spots on the island. In addition, humpback whales migrate to this area to give birth between January and March. Also on the north coast, **Puerto Plata** is one of the country's premier beach resorts.

In the southeast, a more unusual beach experience can be found on the cliff road between Barahona and Oviedo, where visitors have breathtaking views of deserted beaches and small fishing villages.

The coasts offer many other pleasures in addition to lounging on the beach: water sports, golf (Casa de Campo), and spas (near Bayahibe and Punta Cana).

Scuba divers can see multicolored fish and coral near Juan Dolio and Cabarete (also known for surfing and windsurfing). The town of Boca Chica is the departure point for deep-sea fishing excursions.

▶ LANDSCAPE AND HIKES

Hiking is popular in the **Cordillera Central** (highest peaks more than 9,000 feet), especially on Pico Duarte, where the trail begins in the village of La Ciénaga and continues for 11 miles, with an elevation gain of 6,500 feet. A hiker's calves are put to the test here, but the trail to the top is well marked, and if you reach the summit early in the morning, you can watch the sun rise over the lush, green horizon in an amazing spectacle.

In the southwest, **Enriquillo Lake** is home to interesting wildlife (crocodiles, pink flamingos, iguanas), as is muddy **Oviedo Lagoon.** Both offer worthwhile boat tours.

North of Samaná Bay is the peninsula of the same name, where

Traveler's Notebook			
MAIN CONTACTS *Embassy of the Dominican Republic* 1715 22nd Street, NW Washington, DC 20008 (202) 332-6280 www.domrep.org www.godominican republic.com *Embassy of the Dominican Republic* 139 Inverness Terrace Bayswater London W2 6JF, UK + 44 (0) 90 5677 0054 www.dominican embassy.org.uk **TRAVEL DOCUMENTS** For U.S. Citizens: Passport	For U.K. Citizens: Passport and 30-day tourist card issued on arrival **HEALTH ISSUES** No vaccinations required; some risk of malaria in the west **TRAVEL TIME TO DESTINATION & TIME DIFFERENCE** New York to Santo Domingo: 3 hours 45 minutes non-stop flight; EST +1. London to Santo Domingo: 11 hours 55 minutes connecting flight; GMT +4	**AVERAGE TRIP COST** $1,000–$1,275/£650 –£800 for a week's beach vacation **LANGUAGE & CURRENCY** Official language: Spanish; English widely spoken in tourist areas Currency: Dominican peso; U.S. dollars accepted **POPULATION** 9,366,000 inhabitants, 75 percent of mixed race. Capital: Santo Domingo **RELIGION** 92 percent Catholic	**FESTIVALS** January 26: Duarte's Day (father of the country); February: Santo Domingo Carnival; June: Merengue Festival in Puerto Plata; October 12: Discovery of America Day **SHOPPING** Excellent Davidoff cigars; rum and coffee; larimar (turquoise semiprecious stone); naïve paintings; artisanal products from neighboring Haiti

Scuba diving and idling on the beaches are the main activities on the country's southern coast and nearby Isla Saona.

hikers can traverse the hilly terrain. Half an hour to the south, accessible only by boat, is **Los Haitises National Park**, where visitors can see mangroves, wildlife (pelicans, herons), and cave paintings by the island's first inhabitants, the Taínos tribe of Arawak Indians.

When to Go			
	INTERIOR	BEACHES	WHALE-WATCHING
JANUARY	☼		✔
FEBRUARY	☼		✔
MARCH	☼		✔
APRIL	☼		
MAY		☼	
JUNE		☼	
JULY		☼	
AUGUST			
SEPTEMBER			
OCTOBER			
NOVEMBER			
DECEMBER	☼		

▶ CITIES

The capital **Santo Domingo,** domain of Christopher Columbus and his descendants, is home to the imposing Columbus Lighthouse (Faro a Colón) and a monument and museum dedicated to the explorer. A very livable city, Santo Domingo is considered one of the most beautiful in the Caribbean—especially its old quarter, whose colonial-style buildings surround the oldest cathedral in the Americas.

Puerto Plata sits in the shadow of Mount Isabel de Torres and its statue of Christ the Redeemer and is known for its 19th-century Victorian timber houses. Worth the detour is **Santiago,** located in a valley at the foot of the northern cordillera. Throughout the towns and villages of Hispaniola, life moves to the rhythm of the merengue (a dance similar to the samba) and the romantic sounds of the popular bachata music.

Ecuador

Although its archaeological heritage is not widely known, Ecuador represents an excellent microcosm of all that makes travel attractive in South America: the Cordillera of the Andes (trekking), the Amazon (canoeing), Indian markets, and colonial churches and buildings. The Galápagos Islands should feature prominently; it's a paradise for numerous rare species.

What to See and Do in Ecuador

▶ **LANDSCAPE AND EXCURSIONS**
- Avenue of the Volcanoes (Chimborazo, Cotopaxi, Sangay), the Amazon, the Equator

▶ **WILDLIFE**
- Galápagos (flamingos, iguanas, sea lions, seals, tortoises)
- Cotopaxi National Park (condors, pumas, llamas), Sangay National Park (mountain tapirs, condors)

▶ **CITIES AND VILLAGES**
- Quito, Cuenca

▶ **CULTURAL HERITAGE**
- Indian markets (Otavalo), *ferias*

Mountain lakes, Indian traditions, and the Cordillera in the background—that's Ecuador.

▶ LANDSCAPE AND EXCURSIONS

For hikers and climbers, one of the most beautiful pathways in the Andes is the **Avenue of the Volcanoes** from Quito to Riobamba. **Chimborazo,** at a height of 20,702 feet, is Ecuador's highest volcano, followed by **Cotopaxi's** cone of 19,347 feet—it's the most active volcano. These mountains are joined by Pichincha, Pasochoa, Fuya Fuya, and **Sangay.**

For railroad aficionados, the Nariz del Diablo train passes over steep slopes, through semidesert valleys, and along rocky cliffs and ends with a steep descent down the "Devil's Nose."

The **Amazon** offers rain forests, waterfalls, river ports such as Coca (the departure point into the Napo River), many rivers that are navigable only by canoe, and abundant wildlife (freshwater dolphins, anacondas, caimans) for a rewarding journey.

▶ WILDLIFE

About 600 miles from the mainland, the 30 volcanic islands and islets of the **Galápagos** hold protected species unique to them, such as albatrosses, cormorants, pink flamingos, blue-footed boobies, finches, pelicans, penguins, land and marine iguanas, sea lions, seals, and giant tortoises.

Overall, with 7,500 terrestrial and marine animal species and 25,000 plant species, Ecuador is a rare laboratory of nature's treasures. In the national park surrounding **Cotopaxi,** you can spot condors, pumas, llamas, and wild horses. **Sangay National Park** shelters mountain tapirs and condors, and the Amazon region is full of macaws, parakeets, parrots, and other bird species.

▶ CITIES AND VILLAGES

Quito stands out with its baroque and Renaissance colonial architecture (churches, chapels, convents, Spanish patios, Santo Domingo Monastery, San Francisco Church) and is proud of its painting tradition. The city, at an altitude of 9,252 feet, is surrounded by volcanoes and is included on the World Heritage List.

The historic center of **Cuenca** is composed of right angles with an old town of squares, patios, and wooden balconies. Some vestiges of Inca construction were incorporated into the foundations of monasteries by colonists in the 17th century.

▶ CULTURAL HERITAGE

The best examples of Indian crafts in Latin America are in the village markets, especially in **Otavalo** (market for wool and ponchos), Cotacachi (leather market), and Riobamba. Despite its name, the Panama hat was born and continues to be produced in the south of Ecuador.

The Afro-Ecuadorian culture can be found east of Esmeraldas, along the Caypa and Chota Rivers, and in the small town of Borbón.

One tradition that goes back to the colonial period is bullfighting during the feria (fair) held at the beginning of December in Quito. Another ritual is to step on the equator line at the Mittad del Mundo (Middle of the World) monument.

When to Go			
	COAST	ANDES RANGE	GALÁPAGOS
JANUARY			✔
FEBRUARY			✔
MARCH			✔
APRIL			✔
MAY			✔
JUNE	☼	☼	
JULY	☼	☼	
AUGUST	☼	☼	
SEPTEMBER	☼		
OCTOBER	☼		
NOVEMBER	☼		
DECEMBER			

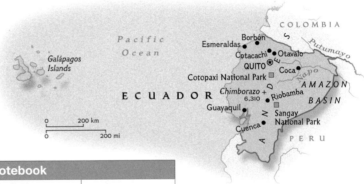

Traveler's Notebook

MAIN CONTACTS
Embassy of Ecuador
2535 15th Street, NW
Washington, DC
20009
(202) 234-7200
www.ecuador.org
www.ecuador
.travel/en/
Embassy of Ecuador
Flat 3B,
3 Hans Crescent
London SW1X 0LS,
UK
+ 44 (0) 20 7584 1367
www.consulado
ecuador.org.uk

TRAVEL DOCUMENTS FOR U.S. & U.K. CITIZENS
Passport

HEALTH ISSUES
Yellow fever immunization is recommended. Malaria prophylaxis is advised for areas below 5,000 feet (no risk in Guayaquil and Quito).

TRAVEL TIME TO DESTINATION & TIME DIFFERENCE
New York to Quito: 8 hours 30 minutes connecting flight; EST. London to Quito: 14 hours connecting flight; GMT +5

AVERAGE TRIP COST
$2,540/£1,640 for a 15-day tour, more if

the Galápagos are included

LANGUAGE & CURRENCY
Official language: Spanish; other languages: Quechua dialects
Currency: sucre; U.S. dollars accepted everywhere

POPULATION
The population of 13,756,000 divides into 40 percent Quechuas, 50 percent people of mixed race, 10 percent Caucasians. Capital: Quito

RELIGION
Almost all Ecuadorians are Catholics.

FESTIVALS
February 27: National Unity Festival; August 10: National Day; November 1: All Saints' Day; beginning of December: Feria de Quito (bullfighting)

SHOPPING
Textiles, embroideries, and hammocks from Indian markets, Panama hats, special bakery goods

Advice

■ **Pros**
• A condensed version of the pleasures of Latin America: colonial heritage, Indian traditions, wildlife, dense forests, trekking to the volcanoes. Outside the Amazon region, the weather is very pleasant.

■ **Cons**
• Cost of travel becomes expensive if the Galápagos are included.

■ **Safety**
• The unsafe north and northeast border regions should be avoided. And, of course, don't flash your valuables.

Egypt

Even for an unrepentant homebody who rarely travels, Egypt must be a destination that sparks considerable interest. This country offers an extraordinary slice of history covering more than five millennia. Although antiquity is the main attraction, another side of Egypt has shown itself in the last few decades—the beaches and diving sites on the Red Sea. Another reason to visit would be to trek through the White Desert or the Sinai.

▶ MONUMENTS

A cruise on the Nile River reveals the country's ancient treasures bit by bit, whether by luxury ship, simple *felucca,* or a larger *dahabiyya* sailboat.

On the outskirts of Cairo, the necropolis of **Giza** with the three pyramids of Pharaohs Khufu, Khafre, and Menkaure watched over by the Great Sphinx, is at the top of Egypt's architectural heritage. But there is so much more. The colossus of Ramses II and Alabaster Sphinx at **Memphis,** the necropolis of **Saqqara** (Step Pyramid of Djoser, Serapeum), and Fayyum with its funerary portraits are also important, nor should the temples and tombs of Tanis in the Nile Delta

What to See and Do in Egypt

▶ **MONUMENTS**

• Pyramids of Giza (Khufu, Khafre, Menkaure), Memphis, Saqqara

• Remnants of ancient Thebes, temples of Luxor and Karnak, Colossi of Memnon, royal tombs (Valley of the Kings, Valley of the Queens)

• Temples of Idfu, Kôm Ombo, and Philae, Kharga Oasis, Abu Simbel

• Monasteries (St. Catherine, St. Simeon), Aswan High Dam

▶ **COASTS**

• Beaches of the Mediterranean and Red Sea

• Diving (Red Sea)

▶ **CITIES AND VILLAGES**

• Cairo, Alexandria

• Nubian villages

▶ **DESERTS AND OASES**

• Sinai Desert (Mount Catherine), White Desert

• Siwa Oasis, Western Desert (Dakhla, Farafra, and Kharga oases)

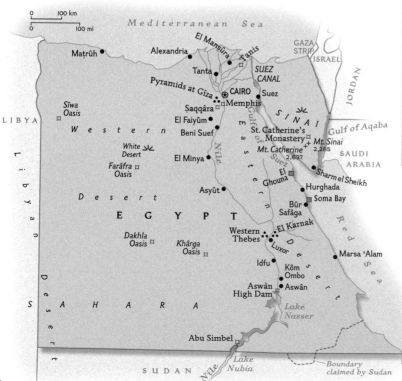

Four giant statues of Ramses II decorate the facade of Abu Simbel, a temple that was relocated above the banks of Lake Nasser.

A Nile River cruise by felucca allows for a leisurely look at Egypt.

be overlooked. More recent excavations at Abusir, not far from Saqqara, are from the fifth pharaonic dynasty, complete with pyramids and royal temples.

The other great archaeological treasures are the ruins of ancient **Thebes,** from the apogee of the New Kingdom period under Amenhotep and Thutmose. Today the temples of **Luxor** and **Karnak** are the most famous remains on the right bank of the Nile. On the other side of the river, Medinet Habu, the **Colossi of Memnon,** the dozens of temples at Gourneh, and Hatshepsut's temple at Dar-el-Bari are only a prelude to the **Valley of the Kings** and **Valley of the Queens.** That's where the royal tombs of the New Kingdom have been excavated, including the treasure-laden tomb of Tutankhamun, opened in 1922. The Mummification Museum in Luxor gives an insight into the process and exhibits artifacts pertaining to death and burial.

Traveling farther south on the Nile, cruise ships pass the temples of **Idfu,** dedicated to the falcon god Horus, and **Kôm Ombo,** founded by Thutmose III and honoring Horus and the crocodile god Sobek.

Upriver at Aswan are the temples of the island of **Philae,** dedicated to the cult of Isis, and Elephantine Island with the Khnum Temple and the Nilometer, a structure for measuring the water level.

North of Aswan, the Coptic **St. Simeon Monastery** (sixth century) offers an architectural contrast. Coptic traces can also be found at the cemetery of El-Bagawat, north of the **Kharga Oasis,** a little-known site boasting ancient temples and Roman fortresses.

Since the **Aswan High Dam** was built, Lake Nasser has flooded the Nubian Valley, but the dismantling and relocation of the historic temples of Ramses II and Nefertari at **Abu Simbel** by UNESCO in the mid-1960s have saved the limestone structures. UNESCO also saved several other Nubian temples including Kalabsha Temple, Kertasi Kiosk, Maharraka Temple, and Daké.

The dam's modern architecture is imposing but has also been a source

Traveler's Notebook

MAIN CONTACTS

Embassy of the Arab Republic of Egypt
3521 International Court, NW
Washington, DC 20008
(202) 895-5400
www.egyptembassy.net
www.egypt.travel/
Embassy of the Arab Republic of Egypt
26 South Street
London W1K 1DW, UK
+ 44 (0) 20 7499 3304
www.egyptembassyuk.org

TRAVEL DOCUMENTS

For U.S. Citizens: Passport and visa
For U.K. Citizens: Passport and 30-day visa issued on arrival

HEALTH ISSUES

Vaccinations are not necessary

TRAVEL TIME TO DESTINATION & TIME DIFFERENCE

New York to Cairo: 10 hours 45 minutes nonstop flight; EST +7.

London to Cairo: 4 hours 45 minutes nonstop flight; GMT +2

AVERAGE TRIP COST

$1,000/£650 for a week's cruise on the Nile

LANGUAGE & CURRENCY

Official language: Arabic
Currency: Egyptian pound

POPULATION

Of the 80,335,000 inhabitants, 15 million live in the capital, Cairo.

RELIGION

94 percent of the population is Muslim; most of the rest are Coptic Christians.

FESTIVALS

February: Sunrise at Abu Simbel Festival (repeated in October), and the Luxor marathon; first Monday after Coptic Easter: Spring Festival; July or August (end of Ramadan): Eid al-Fitr; October 6: National Day;

November: Arab Musical Festival in Cairo.

SHOPPING

Specialties are papyrus and spices, Nubian hibiscus tea leaves, silver jewelry, and traditional textiles (scarves, *galabias,* handwoven silk).

The famous pyramids at Giza in the late afternoon light

of controversy. Today the High Dam (360 feet) controls the Nile floods and forms Lake Nasser, where excursion boats offer rides.

On the Sinai Peninsula, at the foot of Mount Catherine, the Byzantine monastery of **St. Catherine** is the oldest Christian monastery still used for its original purpose. Built in the sixth century by Emperor Justinian, it holds ancient icons and important historic documents on the life of Moses.

▶ COASTS

Beach life on Egypt's shores is not as well known as the country's monuments, even though the sand along the **Mediterranean** near Alexandria or Matrûh is very fine. But the recent development of tourism infrastructures along the **Red Sea** has changed everything. With sunshine 360 days a year, beach vacations at a relatively modest price are the new trend here.

Divers and underwater photographers—even beginners—are documenting the Red Sea's spectacular coral reefs and numerous fish species. Hurghada, a family resort, and Sharm el Sheikh, on the southern tip of the Sinai Peninsula, are popular for diving and snorkeling. Other resorts include Safaga, El Ghouna, Marsa Alam, and Soma Bay, offering

	NILE CRUISES	RED SEA AND DESERT
When to Go		
JANUARY	☼	
FEBRUARY	☼	
MARCH		
APRIL		☼
MAY		☼
JUNE		☼
JULY		
AUGUST		
SEPTEMBER		☼
OCTOBER		☼
NOVEMBER	☼	☼
DECEMBER	☼	

Alexandria's waterfront shows the modern side of the city's historic past.

something for every taste, including spa facilities and golf.

▶ CITIES AND VILLAGES

In **Cairo,** the old neighborhoods, ancient mosques (Ibn Tulun, al-Azhar), and Coptic monuments—including St. Sergius Church (fourth century) on the spot where the Holy Family is said to have stopped on their journey—are the main attractions of a hyperenergized city. A visit to the museums is obligatory, covering culture of the millennia with the National Museum of Antiquities for its mummies and the treasures of Tutankhamun, the Coptic Museum, the Museum of Islamic Art, and the Mahmoud Khalil Museum for Impressionist art.

Alexandria is in search of the lost splendor of the Ptolemies, the last pharaohs, reigning from about 360 to 30 B.C. Excavations have unearthed a necropolis and remains of the famous lighthouse on the harbor bottom. The ancient library, a major center of scholarship until its destruction in 48 B.C. by the Romans, has been reimagined as a futuristic structure, the Bibliotheca Alexandrina, built in 2002, flanked by a Greco-Roman museum. Visitors can stroll along the city's promenade along the Mediterranean or

Like the White Desert, the Siwa Oasis offers stark but stunning vistas.

▶ **DESERTS AND OASES**

The Nile Valley's treasures lead you to forget Egypt's other landscapes, especially the deserts, which are beautiful and attract trekkers of all stripes.

In the **Sinai Desert,** Mount Sinai (7,500 feet), where Moses received the Ten Commandments, is celebrated as the place to watch a sunrise. The higher **Mount St. Catherine** (8,650 feet) is a favorite to explore its surrounding landscape of multicolored sandstone, such as the Colored Canyon near Nuweiba.

In the west, the **White Desert,** so called for its chalk rock formations with astounding color changes, spreads as far as the Libyan border. **Siwa Oasis** lies in the salt lakes at the foot of the Egyptian Sand Sea. The Old Shali fort features prominently above the town, as well as the Mountain of the Dead necropolis (26th dynasty). Other oases with outstanding scenic views are **Dakhla, Farafra,** and **Kharga.**

through the narrow lanes in the Mansheya neighborhood and see the first- and second-century catacombs (Kom el-Shoqafa), Roman amphitheater, Ras el-Tin palace, and necropolis of Anfushi.

Besides Aswan, worth a visit are the nearby Elephantine and Sehel Islands, where the Nubians have been rebuilding their colorful villages that were washed away by the waters of Lake Nasser in 1970.

Advice

■ **Pros**
• The varied choices of travel: luxury cruise or simple sail by felucca, spending time on the Red Sea, or trekking in the desert. Some of the most spectacular coral reefs on the planet.

■ **Cons**
• The heavy police presence and mandatory travel by convoy in certain regions of Egypt.

■ **Safety**
• Despite a few well-publicized attacks on tourists and the presence of land mines along border regions, Egypt is generally a safe country. There are many good reasons to visit; simply use common sense and vigilance.

■ **Special Tip**
• Forget the big cruise boats on the Nile and travel by felucca or some other smaller boat instead and get to really know this river of the gods.

What to See and Do in Ethiopia

▶ **MONUMENTS**

• Historic churches in Lalibela and Aksum, ancient cities of Gondar and Harer

• Archaeological Museum of Addis Ababa

▶ **LANDSCAPE AND WILDLIFE**

• Blue Nile waterfalls, Simien Mountains National Park, Lake Tana, Erta Ale volcano, lakes in the Danakil Depression

• Omo and Awash National Parks

Herdsmen watch their cattle in Simien Mountains National Park.

Ethiopia has long been troubled by political strife, but the country has recovered enough to show off its amazing attractions again: ancient architectural treasures, rugged highlands, beautiful lakes, volcanoes, the Blue Nile, and varied fauna and flora—all in one of the most pleasant climates in Africa.

Ethiopia

Traveler's Notebook

MAIN CONTACTS
Embassy of Ethiopia
3506 International Drive, NW
Washington, DC 20008
(202) 364-1200
www.ethiopian
embassy.org
www.tourism
ethiopia.org
Embassy of Ethiopia
17 Princes Gate
London SW7 1PZ,
UK
+ 44 (0) 20 7838 3897
www.ethioembassy
.org.uk

TRAVEL DOCUMENTS
For U.S. Citizens:
Passport and visa
For U.K.Citizens:
Passport and
3-month visa issued
on arrival

HEALTH ISSUES
Yellow fever immu-nization is strongly recommended; malaria prophy-laxis is necessary in regions below 6,500 feet, but there is no risk in Addis Ababa.

TRAVEL TIME TO DESTINATION & TIME DIFFERENCE
New York to Addis Ababa: 17 hours 45 minutes connecting; EST +8. London to Addis Ababa: 6 hours 45 minutes nonstop; GMT +3

AVERAGE TRIP COST
$3,175/£2,050 for 15 days of all-terrain travel

LANGUAGE & CURRENCY
Official language: Amharic (numerous dialects)
Currency: birr

POPULATION
The 76,512,000 inhabitants are a mixture of Amhara majority and Oromo, Somali, Tigray, and Afar Danakil. Capital: Addis Ababa

RELIGION
Some 52 per-cent of the popula-tion belongs to the Ethiopian Ortho-dox Church, which separated from the Egyptian Copts in the last century; 31

percent follow Islam, 11 percent follow native religions, and a small minority are Jews (Falashas).

FESTIVALS
January 19: Tim-kat procession (Epi-phany; Easter is also an important holi-day); April 6: Victory Day; July or August (end of Ramadan): Eid al-Fitr; Septem-ber 27 or 28: Meskel (Finding of the True Cross)

SHOPPING
Silver and amber jewelry, Ethiopian crosses, parchment paintings, textiles, and coffee

▶ MONUMENTS

Eleven 12th-century churches in **Lalibela** are hewn from rock and connected by underground tunnels. They represent some of the most remarkable architecture in all of Africa. Every January, the town celebrates Timkat, the Ethiopian Orthodox Epiphany. The festival begins with a procession to the sound of drums, when priests and deacons in colorful robes carry the cloth-wrapped Tabot, a model of the Ark of the Covenant, and other stone tablets through the town.

Equally interesting is **Aksum,** the cradle of the kingdom of the Sabaeans, where according to legend the palace of the Queen of Sheba once stood. The city is also famous for its imposing steles; the largest one, dating to the fourth century, dubbed "God's Flute," had been removed by the Italian army and was recently returned. Other attractions include the ruins of the sixth-century Dungur Palace and St. Mary of Zion church.

North of Aksum, the sixth-century monastery of Debre Damo, where six hundred monks still live, is perched on a sheer cliff and accessible only by rope.

Gondar, a city of 44 old churches and a 17th- and 18th-century royal palace, is also worth a visit, as is **Harer,** the old white city enclosed by a town wall, hovering at an altitude of 5,600 feet.

Around Lake Tana, medieval monasteries painted with illustrations from the Bible and churches famed for illuminated manuscripts complete the country's architectural cultural heritage.

The National Museum of Archaeology of **Addis Ababa** exhibits a reproduction of the three-million-year-old skeleton of "Lucy," the famous *Australopithecus afarensis,* which was discovered in the Danakil region.

▶ LANDSCAPE AND WILDLIFE

Ethiopia's natural treasures include the spectacular waterfalls of the Blue Nile, **Blue Nile Falls,** as well as rugged highlands that vary from 5,000 to 15,000 feet in altitude. **Simien**

When to Go		
	CLIMATE	NATURE
JANUARY	☼	
FEBRUARY	☼	
MARCH	☼	
APRIL	☼	⤛
MAY	☼	⤛
JUNE		⤛
JULY		
AUGUST		
SEPTEMBER		⤛
OCTOBER	☼	⤛
NOVEMBER	☼	⤛
DECEMBER	☼	

Mountains National Park offers the most dramatic views north of **Lake Tana,** which harbors a number of islands and a fleet of fishermen's papyrus boats. Other attractions include the Sof Omar Caves carved by the Web River, the **Erta Ale** volcano, the Bale Mountains, and the lakes of the **Danakil Depression.**

The birds of Ethiopia include nearly a thousand species, among them the hooded vulture that is so unafraid of humans that it can be easily approached. The greatest variety of species—such as ospreys, flamingos, ibises, and marabou storks—can be found around the lakes of the Rift Valley about 125 miles south of Addis Ababa.

The classic African wildlife (lions, giraffes, elephants, crocodiles, hippopotamuses) enlivens the **Omo** and **Awash National Parks,** both suitable for a safari. The Omo River ends in a delta at Lake Turkana in Kenya and can be traveled by boat.

Lapland and its different way of life has attracted tourists for years.

Finland

Hikers, skiers, and nature lovers of all stripes unite! This country is for you. Rarely do humans ever have as much space to themselves or so many lakes in one place. Here, visitors can pass summer in the light of the midnight sun, or enjoy themselves in winter with cross-country skiing, reindeer races, and snowmobile rides, not to forget saunas or Santa Claus.

▶ **LANDSCAPE AND EXCURSIONS**

A large section of **Lapland** lies north of the Arctic Circle. Visitors are particularly attracted to this region during Indian summer (Ruska Aika) and winter. From the towns of Levi, Yllas near Kittila, or Saariselka near Ivalo, you can explore the region by snowmobile, dogsled or reindeer sleigh, or even aboard

an icebreaker—as well as by luge, snowshoes, and cross-country skis, the specialty here.

The sacred mountain of the Sami people, **Saana Fell,** rises up from the snow-covered taiga. People flock to the region in summer for excursions by all-terrain vehicle or mountain bike along the Tenojoki River, in Lemmenjoki National Park (the largest wooded area in all of Europe) and Pallas-Ounastunturi National Park, or on the banks of **Lake Inari** with the sacred island of Ukko and a Sami cemetery.

The landscape is dotted with nearly 200,000 lakes, especially in the southeast and in **Karelia,** where two-thirds of the terrain is blanketed by darkly wooded coniferous forests.

The more than 6,500 **Åland** islands and islets form an archipelago in the Baltic Sea across from Turku. A cruise to visit the castles and churches (not to mention the opportunity for tax-free shopping) makes this an attractive excursion.

Between mid-May and the end of July, the sun shines practically without interruption in Lapland—some 73 days of midsummer nights. In winter, on the other hand, darkness prevails, enlivened only by periodic displays of the aurora borealis.

▶ CITIES

Helsinki, at the tip of a peninsula, invites visitors to cruise along its bays and islets in the summer or to wander on its frozen waters in winter. The city's center around Senate Square looks very orderly with its neoclassical buildings, but Uspenski Cathedral and Temppeliaukio Church, which is carved out of the natural bedrock, show a more creative side of Finnish architecture. A 15-minute ferry ride takes visitors to the Suomenlinna sea fortress and its several museums.

Tampere, on an isthmus between two lakes, is worth a visit for its Sara Hilden Art Museum and Kaleva church.

Turku, the oldest city in the country, can attest to its history with a castle, a 13th-century cathedral, and

an open-air museum. Karelia and the border region with Russia merit a detour to **Imatra.** In **Kuopio,** the sites include the market halls and the white cathedral. The small village of **Kerimäki** is known for having the largest wooden church in the world.

▶ CULTURAL HERITAGE

The sauna is a Finnish invention and institution. A sauna begins with a hot steam bath and ends with cooling off by jumping into a cold pool or lake or rolling in snow.

Another institution is Santa Claus or Father Christmas, whose home is said to be in Lapland's Santa Claus Village in Rovaniemi.

More recent traditions include the reindeer races held between January and March.

When to Go			
	SUMMER TOURISM	MIDNIGHT SUN	AURORA BOREALIS
JANUARY			✔
FEBRUARY			✔
MARCH			✔
APRIL			✔
MAY		☼	
JUNE	☼	☼	
JULY	☼	☼	
AUGUST	☼		
SEPTEMBER			
OCTOBER			
NOVEMBER			✔
DECEMBER			✔

France

The most visited country in the world, France's appeal lies in its harmonious landscape, its rich cultural heritage, and its convivial lifestyle. In every region, visitors can find attractive towns and cities, ancient architectural and historic treasures, and fields growing the specialties of its terroir.

▶ LANDSCAPE AND MOUNTAINS

"Harmony" is the key word for describing France's countryside. Moving from west to east, from the lowlands of the Atlantic coast to the hill country in the center and the high peaks in the Alps, France's landscapes complement each other perfectly. Provence and the Côte d'Azur are the most visited regions, followed closely by the Alps, the Pyrenees, and the island of Corsica.

The delicate fragrances and colors of the countryside, odd villages (Les Baux de Provence, Gordes), seasonal markets, the many summer festivals (Aix-en-Provence, Avignon, Orange), and the regional parks

What to See and Do in France

▶ LANDSCAPE

• Provence, the Alps, the Pyrenees

• The Massif Central, the Jura, the Vosges, Corsica

▶ CITIES

• Paris, Lyon, Marseille

• Montpellier, Nice, Toulouse, Bordeaux

• Colmar, Strasbourg

• Dijon, Reims, Lille, Rouen, Rennes

▶ CULTURAL HERITAGE

• Vestiges of the Roman Empire

• Romanesque, Gothic, and Renaissance buildings

• Cathedrals, abbeys, churches

• Palaces (Versailles, Fontainebleau, châteaux in the Loire Valley, Cathar castles of the Languedoc)

• Fortifications (Mont-St.-Michel, Carcassonne, Vauban-designed forts)

▶ COASTS

• Coasts along the Channel, Brittany, and the Vendée

• Basque Coast, Mediterranean

Listed as a World Heritage site, Notre Dame cathedral in Paris is a jewel of sacred art.

The Pont du Gard, a 300-foot-long Roman aqueduct, was built without mortar.

(Camargue, Luberon, Mercantour, Verdon gorges) set **Provence** apart as a vacationland.

Each area in France offers products that are specific to its region, and each can boast gastronomic itineraries—in particular, the wine routes in Bordeaux, Alsace, Burgundy, and Champagne, or one of the 365 towns famous for their cheeses. The town of Roquefort-sur-Soulzon in Aveyron is one example; its sheep's milk blue cheese has a protected designation of origin.

The mountains are as varied as the rest of the country. The Alps and the Pyrenees see as many visitors in summer as in winter.

In the northern **Alps,** the national parks of Vanoise and Vercors, and the lake areas (Lake Annecy, Lake Bourget) are starting points for lengthy hiking tours. Mont Blanc, the highest mountain in Europe at 15,771 feet, sees hikers and climbers all summer long.

In winter, the skiers take over the trails of the Haute-Savoie (Le Grand-Bornand, Megève, Sallanches) and Savoie (Courchevel, La Plagne, Les Arcs, Tignes, Val d'Isère). Ecrins National Park in the southeastern Alps has a rich fauna and flora (ibex, chamois, marmots, and alpine flowers). Queyras National Park is dotted with lakes, waterfalls, and mountain villages, the highest of which is St.-Véran.

The **Pyrenees** stretch for 250 miles from the Basque coast on the Atlantic to the Côte Vermeille (Vermilion Coast) on the Mediterranean. Among the favorite destinations are the hiking areas (Ariège, Cerdagne, Gavarnie, Catalan Pyrenees), ski resorts (Font-Romeu, La Mongie), spas (Bagnères-de-Bigorre, Luchon, Ax-les-Thermes), and Massabielle Grotto, which made the town of Lourdes one of the most important pilgrimage centers for Catholics.

The **Massif Central** offers endless hiking trails in summer, especially in the volcanic landscape of the Auvergne, in the Cevennes Mountains, and in the valleys (caves and gorges of the Ardèche and Tarn Rivers). Elsewhere, regions known for their products (Morvan, Beaujolais, Charolais), emblematic villages

Traveler's Notebook

MAIN CONTACTS

Embassy of France
4101 Reservoir Road, NW
Washington, DC 20007
(202) 944-6000
www.ambafrance-us.org
http://us.france guide.com

Embassy of France
58 Knightsbridge
London SW1X 7JT, UK
+ 44 (0) 20 7073 1000
www.ambafrance-uk.org

TRAVEL DOCUMENTS FOR U.S. & U.K. CITIZENS

Passport

TRAVEL TIME TO DESTINATION & TIME DIFFERENCE

New York to Paris: 7 hours nonstop flight; EST +6.
London to Paris: 1 hour 10 minutes nonstop flight

AVERAGE TRIP COST

a weekend in Paris $380/£250; a week of hiking $1,000/£650

LANGUAGE & CURRENCY

Official language: French
Currency: euro

POPULATION

64,303,000 inhabitants. Capital: Paris

RELIGION

The majority are Catholic; minorities include 6 percent Muslim, 2 percent Protestant, and 1 percent Jewish.

FESTIVALS

February: Carnival (Nice's is well known, as are those in Dunkirk, Lille, and Roubaix); May: Cannes Festival; June 21: Music Festival in Paris (all styles of music in the streets); July 14: Bastille Day (music and dance in all towns and villages); summer: many theater and music festivals (classical and modern), especially in the south

SHOPPING

Leaving France without some cheese, wine, or one of the many regional specialties could be seen as heresy. The AOC designation *(appellation d'origine contrôlée,* or protected designation of origin) guarantees the product's source. Regional arts and crafts include jewelry, faience, *santons* (painted ceramic crèche figures from Provence), and pottery.

One of the most popular beaches in Corsica is Palombaggia in Porto Vecchio, with its striking blue water.

(Rocamadour), or natural attractions (Padirac Abyss, Aven Armand Cave) draw many visitors.

The **Jura** and **Vosges Mountains** offer additional fine alternatives to hikers, with quiet and remote valleys, or balloon flights above the Vosges.

Corsica's geography, on the other hand, has something for everyone, whether hiker or beach lover. It may take just a little while to get from the rugged mountains (Vizzavona forest, Col de Bavella) via the long-distance GR 20 trail to the splendid coast. The hinterlands are equally amazing with the Agriate desert and the rock formations of the Calanques de Piana.

▶ CITIES

The classic tour of **Paris** begins at the Arc de Triomphe, then heads down the Champs-Elysées to the Place de la Concorde and the Louvre Museum, followed by a quick visit to the Latin Quarter on the Left Bank. After the major sites, a visit to some of the more traditional neighborhoods is in order, such as the Marais, Les Halles, Bastille, and Menilmontant, or the flea market in Clignancourt. Other famous places are Montmartre, the Church of the Madeleine, Notre Dame Cathedral, and Place des Vosges. Of the many famous monuments and museums, the most important ones are the

Orsay Museum with its Impressionist art; the Pompidou Center, which holds, among others, the National Museum of Modern Art; and the Grand Palais and Petit Palais, housing temporary exhibits.

Other French cities can hold their own with Paris. **Lyon**'s panorama looks grand from Fourvière hill. In the old town, the interior courtyards of the St.-Jean quarter and the cathedral stand out. Characteristic of this former capital of ancient Gaul are the *traboules*, alleys to connect backyards; the *bouchons,* typical restaurants; and Croix-Rousse, the historic quarter of the silk weavers, the *canuts.*

The abbey of Mont-St.-Michel sits on a rocky tidal island in Normandy.

In the south, **Marseille** attracts interest with the broad boulevard La Canebière, Notre Dame de la Garde basilica, the old harbor, and Château d'If, the offshore fortress made famous in *The Count of Monte Cristo.* Other pleasures await the visitor in the oldest quarter, the Panier, with the architectural masterpieces of the Diamantée House and Vielle Charité, now a museum and cultural center. Other important destinations in the south include the city of **Montpellier** and its Place de la Comédie, Avignon and its Papal Palace, **Nice** with the Promenade des Anglais and old town, **Toulouse**'s Capitole (city hall) and St.-Sernin Church, and **Bordeaux** (St.-André Cathedral, St.-Michel Church and tower, Grand Théâtre).

On the other side of the country, **Strasbourg** (Notre Dame Cathedral, half-timbered houses in the Petite France quarter), **Colmar** (half-timbered houses, Unterlinden Museum), and **Nancy** (Stanislas Place, Golden Gates, Nancy School of Art Nouveau) underline the diversity of urban France.

Such a tour should not exclude some of the sights in **Dijon** (Palace of the Dukes of Burgundy, St.-Bénigne Cathedral), **Reims** (cathedral and St.-Remi basilica; Porte de Mars, a Roman triumphal arch), **Lille** (churches; Vieille Bourse, the old stock exchange), **Rouen** (Gros Horloge, an astronomical clock; Notre Dame Cathedral), or **Rennes** (court house, churches, Old Town).

▶ **MONUMENTS**

France's architecture is so rich because all great eras of European history—the Roman Empire, Romanesque, Gothic, Renaissance, classicism—have been represented in the country. This makes for a long list of things to see.

The Romans left quite a few of their grand structures in the south, among them the Pont du Gard and the amphitheater at Orange; the arenas, the "Square House," and the Temple of Diana in Nîmes; and the arena and amphitheater in Arles.

The Christian heritage is represented by the cathedrals of Albi, Amiens, Bourges, Chartres, Reims, Rouen, and Strasbourg; countless smaller churches in the Romanesque and Gothic styles; and abbeys

When to Go			
	NORTH	SOUTH	WINTER SPORTS
JANUARY			❄
FEBRUARY			❄
MARCH			❄
APRIL		☼	❄
MAY	☼	☼	
JUNE	☼	☼	
JULY	☼	☼	
AUGUST	☼	☼	
SEPTEMBER	☼	☼	
OCTOBER		☼	
NOVEMBER			❄
DECEMBER			❄

such as Cluny and Fontenay in Burgundy, St.-Michel-de-Cuxa in Roussillon, and Senanque in Provence. The basilica of the Madeleine in Vézelay, in a subtle mix of Romanesque and Gothic, is one of the pilgrimage stops on the way to Santiago de Compostela in Spain.

Other favorite landmarks are the châteaux: First in line is **Versailles** (Louis XIV) with some five million visitors per year, followed by **Fontainebleau** (François I) and the great châteaux of the **Loire Valley,** built in the 15th and 16th centuries—Amboise, Azay-le-Rideau, Blois, Chambord, Chenonceau, and others. The castles that preceded them are equally outstanding, such as the châteaux of the Auvergne or the Cathar castles of the **Languedoc**—veritable

eagles' nests such as Peyrepertuse or Montségur.

Two fortified complexes should be included in any itinerary: **Mont-St.-Michel,** located on a rocky tidal island in Normandy, hides a Benedictine abbey and church behind its fortified walls; and, in the south of the country, **Carcassonne,** an early medieval fortified citadel that, although much restored over the years, boasts architecture that remains true to its origin. The forts built by military engineer Vauban, the 17th-century inventor of the pentagonal structure of fortifications, are well worth a visit, as well; 12 of them are listed as World Heritage monuments such as the citadel of Besançon in the Franche-Comté or Briançon in the Alps.

▶ COASTS

The coast along the **Channel** in the north is either sandy and flat or steep and rocky (Cap Gris-Nez, cliffs of Étretat). Allied forces landed on the beaches of Normandy in June 1944. Many of the resorts (Le Touquet-Paris-Plage, Deauville) are weekend haunts for Parisians. The north and

west coasts of **Brittany** are steadily battered by winds; the south coast enjoys gentler conditions and is flanked by islets (Île de Groix, Belle-Île). The fishing ports of Dinard, St.-Malo, Bénodet, and Camaret draw romantics and fans of thalassotherapy.

Along the Atlantic coast toward the south lies the **Vendée** region (Les Sables-d'Olonne, La Baule) and islands (Île de Ré, Île d'Oléron). In succession follow the Côte Sauvage, or Wild Coast (Royan), and the Côte d'Argent, the Silver Coast, which ends at the Bassin d'Arcachon with its large sand dunes. The Landes coast is suitable for surfing, and the **Basque Coast** boasts the beach town of Biarritz and the charming St.-Jean-de-Luz.

The Côte d'Azur stretches along the **Mediterranean** coast from Menton to St.-Tropez. This is where high society convenes. A more modest clientele vacations on the coast from Hérault (La Grande Motte, Le Cap d'Agde) and Aude (Gruissan, Leucate) all the way to Roussillon (Argelès-sur-Mer, Canet-Plage).

Advice

■ Pros

• France has everything to offer: beautiful countryside, a long cultural heritage, and beaches. Paris always has a special allure. The reputation of convivial living in France never seems in dispute.

■ Cons

• On the expensive side.

■ Special Tips

• Many seaside resorts have spas with thalassotherapy and balneotherapy treatments.

• Active vacations and exploration of nature rather than beaches or visits to the big cities seem to be attracting more new fans.

What to See and Do in French Guiana

▶ **EXCURSIONS**

- Traveling by dugout canoe up the rivers

▶ **WILDLIFE**

- Agoutis, anacondas, black caimans, sloths, leatherback turtles, scarlet ibis, parakeets, vultures, toucans

▶ **CULTURAL HERITAGE**

- Penal Colony of Île Royale, prison of St.-Laurent-du-Maroni
- Space center in Kourou

The view from Île Royale to Devil's Island, the notorious French penal colony

French Guiana

■ *French Guiana is part of the "green hell" of the Amazon, which is the reason for some of its allure. The dense rain forest lends itself to exploration via dugout canoe. Other highlights include a visit to the former penal colony on Île Royale and the space center in Kourou.*

Traveler's Notebook

MAIN CONTACTS

Embassy of France
4101 Reservoir Road, NW
Washington, DC 20007
(202) 944-6000
www.ambafrance-us.org
http://us.france guide.com

Embassy of France
58 Knightsbridge
London SW1X 7JT, UK
+ 44 (0) 20 7073 1000
www.ambafrance-uk.org

TRAVEL DOCUMENTS FOR U.S. & U.K. CITIZENS

Passport

HEALTH ISSUES

Yellow fever immunization recommended; malaria prophylaxis is strongly recommended for the interior

TRAVEL TIME TO DESTINATION & TIME DIFFERENCE

New York to Cayenne: 20 hours 30 minutes connecting flight; EST +2. London to Cayenne: 22 hours 55 minutes connecting flight; GMT -3

AVERAGE TRIP COST

$2,550/£1,650 for a 15-day rain forest adventure

LANGUAGE & CURRENCY

Official language: French, but 90 percent speak Creole; Taki-Taki is spoken around Maroni
Currency: euro

POPULATION

199,500 inhabitants, a low population density; a quarter of the population lives in the capital, Cayenne.

RELIGION

Catholics: 87 percent; others include Protestants (including an increasing number of evangelicals), animists, Muslims, spiritists, and Baha'is

FESTIVALS

February or March: Carnival is all about "King Vaval" between the weekends of Epiphany and Ash Wednesday and four days of follies preceding Ash Wednesday; June 10: Abolition Day

SHOPPING

A hammock, a calabash, and a few tiny gold nuggets are favorite souvenirs.

▶ RIVERS

The rivers of the Amazon region, which have seen the vanished dreams of clandestine gold diggers, are of major interest in French Guiana. The rivers are full of rapids but lend themselves to exploration by canoe or other watercraft. Best known is the Maroni River (it takes four days to travel by dugout from St.-Laurent-du-Maroni on the coast to the town of Maripasoula halfway up the river). Other rivers include the Oyapock, Approuague, Mana, and Inini.

The dugout canoe is both the local transport and a tourist attraction, as is the *carbet,* a large open hut that serves as shelter and camp (sleeping in hammocks). Besides its adventurous and sporty aspect, this kind of travel allows for swimming in the rivers and the occasional meeting with Amerindian populations such as the Wayana.

▶ WILDLIFE

Unless you are a wildlife specialist, you will have trouble recognizing the hundreds of species of reptiles, fish, and birds in this 30,000-square-mile protected rain forest territory teeming with agoutis, anacondas, and black caimans, the latter present in large numbers in the Kaw Swamps.

Hikers should hire a guide to keep from getting lost and because at every curve of the river there are new animal species to discover—especially around the Saül region, where sloths, parakeets, vultures, jacanas, scarlet ibis (in the estuary of the Sinnamary River), and toucans can be spotted.

Another highlight is the egg-laying period of the endangered leatherback turtles, between April and July, both in Mana and on the beaches of Les Hattes in the Awala-Yalimapo commune.

Tourists who didn't find many exotic species in their explorations can visit the Eugène-Bellony Zoo, the Franconi Museum, or the Fauna Flora Amazonica in Cayenne to catch up.

▶ CULTURAL HERITAGE

The penal colony off the coast from Kourou on the **Île Royale** (closed in 1954), St. Joseph Island, and Devil's Island together form the island group Îles du Salut. The prison buildings, where Alfred Dreyfus was incarcerated, are an eerie sight; a small museum explains their history. The prison in **St.-Laurent-du-Maroni** recalls its most famous inmate, Papillon, who eventually escaped.

The Guiana Space Center in Kourou is open Wednesdays for visitors with reservations. With sufficient early reservations, it is possible to watch the launch of an Ariane rocket. The space museum in Kourou simply has to be part of such a visit.

Advice

▪ Pros
• The true Amazon region can be explored by dugout canoe. Well-established infrastructure.

▪ Cons
• Excessive heat and humidity. For river exploration, tourists must be prepared to sleep in hammocks or at least out in the open. The mangrove coasts are not accessible to tourists and not suitable for swimming.

▪ Safety
• It is not safe to explore the rivers and forests on one's own without a guide.

▪ Special Tip
• Anyone who hasn't traveled by dugout on a river and met some village people hasn't really experienced French Guiana.

When to Go		
	CLIMATE	LEATHERBACK TURTLE NESTING SEASON
JANUARY		
FEBRUARY		
MARCH		
APRIL		✔
MAY		✔
JUNE		✔
JULY		✔
AUGUST	☼	
SEPTEMBER	☼	
OCTOBER	☼	
NOVEMBER	☼	
DECEMBER		

What to See and Do in French Polynesia

▶ **COASTS**

• Society Islands lagoons

• Bora Bora (luxury resorts; tropical fish), Moorea (beaches and scenic excursions), Huahine

• Marquesas

• Rangiroa (scuba diving)

▶ **CULTURAL HERITAGE**

• Tikis on the Marquesas

• Gauguin Museum and Pearl Museum, Tahiti

Whether visiting the Marquesas or other islands, Polynesia is a paradise.

French Polynesia

Tahitian women (wahine), the emerald ocean, and the perfume of Tahitian flowers may linger in one's mind— reinforced by the influence of painter Paul Gauguin— although these romantic images have given way to conventional tourism. But that is no reason not to go: The beauty of this earthly paradise, with its 118 islands, remains.

Traveler's Notebook

MAIN CONTACTS
Embassy of France
4101 Reservoir Road, NW
Washington, DC 20007
(202) 944-6000
www.ambafrance-us.org
Embassy of France
58 Knightsbridge London SW1X 7JT, UK
+ 44 (0) 20 7073 1000
www.ambafrance-uk.org

TRAVEL DOCUMENTS FOR U.S. & U.K. CITIZENS
Passport

TRAVEL TIME TO DESTINATION & TIME DIFFERENCE
New York to Papeete: 16 hours 45 minutes connecting flight; EST –5. London to Papeete: 22 hours 45 minutes connecting flight; GMT -10

AVERAGE TRIP COST
$3,810/£2,460 for 12 days of cruising

LANGUAGE & CURRENCY
Official language: French; unofficial language: Tahitian

Currency: Pacific franc

POPULATION
279,000 inhabitants; 80 percent are Polynesian, 9 percent Asian, and 10 percent European. Capital: Papeete

RELIGION
Protestants slightly outnumber Catholics; Mormons are well represented

FESTIVALS
March 5: Missionary Day; June 29: Anniversary of Internal Autonomy

(Heiva); October: Carnival in Tahiti; Hawaiki Nui Va'a canoe race, Tahiti; December: Tahiti Flower Festival (Tiaré)

SHOPPING
Tahitian Monoi-oil, black pearls, and a pareo (beach wrap) are the typical souvenirs, besides all kinds of basketware.

▶ COASTS

Society Islands

Contrary to common belief, Tahiti is not the most beautiful island in the Society Islands, or in French Polynesia in general. Many visitors prefer Bora Bora, christened "Pearl of the Pacific," with its turquoise lagoon surrounded by coral reefs—ideal for snorkeling and scuba diving; it is also the premier luxury destination in the islands. Some people prefer to relax on the beaches and explore the scenic landscape of **Moorea,** others to discover the hidden beaches and more traditional way of life on **Huahine.**

Marquesas Islands

Unlike most other Pacific archipelagos, the more than 20 islands of the Marquesas (six of which are inhabited) have neither coral reefs nor lagoons, but rather high cliffs and pebble beaches. This landscape is unique to the Marquesas and attracts those who prefer the road less traveled.

Ua Huka, Fatu Hiva, and Nuku Hiva are often cited as the islands' most beautiful places, but not to be missed are Hiva Oa and Atuona, the village where Gauguin lived.

Other Islands

In the north, the atoll of **Rangiroa** wins the award for best scuba diving spot. Near the area's 78 coral islets *(motu),* travelers can see manta rays and hammerhead sharks.

In the extreme south of French Polynesia, the Austral Islands and Gambier Islands have become less popular with tourists—a good opportunity to buck the trend!

Cruising the islands on ships such as the *Aranui III* and the *Paul-Gauguin* is a good way for travelers to see all the sites, most of them in the Marquesas.

Map

500 km
500 mi

Marquesas Islands

KIRIBATI

Pacific

Ocean

Rangiroa
Huahine
ora Bora
Tuamotu Archipelago
Moorea
Tahiti
PAPEETE
Society
Islands

Austral Islands

Gambier Islands

FRENCH POLYNESIA
(France)

Advice

■ Pros

• The enduring myth of distant horizons, which can be found here with dreamlike images and places. When money is no object, the abundance of luxury hotels and spas that feature local culture and decor.

■ Cons

• The cost of travel and accommodations remains high; this is high-end tourism.

■ Special Tip

• French Polynesia is an increasingly popular destination for honeymoons and wedding anniversaries, including travel by cruise ship. Everyone has an idea of heaven on Earth.

▶ CULTURAL HERITAGE

In addition to music and dance, the Marquesas are known for their tikis. These wood or stone statues can stand over 6 feet high and are carved in humanoid forms.

Not to be missed in Tahiti are the Gauguin Museum (25 original paintings) and the Pearl Museum (the island has numerous black pearl farms).

When to Go		
	CLIMATE	DIVING
JANUARY		
FEBRUARY		
MARCH		
APRIL		✔
MAY	☼	✔
JUNE	☼	✔
JULY	☼	
AUGUST	☼	
SEPTEMBER	☼	
OCTOBER	☼	
NOVEMBER		
DECEMBER		

Germany

What to See and Do in Germany

▶ **CITIES AND MONUMENTS**

• Hamburg, Berlin, Potsdam, Dresden, Weimar, Cologne, Rothenburg, Heidelberg, Munich, Bremen, Lübeck, Frankfurt, Mainz, Würzburg, Nuremberg, Trier, Aachen, Bayreuth, Bamberg, Berchtesgaden

• Neuschwanstein in Bavaria, Hohenzollern castles

▶ **LANDSCAPE**

• Bavarian Alps, Rhine Valley, Harz Mountains, Saxon Switzerland, Lake Laach

• Valleys of the Mosel, Elbe, Weser, and Danube Rivers

• Externsteine, Black Forest, Thuringian Forest, Frisian Islands

▶ **FESTIVALS**

• Carnival, Christmas markets

• Oktoberfest in Munich

Since reunification in 1990, Germany has been showcasing some 20 cities that are worth a visit, with Berlin as the standard-bearer. The romantic vistas along the Rhine Valley, the extravagance of the castles in Bavaria, and the Alps hold a special charm.

▶ CITIES AND MONUMENTS

Hamburg is known as the "red Venice" for its redbrick buildings, its numerous canals and bridges, and its mercantile tradition.

Berlin, a perpetual construction site since the fall of the Berlin Wall, now offers visitors ultramodern architecture in the Mitte district and the Potsdamer Platz area, while preserving the old sections of the city with an alternative lifestyle (Kreuzberg and Prenzlauer Berg). Modern buildings (Reichstag, Jewish Memorial) surround the symbolic Brandenburg Gate, in a city where cultural life plays a strong role (Museum Island, Neue Galerie art museum).

Potsdam, south of Berlin, was once known as the "Prussian Versailles" and includes Sanssouci Park (Sanssouci Palace, Neues Palais).

Dresden, nicknamed "Florence on the Elbe" for its baroque architecture and ocher colors, was known as one of the most beautiful cities in Germany from the 17th century until the Allies bombed it in 1945. The reconstruction of its buildings (Zwinger Palace, Semper Opera, and the emblematic Lutheran Frauenkirche, which only recently has been rebuilt) shows them convincingly just as they used to be.

Weimar had its time of glory and preserves its cultural heritage from the time of writer Johann Wolfgang von Goethe. **Cologne** (Köln), advantageously situated along the Rhine River, has the most beautiful cathedral in the country. The walled town of **Rothenburg** is one of the best examples of a small, medieval town in Germany. Not far from there, **Heidelberg** still epitomizes the era of German romanticism (castle, Old Town, Old Bridge).

Munich boasts the old city around Marienplatz, the Wittelsbach

The Altes Museum (left), built in 1830, and the Berlin Cathedral, built in 1894–1905, dominate Berlin's Museum Island.

Residence, and baroque churches, as well as futuristic structures (Allianz Arena stadium, BMW-World).

Other historic places in Germany include the Hansa cities of **Bremen** and **Lübeck, Frankfurt** (Goethe Haus, cathedral, museums), **Mainz** (13th-century Romanesque cathedral, castle of the prince-electors), **Würzburg** (Marienberg fortress, residence of the prince-bishops, decorated with frescoes by Tiepolo), **Nuremberg** (castle, St. Sebaldus and St. Lorenz churches, Beautiful Fountain), **Trier** (well-preserved Roman buildings such as the Porta Nigra and baths, cathedral), **Aachen**

(Gothic cathedral and Palatine Chapel of Charlemagne), **Bayreuth** (theater built by Ludwig II and the annual festival of Richard Wagner's operas), **Bamberg** (medieval cathedral, old city hall), and **Berchtesgaden** (Wittelsbach castle, churches, old salt mines).

The following sites also merit a detour: the extravagant castles built by Ludwig II of Bavaria (Hohenschwangau, Neuschwanstein), the Hohenzollern castles (Sigmaringen in Baden-Württemberg), the romantic castles of Thuringia (Wartburg, where Martin Luther translated the Bible and the site of

the Meistersinger contest, around which Wagner's opera Tannhäuser revolves), the fortified castles in the Rhine Valley, and the marvelous baroque architecture of Ottobeuren Abbey in Bavaria.

Each big city has at least one important museum. Major examples include the Kunsthalle and history museum in Hamburg; the Pergamon Museum, Bode Museum, Modern Art Museum (Rembrandt, Van Eyck, Vermeer, Watteau), and Wall Museum in Berlin; the Romano-Germanic Museum and Museum Ludwig in Cologne; the Gemäldegalerie in Dresden

Between Mainz and Koblenz, the Rhine narrows at the Lorelei rock, which gave rise to the legend of the siren.

(Raphael, Titian, Poussin, Rembrandt, Rubens, Vermeer); and the Gutenberg Museum (museum of printing) in Mainz. Munich's museums include Alte Pinakothek (Dürer, Grünewald, Hieronymus Bosch, Fragonard, Tintoretto, Rembrandt, Rubens, Van der Weyden), Neue Pinakothek (Cézanne, Degas, Delacroix, Gauguin, Géricault, Manet, Van Gogh), and the new Pinakothek der Moderne, housing the best collection of modern art in the country.

▶ LANDSCAPE

Two geographic features dominate Germany's important destinations: the Alps and the Rhine River. The **Bavarian Alps** give one pause with their grand panorama in the Bayerischer Wald National Park—its wildlife, including brown bears and the rare European lynx—as well as the scenic road leading from Lake Constance (Bodensee) to Berchtesgaden, taking in the Königsee and Staffelsee lakes, the ski resort Garmisch-Partenkirchen, and the Zugspitze, at 9,721 feet the highest mountain in the country, which can be reached via cable car for breathtaking views over the subalpine ranges.

Farther north, Bavaria presents a pleasant mixture of scenic views and ancient castles on the Romantic Road (Augsburg, Spessart Mountains, Nördlingen, Rothenburg, Würzburg). The number of modern

Traveler's Notebook

MAIN CONTACTS
Embassy of the Federal Republic of Germany
4645 Reservoir Road, NW
Washington, DC 20007
(202) 298-4000
www.germany.info
www.germany-tourism.de
Embassy of the Federal Republic of Germany
23 Belgrave Square
London SW1X 8PZ, UK
+ 44 (0) 20 7824 1300
www.london.diplo.de

TRAVEL DOCUMENTS FOR U.S. & U.K. CITIZENS
Passport

TRAVEL TIME TO DESTINATION & TIME DIFFERENCE
New York to Berlin: 8 hours 35 minutes nonstop; EST +6.
London to Berlin: 1 hour 50 minutes nonstop; GMT +1

AVERAGE TRIP COST
$800/£500 for a week's cruise on the Rhine

LANGUAGE & CURRENCY
Official language: German; English is frequently spoken, as is Russian in the former East Germany
Currency: euro

POPULATION
With 82,401,000 inhabitants, Germany is Europe's most densely populated country. There are many Turkish and ex-Yugoslavian immigrants. Capital: Berlin

RELIGION
Lutherans represent 40 percent, especially in the north of the country; 45 percent in the former West Germany are Catholic, far fewer in the former East Germany.

FESTIVALS
February: Carnival; September: Oktoberfest in Munich; December: Christmas markets

SHOPPING
The city of Nuremberg is the toy capital for buying porcelain dolls, wooden toys, and stuffed animals. In Bavaria, linen dresses and loden jackets are in fashion.

health spa resorts in the Allgäu Alps near Kempten and Murnau is increasing steadily.

The **Rhine Valley,** which could entail a three- or four-day river cruise, is known for its steeply rising vineyards, often topped by medieval fortresses. The most interesting section lies between Mainz and Koblenz (with the legendary narrows at the rock of the Lorelei).

But there is more: In the former East Germany, don't miss the granite boulders and pine forests of the **Harz Mountains** and the sandstone towers of **Saxon Switzerland,** a lovely region in southern Saxony that straddles the Elbe River and stretches to the borders of Poland and the Czech Republic. In western Germany, highlights include **Lake Laach** in the Eifel hills and the **Mosel Valley.** In the north, visit the valley of the **Elbe River,** the upper reaches of the **Weser River** with its Porta Westfalica, and the rock formations of the **Externsteine.** And in the south, top sights include the **Danube River** (Ulm,

Passau) and the **Black Forest and Thuringian Forest**.

The North Sea Coast features resorts on the **Frisian Islands** and Helgoland island across from the mouth of the Elbe (red sandstone cliffs). Activities include fishing and bird-watching along the salt marshes, sand dunes, and miles of tidal mud flats, an ecosystem now protected as three national parks.

▶ FESTIVALS

Celebrating Carnival is one of Germany's great traditions. The liveliest festivals take place in Cologne (Rose Monday), Düsseldorf, Mainz, and Aachen.

In September, Munich's Oktoberfest with six million annual visitors is very colorful and well lubricated, but it is no less famous than the Christmas markets, which warm up the hearts of the large cities from the beginning of December until Christmas Eve. Among the roasted almonds, mulled wine, marzipan figurines, and array of stalls filled with Christmas gift ideas, you can catch

glimpses that are unique to this part of Europe. Munich, Cologne, Lübeck, Augsburg, and Dresden hold the most famous markets.

Germany is also one of the great venues of classical music, as the numerous music festivals attest. Two of the most famous are Bayreuth's Wagner festival and Dresden's Musikfestspiele (concerts and operas, beginning of June).

The teahouse in the park of Frederick the Great's Sanssouci Palace in Potsdam

When to Go			
	NORTH	SOUTH	RHINE OR DANUBE RIVER CRUISE
JANUARY		❄	
FEBRUARY		❄	
MARCH			
APRIL			✔
MAY		☼	✔
JUNE	☼	☼	✔
JULY	☼	☼	✔
AUGUST	☼	☼	✔
SEPTEMBER	☼	☼	✔
OCTOBER			✔
NOVEMBER			
DECEMBER		❄	

Greece

Mainland Greece

▶ MONUMENTS AND CLASSICAL SITES

Traveling north to south a visitor can hardly overlook the archaeological treasures of Greece. They include:

• **Philippi** for its Roman ruins (amphitheater, forum, baths);
• **Delphi** for the site of the Delphic oracle and worship of Apollo;
• **Athens** for its monuments;
• **Cape Sounion** for the 15 columns of the Temple of Poseidon;
• **Olympia** for the Temple of Zeus and the site of the first Olympic games 2,500 years ago (gymnasium, palestra, archaeological museum);
• **Corinth** for the Apollo Temple, Peirene Fountain, and acropolis;
• **Mycenae,** according to Homer "rich in gold," the former kingdom of the Atreides (second millennium B.C.), for the Lion Gate,

What to See and Do in Mainland Greece

▶ MONUMENTS AND CLASSICAL SITES

• Ancient Greek ruins at Philippi, Delphi, Athens, Cape Sounion, Olympia, Corinth, Mycenae, Epidaurus

• Mount Athos, Meteora, Nafplio, Mystras

▶ CITIES

• Athens, Thessaloniki, Ioannina

▶ LANDSCAPE

• Pindus Mountains (Vikos Gorge), Mount Pelion, Mount Olympus

• The Peloponnese, Corinth Canal, Mani Peninsula

▶ COASTS

• Peloponnese, Macedonia, Chalkidiki

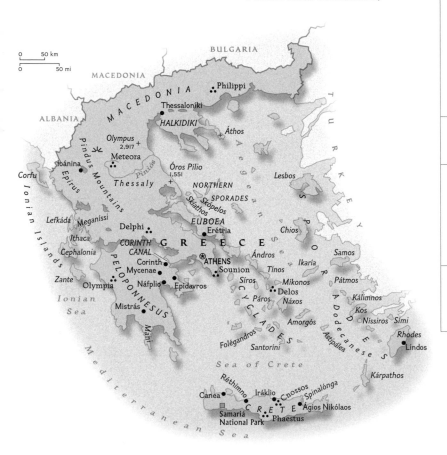

With cliffs rising sharply from the plains of Thessaly, Meteora and its monasteries— here the Agia Triada, or Holy Trinity—seem suspended in the air.

The famous caryatids of the Erechtheion on the Acropolis in Athens

which recalls the names of Menelaus, Agamemnon, Clytemnestra, and Orestes; and

• **Epidaurus,** for the sanctuary of Asclepius, god of healing, and the best preserved theater—in use again for its amazing acoustics.

▶ OTHER IMPORTANT SITES

Mount Athos is a sort of self-governed state, home to more than a thousand monks, guardians of the Orthodox faith, and all kinds of art treasures spread over 20 monasteries. Unfortunately, it is rarely possible to visit here or to enter into a discussion with the monks, and women (and even female animals) have not been admitted for the last thousand years.

Meteora is a complex of seven monastic buildings perched on top of an enormous rock above the Pinios Valley in the Plain of Thessaly.

Not far from Mycenae is **Nafplio,** a pleasant resort town overshadowed by two hilltop fortresses, the Greek Acronafplia and the Venetian Palamidi.

Near ancient Sparta rises the fortified citadel of **Mystras,** conquered by the crusaders in 1204 and once the pride of the despot of Morea. The town's Byzantine monasteries, palaces, and 14th- and 15th-century churches are inscribed on the World Heritage list.

▶ CITIES

When you hear the name **Athens,** you picture the Acropolis. The temple complex was built above the city by order of Pericles some 2,500 years ago and is one of the most visited sites in the world: The Propylaea opens the way to the Parthenon, sanctuary of Athena, followed by the Erechtheum, with its porch of the Caryatids. A few steps away lie the Temple of Athena Nike and the new Acropolis Museum. On the lower slopes of the Areopagus hill range the Theater of Dionysus and the Odeon of Herodes Atticus, site of the annual Athens Festival. Below the Acropolis, the Agora and the Theseion add more archaeological treasures to the Greek capital.

The modern city is best seen from Mount Lycabettus, known as Wolf Hill, or from Philopappos Hill. Since before the Olympic Games of 2004, Athens has been busy in cleaning up its image as a heavy

Traveler's Notebook

MAIN CONTACTS	**HEALTH ISSUES**	**AVERAGE TRIP COST**	Crete, and Kathari
Embassy of Greece	No major problems	$775/£500 for a	Deftera (Clean Mon-
2228 Massachu-	except for the heavy	week on the beach	day, the first day
setts Avenue, NW	pollution in Athens		of Lent); March 25:
Washington, DC	in summer	**LANGUAGE &**	National Day; April
20008		**CURRENCY**	or May: Ortho-
(202) 332-8145	**TRAVEL TIME TO**	Official language:	dox Easter; August:
www.mfa.gr/	**DESTINATION & TIME**	Greek	wine festival on
washington	**DIFFERENCE**	Currency: euro	Crete; November:
www.gnto.gr	New York to Athens:		olive harvest on
Embassy of Greece	10 hours 5 minutes	**POPULATION**	Crete
1A Holland Park	nonstop flight; New	10,706,000 inhab-	
London W11 3TP,	York to Heraklion:	itants, a third of	**SHOPPING**
UK	13 hours 40 minutes	whom live in metro-	Classic handi-
+ 44 (0) 20 7229	connecting flight;	politan Athens, the	crafts—pottery,
3850	EST +7. London to	capital	silver jewelry,
www.greek	Athens: 3 hours 35		leather—ouzo, ret-
embassy.org.uk	minutes nonstop	**RELIGION**	sina, and olives
	flight; London to	The majority is	
TRAVEL DOCUMENTS	Heraklion: 6 hours 5	Greek Orthodox	
FOR U.S. & U.K.	minutes connecting		
CITIZENS	flight; GMT +2	**FESTIVALS**	
Passport		January 6: Epi-	
		phany; February or	
		March: Carnival on	

The Acropolis and its three famous monuments: the Parthenon, Propylaea, and Erechtheion

polluter, and run-down neighborhoods have been revitalized—especially the narrow lanes and squares of the medieval Plaka and Monastiraki neighborhoods. Fashionable boutiques and cafés can be found in the Kolonaki neighborhood around Syntagma Square.

Museums of renown are scattered all over town: the National Archaeological Museum, which holds almost all of the important art of Greek antiquity, especially the treasures of Mycenae; the Benaki Museum, featuring Hellenic and Byzantine art; the Cycladic Art Museum; the Byzantine and Christian Museum; the Melina Mercouri Collection; and the new Frissiras Museum for contemporary art.

Other Greek cities can hardly compete, but the churches, former mosques, and museums (archaeology and Byzantine art) in **Thessaloniki** should not be overlooked. **Ioannina** on Lake Pamvotis also has much to offer, with six monasteries, a mosque, and a castle complex.

▶ LANDSCAPE

North

The mountainous landscapes in the north and on the Peloponnese see fewer tourist crowds than the classical sites or the beaches. It would be a pity to miss out on certain unique regions such as Epirus in the northwest and the Pindus Mountains, where the area around Zagoria boasts charming villages (Vitsa, Monodendri), old bridges, and the Vikos Gorge, whose sheer cliff walls rise 3,000 feet above the river.

Mount Pelion in the east offers pleasant trails for hiking through mountain villages, forests, and orchards. More visitors go to **Mount Olympus,** home of the gods, where climbing the mountain's 9,577 feet is considered a nontechnical hike.

The Peloponnese

The **Peloponnese** begins at the narrow, steep-walled **Corinth Canal** that leads into the gulf of the same name and to the discovery of Cape Iraion. The peninsula's secrets are

When to Go			
	COASTS	CULTURAL VISITS	NATURE
JANUARY			
FEBRUARY			
MARCH			
APRIL		✔	⟨⟨
MAY		✔	⟨⟨
JUNE	☼		⟨⟨
JULY	☼		
AUGUST	☼		
SEPTEMBER	☼	✔	⟨⟨
OCTOBER		✔	
NOVEMBER			
DECEMBER			

the three "fingers" to the south, especially the remote and wild **Mani Peninsula** and its villages with Byzantine churches and tower houses.

▶ COASTS

The beaches along the Peloponnese, the Arcadian coast in the east, and Macedonia are not well known, but the situation is different on the Halkidiki Peninsula, where there are as many foreign beach lovers as Greeks.

Crete

▶ LANDSCAPE

The interior of Crete is ideal for backpackers and lovers of unspoiled scenery. A few paths lead to unique areas such as the **Samaria Gorge,** ancient monasteries, and traditional villages with small chapels. Serious hikers should consult with an agency specializing in lengthy tours to discover less well known areas than Samaria—for instance, the Lasithi Plateau with its landmark windmills.

▶ COASTS

The crowded beaches of the north coast are playgrounds of the beautiful people in places such as **Agios Nikolaos,** and even more so Elounda. Exceptions are the familiar beaches of Gouves and Hersonissos and the island Spinalonga with its Venetian fortress. West of Heraklion, the beaches of Agia, Pelagia, **Chania,** and **Rethymnon** have an easy feel. The south coast is not as sandy and lacks some tourist amenities, but will serve someone in search of quiet relaxation.

▶ ARCHAEOLOGY

Knossos is the most important archaeological site on Crete. This

---

What to See and Do in the Greek Islands

Crete

▶ LANDSCAPE
- Samaria Gorge, monasteries, villages

▶ COASTS
- Beaches along the north coast (Agios Nikolaos, Chania, Rethymnon)

▶ ARCHAEOLOGY
- Knossos, Phaistos, Heraklion Museum

The Cyclades

▶ COASTS
- Beaches of Mykonos, Santorini, Naxos, and Paros

▶ CULTURAL HERITAGE
- Island of Delos (Apollo sanctuary), Santorini (Akrotiri)

Euboea

▶ COASTS
- Large and small bays

▶ CULTURAL HERITAGE
- Eretria

Ionian Islands

▶ COASTS
- Beaches of Corfu, Cephalonia, Ithaca, and Meganisi

▶ CULTURAL HERITAGE
- Artemis Temple

The Sporades

- Coastal landscapes of Skiathos and Skopelos
- Beaches of Kos, Patmos, and Rhodes

▶ MONUMENTS
- Rhodes

---

is where the Minoan culture developed, as evidenced by the ruins of the palace of Minos. Another important Minoan site is **Phaistos,** whose artifacts are displayed in a museum in Heraklion, the most important

among them the clay disk with 210 pictograph inscriptions. A visit to this museum is a must for anyone interested in the culture of Crete.

The Cyclades

▶ COASTS

Mykonos, Santorini, Naxos, Paros—these names evoke images of the sun, blue sea, sand, and white sugar-cube houses. Together

The village of Oia and the blue domes of its churches on Santorini represent an ideal image of the Cyclades and the Aegean Sea.

with Crete, the 34 Cyclades are the most popular tourist destinations in Greece.

Syros, Amorgos, Folegandros, Tinos, and Andros are not crowded. By contrast, nightlife on Mykonos is exceptionally lively. The attractions of Santorini lie in its topography, caused by a volcanic eruption that left only its crater's rim, creating a wide bay rimmed with white, ochre-colored, and black rock.

It is easy to travel from island to island by ferry, cruise ship, or sailboat around the Cyclades, as well as the other Greek islands.

▶ CULTURAL HERITAGE

The island of **Delos** holds the important Apollo sanctuary. Here you can wander among the ruins to see temples, the treasury, a theater, and statuary. The most important artifacts are exhibited in the museum.

On **Santorini,** the town of Akrotiri protects the remains of a settlement buried by the ash of the volcano's eruption in 1500 B.C.

Euboea

▶ COASTS AND LANDSCAPE

Less well known than the Cyclades islands and with fewer sandy beaches, but with many more coves

The Ionian island of Zakinthos has seen Sicilians, Neapolitans, and Venetians as overlords.

(especially in the south), the shores of Euboea present a great alternative to the crowded Aegean beaches. Picturesque fishing ports dot the coasts, and the interior mountains, especially Mount Dirfi, offer hiking trails.

▶ CULTURAL HERITAGE

The ruins of the acropolis, amphitheater, and temple in **Eretria** add to the island's allure. More

modern times are reflected in the Byzantine churches, chapels, and monasteries.

Ionian Islands

▶ COASTS

Corfu stands out in the islands of the Ionian Sea. As in the Northern Sporades, tourism is not as chaotic here as in the Aegean Sea. The

southerly islands of **Cephalonia, Ithaca,** and **Meganisi** see even less of the tourist invasion.

▶ CULTURAL HERITAGE

The best known monuments are on Corfu, where the famous pediment from the Temple of Artemis depicted the Gorgon just before her beheading by Perseus. The head is now exhibited in the Archaeological Museum.

The columns of the Acropolis of Lindos on the island of Rhodes

The Sporades

▶ COASTS

The Southern Sporades is the group of islands closest to the Turkish coast, including the Dodecanese. The islands are located south of the trio of Lesbos (island of famed female poet Sappho), Chiros, and Samos and are as much in demand. **Kos, Patmos,** and especially

Rhodes (Faliraki and Kolymbia beaches on the east coast) are summer playgrounds. Mountainous Kalymnos is ideal for climbing, but its beaches also offer scuba diving. Karpathos, Niros, and Symi are quiet resorts.

The Northern Sporades, in the middle of the Aegean Sea, are far less fashionable than Crete or the Cyclades. Even so, **Skiathos** and **Skopelos** are tourist favorites.

▶ CULTURAL HERITAGE

The Colossus of **Rhodes,** one of the Seven Wonders of the Ancient World, was destroyed by an earthquake in 277 B.C. But the town walls, the Palace of the Grand Master of the Knights Hospitaller, and the walled medieval city are still standing.

Another site not to be forgotten is the acropolis above the town of Lindos.

Advice

▪ Pros

• Its archaeological treasures make Greece one of the preferred destinations in the world. Numerous islands and islets with some 10,000 miles of coastline and modern tourist amenities.

▪ Cons

• Last-minute booking during high season is practically impossible. Hotels and, depending on location, transport to the islands have to be booked far in advance.

▪ Safety

• Be careful in crowded tourist venues in Athens. Drive with utmost care. Greece has the highest percentage of fatal car crashes in Europe.

▪ Special Tip

• Mykonos rivals Ibiza, Spain, for the crown of hottest nightlife in summer, but you don't need to follow the crowd. Other islands and especially northern Greece have much to offer beyond the tourist itineraries.

What to See and Do in Guadeloupe

Basse-Terre

▶ **LANDSCAPE**

• Rain forest, Carbet Falls, Soufrière volcano

▶ **COAST**

• From Pointe-Noire to Ste.-Rose

Grande-Terre

• Ste.-Anne, St.-François, Le Gosier

Other Islands and Islets

• Les Saintes, La Désirade, Marie-Galante, St.-Barthélemy, and the north of St. Martin

Palm trees and green hills frame the beaches of Les Saintes.

Guadeloupe

■ The two almost-touching main islands of Guadeloupe, forming what looks like the wings of a butterfly, are very different: The flat eastern Grande-Terre is suitable for beach lovers, whereas Basse-Terre, the mountainous western part, is preferred by backpackers and ecotourists. The islands of La Désirade, Les Saintes, Marie-Galante, St.-Barthélemy, and the French part of St. Martin (the Dutch part is on the south side) complete the French overseas region of the area.

Traveler's Notebook

MAIN CONTACTS
Embassy of France
4101 Reservoir Road, NW
Washington, DC 20007
(202) 944-6000
www.ambafrance-us.org
http://us.france guide.com
Embassy of France
58 Knightsbridge
London SW1X 7JT, UK
+ 44 (0) 20 7073 1000
www.ambafrance-uk.org

TRAVEL DOCUMENTS FOR U.S. & U.K. CITIZENS
Passport

HEALTH ISSUES
No problems except for pesky mosquitoes in the evening

TRAVEL TIME TO DESTINATION & TIME DIFFERENCE
New York to Point-à-Pitre: 8 hours 15 minutes connecting; EST +1. London to Point-à-Pitre: 15 hours 20 minutes connecting; GMT +4

AVERAGE TRIP COST
$1,000/£650 for a week's beach vacation

LANGUAGE & CURRENCY
Official language: French, Creole spoken in the streets
Currency: euro

POPULATION
431,000 inhabitants on the main island Basse-Terre, 90 percent black and mulatto, 5 percent Caucasian. Capital: Basse-Terre

RELIGION
Catholics in the majority

FESTIVALS
January and February: Carnival, climaxing on Mardi Gras; April: Festival of Creole Gastronomy; June 27: Abolition Day

SHOPPING
Rum, jewelry (creole design), spices, fabric (Madras)

Basse-Terre

▶ LANDSCAPE

The rain forest, flower park, **Carbet Falls,** and trails up **Soufrière** volcano, all in Guadeloupe National Park, invite hiking, canyoneering, and zip-lining. Ecotourism is growing here.

▶ COASTS

Less crowded than the beaches of Grande-Terre, Basse-Terre's beaches are worth a vacation on the south coast at Grande-Anse, near Trois-Rivières, or on the island's "left shoulder" from **Pointe-Noire** to **Ste.-Rose** via Deshaies.

The famous coral barrier reef near Pigeon Island has been turned into the Jacques Cousteau Underwater Reserve.

Grande-Terre

The beaches of Grande-Terre are simply fabulous, as much at **Ste.-Anne** as at **St.-François. Le Gosier** with its shorter beach is also pleasant and suitable for diving. Less populated beaches can be found in the east at Le Moule and in the north at Anse-Bertrand.

Other Islands and Islets

The islands of **Les Saintes** are split into Terre-de-Haut and Terre-de-Bas.

When to Go		
	CLIMATE	FLORA AND PHOTOGRAPHY
JANUARY	☼	
FEBRUARY	☼	
MARCH	☼	
APRIL	☼	
MAY		
JUNE		⤚
JULY		⤚
AUGUST		⤚
SEPTEMBER		⤚
OCTOBER		
NOVEMBER		
DECEMBER		

Together they provide everything that makes island life desirable: beaches bordered by coconut palms, small boats for ocean excursions, and hills with hiking trails.

Life moves to the rhythm of its fishermen on the small island of **La Désirade** (7 miles by 1.2 miles). The island, with its marine cemetery in Grande-Anse and its lagoons, represents a different image from the usual beach life.

Marie-Galante is said to produce the best rum in the West Indies, and the island's Murat Castle is the former master's house of a sugarcane plantation.

Two additional islands were named overseas collectivities of France in 2007: **St.-Barthélemy,** situated about 100 miles northwest of the archipelago, keeps tourism relatively in check with its reputation as the island of billionaires. A touch of Swedish colonialism is still apparent here with bright red roofs and pastel-colored houses. The French part of **St. Martin** about 15 miles north of St.-Barthélemy, fulfills all expectations: perfect beaches, a tax haven, and casinos.

All around Lake Atitlán, travelers come face-to-face with Maya traditions and a harmonious landscape.

 Guatemala is often overshadowed by neighboring Mexico, but it is proud of its reputation as the most beautiful country in Central America, thanks to its volcanic lakes, rain forests, and archaeological treasures in Tikal and other Maya sites.

Guatemala

▶ LANDSCAPE

Lake Atitlán is surrounded by three volcanoes (Atitlán, San Pedro, Tolimán) and colorful Maya villages. Several volcanoes (Acatenango, Fuego, Pacaya, San Pedro, and Santa Maria) offer relatively easy, scenic hikes. The **Volcán de Agua,** with its nearly perfect cone, is a feast for the eyes. The extensive **Sierra de los Cuchumatanes,** covered with montane forests, is the highest nonvolcanic mountain range in Central America.

Traveler's Notebook

MAIN CONTACTS
Embassy of Guatemala
2220 R Street, NW
Washington, DC 20008
(202) 745-4952
www.visitguatemala.com
Embassy of Guatemala
13 Fawcett Street
London SW10 9HN, UK
+ 44 (0) 20 7351 3042

TRAVEL DOCUMENTS FOR U.S. & U.K. CITIZENS
Passport

HEALTH ISSUES
Malaria prophylaxis recommended for visits

to elevations below 5,000 feet; dengue fever vaccination advised

TRAVEL TIME TO DESTINATION & TIME DIFFERENCE
New York to Guatemala City: 7 hours 21 minutes connecting flight; EST –1. London to Guatemala City: 15 hours 5 minutes connecting flight; GMT -6

AVERAGE TRIP COST
$2,540–$3,175/£1,640–£2,010 for 15 days of classic touring

LANGUAGE & CURRENCY
Official language: Spanish; Indian languages are also spoken
Currency: quetzal; U.S. dollars widely accepted (limited use of credit cards)

POPULATION
12,728,000 inhabitants, divided into the mountainous west (where 56 percent are Maya, the largest Indian population in all of Latin America) and the east, with

Ladinos (people of mixed race) and people of Spanish descent. Capital: Guatemala City

RELIGION
Catholic: 75 percent; Protestant: 25 percent; Mayan rites are recognized

FESTIVALS
Mid-January: Pilgrimage to the Black Christ of Esquipulas; April: Good Friday procession in Antigua Guatemala; November: All Saints'

Day in the Maya villages of the high plateau, and a week's celebration of the Day of the Dead in Todos Santos Cuchumatán; December: Santo Tomás festival in Chichicastenango

SHOPPING
You can buy handwoven, colorful textiles in the traditional markets, as well as silver jewelry, pottery, jade objects, and leather goods.

<table>
<tr><td colspan="2">

What to See and Do in Guatemala

▶ **LANDSCAPE**

- Lakes (Atitlán)
- Hiking, volcanoes (Agua)
- Sierra de los Cuchumatanes

▶ **CULTURAL HERITAGE**

- Maya traditions (villages, markets), Carib population (Livingston)

▶ **MONUMENTS**

- Maya temple-pyramids of Tikal, El Mirador, Uaxactún, El Ceibal, Antigua Guatemala

</td></tr>
</table>

Advice

■ **Pros**

- Though a small country, Guatemala is full of important sites that make it one of the most interesting destinations in all of Latin America. The civil war is over, and peace seems to be holding.

■ **Cons**

- The Pacific coast is of limited interest.

■ **Safety**

- Guatemala has long been known to present some problems for individual travelers. Warnings of possible theft or even armed robbery should be taken seriously.

In the area of **Antigua Guatemala** and **Cobán,** where the Río Candelaria goes underground, are limestone caves and gorges. The wildlife is remarkable in the north, where visitors may catch a glimpse of coatis and toucans, and maybe even a jaguar.

▶ **CULTURAL HERITAGE**

Nearly half the population is of Indian, mostly Maya, descent. In the villages and markets, Maya people exhibit many handicrafts, ranging from carved wooden masks to handwoven textiles in bright colors. The largest markets are held in Chichicastenango and Antigua Guatemala. The ancient traditions are especially in evidence during religious holidays. Some villages, though, in particular those around Lake Atitlán (e.g., Santa Cruz, San Pedro), are visited by tourists in droves and are losing their authenticity.

Near the town of **Livingston** on the Gulf of Honduras, an unusual mix of Garifuno, Maya, and Ladino people have combined into a culture that is different from the customs and traditions of the rest of the country.

▶ **MONUMENTS**

From A.D. 430 to 830, **Tikal** was one of the largest urban centers of Maya civilization. Of the thousands of ancient structures now overgrown by tropical rain forest, two pyramids stand out at 230 feet and 180 feet high, as do Tikal's large royal palaces, residential buildings, royal tombs, ball courts, and causeways. Archaeologists have deciphered inscriptions of a dynastic list that began in the year 378 and ended in 869.

North of Tikal lies the even earlier Maya settlement of **El Mirador,** with one of the most massive ancient structures in the world, founded about the sixth century B.C. Although the site is not accessible to general tourism, its importance should be noted as a probable cradle of Maya civilization. Other Maya sites include **Uaxactún** and **El Ceibal** in the Maya lowlands of the Petén.

The importance of the Maya sites sometimes makes the modern cities pale by comparison. But the architecture of the colonial period was also impressive, as can be seen in **Antigua Guatemala,** the former capital, built under the influence of the Italian Renaissance with remarkable baroque buildings such as the Palace of the Captains-general, the Cathedral of Santiago, and other churches and monasteries.

When to Go		
	CLIMATE	PETEN AND TIKAL
JANUARY	☼	≼
FEBRUARY	☼	≼
MARCH	☼	
APRIL	☼	
MAY		
JUNE		
JULY		
AUGUST		
SEPTEMBER		
OCTOBER		
NOVEMBER	☼	≼
DECEMBER	☼	≼

Hong Kong Island, with its famous skyline, is Hong Kong's major draw, but its other islands and the New Territories are worth a visit as well.

Hong Kong

What to See and Do in Hong Kong

▶ **SIGHTS**
- Victoria Peak, New Territories (Kowloon), islands

▶ **SHOPPING**
- Jewelry, photo and stereo equipment

▶ **COAST**
- Beaches (Lantau), ports

The handover of Hong Kong from Britain to China in 1997 changed everything and nothing. The lively streets and nighttime neon lights and the contrasts between tradition and modern life are still part of the city's allure.

Traveler's Notebook

MAIN CONTACTS
Embassy of the People's Republic of China
3505 International Place, NW
Washington, DC 20008
(202) 495-2266
www.china-embassy.org
www.cnto.org
Embassy of the People's Republic of China
49 Portland Place
London W1B 1JL, UK
+ 44 (0) 20 7299 4049
www.chinese-embassy.org.uk

TRAVEL DOCUMENTS FOR U.S. & U.K. CITIZENS
Passport

TRAVEL TIME TO DESTINATION & TIME DIFFERENCE
New York to Hong Kong: 16 hours 5 minutes nonstop flight; EST +13. London to Hong Kong: 11 hours 35 minutes nonstop flight; GMT +8

AVERAGE TRIP COST
$900/£575 for 3 days and 2 nights

LANGUAGE & CURRENCY
Official languages:
Chinese and English
Currency: Hong Kong dollar

POPULATION
6,980,000 inhabitants, almost all Chinese

RELIGION
Buddhists and Taoists are in the majority; minorities of Christians (10 percent), Muslims, Hindus, Sikhs, and Jews

FESTIVALS
January or February: Lantern Festival (last day of Chinese New Year); February or March:
Carnival; March: Chung Ming festival (ancestor cult); June: Dragonboat Festival; October: Moon Cake Festival

SHOPPING
The choices in electronics—computers, cameras, stereo equipment—are endless. It's important to choose carefully and not overlook the small markets.

▶ SIGHTS

Hong Kong is a global center of trade and one of the most densely populated areas in the world. The heart of it is the Central District, with its skyline featuring more than 7,000 skyscrapers with 36 of the world's 100 tallest residential buildings. The sidewalks are teeming with shoppers and people engaged in business. Towering above Central, Victoria Peak, reached by the Peak Tram, affords a spectacular view over Hong Kong and the New Territories. This view is Hong Kong's calling card.

But the island has much more to offer: Aberdeen, known for its floating villages and harbor of junks and sampans; Ocean Park and its replicas of ancient Middle Kingdom architecture and the statue of the Datong Buddha; the museums, including the Hong Kong Museum of History, Flagstaff House Museum of Tea Ware, Maritime Museum, and Hong Kong Museum of Art; and the venerable Peninsula Hotel.

In Hong Kong, urbanism has reached great heights, but Chinese traditions are still apparent in the diverse landscape of the **New Territories.** Here, visitors can hike in the mountainous parks and visit the monastery of the Ten Thousand Buddhas, the Kadoorie Farm and Botanic Garden, and the Tai Po Kau Nature Reserve, home to rare birds and plants.

The islands south of Hong Kong have many national parks, for example, the recently opened Wetland Park, a favorite of bird-watchers; others are on Lantau, Cheung Chau (no cars allowed), Lamma, and the Sai Kung peninsula. Signs of Buddhism are everywhere, as in the Po Lin Monastery with its imposing Buddha.

The Pearl River Delta, one of the leading economic regions, combines the "three Chinas"—Hong Kong, Macao, and Guangzhou—into one.

▶ SHOPPING

Commerce plays a large role here. Luxurious shopping centers are big business everywhere in Hong Kong and Kowloon (New Territories).

Some merchandise purchases are tax free, among them jewelry, computer gear, and photo and stereo equipment. Special sales are offered in winter. The best shopping area is the Golden Mile on Nathan Road (Central) in the Tsim Sha Tsui neighborhood. But it's also worthwhile to shop in the large centers on Hollywood Street and Cat Street and in the night markets on Temple Street and in the Mongkok neighborhood.

The tourist office has produced an official shopping guide that guarantees quality (the agency's stamp guarantees the authenticity of an item), specifies Western standards or not, and states the quantities of an item that can be exported. Prices for electronics, however, have risen in the last few years.

▶ COASTS

The beaches are rather a surprise. On the islands south of Hong Kong are numerous pleasant spots, especially on **Lantau.** There you can discover traditional villages and small ports in unexpected areas. But this is not a corner of the world for solitude; Hong Kong clearly shows signs of overpopulation.

Advice

■ Pros
• The location, atmosphere, and extravagance of Hong Kong are unique (only Singapore comes close). Ecotourism is rather new here, but is succeeding quite well.

■ Cons
• Lodging is expensive, and Hong Kong is not a place for bargain shopping anymore. In summer, the weather is hot and humid.

■ Safety
• There are really no safety problems, but as in all large cities, wallets and purses should be kept safe.

When to Go		
	CLIMATE	SALES
JANUARY	☼	✔
FEBRUARY	☼	
MARCH	☼	
APRIL		
MAY		
JUNE		
JULY		
AUGUST		
SEPTEMBER		
OCTOBER		
NOVEMBER	☼	✔
DECEMBER	☼	✔

CHINA

0   10 km
0   10 mi

Wetland Park
Tai Po Kau Nature Reserve
Grass Island
Sai Kung Peninsula
NEW TERRITORIES
HONG KONG
Kowloon
Po Lin Monastery
Lantau Island
Victoria Peak 552
Hong Kong
Aberdeen
Hong Kong Island
Cheung Chau
Lamma Island
SOUTH CHINA SEA

What to See and Do in Hungary

▶ **CITIES AND MONUMENTS**

• Budapest, Hollókö, Szentendre, Sopron, Fertöd, Eger, Györ, Székesfehérvar, Pécs

▶ **LANDSCAPES**

• Puszta (Hortobágy, Bugac), lakes (Balaton, Velence)

• Mátra Mountains (thermal springs), Danube Bend, Tokaj

Budapest is known as one of the most beautiful cities in Europe and had its share of tourists even during Soviet times. The trend continues, but travelers should plan to include other parts of Hungary during a visit.

Chain Bridge is perhaps Budapest's most famous of its nine bridges spanning the Danube.

Hungary

Traveler's Notebook

MAIN CONTACTS

Embassy of Hungary
3910 Shoemaker Street, NW
Washington, DC 20008
(202) 362-6730
www.huembwas.org
www.hungary.com
Embassy of Hungary
35 Eaton Place
London SW1X 8BY, UK
+ 44 (0) 20 7201 3440
www.mfa.gov.hu/kulkepviselet/UK/en/

TRAVEL DOCUMENTS FOR U.S. & U.K. CITIZENS
Passport

TRAVEL TIME TO DESTINATION & TIME DIFFERENCE
New York to Budapest: 11 hours connecting flight; EST +6. London to Budapest: 2 hours 30 minutes nonstop flight; GMT +1

AVERAGE TRIP COST
$2,200/£1,400 for a 10-day cruise on the Danube

LANGUAGE & CURRENCY
Official language: Magyar (related to Finnish; both are Finno-Ugric languages). Two percent of the population speaks Romani.
Currency: forint

POPULATION
9,956,000 inhabitants; one-fifth of the population lives in Budapest, the capital. The country counts 13 minorities, including 8 percent Roma.

RELIGION
Two-thirds of the population is Catholic; one quarter is Calvinist Protestant; and there are also Lutheran, Orthodox, and Jewish minorities.

FESTIVALS
February or March: Carnival; March 15: spring festival in Budapest; August: Nagykálló Folklore Festival

SHOPPING
Embroidery, porcelain, wooden toys, pottery items, Tokaji wine

▶ CITIES AND MONUMENTS

Nine bridges cross the Danube River in **Budapest.** The "Pearl of the Danube" is actually a combination of three cities: Buda and Obuda on one side of the river, and Pest on the other. History buffs will enjoy strolling through the quiet Buda neighborhood with its cobbled streets, the former Royal Palace (National Gallery and History Museum), and the famous Matthias Church next to the Fisherman's Bastion. At the top of Gellert Hill is the citadel, affording a splendid view over the city and Chain Bridge. Pest presents a different picture; it's the historic and economic heart of the city. In the downtown area, Art Nouveau facades predominate on Vorosmarty Square and Váci Street, and the early 20th-century neo-Gothic parliament building rises grandly alongside the Danube.

The city really deserves a visit of no less than three days to see the Jewish Quarter, the National Museum, Andrássy Street and the opera house, Hero Square and the Museum of Fine Arts (Raphael, Dürer, El Greco, Manet, Monet, Gauguin), and Varosliget, the city park. An excursion on the Danube is a pleasant option. The 50 baths—last echoes of the Romans and Turks—and roughly 100 thermal springs around Budapest represent an institution; some simple, some luxurious, they add to Budapest's fame as a spa city. The Gellert Bath (Art Nouveau style) is legendary and Szecheny Bath in Pest is the largest of its kind in all of Europe.

North of Budapest, **Hollókö** keeps to its traditions, and

Szentendre is famed for the colorful houses that make it the most beautiful city in the area. In the west, the medieval cities of **Sopron** and **Fertöd** (baroque castle of the Esterhazys) have Roman roots. Other attractive cities are **Eger** for its location in the Matra Mountains, its cathedral, and baroque architecture; **Györ** (baroque cityscape); **Székesfehérvar** (baroque and neoclassicist architecture); and **Pécs** with its Ottoman cultural monuments.

▶ LANDSCAPE

The **Puszta** is the largest steppe in Europe; most of it is now protected

When to Go		
	CLIMATE	BUDAPEST
JANUARY		
FEBRUARY		
MARCH		
APRIL	☼	✔
MAY	☼	✔
JUNE	☼	✔
JULY	☼	
AUGUST	☼	
SEPTEMBER	☼	✔
OCTOBER		
NOVEMBER		
DECEMBER		

Advice

■ **Pros**
• The style and beauty of Budapest, as well as numerous attractions in the country.

■ **Cons**
• No negatives.

■ **Safety**
• Hungary does not present any problems, though as always, certain precautions are advisable in the cities.

■ **Special Tip**
• Most hotels offer spa services, from simple to luxurious.

in national parks. Covering the east is the **Hortobágy National Park,** with horses and cattle tended by herdsmen, and in the south, Kiskunsag National Park, with the **Bugac** area of moors, dunes, and woods.

Lake Balaton is the largest freshwater reservoir in Europe. It is as beautiful in summer as in winter, whether seen from the Bakony Mountains or the Tihany Peninsula. Here swimming and water sports were long the privilege of vacationers from the Eastern Bloc countries.

Lake Velence, with its lagoons and reeds, and mountains in the background, is only 30 miles from Budapest, and makes for a favorite day trip from the capital.

Hundreds of thermal springs flow in the **Mátra Mountains,** attracting many new visitors from Western Europe.

The **Danube Bend** region just north of Budapest, with its picturesque small towns, had its heyday in the Middle Ages. Must-sees include Szentendre, the ruins of the royal palace at Visegrad, and the basilica of the archbishop of Esztergom. The **Tokaj** region still produces its famous sweet wine.

What to See and Do in Iceland

▶ **LANDSCAPE AND EXCURSIONS**

• Geysers, fumaroles, water-falls, glaciers (Vatnajökull), lakes (Myvatn), fjords (Breidafjördur, Isafjördur)

• Walking tours, bicycle excursions, cross-country skiing, snowmobiling, horseback riding, fishing, aurora borealis

▶ **WILDLIFE**

• Puffins, sea eagles, gyrfalcons, reindeer, arctic foxes, sperm whales, seals, fin whales

▶ **CAPITAL**

• Reykjavík

Iceland's unstable geology has created a peculiar terrain with active volcanoes, many geysers and waterfalls, a strange desert touched with black and green, glacial valleys, and fjords. Due to its northern latitude, the aurora borealis is frequently seen. A walking tour or bicycle excursion across the plateaus under the midsummer light is an unforgettable experience.

The thermal waters of the famous Blue Lagoon, near Reykjavík

Iceland

Traveler's Notebook

MAIN CONTACTS
Embassy of Iceland
2900 K Street, NW
Washington, DC 20007
(202) 265-6653
www.iceland.org/us/
www.goiceland.org
Embassy of Iceland
2A Hans Street
London SW1X 0JE, UK
+ 44 (0) 20 7259 3999
www.iceland.org/uk/

TRAVEL DOCUMENTS FOR U.S. & U.K. CITIZENS
Passport

TRAVEL TIME TO DESTINATION & TIME DIFFERENCE
New York to Reykjavik: 5 hours 45 minutes nonstop flight; EST +5. London to Reykjavík: 3 hours nonstop flight; GMT

AVERAGE TRIP COST
$1,200/£800 for a week of hiking

LANGUAGE & CURRENCY
Official language: Icelandic (a Germanic language that has changed little since the Middle Ages)
Currency: krona (exchange money in Iceland rather than at home)

POPULATION
Statistically, the population density for the 301,900

Icelanders is very low—nearly a square mile per person—but most people live in a few places along the coast. Four-fifths of the island is uninhabited. Nearly half the population lives in the capital, Reykjavík, and its surroundings.

RELIGION
Nearly everyone belongs to the Icelandic Lutheran Church (93 percent).

FESTIVALS
February: Festival of Lights, Food and Fun Festival; June:

Sjømannadagurinn (Sailors' Day); August 20: Arts Festival in Reykjavík; September: Drive for Bringing in the Sheep

SHOPPING
Traditional sweaters and other knitwear of Icelandic wool can be bought, and the smoked salmon is in a class with Scottish and Norwegian salmon.

famous and most active Icelandic volcano, actually puts out so much lava it creates new land. Surtsey, an island of the Westman archipelago, was formed through such an eruption and can be visited only by plane or boat.

Visitors can explore Iceland on foot, by mountain bike, or on the back of an Icelandic pony. Once you've left the coastal area, you will barely find another person. Winter is for cross-country skiing, snowmobiling, and a chance to see the aurora borealis—the northern lights.

Fishing enthusiasts find lakes and rivers full of char, trout, and salmon.

▶ WILDLIFE

Iceland has more than 200 bird species, including puffins, murres, sea eagles, and petrels. Lake Myvatn and the Westman Islands are ideal spots for bird-watching, especially in spring during the breeding season. Along the south coast, visitors can spot sperm whales, seals, and fin whales. Reindeer live on the plains, and with a little luck you may see polar foxes.

▶ LANDSCAPE AND EXCURSIONS

Iceland's volcanic origin has determined its surface. Characteristic features include geysers, like Strokkur, which sends up bubbling hot water as much as a hundred feet high every six to ten minutes; fumaroles, volcanic vents that emit sulfuric gases; waterfalls such as Godhafoss, Gullfoss, and Dettifoss, which cascade for more than a hundred feet over granite shelves; and natural pools of hot, sulfurous water that invite local bathers and tourists alike.

The island's far northern latitude has also created many glaciers, including **Vatnajökull** (the largest in Europe) and the glacial valley of Thorsmörk; lakes like **Myvatn;** and fjords such as **Breidafjördur** and **Isafjördur** at the northwestern point.

The eruption of Eyjafjallajökull volcano in 2010 spewed so much black ash that it disrupted air travel throughout Europe and the North Atlantic, whereas Hekla, the most

When to Go			
	CLIMATE	SKIING	MIDNIGHT SUN/AURORA BOREALIS
JANUARY			⇐
FEBRUARY			⇐
MARCH		❄	⇐
APRIL		❄	
MAY			
JUNE	☼		⇐
JULY	☼		⇐
AUGUST	☼		
SEPTEMBER	☼		⇐
OCTOBER			⇐
NOVEMBER			⇐
DECEMBER			⇐

▶ CAPITAL

Reykjavík is a lively city, especially on the weekends. On Friday and Saturday nights, young people roam the city streets and celebrate with plenty of beer or whiskey until dawn. The outdoor geothermal pool, Reykjavík Spa City, is an institution and always an attraction, even in winter. Nightlife in the city is even more intense—and much longer—in the wintertime.

Because Reykjavík lies only two degrees south of the Arctic Circle, it sees no more than four hours of sunlight during the winter, but in summer the nights have the full benefit of the round-the-clock midsummer night sunlight, not just during the summer solstice.

Although the city is said to have been founded around 870 by the Norwegian settler Ingólfur Arnarson and his family—who named the place for its geothermal vents Bay of Smoke, or Reykjavík—it did not become a city until 1786, and thus still feels young and new.

India

🏳 *India has always intrigued foreigners. Its architectural splendor, spirituality, stunning landscapes, and deep-rooted culture assault the senses, stretching them further than you may have thought possible.*

Bihar

▶ CULTURAL HERITAGE

The Bodhi Tree *(Ficus religiosa)* in Bodh Gaya is one of the most revered trees anywhere: Under its shade, Buddha is said to have experienced enlightenment, and the Mahabodhi Temple was built there. This sanctuary makes Bodhgaya one of Buddhism's most important pilgrimage sites.

What to See and Do in Northeastern India

Bihar

▶ **CULTURAL HERITAGE**

• Bodh Gaya

▶ **WILDLIFE**

• Leopards, tigers (Palamau National Park)

West Bengal

▶ **WILDLIFE**

• Tigers (Sundarbans Tiger Reserve)

▶ **CITIES**

• Kolkata, Darjiling

Sikkim

▶ **CULTURAL HERITAGE**

• Tibetan monasteries

▶ **TREKKING**

• Gocha Pass region

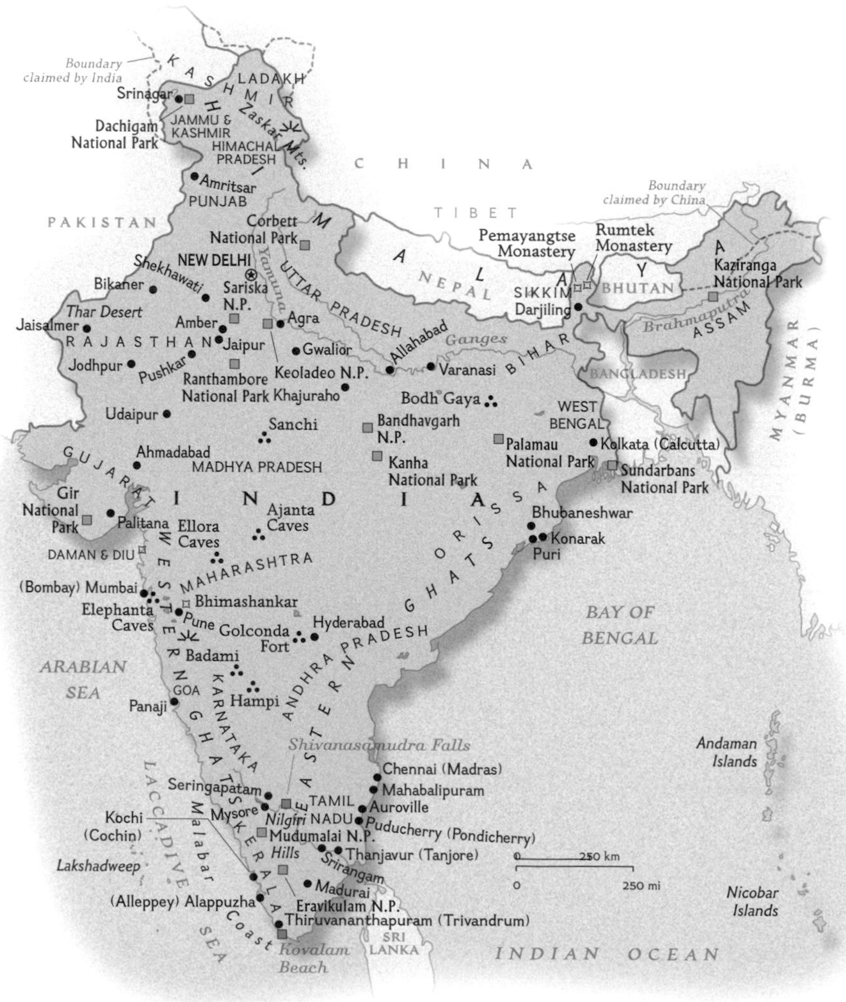

The Mahabodhi Temple towers above Bodh Gaya in Bihar: This is where Siddhartha Gautama, the Buddha, found enlightenment.

Rickshaws, porters, bicycles—the streets of Kolkata are in perpetual motion.

trains; the Victoria Memorial; and the Indian Museum. Dating to the British raj, the Maidan, the "lungs of Kolkata," is a large green park in this heavily polluted city.

By contrast, **Darjiling** (Darjeeling) is a peaceful hill station, known for its quality tea and splendid views of the Himalaya.

▶ WILDLIFE

Leopards and tigers hide out in **Palamau National Park,** but it is rather difficult to spot them.

West Bengal

▶ WILDLIFE

Although it may not be easy to spot, the Bengal tiger is the reason to travel to the **Sundarbans Tiger Reserve,** about 60 miles south of Kolkata.

▶ CITIES

Kolkata (Calcutta), the capital of India until 1912, one of the most populous urban centers in the world, is at once fascinating and disturbing. The vast difference between rich and poor is clearly apparent in the train station of Howrah, where hundreds of homeless people live. The Howrah Bridge spans the Hoogli River, connecting Kolkata and Howrah. On the Kolkata side, the attractions include the lively market on Mahatma Gandhi Road; a temple to the goddess Kali, who has to be soothed with animal sacrifices; Kumartuli, the potter's town, where statues of Hindu gods take shape; the Metro, the first of India's underground

Sikkim

▶ CULTURAL HERITAGE

Since the 13th century, Tibetan Buddhism has been the cultural foundation of this small state bordering Bhutan, Nepal, and Tibet. Rumtek and Pemayangtse are the most impressive of the more than two hundred monasteries.

▶ TREKKING

Trekking in Sikkim is less common than in Ladakh or Zanskar, because most of the state is not accessible from base camp at Kangchenjunga, but is popular around the **Gocha Pass.**

Traveler's Notebook

MAIN CONTACTS

Embassy of India
2107 Massachusetts Avenue, NW
Washington, DC 20008
(202) 939-7000
www.indianembassy.org
www.incredibleindia.org
High Commission of India
India House
Aldwych
London WC2B 4NA, UK
+ 44 (0) 20 7836 8484
http://hcilondon.in

TRAVEL DOCUMENTS FOR U.S. & U.K. CITIZENS
Passport and visa

HEALTH ISSUES
Vaccinations are not required, but malaria prophylaxis is recommended,

especially during monsoon weather and for areas below 6,000 feet.

TRAVEL TIME TO DESTINATION & TIME DIFFERENCE
New York to Mumbai: 14 hours 15 minutes nonstop flight; New York to Kolkata: 18 hours 35 minutes connecting flight; EST +10:30; London to Mumbai: 8 hours 15 minutes nonstop flight; London to Kolkata: 12 hours connecting flight; GMT +5:30

AVERAGE TRIP COST
$2,550/£1,650 for 15 days of touring

LANGUAGE & CURRENCY
Official language: Hindi;

some 15 other languages, along with numerous dialects, are spoken by a third of the population. English is widely spoken. Currency: rupee

POPULATION
Well over a billion people (1,129,866,000) live in India, which makes India the largest democracy in the world. The population is 70 percent rural, living in some 700,000 villages. The largest cities are Mumbai (Bombay; 18,000,000) and Kolkata (Calcutta; 14,000,000). Capital: New Delhi (population 9,500,000)

RELIGION
For years, religion has been the cause of conflict in India between the majority Hindus (83 percent) and the Muslims (11 percent). Christians live largely in the south; Sikhs in the Punjab; Jains in Gujarat, Bihar, and the state of Mysore. Buddhists, Parsis, and Jews add to one of the greatest religious diversities in the world.

FESTIVALS
February to March: Tibetan New Year; June: Pilgrimage to Jagannath Temple in Puri (Orissa); November:

Dasara festival in Karnataka (Mysore); full moon in November: Pushkar Camel Fair in Rajasthan.

SHOPPING
From silk to jewelry and precious gems, sandalwood objects, and cashmere, the merchandise on offer is as wide as the country. Items selected under quality control can be found in the government emporia.

The Golden Temple of Amritsar is the most sacred shrine in Sikhism.

Assam

▶ WILDLIFE

Kaziranga National Park, between Jorhat and Gauhati, is known for its one-horned rhinos and water buffalo, as well as tigers, leopards, and Hangul deer. Visitors can explore the park by elephant. The nearby Manas Wildlife Sanctuary is home to many rare birds.

Punjab

▶ CITY

Amritsar, the holy city of the Sikhs, is the main attraction in the Punjab, the Land of Five Rivers. The Golden Temple, covered in gold plate and sitting in the middle of the "Lake of Holy Nectar," is the spiritual center of the Sikh religion.

Delhi

▶ CITIES

Delhi has some quiet spots—such as the Red Fort, the Gandhi memorial, and the Jama-Masjid mosque, the largest one in the country—but most of the streets are teeming with people, especially around the Chandni Chowk market, where sellers mix with buyers and sacred cows.

New Delhi in the south of Delhi was created by the British as the new capital after Kolkata. The streets seem unremarkable until you get to the India Gate, parliament, and the 13th-century Qutub-Mina minaret.

Himachal Pradesh

▶ LANDSCAPE AND CULTURAL HERITAGE

This small state in the Himalaya between Kashmir and Nepal is of interest to mountain climbers for peaks up to 26,000 feet. The legendary Nanda Devi, for example, although off limits to climbers, is often scaled anyway. The Tibetan monasteries on the heights and the spectacular views along the Parvati and Spiti Rivers are prime reasons for visiting this state, as is Dharamsala,

What to See and Do in Northern India

Assam

▶ **WILDLIFE**

- Rhinoceroses, water buffalo, tigers (Kaziranga National Park)

Punjab

▶ **CITY**

- Amritsar (Golden Temple)

Delhi (National Capital Territory)

▶ **CITIES**

- Delhi, New Delhi

Himachal Pradesh

▶ **LANDSCAPE AND CULTURAL HERITAGE**

- Trekking in the Himalaya, Tibetan monasteries

Jammu and Kashmir

▶ **LANDSCAPE AND TREKKING**

- Kashmir Valley, Srinagar (Dal and Nagin Lakes, Shalimar Gardens), Ladakh, Zaskar

▶ **CULTURAL HERITAGE**

- Ladakh monasteries

▶ **WILDLIFE**

- Hangul deer, brown bears, leopards (Dachigam National Park)

A Tibetan monastery in Ladakh fits harmoniously into the Himalaya landscape.

home of the Dalai Lama and the exiled Tibetan government.

Jammu and Kashmir

▶ LANDSCAPE AND TREKKING

The **Kashmir Valley,** encircled by Himalayan peaks, is called Happy Valley. But the region has been plagued by political tensions since 1989, and safety warnings should be heeded. **Srinagar,** the largest city, is known for its picturesque houses along the Jhelum River, wooden mosques, green pastures dominated by the Shalimar Gardens, sparkling rivers, and Dal and Nagin Lakes. Depending on the political situation, renting a houseboat moored at the edge of these lakes can make for a heavenly vacation.

The **Ladakh** region, a high-elevation desert where Tibetan religious traditions and monasteries are entrenched, is a destination for hikers, who may encounter festivals such as Losar, the New Year's celebration. The neighboring **Zaskar** region, at an altitude of 16,400 feet, is another target for serious trekkers.

▶ CULTURAL HERITAGE

Most of the monasteries in Ladakh (Lamayuri, Phuktal) lie in the surroundings of Leh, the capital, and represent the architectural treasures of the state. In some monasteries, visitors can observe religious celebrations, such as the Hemis Tse Chu, celebrating the birthday of the founder of Tibetan Buddhism.

▶ WILDLIFE

Dachigam National Park near Srinagar is a special reserve for Hangul deer, but also holds brown bears and leopards.

Rajasthan

▶ COLORS

The yellow of the sun in the **Thar Desert,** the eternal blue sky, the pink houses of the state capital Jaipur, the traditional red clothing and multicolored houses in the villages of the **Shekawati** region, all combine to make Rajasthan one of the most colorful places in India. Daily life here is governed by the traditions of the old ruling caste.

▶ CITIES

Rajasthan is the home of kings, fortresses, and maharajah's palaces. There

What to See and Do in Northwestern India

Rajasthan

▶ **COLORS**
- Traditional dress, Thar Desert, villages of the Shekawati region

▶ **CITIES**
- Jaipur, Udaipur, Amber, Jodhpur, Bikaner, Jaisalmer

▶ **WILDLIFE**
- Deer, antelopes, tigers (Ranthambore, Sariska, and Keoladeo National Parks)

▶ **FESTIVALS**
- Pushkar Camel Fair

Uttar Pradesh

▶ **CITIES AND MONUMENTS**
- Agra (Taj Mahal, Red Fort, Jama Masjid mosque), Fatehpur Sikri, Varanasi (temples, *ghats*), Allahabad

▶ **LANDSCAPE**
- Tehri Garhwal glaciers, source of the Ganges River

▶ **WILDLIFE**
- Tigers, elephants, leopards, Axis deer (Corbett and Dudhwa National Parks)

are numerous important buildings, especially in **Jaipur,** known for its Hawa Mahal (Palace of the Winds) and pink stone, and **Udaipur,** site of palace complexes in typical Rajput style. Equally famous are **Amber** with its palace of the Mughal period and **Jodhpur** and its citadel. Elsewhere, the cities of **Bikaner** and **Jaisalmer** on the caravan route through the Thar Desert have become great tourist magnets.

Pink stone adorns the Palace of the Winds in Jaipur; comparably delicate architecture can be found only in neighboring Udaipur.

The Taj Mahal, in Agra, is both an artistic masterpiece and an ode to love.

▶ WILDLIFE

Only some 30 Bengal tigers (*Panthera tigris*), a highly threatened species, still survive in **Ranthambore National Park,** where they are carefully protected. Chances to see them are rare. This used to be the hunting ground of the maharajahs, but today it is a much loved animal park (closed between June and October) where Indian gazelles, macaques, jackals, and sloths can be spotted.

In **Sariska National Park,** the Sambar deer and Nilgai antelope dominate, but it is also a tiger reserve. **Keoladeo National Park** is a major wintering area for birds, including herons, ibis, storks, Siberian cranes, and geese.

▶ FESTIVALS

The largest assemblage of camels in the world can be found each year in **Pushkar** at the fair, when everyone from desert herders to bear tamers comes together. The festival begins on the day of the full moon in November, and it attracts thousands of buyers, sellers, onlookers, and pilgrims who come to get purified in the sacred lake at Pushkar.

Uttar Pradesh

▶ CITIES AND MONUMENTS

The **Taj Mahal,** in **Agra,** is the signature monument of India. This mausoleum of white marble, built by Mughal emperor Shah Jahan in memory of his wife, is even more impressive to see at sundown, when the walls, which unfortunately show signs of decay from pollution, take on a pink glow. Other must-see monuments include the **Red Fort** and the **Great Mosque.** The city of Agra, which excels in handicrafts, should be on every tourist itinerary.

Fatehpur Sikri, the ancient capital of the emperor Akbar the Great, is another example of typical Mughal architecture, with its great mosque, the Jama Masjid, and the tomb of Sufi saint Salim Chishti.

Another highlight is a journey to **Varanasi,** a city of 1,500 temples, the place where Buddha gave his first sermon and where the study of Sanskrit and the sciences is still important. But foremost in Varanasi is the observance of Hindu rites along its famous ghats (stairs) that lead to the Ganges, the sacred river, where millions of pilgrims come to undergo purification by bathing in the river and where, at the so-called burning ghats, families assist in cremation rites for the deceased.

The lesser-known but equally important city of **Allahabad** is situated at the confluence of the Ganges and the Yamuna, both sacred rivers to the Hindus. At Allahabad Fort stands a pillar erected by Mauryan king Ashoka in the third century B.C. But the city's importance rests on the Kumbh Mela, held every 12 years, when millions of Hindus come for purification in the rivers. The next gathering will take place in 2013.

▶ LANDSCAPE

The Himalayan glaciers in the **Tehri Garhwal** district form many small streams that constitute the headwaters of the **Ganges River,** a favorite haunt of pilgrims.

▶ WILDLIFE

Corbett National Park, in the foothills of the Himalaya, is home to tigers, elephants, leopards, and deer, among them the chital, considered the most beautiful of the species. **Dudhwa National Park** on the border with Nepal also harbors tigers, panthers, and several species of deer.

Agra is worth a visit for its artisans and its brilliant colors.

What to See and Do in Central India

Andhra Pradesh

▶ **CITIES**

• Hyderabad, Golkonda

Goa, Daman, and Diu

▶ **COAST**

• Beaches

▶ **MONUMENTS**

• Goa

Gujarat

▶ **CITY**

• Ahmadabad (mausoleums, temples, Gandhi ashram)

▶ **MONUMENTS**

• Palitana

▶ **WILDLIFE**

• Asian lions (Gir National Park)

Madhya Pradesh

▶ **MONUMENTS**

• Khajuraho (Hindu and Jain temples), Gwalior, Sanchi (Great Stupa)

▶ **WILDLIFE**

• Tigers, leopards, Barasingha deer, birds (Kanha and Bandhavgarh National Parks)

Maharashtra

▶ **MONUMENTS**

• Cave-temples (Ajanta, Ellora, Elephanta Island)

▶ **CITIES**

• Mumbai, Pune

▶ **LANDSCAPE**

• Western Ghats

Orissa

▶ **MONUMENTS**

• Brahmin temples of Bhubaneswar, Sun Temple in Konarak, Jagannath Temple in Puri

▶ **BEACHES**

• Puri

Andhra Pradesh

▶ **CITIES**

Starting in 1725, **Hyderabad** was governed for two centuries by Muslim rulers of the Nizam dynasty, whose palaces are still showplaces today. The city can also boast of splendid mosques of an earlier period, especially Charminar from 1591.

Golkonda was an important sultanate at the beginning of the 16th century and has a fortress, mausoleums, and mosques from that era.

Goa, Daman, and Diu

▶ **COAST**

During the 1960s and 1970s, the long beaches of Goa were invaded

The Chhatrapati Shivaji train station in Mumbai is always crowded.

by hippies, followed by backpackers. Over the years, this "alternative" lifestyle became dated and has made room for more luxurious beach life, even if youthful exuberance, loud music, and lively nightlife remain.

▶ MONUMENTS
Until the 14th century, Old Goa (Velha Goa) was a prosperous city of commerce; today, only ruins are left. **Goa** (Nova Goa), on the other hand, in its capital, Panaji, preserves traces of its Portuguese past (arcaded streets, balconies). Religious buildings (St. Catherine Cathedral, the church of St. Francis of Assisi with its ceramic tile walls) attest to the Indo-Portuguese style of architecture of the 16th and 17th centuries.

Gujarat

▶ CITY
Rich in mausoleums, temples (Jain temple of Hathee Singh), an ashram founded by Mahatma Gandhi (who lived here from 1918 to 1930), and many mosques (Great Mosque, Muhafiz Khan), **Ahmadabad** was one of the great tourist destinations before the earthquake of 2001.

▶ MONUMENTS
It's in Gujarat that Jainism has left its deepest imprint. In the sacred Shatrunjaya hills of **Palitana,** a major pilgrimage center, there are more than 1,300 temples.

▶ WILDLIFE
The **Gir National Park** near Junagadh is the last home of the Asiatic lion *(Panthera leo persica)*, which once roamed all over India; today there are only about 200 left.

Madhya Pradesh

▶ MONUMENTS
Built between the 9th and the 11th centuries, the 30 Hindu and Jain temples in **Khajuraho,** ancient capital of the Candela dynasty, are replete with sculptures. Some of these on the temples' exterior walls are depicted in erotic poses, which always draws a crowd of admirers.

Two other sites merit a detour: **Gwalior** for its temples and fortified Man Mandir palace, and **Sanchi** for its Great Stupa of the second

century B.C. and Buddhist monasteries and temples.

▶ WILDLIFE
Kanha National Park and Tiger Reserve harbors Barasingha deer, a threatened species, and that other rarity: the Bengal tiger. **Bandhavgarh National Park** fortunately still has a dense tiger population, together with leopards and a great number of bird species.

Maharashtra

▶ MONUMENTS
Hewn into the **Ajanta** hills are rock-cut *viharas* (monasteries with a sanctuary in the rear) that sheltered Buddhist monks during the rainy season and *chaityas,* larger temple sites, some of which date to the second century B.C. Several of these caves are decorated with murals that are still in a reasonable state of conservation.

At **Ellora,** there are 34 rock-cut sanctuaries dating from the fourth to ninth centuries. Some are Buddhist, some Brahman, and some Jain. The most famous one is Kailasa, a monolithic temple dedicated to the god Shiva.

Near Mumbai, on **Elephanta Island,** are similar cave temples with statues and sculptures dedicated to Shiva.

▶ CITIES
Mumbai, formerly known as Bombay, is the most anglicized Indian city. Opulence and poverty dwell side by side in this most populous city, where the highlights include the elegant Marine Drive along the bay and its buildings, such as the Gateway of India, Juhu Beach, and Crawford Market.

Millions of Hindus come to Varanasi for purification in the Ganges River.

Pune, the old capital of the Maratha Empire (18th century), boasts the Shaniwarwada Palace from the Peshwa dynasty. The city, where Sanskrit was developed, has a long tradition of learning and is dedicated to preserving its arts and crafts and cultural heritage.

▶ LANDSCAPE

Along the Arabian Sea rise the **Western Ghats** of red and black sandstone, extending up to Kerala. Around the Bhimashankar temple, northwest of Pune, the view of the surrounding mountains is awesome.

Orissa

▶ MONUMENTS

The temples in Orissa are as amazing as those in Tamil Nadu. Of the numerous Brahmin temples in the state capital, **Bhubaneswar,** the Lingaraja temple stands out. In **Konarak,** it's the Sun Temple in the shape of

the chariot of Surya, the sun god. In **Puri,** the Jagannath Temple takes center stage in a celebration each June, when pilgrims in a procession pull three huge chariots bearing idols of the gods through the city.

▶ BEACHES

Puri is a popular beach resort with fine, sandy beaches along the Bay of Bengal.

Andaman and Nicobar (Indian Ocean)

▶ COASTS

This archipelago of 328 islands, 28 of which are inhabited, was seriously devastated in the tsunami of 2004. Having served as a penal colony for the British at the end of the 18th century, the islands' coconut palm-fringed shores, coral reefs, and lively underwater world

attract beach lovers today because the setting compares favorably with the Maldives.

Karnataka

▶ CITIES AND MONUMENTS

Besides its Indo-Muslim-style palace and Chamundi Hills, with a statue of Nandi the Bull, who served as a *vahana* (vehicle) for Shiva, the city of **Mysore** takes center stage during the Dasara festival to honor the goddess Devi. That's when a procession with highly decorated elephants, camels, and horses winds its way through town, accompanied by dancers and musicians.

In the north of the state is the archaeological site of **Hampi** (Vijayanagar). Believed to have been the largest city in India by the end of the 15th century, it was destroyed in a conflict with a kingdom in the northern Deccan. The ruins include fortresses, palaces, pavilions, and sanctuaries.

The Virupaksha Temple towers above Hampi, the capital of the last Hindu kingdom of Vijayanagar.

All festivals or processions of importance include elephants.

In **Badami,** the main attractions are four rock-cut Hindu sanctuaries of the Chalukya kingdom.

On the return trip to Mysore, you will pass **Seringapatam,** the old capital of the state, and its many temples dedicated to Vishnu.

▶ LANDSCAPE

Near the town of Shivanasamudram, the Kaveri River splits in two to form the powerful **Shivanasamudra Falls,** the Sea of Shiva. The river travels precipitously through gorges and rapids, only to calm itself again for its last 50-mile stretch.

The hillsides of the **Western Ghats** traverse the state, whose forests include protected areas for some of the last tracts of virgin tropical forests.

▶ WILDLIFE

In the north of Karnataka, Bhadra Wildlife Sanctuary and Kudremukh National Park are tiger reserves that also hold the rare bonnet macaque.

Six islets in the Kaveri River not far from Mysore, make up the Ranganathittu Bird Sanctuary. The south has its Bandipur National Park, home to chital deer, leopards, and tigers.

Kerala

▶ LANDSCAPE

Kerala is exceptionally green. On the Malabar coast, visitors can glide along in boats traveling through the canals and backwaters to see fishing villages surrounded by coconut palms and rice fields.

In the east, the plains become the midlands of the **Nilgiri Mountains** and **Cardamom Hills,** lush with coffee and tea plantations.

▶ COAST

Kovalam Beach, with its coconut palms, is one of the most beautiful beaches in all of India. North of there in Kannur is another famous beach. Less grandiose, but more typical, are the lagoons of **Alappuzha** and Kottayam.

▶ CULTURAL HERITAGE

The Chinese fishing nets of **Kochi** and the peninsula of Fort Kochi are only a few of the charming sites in

Kerala. The state also has numerous monuments of Portuguese and Dutch origin from the colonial period between the 16th and 18th centuries.

A different tradition is honored in **Thiruvananthapuram** (Trivandrum) when Hindu pilgrims head for the Vishnu temple in the fortress.

The most populous state (70 percent of the population), Kerala combines a long democratic and communist tradition with great religious tolerance. Over the centuries, diverse religious groups have settled here, including Christians.

Kerala also preserves a number of traditional Hindu theatrical arts such as *Kutiyattam,* Sanskrit dance, and the newer *Kathakali,* the classical dance drama. Simpler versions of these dances are also produced for tourists.

▶ WILDLIFE

Safely installed on a boat on the lake in the Periyar Wildlife Sanctuary and Tiger Reserve, visitors can enjoy a safari to see elephants and other wildlife in the park.

In the Nilgiri Mountains, Eravikulam National Park provides a sanctuary for some of the last Nilgiri ibex.

Lakshadweep Islands

▶ DIVING

The Lakshadweep Islands, the tiniest united territory of India, whose atolls lie far from the coast off Kerala in the Arabian Sea, hopes to challenge the Maldives as a tourist attraction with great beaches, water sports, and diving centers.

The fishermen and their nets are a symbol of the "green state" of Kerala.

Tamil Nadu

▶ MONUMENTS

In Tamil Nadu, the most famous temples are gathered in one spot. There are the rock-cut sanctuaries of **Mahabalipuram** right by the ocean, including the Shore Temple and the giant open-air bas-relief called Descent of the Ganges, all relics of the Pallava dynasty, including parts of a temple uncovered by the receding waters of the tsunami of 2004. The god Vishnu is honored each year in Srirangam by pilgrims who gather at the **Sri Ranganathaswamy Temple,** famous

Advice

■ **Pros**
• The wide-ranging styles of architecture in India. No other country can boast as many cultural heritage sites, including temples, mosques, and pilgrim shrines.

■ **Cons**
• Sporadic problems between various religious groups. There are always tensions in Kashmir and the northern states. Between June and September, during monsoon season, the climate is pleasant only in the Himalaya region and in Kashmir and Ladakh.

■ **Safety**
• The political situation in Jammu and Kashmir is unstable. For that reason, several northern states should be avoided (possible terrorist attacks). In some regions, there is a danger of dengue and Chikungunya fever.

■ **Special Tip**
• Thanks to the camel fair in Pushkar and Ranthambore National Park, Rajasthan is a favorite destination. Other highlights are the boat excursions through the backwaters of Kerala and alongside drying Chinese fishing nets in Kochi.

In the **Mudumalai National Park,** visitors can spend a day on the back of an elephant in search of tigers and black panthers.

▶ CITIES

Chennai (formerly Madras) has many museums. Its important film studios are open to visitors.

Puducherry (Pondicherry) is beloved for its colonial charm. In 1968, Mirra Alfassa founded an ashram there near Auroville to honor the philosopher Sri Aurobindo in an attempt to achieve human unity and in the hope of having some 50,000 people live there in harmony.

for its grandiose architecture and hall of a thousand horse sculpture pillars. In **Thanjavur,** the temple of Shiva Brihadeeshvara has a 13-story-high *vimana* (tower). The temple in Tiruchirapalli is dedicated to Ranganatha. And the temple of **Madurai** is considered the best example of Dravidian art.

▶ LANDSCAPE AND WILDLIFE
The **Nilgiri Mountains** (Blue Mountains) are a cool oasis in southern India's tropical climate, lush with forests, tea and coffee plantations, and eucalyptus groves, and an ideal setting for the hill stations of **Ootacamund** and **Coonor.** The area is great for hiking.

Indonesia

In recent years, Indonesia's image as a serene vacationland has been affected by political tensions and terror attacks. But the islands of Java and Bali continue to be favorite destinations, and travelers in search of a taste of the unusual go to the Lesser Sunda Islands, Sumatra, and Sulawesi. Adventurers may prefer Irian Jaya and Borneo.

The Buddhist temple of Borobudur has bas-reliefs relating the stories of the Buddha's past and present lives.

Sumatra

▶ LANDSCAPE AND EXCURSIONS

Travelers in search of adventure can find plenty to do on the island of Sumatra, with its dense tropical rain forest, volcanoes, and volcanic lakes. **Lake Toba,** for example, in the region of the Batak ethnic group, is surrounded by steep cliffs and water-falls. The villages of the Minang-kabau people along **Lake Maninjau** are a special tourist attraction.

It takes some stamina, though, to explore the highlands on foot and visit with some of the eth-nic groups. The Minangkabau of the Padang and Bukittinggi region keep to their traditional way of life in remote villages. Their large com-munal houses stand out for their distinctive roof architecture with upswept gables that look like water buffalo horns. The emblematic buffalo horns also feature on seals and coats of arms and, during fes-tivals, in real combat between buf-faloes. The critically endangered

What to See and Do in Southern Indonesia

Sumatra

▶ **LANDSCAPE AND EXCURSIONS**

- Volcanoes, lakes, Bintan Island
- Hiking tours to the Batak, Minangkabau, Nias, and Mentawi peoples

Java

▶ **MONUMENTS**

- Borobudur Buddhist complex, Prambanan temple, Dieng temples

▶ **VOLCANOES**

- Merapi, Semeru, Papandayan, Kawah Ijen, Bromo, Krakatau

▶ **CITIES**

- Solo, Yogyakarta, Jakarta

Madura

- Bull racing

Lesser Sunda Islands

▶ **COASTS AND LANDSCAPE**

- Flores, Lombok, Sumbawa, Sumba

▶ **WILDLIFE**

- Komodo dragons

Bali

▶ **CULTURAL HERITAGE**

- Traditional handicrafts, religious festivals, cremations, dance

▶ **LANDSCAPE**

- Rice fields, volcanoes

▶ **COASTS**

- Beaches, surf

For fans of volcanology, Java is a paradise; even the fatigue after climbing Mount Bromo is quickly forgotten.

Traveler's Notebook

MAIN CONTACTS

Embassy of the Republic of Indonesia
2020 Massachusetts Avenue, NW
Washington, DC 20036
(202) 775-5200
www.embassyof
indonesia.org

Embassy of the Republic of Indonesia
38 Grosvenor Square
London W1K 2HW, UK
+ 44 (0) 20 7499 7661
www.indonesian
embassy.org.uk

TRAVEL DOCUMENTS
U.S. Citizens: Passport and visa; U.K. Citizens: Passport and 30-day visa issued on arrival

HEALTH ISSUES
No immunizations necessary, but malaria prophylaxis is required outside of Jakarta and other large cities on Java and Bali.

TRAVEL TIME TO DESTINATION & TIME DIFFERENCE
New York to Jakarta: 22 hours 45 minutes connecting flight; EST +12; London to Jakarta: 15 hours 10 minutes connecting flight; GMT +7

AVERAGE TRIP COST
$2,800/£1,800 for 15 days in Java and Bali

LANGUAGE & CURRENCY
Official language: Bahasa Indonesia. Although Bahasa Indonesia is spoken by 80 million people, it is the secondary language on most islands. On Java, which has its own language, Bahasa is barely used. Another 250 languages are heard in the country. English is widely spoken.
Currency: rupiah; U.S. dollars accepted

POPULATION
Population density is high with 234,694,000 inhabitants. Capital: Jakarta.

RELIGION
87 percent of

Indonesians are Muslim, 9 percent Christian (Protestant mostly in the north of Sulawesi, Catholic in Timor and Irian Jaya), 2 percent Hindu, and 1 percent Buddhist. Bali is the exception, with a strong Hindu majority, where the many rites and traditions have added to the island's reputation.

FESTIVALS
February: Sea Festival in Lombok; June: Festival of Borobudur; August 17: National Day; December: pilgrimage to Mount Bromo (Java); all year long: religious

ceremonies in Bali (processions, cremations), bull races (Karapan Sapi) in Madura

SHOPPING
One specialty above all else is batik—cloth dyed in a wax-resist technique—whether as fabric, tablecloth, or painting. The best selections can be found in Yogyakarta (Java). Also on the to-buy list are the leather shadow-puppet figures from the *Ramayana* epic that are very popular in Southeast Asia.

orangutan, however, is threatened ever more by wildfires and deforestation.

The villages on the mountainous island of Nias were a favorite tourist stop until the tsunami of 2004, and then an earthquake in 2005, devastated the island. The Nias people have largely kept to their culture of fishing, hunting, and trading. Some unusual sculpted megaliths representing ancestors are found around the island.

The Mentawai people on the island of Siberut are known for their flower necklaces and tattoos. Like the Nias, they have kept to their ancient livelihoods as hunters and fishermen and live in communal settlements.

By contrast, on the islands of Batam and **Bintan** not far from Sumatra—and even closer to Singapore (less than an hour by ferry)— luxurious resorts have sprung up, many with golf courses.

Java

▶ MONUMENTS

The vast Buddhist complex of **Borobudur** (ninth century), rising like a pyramid, is one of the great masterpieces of world architecture. It consists of four rectangular levels of galleries decorated with 1,640 bas-reliefs telling of the Buddha's past and present lives, topped with three circular terraces enclosed by 72 stupas and crowned with one great stupa. Each year between May and October, the full *Ramayana* epic is performed at Borobudur.

Not far from there, the **Prambanan** Hindu temple (eighth and ninth centuries) is equally impressive. The two complexes are the

Bali offers picturesque terraced countryside.

cultural must-sees on Java. The eight Hindu temples on the high plateau of **Dieng** are also well worth a visit, but the region is even better known for its mini-geysers.

▶ VOLCANOES

For volcanologists, Indonesia is the center of the world. More than a hundred volcanoes rise from Java, 25 of which are active. The classic volcanoes that can be watched during an eruption and are suitable for a hike to the summit are **Mount Merapi,** which erupted in 2010; **Mount Semeru,** the highest mountain on the island; **Mount Papandayan,** which grumbles so regularly that it's been named "the forge"; and the active crater **Kawah Ijen.** A hike of several hours leads to **Mount Bromo** and its craters in the Tengger massif surrounded by the Sand Sea, where thousands of Hindus make an annual pilgrimage in December.

Not to be forgotten is the island of **Krakatau,** whose volcanic eruption in 1883 has no modern equal. Anak Krakatau, or Child of Krakatau, is a new island that has risen from the earlier eruption

When to Go		
	CLIMATE	FEWER CROWDS
JANUARY		
FEBRUARY		
MARCH		
APRIL	☼	✔
MAY	☼	✔
JUNE	☼	
JULY	☼	
AUGUST	☼	
SEPTEMBER	☼	✔
OCTOBER	☼	✔
NOVEMBER		
DECEMBER		

Amed Beach is not well known, but it has the tranquillity that Kuta Beach has lost.

and continues to grow about 18 feet per year, with frequent minor eruptions.

Easy hikes can be taken on Papandayan, Bromo, and Kawah Ijen, difficult ones on Merapi (often dangerous) and Semeru.

Cities

Solo, the ancient capital of Java, and bustling **Yogyakarta** are more pleasant than the huge capital city of **Jakarta** (although the latter's National Museum is not to be missed). Cultural interests, crafts (batik), and traditions (dances, shadow-puppet plays) relate directly to Indonesian epics and political themes. This makes the two cities of the interior some of the best places to stay.

Madura

On this small island near Java, visitors can participate in an unusual event: the Karapan Sapi, or bull race. This competition differs from the running of the bulls in Europe: here, each pair of bulls is pulling a jockey on a cart. It's one of the island's unique traditions and fun to watch.

Lesser Sunda Islands

▶ COASTS AND LANDSCAPE

The Lesser Sunda Islands link Indonesia with Australia ("lesser" is to distinguish them from their larger neighbors, Java and Sumatra). The

northern islands (Flores, Lombok, Sumbawa) see the most tourists.

Several coves make up the south coast of **Flores,** which is bordered by active volcanoes. The most famous volcano is the Kelimutu, flanked by three crater lakes that change colors with the seasons. The landscape of Flores is thickly wooded and cut through by deep gorges. During excursions, visitors can explore fishing villages and traditional settlements and meet tribal people of the interior.

Lombok's landscape is dominated by the much-scaled, 12,224-foot-high Mount Rinjani. Because of its volcanoes and terraced rice fields, Lombok is often compared to its neighbor Bali. The island's white sandy beaches (Sengigi), its south

Even if the barong dance is often somewhat altered for tourists, it remains a moving spectacle.

coast that's ideal for surfing, and its coral reefs (Gillis Islands) for diving bring many tourists who want to escape the crowds on Bali.

Sumbawa and **Sumba** are also worth a visit because of their scenic landscape and beaches. Other attractions are the traditional homes and craft workshops, especially for ikat weaving in the villages of Sumba.

▶ WILDLIFE

Komodo Island is known for *Varanus komodoensis,* the Komodo dragon, which at full maturity reaches ten feet in length and can weigh 250 pounds. The creature is a large prehistoric lizard that is a modern link to the dinosaurs. This species occurs only on Komodo and a few neighboring islands. Visitors can observe the

lizards on a guided tour in Komodo National Park, which also covers the islands of Sumbawa and Flores.

Bali

▶ CULTURAL HERITAGE

Bali's reputation is linked to its traditions and spirituality, including traditional dances (to preserve harmony and transmit sacred myths), crafts in the villages (painters' studios and galleries in Ubud), and religious festivals (processions; temple feasts; cremations in the presence of family, the village, and tourists).

Although sometimes "prefabricated" for the tourists, the dance performances (barong, kecak, legong) are deeply moving and relate to the

Ramayana, the famous Indian epic known all over Southeast Asia.

In another tradition, musicians from the villages gather to form a gamelan ensemble, a typical group of bamboo xylophone players and drummers.

▶ LANDSCAPE

The green, terraced rice fields on volcanic soil have shaped Bali's topography into an artistic masterpiece. As if to top this perfection, the caldera and crater lake of Mount Batur, one of the island's two sacred volcanoes along with Mount Agung, are ideal hiking areas.

▶ COASTS

Most of Bali's beaches have strong surf, a plus for surfers. The beaches

In Kalimantan, the Dayak people are trying to preserve their rituals.

on the south side, such as Kuta, Legian, and Sanur, show strong Western influence and are a long way from being deserted. They have been joined by new resorts such as Nusa Dua, Tanah Lot, and Tuban.

An excursion by *bemo* (group taxi) to the beaches in the north lets visitors explore quieter shores. But tranquillity is never a given; although Bali suffered terrorist attacks in 2002 and 2005, the island still counts some four million tourists per year.

Kalimantan (Borneo)

▶ **LANDSCAPE AND WILDLIFE**

The rain forest and river routes are the main attractions of Kalimantan, the Indonesian part of the island of Borneo. Two rivers, the Kapuas and the Mahakam, can be traveled by dugout canoe. A trip that takes several days can include hikes through the rain forest and a visit to a village of the Dayak people.

Tanjung Puting National Park is a popular ecotourism destination; its wildlife includes crocodiles, dolphins, pythons, hornbills, and the endangered orangutans. Near Banjarmasin, the Pulau-Kaget Reserve protects the threatened proboscis monkeys.

▶ **TOWNS**

The large port of **Banjarmasin,** the capital of South Kalimantan, built on wooden piles and boasting a floating market, has often been compared to Venice. Some 120 miles away, in the village of **Tamianglayang,** the Dayak people still hold their animist traditions, and they see a steady influx of visitors to their colorful market. Writer Joseph Conrad is said to have made four trips up the Berau River through the dense forest to **Berau** when he was in the merchant marine.

Moluccas

▶ **CULTURAL HERITAGE**

Nutmeg and cloves gave the Moluccas the name "Spice Islands" and let Europeans of the 16th century dream of exotic locales. Magellan was among the famous navigators who stopped here. Today the islands are hardly known except to tourists who pause here on cruise ships coming from the northeast of Sulawesi, whenever the political situation allows.

Sulawesi (Celebes)

▶ **CULTURAL HERITAGE**

Among the islands' ethnic groups, the Toraja are the most well known people because of their funeral rites (rock-cut tombs, wooden effigies) and sacrifices (buffalo, pigs). Their longhouses on wooden piles

Banjarmasin, one of the few cities on Kalimantan, has a floating market.

(tongkonan) with roofs swooping upward like the prow of a ship, are the most unusual in all of Indonesia.

▶ LANDSCAPE

Rice fields, orchids, carnivorous plants—these are just some of the discoveries on a nature hike across the island from the Torajas' traditional villages. The area around **Lake Poso** in central Sulawesi has seen few tourists until recently,

but in the future guided treks will be led here and to **Lore Lindu National Park,** a UNESCO Biosphere Reserve.

The **Togian Islands** (beaches, lagoons, marine life) are still a secret destination.

Irian Jaya

▶ TREKKING

Except for ethnologists, few people

have visited the western part of New Guinea. Today the region can be explored by rather arduous treks in hopes of meeting some tribal people. But Irian Jaya remains the most unusual destination in all of Indonesia.

▶ WILDLIFE

Together with its neighbor Papua New Guinea, Irian Jaya—or more precisely the Biak Archipelago—is the one of the few places where you can find birds of paradise.

Ireland

It's hard to imagine how green the countryside really is—green and damp. The changeable weather should not be a reason to avoid this country of marvelous sights and activities, be they walking tours, bicycle excursions, river cruises, or playing a round of golf.

What to See and Do in Ireland

▶ **LANDSCAPE**

• Heaths, bogs, and lakes of Connemara, the Aran Islands, the Burren, Dingle Peninsula, sea cliffs (Slieve League), Benbulbin

• Wicklow and Waterford Counties

▶ **ACTIVITIES**

• Golfing, horseback riding, fishing (salmon)

• Excursions on foot, horse, or bicycle

• Riverboat tours on the Shannon

▶ **MONUMENTS AND CULTURAL HERITAGE**

• Dolmens, castles, ancient ruins (Staigue Fort)

• St. Patrick's Day

▶ **CITIES**

• Dublin, Waterford, Kilkenny, Cork

▶ **LANDSCAPE**

Ireland's tourism is focused on the landscape, which is never more beautiful than when the sun appears over the hills and dales after a rainstorm. **Connemara** takes prime position in this regard, thanks to its heaths, blanket bogs, lakes, and fishing coves, along with its Gaelic language, special light, and country houses.

The west coast is well known for its scenic cliffs (the Cliffs of Moher rise to 394 feet), rocky bays, the rough **Aran Islands,** and the **Burren** with its strangely formed limestone outcrops and grottoes. County Kerry in the southwest has a gentle climate,

Connemara, with its flowers, heath, and blanket bogs, epitomizes the west coast of Ireland.

ideal for clumps of blooming rhododendrons in the beginning of June, and boasts the lakes of Killarney, sandy beaches at Inch on the **Dingle Peninsula,** and tremendous views from the cliffs. At 3,406 feet, the Carrantuohill is the highest peak of the Macgillycuddy's Reeks range and the highest mountain in Ireland.

On the north coast, the cliffs of **Slieve League** form in some places the highest coastal relief in Europe. **Benbulbin,** its limestone formations resembling the prow of a ship, is nestled at the foot of the Dartry Mountains.

South of Dublin, County **Wicklow** stands out for its gardens (Kilruddery, Powercourt) and heaths.

County **Waterford** in the southeast features a riverine landscape formed by the Barrow, Suir, and Blackwater Rivers. John F. Kennedy's great-grandparents emigrated from New Ross in this region to the United States. Sailing from Cobh, near Cork, nearly three million Irish left for the New World, and the legendary *Titanic* made it its last port of call. Midleton is home to the Jameson Heritage Center, with exhibits about the famous

whiskey distillery and the largest still in the world.

▶ ACTIVITIES

The country's many attractions have led to the development of varied activities. Many sites can be visited on foot, by horse or bicycle, or by boat on the Shannon or the Blackwater.

Golf is a widespread leisure activity, and many famous golf courses beckon, including Tralee, Ballybunion, Clifden, and especially Waterville, which also has one of the most beautiful beaches in Ireland.

The lanes and pubs along the River Liffey in Dublin give the town its special flair and charm.

Traveler's Notebook

MAIN CONTACTS

Embassy of Ireland
2234 Massachusetts Avenue, NW
Washington, DC
20008
(202) 462-3939
www.embassyof
ireland.org
www.discover
ireland.com/us/
Embassy of Ireland
17 Grosvenor Place
London SW1X 7HR,
UK
+ 44 (0) 20 7235 2171
www.embassyof
ireland.co.uk

TRAVEL DOCUMENTS FOR U.S. & U.K. CITIZENS
Passport

TRAVEL TIME TO DESTINATION & TIME DIFFERENCE
New York to Dublin: 6 hours 40 minutes nonstop flight; EST +5. London to Dublin: 1 hour 15 minutes nonstop flight; GMT

AVERAGE TRIP COST
$1,500/£1,000 for a 10-day excursion

LANGUAGE & CURRENCY
Official languages: Gaelic and English Currency: euro

POPULATION
During the last 150 years, the population decreased by half. A century of famine and poverty had forced people to emigrate, and

most headed for the United States. The recent economic upswing in Ireland, however, attracted people from all over Europe. Today the population stands at 4,109,000. Capital: Dublin (metropolitan population: 1,100,000)

RELIGION
93 percent are Catholic; the major Protestant faiths are Church of Ireland (Anglican), Presbyterian, and Methodist.

FESTIVALS
March 17 (and days leading up to it): St. Patrick's Day; June 16: Bloomsday in Dublin; August:

Rose of Tralee Festival; September: All Ireland Hurling Finals; October: Guinness Cork Jazz Festival; end of October: Dublin Marathon

SHOPPING
Favorite souvenirs are tweed clothing, wool sweaters, Guinness, whiskey, and smoked salmon. Good handicrafts include jewelry, pottery, crystal, and other glass objects.

Visitors can ride horseback through Kerry, Connemara, and Donegal, to the sandy beaches of the Dingle Peninsula, or into narrow passes such as the Gap of Dunloe. Touring by old-fashioned covered wagon is yet another option.

Fishing aficionados can rent boats to catch salmon in the Blackwater River or pike in the Shannon.

▶ MONUMENTS AND CULTURAL HERITAGE

Dolmens, castles (Kilkenny), ancient ruins (**Staigue Fort**)—tourists have not yet discovered all the monuments of Ireland's long history.

Each year, on March 17, St. Patrick is celebrated for having brought Christianity to Ireland in the fifth century. Especially in Dublin, the festivities include parades, street theater, fireworks, and traditional *ceili* dance. The Irish hold tight to their traditions and manage to sweep tourists along in their exuberance.

► CITIES

Located in a pleasant bay surrounded by hillsides, **Dublin** is not known as one of the huge urban destinations in Europe, but it is ranked among the top 25 cities in the world. Dublin's narrow streets, pubs, and the fashionable area around Temple Bar south of the River Liffey attract crowds. The river flows through the center of the city, the two halves connected with graceful bridges such as the Half-Penny Bridge.

Three signposted itineraries lead through the city—the Georgina Trail, Old City Trail, and the Cultural Trail—inviting tourists to explore the old quarters.

The capital has a famous university, Trinity College, and numerous museums, including the National Museum of Ireland with Irish archaeology exhibits and the Dublin City Gallery with works by Corot, Monet, Osborne, and Renoir. Between squares and gardens,

comfy pubs entice visitors to a pint of Guinness. The Guinness Storehouse, a museum dedicated to the brew, is on the site of the brewery. There is also a museum to Jameson's Whiskey in Smithfield Village.

The port city of **Waterford,** in the southeast, is known for its crystal, but the city's glassmaking works closed in 2009. **Kilkenny** is a typical small Irish town with colorful facades and crowded pubs dedicated to Guinness. The university town and port city of **Cork** in the south, with its Victorian cityscape and many churches, was named European Capital of Culture in 2005.

When to Go		
	CLIMATE	FLORA ON THE WEST COAST
JANUARY		
FEBRUARY		
MARCH		
APRIL		
MAY		☘
JUNE	☼	☘
JULY	☼	
AUGUST	☼	
SEPTEMBER	☼	
OCTOBER		
NOVEMBER		
DECEMBER		

Advice

■ **Pros**
 • Very diverse activities. Tourists are received with legendary warmth and goodwill. Beautiful, unspoiled countryside.

■ **Cons**
 • The weather is rather changeable.

■ **Safety**
 • No particular problems, unless too much Guinness plays a role.

■ **Special Tip**
 • Lodging in Ireland covers a wide spectrum, including cottages, guest houses, manors, country houses, and farms.

The cliffs rise steeply at Fort Dun Aengus in the Aran Islands.

Jerusalem, the holy city, features many exceptional religious structures.

📧 *Despite political tensions, Israel is a compelling destination thanks to its historical sites, ancient and modern architecture, pleasant beaches, and, for hikers, the Judean Desert and the Negev.*

Israel

▶ CULTURAL HERITAGE

The Old City of **Jerusalem** is divided into Christian, Armenian, Jewish, and Muslim quarters and thus unites adherents of the three Abrahamic religions. Among its many historic sites are the Dome of the Rock (also known as Omar Mosque) dating to the seventh century; the al-Aqua Mosque, the largest mosque in the city; the Temple Mount and Western Wall, the

---

What to See and Do in Israel

▶ **CULTURAL HERITAGE**

- Jerusalem

- Holy Land and pilgrimages: Bethlehem, Nazareth, Capernaum, Mount Tabor, Sea of Galilee

- Mount Carmel, Acre, Qumran, Masada

▶ **LANDSCAPE**

- Dead Sea (spa treatments and thalassotherapy), Judean Desert, Negev

- Kibbutzim

▶ **COASTS**

- Mediterranean beaches (Netanya, Caesarea), Red Sea (Elat)

Traveler's Notebook

MAIN CONTACTS
Embassy of Israel
3514 International Drive, NW
Washington, DC 20008
(202) 364-5500
www.israelemb.org
www.goisrael.com/tourism_eng/
Embassy of Israel
2 Palace Green
Kensington W8 4QB, UK
+ 44 (0) 20 7957 9500
http://london.mfa.gov.il

TRAVEL DOCUMENTS FOR U.S. & U.K. CITIZENS
Passport and visa

TRAVEL TIME TO DESTINATION & TIME DIFFERENCE
New York to Tel Aviv: 10 hours 40 minutes nonstop flight; EST +7. London to Tel Aviv: 4 hours 55 minutes nonstop flight; GMT +2

AVERAGE TRIP COST
$1,400/£900 for a week of excursions

LANGUAGE & CURRENCY
Official languages: Hebrew and Arabic; English widely spoken
Currency: shekel

POPULATION
Jewish immigrants from Europe, North Africa, the Middle East, Eastern Europe, the United States, and countries of the former Soviet Union represent five-sixths of the population of 6,427,000. Capital: In 1980, the Knesset voted to move the capital from Tel Aviv–Yavo to a reunited Jerusalem.

RELIGION
About 80 percent are Jewish; Islam and Christianity are both well represented.

FESTIVALS
January: Dance Festival in Eilat; June: Jerusalem Festival of Lights; Jewish holidays: Jewish New Year (Rosh Hashanah), Passover, Shavuot, Sukkoth, Yom Kippur

SHOPPING
Objects made from olive wood, leather goods, spices, and of course religious keepsakes are favorite souvenirs.

LEBANON
Boundary claimed by Syria
SYRIA
Mediterranean Sea
Capernaum
Acre
Sea of Galilee
Mt. Carmel
Nazareth
Mt. Tabor
Caesarea
Netanya
Tel Aviv-Yafo
WEST BANK
Jordan
JERUSALEM
Bethlehem
Khirbat Qumrān
GAZA STRIP
Judaean Desert
Dead Sea
Beersheba
Masada
ISRAEL
JORDAN
NEGEV
EGYPT
0
40 km
0
40 mi
Elat
Gulf of Aqaba

remains of Herod's Temple begun in 19 B.C. and an important Jewish prayer area; the Church of the Holy Sepulcher, where Christ is said to have been buried; the walls of the Old City; and the Via Dolorosa and Stations of the Cross. The Mount of Olives, east of the old city across the Kidron Valley, overlooks many of these sites in a stunning panorama.

Jerusalem's two most important museums are the Yad Vashem Holocaust Memorial and the Israel Museum. Among the precious artifacts in the latter are the Dead Sea Scrolls, biblical texts and apocrypha discovered in 1946 in the Qumran caves and associated with the ancient Jewish sect of the Essenes.

The holy sites of the three major monotheistic religions—Judaism, Christianity, and Islam—are Israel's main attractions. Christians from around the world gather in Jerusalem to visit Christ's tomb and in **Bethlehem** to see the Holy Crypt in the Church of the Nativity. Other important Christian destinations are **Nazareth; Capernaum; Mount Tabor,** where according to the Bible the Transfiguration of Christ occurred; and the **Sea of Galilee.**

Other places of interest include **Mount Carmel; Acre,** one of the oldest crusader fortresses; the **Qumran** caves of the Dead Sea Scrolls; and the plateau of **Masada,** where Herod built his fortress.

▶ LANDSCAPE

The salt content, the cliffs, and the blue of sky and water attract both the curious and health spa aficianados to the **Dead Sea.** The Dead Sea lies 1,300 feet below sea level; its high mineral content is said to have therapeutic effects, especially for neurodermatitis and rheumatism, and resorts offer various treatments.

When to Go

	JERUSALEM AND THE COAST	EAST AND SOUTHERN DESERT	DIVING IN THE RED SEA
JANUARY		☼	
FEBRUARY		☼	
MARCH		☼	✔
APRIL	☼	☼	✔
MAY	☼		
JUNE	☼		
JULY	☼		
AUGUST	☼		
SEPTEMBER	☼		
OCTOBER	☼	☼	
NOVEMBER	☼	☼	✔
DECEMBER		☼	✔

Advice

Pros

- Tourism in Israel is unique, pleasant, and dynamic. Visitors can spend a night in a kibbutz or combine a spa vacation with desert hikes.

Cons

- Political tensions can on occasion disturb a vacation.

Safety

- Because of the political situation, it is wise to always check with the U.S. State Department before traveling to Israel.

The **Judean Desert** extends west of the Dead Sea and presents an attractive profile of high plateau and deep gorges.

The **Negev**—with its gorges (Red Canyon), pastel-colored rock, and sandstone sculptures created by erosion—covers more than half of Israel. This desert was once the crossroads of traders in frankincense.

Other sites are entirely new, such as the kibbutzim. In the 1960s, many young people, especially Americans, came here for several months at a time to work communally in agriculture. Today farming has been largely supplanted by other enterprises, but tourists are still invited to visit a kibbutz.

▶ COASTS

Israel has beautiful beaches on the **Mediterranean** coast, including Netanya, Caesarea Maritima, and Tel Aviv–Yafo, and on the **Red Sea** near Eilat, as well as inland on the Dead Sea and the Sea of Galilee. The resorts offer all kinds of water sports.

Elat far to the south welcomes most of its visitors in winter. From here scuba dive to the coral reefs of the Red Sea to watch dolphins and colorful fish.

Italy

Mainland Italy

▶ **CITIES**

Florence, Rome, and Venice with their historic buildings and art collections attract art lovers from the world over.

To get a panoramic view of **Florence,** go up to the nearby town of Fiesole and see the city unfold below you. The old heart of the city was built during the Medici era, between the 12th and 16th centuries. It includes the Piazza della Signoria—with the Palazzo Vecchio, Loggia dei Lanzi, and a reproduction of Michelangelo's *David*—the most beautiful architectural ensemble of the city; the Palazzo Medici; and Palazzo Pitti with the famous Medici frescoes.

The dome of Cathedral Santa Maria del Fiore was designed by Brunelleschi and the Campanile by Giotto. Florence's churches—such as San Marco and its works by Fra Angelico, Santa Croce, and Santa Maria Novella—are also famous. The Uffizi Gallery with works by Botticelli, Dürer, Michelangelo, Raphael, and Rembrandt is the most important museum in the city.

Rome is spread out over seven hills. Practically every square inch of space is of historic importance, especially the Palatine Hill, which has been occupied since the seventh century B.C. Many impressive buildings of Imperial Rome are

What to See and Do in Mainland Italy
▶ **CITIES AND CULTURAL HERITAGE**
• Florence, Rome, Venice, Naples, Verona, Pisa, Siena, Assisi, Milan, Bologna, Padua, Vicenza, Ravenna, Turin, Trieste
• Pompeii, Herculaneum, Paestum
▶ **COASTS**
• Picturesque and popular beaches (Amalfi Coast, Capri, Ligurian and Adriatic coasts)
▶ **LANDSCAPE**
• Alps (Cervinia, Dolomites, Valle d'Aosta)
• Abruzzo, lakes (Como, Maggiore, Garda), Tuscany

Italy's architectural and artistic heritage, together with its long coastlines, celebrated cuisine, and deep-seated culture, gives the country a special charm. There is something for everyone: historic cities, popular beaches, beautiful landscapes, active volcanoes, and much more. If that's not enough, its many islands offer a mix of culture and beach relaxation.

Map labels:
SWITZERLAND, Lake Maggiore, Lake Como, Lake Garda, Dolomites, AUSTRIA, SLOVENIA, Trieste, Cervinia, VALLE D'AOSTA, Milan, Vicenza, Verona, Padua, Venice, FRANCE, Turin, Po, Bologna, Ravenna, Rimini, Adriatic Riviera, Genoa, Ligurian Coast, Pisa, Florence, Arno, SAN MARINO, Ligurian Sea, Siena, TUSCANY, Assisi, UMBRIA, Adriatic Sea, Corsica (FRANCE), ITALY, ABRUZZI, ROME, La Maddalena Archipelago, Costa Smeralda, Ischia, Capri, Naples, Mount Vesuvius 1,281, Pompeii, Amalfi Coast, Paestum, Nuraghes, Alghero, Tyrrhenian Sea, Sardinia, Villasimius, Stromboli, Lipari Islands, Salina, Lipari, Vulcano, Ionian Sea, Pula, Palermo, Mount Etna 3,322, Taormina, Sicily, Piazza Armerina, Agrigento, Syracuse, Mediterranean Sea, 0 100 km, 0 100 mi

Venice, "La Serenissima," enchants its visitors in every season, from every vantage point.

Rome's Castel Sant'Angelo, on the right bank of the Tiber River, was built as a mausoleum for Emperor Hadrian.

still standing, including the Colosseum, the Pantheon, Trajan's Column and its storied bas-relief, and the baths of Diocletian and Caracalla. These were followed in time by the oldest churches, the Basilica San Giovanni in Laterano and San Lorenzo fuori le Mura. The Renaissance produced the Palazzo Venezia, the Sistine Chapel with art by Michelangelo and Raphael, the present appearance of St. Peter's Basilica, and the Farnese Palace. Baroque art is found at the Piazza Navona in the form of the Bernini fountain. The most famous museums are the Vatican Museums, the Borghese Gallery, and the National Gallery of Ancient Art (Barberini and Corsini Palace).

Doomsayers perennially predict the end of **Venice,** sinking under the rising waters and the tourist crowds, but the city continues on. Its famous sites include St. Mark's Square, the Doges' Palace, the Bridge of Sighs, the palazzos along the Grand Canal, and the Rialto Bridge. In addition, there are the Academy, where the Venetian school began with Titian, Veronese, and Tintoretto; the Palazzo Grassi, with its famous exhibitions; La Fenice opera house; and about a hundred churches. All these can easily be visited on foot or by gondola.

"See **Naples** and die"—you will understand this famous phrase as soon as you see the Bay of Naples. This city, where pizza was invented, is overshadowed by Mount Vesuvius, the volcano that always looms as somewhat of a threat. The city's narrow lanes lead to discoveries such as the Palazzo Reale, San Pietro a Maiella church, Santa Chiara monastery, Castel Nuovo—the architectural symbol of Naples—and San Carlo opera house. The museums include the National

Traveler's Notebook

MAIN CONTACTS

Embassy of Italy
3000 Whitehaven Street, NW Washington, DC 20008
(202) 612-4400
www.amb
washingtondc
.esteri.it
www.enit.it
www.italia.it/en/
home.html
Embassy of Italy
14 Three Kings Yard London W1K 4EH, UK
+ 44 (0) 20 7312 2200
www.amblondra.
esteri.it

TRAVEL DOCUMENTS FOR U.S. & U.K. CITIZENS
Passport

TRAVEL TIME TO DESTINATION & TIME DIFFERENCE
New York to Rome: 8 hours 10 minutes nonstop flight; EST +6. London to Rome: 2 hours 20 minutes nonstop flight; GMT +1

AVERAGE TRIP COST
$1,400/£900 for a week of excursions

LANGUAGE & CURRENCY
Official language: Italian
Currency: euro

POPULATION
58,148,000 inhabitants. In recent times, Italy has seen heavy immigration, although for a long time it was a country of net emigration.
Capital: Rome

RELIGION
Most Italians are Catholic.

FESTIVALS
February: Mostra, the biannual Venice Film Festival; February or March: Carnival in Venice; June: Festival of St. John in Florence; mid-June to the end of August: Shakespeare Festival in Verona; July: Feast of Our Lady of Mount Carmel in Naples, and Redentore Festival in Venice (decorated boats on the Giudecca Canal and the waters around St. Mark's Square); September: Regata Storica in Venice

SHOPPING
Classic shopping items include a silk tie, leather gloves, and shoes—some of the things Italy is famous for. Other items could be jewelry from Florence, Carnival masks from Venice; Murano glass; crèche figurines from Naples; or coral jewelry from Sardinia.

Bridging Florence's Arno River, the Ponte Vecchio has sheltered goldsmith's stores and workshops since the 16th century.

Archaeological Museum, which houses artifacts from Pompeii and Herculaneum such as gold jewelry, Greek vases, sculptures, mosaics, and frescoes. There is even a museum of nativity scenes and the National Museum of Capodimonte, featuring Neapolitan painting and decorative arts.

The following cities should also be part of any journey through Italy:
• **Verona** has a huge arena from the first century, a Roman theater above the Adige River, the Piazza delle Erbe (former site of the Roman forum), the Piazza dei Signori with its Gothic and Renaissance architecture, the churches of San Zeno Maggiore and Sant' Anastasia, libraries, the Castelvecchio Museum with paintings of the Veronese and Venetian schools, and the legendary

balcony from which Juliet supposedly spoke to Romeo.
• In **Pisa,** the main attraction is, of course, the well-restored, 12th-century Leaning Tower, next to the beautiful cathedral on the Piazza del Duomo.
• **Siena** has the beautiful medieval Piazza del Campo in its historic center, with which only the cathedral square in Lecce can compete.
• **Assisi** was terribly damaged by an earthquake in 1997, but it is still worth visiting for its many monuments: the Roman ruins (amphitheater, temple of Minerva), as well as the Basilica of St. Francis with famous frescoes by Cimabue and Giotto.
• A visit to **Milan,** the fashion capital, should include stops at the La Scala opera house and the Sforza Castle.

• **Bologna** is known for its historic center of medieval and Renaissance palaces, museums, and churches.

When to Go			
	NORTH	SOUTH AND ISLANDS	FLORENCE, ROME, VENICE
JANUARY			
FEBRUARY			✔
MARCH			✔
APRIL		☼	
MAY	☼	☼	✔
JUNE	☼	☼	✔
JULY	☼		
AUGUST	☼		
SEPTEMBER	☼	☼	✔
OCTOBER		☼	✔
NOVEMBER			
DECEMBER			

• **Padua** should be seen for its Palazzo della Ragione and sacred buildings; **Vicenza** for its municipal building, the 15th-century basilica and the Teatro Olimpico, both by Palladio, and the Palladian villas in the surrounding region; and **Ravenna** for its Roman amphitheater and aqueduct and its Byzantine churches richly ornamented with mosaics.

• **Turin** is admired for its baroque architecture, the Egyptian Museum with one of the largest collections

The rugged Dolomites characterize the Alto Adige region.

of ancient Egyptian artifacts outside Egypt, and the Shroud of Turin, the linen cloth that is said to have covered Jesus at his burial. Skiing in the nearby Alps is a huge winter draw.

• **Trieste**'s varied architecture ranges from Roman ruins to a medieval fortified castle, a cathedral of multiple period styles, and Romanesque and baroque churches.

Remnants of the Roman Empire, the Middle Ages, and the Renaissance crop up wherever you go in Italy. Umbria has splendid medieval

sites at Spoleto, Orvieto, and Città della Pieve, for example. In the Camonica Valley in Lombardy, even earlier history is recorded in a number of rock drawings from the Neolithic period.

The cultural heritage of Roman antiquity in all regions of Italy particularly surprises and delights visitors from around the world.

Pompeii was covered by ash from Mount Vesuvius in A.D. 79. Many ruins have been uncovered, including the forum and houses such as the Villa of the Mysteries. In **Herculaneum,** buried by the same volcanic eruption, the Houses of Neptune and Amphitrite have been excavated in good condition.

Ostia, Rome's ancient seaport, is now silted up, but several of the buildings stand still intact around the Square of the Guilds (Piazzale delle Corporazioni). The town of **Paestum** has preserved its Poseidon Temple.

▶ COASTS

Italy, along with Spain and Greece, is one of the favorite destinations for Mediterranean beach tourism and for cruise ships between spring and October, leaving from Venice, Genoa, Naples, and Palermo.

The **Amalfi Coast,** south of Naples, is most picturesque, with the famous beaches of Ravello and Positano and the Sorrento peninsula. From Naples or Sorrento, ferries take visitors to the island of **Capri,** which is as much admired for its luxurious ambiance as for its limestone sea grottos that feature strange effects of light. North of Capri, the island of Ischia attracts a similar clientele.

The beaches on the **Ligurian** coast stretch from La Spezia to Levanto, with famous resorts including Portofino and the five hillside towns of **Cinque Terre,** featuring steep, rocky terraces and vineyards.

The coast of Tuscany profits from its beaches in towns like Viareggio and Forte dei Marmi. Every summer, tourist crowds spread out over the beaches of the **Adriatic** Riviera around Rimini, although since 1989 its waters have been frequently plagued by algae.

▶ LANDSCAPE

Between the Valle d'Aosta and Piedmont regions in northwest Italy, Gran Paradiso National Park encompasses glacial valleys, forests, torrential streams, and endless hiking trails. The ski area of **Cervinia** lies at the foot of the Matterhorn (Cervino), one of the highest peaks in the Alps. Farther east, the **Dolomites** raise their rugged peaks above gentler valleys of pine woods.

Tuscany's landscape and historic buildings are bathed in a unique light.

The mountains are a mecca for sports enthusiasts. In **Valle d'Aosta,** winter sports have a long tradition, covering everything from alpine skiing to heli-skiing and cross-country skiing, starting out from small towns like Breuil-Cervinia and Pila in France. During the summer, tourists can visit historic monuments or hike in Gran Paradiso to see ibex, chamois, and marmots.

The **Abruzzo** mountains' limestone massif and the National Park of Abruzzo, Latium, and Molise embrace the highest mountains of central Italy, where you can find wolves, lynx, and bears and opportunities for extended hikes.

The area around **Lake Como** is enchanting as much for its idyllic setting as for its historic sites and sumptuous villas—Villa d'Este, Villa Carlotta, and Villa d'Erba, where young Luchino Visconti, the film director, lived. Other favorite tourist destinations include **Lake Garda**—known as the Olive Riviera—and **Lake Maggiore** with surprisingly Mediterranean flora and attractive villas.

A combination of Mediterranean climate, rolling hills planted with vineyards, and olive trees gives **Tuscany** a harmonious, luminous aspect, rarely equaled anywhere—although the neighboring region of Umbria, which is much less well known, comes close.

Lipari Islands

These seven islands, north of Sicily, can be reached by hydrofoil. The volcanic islands **Stromboli** and **Vulcano** offer interesting hikes around the volcanic peaks and quiet bays, ideal for bathing. Other destinations include the fishing island of **Filicudi, Panarea** and its hot

What to See and Do on the Italian Islands

Lipari Islands

▶ **LANDSCAPE AND COASTS**

- Volcanoes (Stromboli, Vulcano)
- Filicudi, Panarea, Salina, Lipari

Sardinia

▶ **COASTS**

- La Maddalena Archipelago, Costa Smeralda
- South Coast (Pula, Villasimius)

▶ **CULTURAL HERITAGE**

- Stone towers (nuraghes)

Sicily

▶ **COASTS**

- Taormina and beaches on the east coast

▶ **LANDSCAPE**

- Mount Etna

▶ **MONUMENTS**

- Ancient cities (Taormina, Syracuse, Agrigento, Palermo, Piazza Armerina)

springs, and **Salina,** known as the island where the movie *Il Postino* was filmed.

The Lipari Islands have long rested in obscurity because of their isolation and few sandy beaches, but tourists treasure them for their scenic beauty and tranquillity, especially **Lipari.**

Sardinia

▶ COASTS

Sardinia has quiet coves to offer. The beaches in the north are rather rocky, whereas the southern beaches are long and sandy.

To the northeast, the 62 islets of **La Maddalena Archipelago,** which are covered in a kind of scrubland, are an ideal setting for long walks.

The Aga Khan transformed a forgotten coast in Sardinia's northern region into a luxurious tourism paradise, called **Costa Smeralda.** Hotels and vacation villages are legion, but the rocky coast allows for diverse activities; particular favorites are sailing, diving, and surfing. The long rocky coast on the west side sees fewer tourists than the beaches of **Pula** and **Villasimius.**

▶ CULTURAL HERITAGE

The town of Alghero with its fortified town wall and narrow lanes is worth a detour. But it is the 6,000 dry-stone towers, called *nuraghes,* erected all over the island between the 18th and 15th centuries B.C., that draw every visitor's curiosity. Other civilizations have also left their mark here: There are ruins of Punic temples in Antas and Nora, Romanesque churches in Sassari and San

Ancient Cefalù in Sicily attracts visitors with its architecture and beaches.

Giusta, a Gothic church in Alghero, the tomb of Italian national hero Giuseppe Garibaldi on the island of Caprera, and a castle and baroque cathedral in Cagliari.

Sicily

▶ COASTS

Sicily, the largest island in the Mediterranean, is a top tourist destination. The town of **Taormina** exemplifies the combination of scenic beauty along a bay with a rich and varied history. The beach towns on the east coast always draw the most visitors, but it is still possible to find secluded spots.

▶ LANDSCAPE

It takes about two and a half hours to hike up **Mount Etna,** the most active volcano in Europe. A hike traditionally begins at the Refugio Sapienza tourist station, which can be reached by cable car. This is not a particularly trying hike, but visitors should get all necessary safety information and be prepared for the weather. The volcano's slopes change from green fields, vineyards, and orchards to rough lava deserts.

▶ CULTURAL HERITAGE

Traces of Sicily's stormy history can be found everywhere: **Taormina** has a famous Greek theater and many ancient city lanes. **Syracuse** boasts an amphitheater, a Doric Temple of Apollo on the island of Ortigia, a massive 13th-century fortress, the Castello Maniace, the Palazzo Beventano del Bosco, the Pantalica Necropolis, and the

Archaeological Museum with Greek artifacts.

Agrigento's sites include the Valley of the Temples, site of seven seventh- and sixth-century B.C. Doric temples and other sanctuaries of the fourth century B.C. Local writer Luigi Pirandello is celebrated in the Pirandello Literature Park.

Palermo was strongly influenced by three cultures in its history: Greek, Roman, and Muslim. The city's most glorious time was the 12th century, as shown in many of its buildings: the Cappella Palatina (mosaics), the Byzantine church of La Martorana, San Giovanni and San Cataldo churches, and the cathedral built by Norman king William II (Byzantine mosaics). Outside Piazza Armerina stands the Villa Romana del Casale, with the largest and most complex Roman mosaics in the world.

The Doric Temple of Ceres in Segesta is a vestige of its Greek past, as is the case with Selinunte's ruins of ancient Greek temples.

Jamaica

✖ *The third largest island in the Caribbean, after Cuba and Hispaniola, Jamaica offers an array of waterfalls and mountains, fascinating historic sites, a vibrant cultural life, and beautiful beaches.*

What to See and Do in Jamaica

▶ **LANDSCAPE**
- Blue Mountains, plateaus, plantations

▶ **CITIES AND BEACHES**
- Kingston, Ocho Rios (Turtle Beach), Montego Bay (Doctor's Cave Beach), Spanish Town
- Port Antonio (Frenchman's Cove, San San Beach, Blue Lagoon, Dragon Bay), Negril

---

▶ LANDSCAPE

Like many of its neighbors, Jamaica evolved from a broad arc of volcanoes rising from the seabed billions of years ago. This igneous rock forms the **Blue Mountains,** which traverse the eastern part of the island. Limestone plateaus, carved into sinkholes, caves, and gullies by more than a hundred rivers, cover about two-thirds of the country. Lush vegetation and huge plantations spread across the remaining land.

▶ CITIES, BEACHES, AND COASTS

Kingston, the capital, throbs with the energy of more than half a million citizens. The heart of the city lies downtown near the waterfront, with historic sites such as the former British army parade grounds and submerged Port Royal. At Gordon House, visitors can observe debate in the House of Representatives or the Senate. The National Gallery exhibits an impressive, permanent collection of African-style art. Reggae aficionados should go into New Kingston for a tour of the Bob Marley Museum.

Ocho Rios is notable for both its bauxite industry and its overwhelming natural wonders. Dunn's River Falls, a 600-foot-long cascade, and the area's renowned gardens (Coyaba River Garden and Museum, Fern Gulley, Shaw Park Botanical Gardens) are all located within a few miles of the city. **Turtle Beach** buzzes with activity, including water sports and plenty of shopping.

Montego Bay attracts tourists with its historic charm and

Traveler's Notebook

MAIN CONTACTS *Embassy of Jamaica* 1520 New Hampshire Avenue, NW Washington, DC 20036 (202) 452-0660 www.embassyofjamaica.org *Jamaican High Commission* 1–2 Prince Consort Road London SW7 2BZ + 44 (0) 20 7823 9911 www.jhcuk.org	**TRAVEL DOCUMENTS FOR U.S. & U.K. CITIZENS** Passport **TRAVEL TIME TO DESTINATION & TIME DIFFERENCE** New York to Kingston: 3 hours 45 minutes nonstop flight; EST. London to Kingston: 13 hours 45 minutes connecting flight; GMT –5 **AVERAGE TRIP COST** $1,275–$2,500/£800–	£1,600 for seven days at an all-inclusive resort **LANGUAGE & CURRENCY** Official language: English; English-African Creole is heard on the streets Currency: Jamaican dollar; U.S. dollars accepted **POPULATION** 2,687,200 inhabitants. The majority of the population is of African descent; the largest minority groups are of Indian and	Chinese descent. Capital: Kingston **RELIGION** The majority are Christians; Rastafarians have about 24,000 adherents. **FESTIVALS** January 6: Accompong Maroon Festival (honoring the Jamaican Maroons, runaway slaves who helped defeat the English army during the 1700s); July: Reggae	Sumfest, a three-day music festival; all summer: National Festival of the Arts, a celebration showcasing the work of native artists **SHOPPING** Local art and crafts, baskets, coffee, spices (be prepared to bargain)

Map: Frenchman's Cove Beach, San San Beach, Dragon Bay, Blue Lagoon; Doctor's Cave Beach; Falmouth; Dunn's River Falls; Turtle Beach; Montego Bay; Oyster Bay; Oracabessa; Negril; Nine Mile; Ocho Rios; Port Antonio; JAMAICA; Mandeville; Spanish Town; Blue Mts.; KINGSTON; Port Royal; Caribbean Sea; 0 20 km; 0 20 mi

Winnifred Beach in Jamaica is a public beach, open to all.

contemporary accommodations. The mineral springs at **Doctor's Cave Beach** brought Jamaica international recognition as a spa, and the lively downtown square, named for slave rebellion leader Sam Sharpe, reminds visitors of the country's tumultuous past. Rose Hall Great House—said to be haunted—is furnished with antiques from its heyday as a sugar plantation. Montego Bay Marine Park offers snorkeling, diving, and glass-bottom boat tours of an extensive ocean reef.

Spanish Town, the former capital, is largely a modern city,

embellished with Georgian architecture. Parade Square in the city center boasts several historic buildings, including King's House, the governor's mansion dating from 1762, and the Cathedral of St. Jago de la Vega, the oldest Anglican cathedral outside England.

Port Antonio is a quiet backwater mostly visited by independent travelers. The city abounds with old forts (Fort George), lodges (DeMontevin Lodge), and wharves (Boundbrook Wharf), but generally draws crowds with its coastal scenery. East of the port lie **Frenchman's Cove** and **San San Beach,** as well as the **Blue Lagoon** and **Dragon Bay,** two locations made famous by 1980s-era movies (*Blue Lagoon, Club Paradise,* and *Cocktail*). In the Rio Grande Valley, tourists float down the river on 30-foot-long bamboo rafts.

Other cities worth a visit are: sleepy Oracabessa, where authors Ian Fleming and Sir Noël Coward lived; Falmouth with its bioluminescent lagoon (Oyster Bay); Falmouth for Good Hope Plantation; Nine Mile for Bob Marley's mausoleum; **Negril** with its famous Long Bay; and Mandeville, known for its food (High Mountain Coffee, Pioneer Chocolate, Pickapeppa) and old mansions (Marshall's Pen Great House, Huntingdon Summit).

An offshore coral reef shields the white, sandy beaches of Jamaica's north shore, dotted with many resorts. The eastern coastline, unprotected from ocean swells, is far more rugged and dramatic. With a few exceptions, the south and west coasts are volcanic black-sand beaches.

Advice

■ Pros
• Beautiful, sandy beaches and verdant landscapes. A great variety of tourist accommodations. Temperatures average 77 to 86 degrees Fahrenheit year-round.

■ Cons
• Largely mass tourism.

■ Safety
• Travelers are advised not to walk around alone at night, to keep cars locked, and to beware of pickpockets.

■ Special Tip
• Don't forget to try authentic Jamaican recipes. Jerk cuisine is found all over the island and is one of Jamaica's most distinctive styles of cooking. Meat, usually chicken or pork, is marinated in a special blend of spices (including peppers, cinnamon, and nutmeg) and then slowly grilled over a pimento-wood fire.

When to Go		
	CLIMATE	LOCAL FESTIVALS
JANUARY	☼	✔
FEBRUARY	☼	
MARCH	☼	
APRIL	☼	
MAY		
JUNE		✔
JULY		✔
AUGUST		✔
SEPTEMBER		
OCTOBER		
NOVEMBER		
DECEMBER	☼	

Japan

<table>
<tr><th colspan="2">What to See and Do in Japan</th></tr>
</table>

► **LANDSCAPE**

• Mountains (Mount Fuji, the Japanese Alps, Mount Aso, Mount Asama, Hokkaido Island)

• Matsushima, hot springs (Beppu), lakes, gorges (Yabakei), gardens (Kenrokuen), Yoshino-Kumano National Park

► **CITIES AND MONUMENTS**

• Tokyo, Kyoto, Osaka, Kobe, Hiroshima, Himeji

• Shinto and Buddhist sanctuaries (Ise, Nara, Kamakura, Kyoto, Nikko, Miyajima)

● *The stereotypical view of Japan is that of dutiful geishas and the perfect cone of Mount Fuji. If the first idea is pure fancy, Mount Fuji with its temples and sanctuaries is indeed a perfect example of scenic beauty.*

► **LANDSCAPE**

The volcanic landscape of Japan has produced the legendary **Mount Fuji,** which is part of the **Japanese Alps.** Mount Fuji is the symbol of the country and a pilgrim destination. The perfection of its extinct volcanic cone (12,388 feet) has inspired traditional artists to portray it in countless woodblock prints (such as those by Hokusai). **Mount Asama** is an active volcano complex, as is **Mount Aso** with one of the largest calderas in the world. The peaks on **Hokkaido** are a well-known skiing mecca (Sapporo).

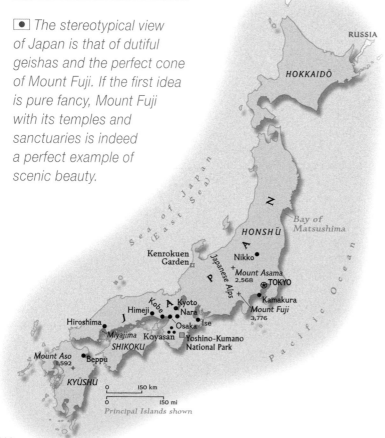

One of Japan's iconic sights lies in the bay of **Matsushima,** where the ocean, islets, and temples combine to one of the "Three Views of Japan." **Beppu** boasts hot springs and pristine lakes. Other sites not far from Beppu are the **Yabakei** gorge and the **Kenrokuen** and Kanazawa landscape gardens. The **Yoshino-Kumano National Park** symbolizes "pure land," where pilgrims commune with nature at the temples.

Legendary Mount Fuji, the pilgrimage site and artist's subject, remains a place of veneration.

But it is in the first two weeks of April, when the cherry blossoms are at peak bloom, that all of Japan celebrates nature.

▶ CITIES AND MONUMENTS

Tokyo presents a sort of encapsulated image of its history with three main sites: the Imperial Palace (near the Ginza business district), the Meiji shrine, and the Buddhist temple of Asakusa. The city offers many contrasts between its modern quarters (Century Tower) and the small, old houses with gardens that have not changed but are in danger of being torn down.

Visitors should not skip a visit to the Tsukiji fish market, the largest in the world, which is slated to move out of the city center in a few years. Equally important is a stop at the Tokyo National Museum for its traditional Japanese arts.

Kyoto, with its cherry orchards, is often compared to a living museum for its 1,500 Buddhist temples—the most famous of which is the Golden Pavilion—and 400 Shinto shrines.

Osaka is home to the Shitenno-ji, the oldest temple in Japan, as well as Osaka Castle and several museums. Before the earthquake of 1995, **Kobe** stood out for the historic Meiji-era Kitano-Cho district.

The Kiyomizu Dera temple overlooks Kyoto, a city of 1,500 temples.

Visitors can spend a night along with pilgrims in one of the hundred temples on Mount Koya in the Osaka region, the headquarters of the Shingon sect of Japanese Buddhism.

A moving experience is a visit to **Hiroshima**'s Peace Memorial Park, at the site of the 1945 atomic blast. In the park is the A-Bomb Dome and museum, which is listed as a World Heritage site.

In the south of Honshu Island, on a hilltop of the ancient city of **Himeji** stands a brilliant white castle complex of the 14th and 15th centuries comprising 83 wooden buildings known as the White Heron Castle.

Traveler's Notebook

MAIN CONTACTS
Embassy of Japan
2520 Massachusetts Avenue, NW
Washington, DC 20008
(202) 238-6700
www.us.emb-japan.go.jp
www.jnto.go.jp
Embassy of Japan
101–104 Piccadilly
London W1J 7JT
+ 44 (0) 20 7465 6500
www.uk.emb-japan.go.jp

TRAVEL DOCUMENTS FOR U.S. & U.K. CITIZENS
Passport

TRAVEL TIME TO DESTINATION & TIME DIFFERENCE
New York to Tokyo: 14 hours nonstop flight; EST -14. London to Tokyo: 11 hours 35 minutes nonstop flight; GMT +9

AVERAGE TRIP COST
$3,800/£2,450 for 15 days of touring

LANGUAGE & CURRENCY
Official language: Japanese
Currency: yen

POPULATION
127,433,000 inhabitants; the cities are densely populated, home to about 80 percent of the population. Capital:

Tokyo (metropolitan area population: 26,500,000)

RELIGION
Both Shintoism and Buddhism are practiced in Japan; these ancient religions are, in their way, unique to Japan.

FESTIVALS
January: The New Year (Ganjitsu) is celebrated over several days; February: Lantern

Festival in Nara; April to May (depending on the region): Cherry Blossom festivals; June: Summer solstice (Geshi); October or November: Tokyo Tori-no-Ichi (Rake Fair) Festival; December 23: National Day

SHOPPING
Dolls and kimonos

Japan's religious traditions encompass both Shintoism and Buddhism. Shintoism is best represented in the **Ise** Grand Shrine. An expression of Buddhist piety is found in the many Daibatsu ("large Buddha") statues and temples all over Japan, including the **Nara** Temple in Toda-ji, the most important and largest wooden temple complex, and Horyu-ji, the cradle of Japanese Buddhism.

Buddha is also represented in **Kamakura,** where a 46-foot-high 13th-century bronze Buddha resides outdoors, and in Kyoto. In **Nikko,** besides temples, the historic sites include mausoleums of the Tokugawa family, shoguns of the Edo period. And on the island of **Miyajima,** the Itsukushima Shrine is a sacred site of both Shintoism and Buddhism.

Advice

■ Pros

• The contrast between tradition and modernism in Japan makes it an attractive destination. It is possible to book typical Japanese accommodations, such as *ryokans,* traditional inns with tatami-matted rooms, and *minshukus,* the budget version.

■ Cons

• Communication is complicated; few people speak English. Japanese signs can be difficult to understand.

■ Safety

• Japan is a safe country. However, medical costs are high, and travelers are advised to consider travel insurance.

■ Special Tips

• Japan has been discovered as a special destination, especially during the short cherry blossom time, which is highly celebrated and of great importance to the Japanese.
• It is easier to purchase yen before your trip and to carry traveler's checks in yen or dollars.

The galloping urbanization of Tokyo is a challenge to its traditional homes.

When to Go		
	IN GENERAL	TOKYO AND THE SOUTH
JANUARY		
FEBRUARY		
MARCH	☼	
APRIL	☼	☼
MAY	☼	☼
JUNE		☼
JULY		
AUGUST		
SEPTEMBER		
OCTOBER	☼	☼
NOVEMBER	☼	☼
DECEMBER		

Extending over several miles, Petra is a history lesson in architecture.

▶ The ancient city of Petra was founded by the Nabataeans, an Arabic people from southern Jordan. The city lies not far from Wadi Rum, another jewel of the Middle East, made famous by the film *Lawrence of Arabia* and a favorite destination for trekkers.

Jordan

▶ MONUMENTS

In **Petra,** the funerary temples and tombs that are witnesses to its illustrious Nabataean past (fourth to second centuries B.C.) are all cut from the same pink and red limestone sitting in a sort of rocky circle nearly two miles across. This site on the incense trade route was chosen because of its inhospitable terrain enclosed by towering rocks, entered though a gorge *(siq)* so narrow that the sun shines in for no more than three-quarters of an hour.

Visitors need at least two days and must hike for several miles to see all of Petra: the temples, mausoleums, funerary chambers, and al-Deir (the

Traveler's Notebook				
MAIN CONTACTS	Gardens	nonstop flight; EST +7.	**POPULATION**	**FESTIVALS**
Embassy of the Hashe-mite Kingdom of Jordan	London W8 7HA	London to Amman: 5	6,053,000 inhabitants,	May 25: Independence
3504 International Drive, NW	+ 44 (0) 20 7937 3685	hours nonstop flight;	60 percent of whom are	Day; July or August (end of Ramadan): Eid al-Fitr
Washington, DC 20008	www.jordanembassy.org.uk	GMT +2	Palestinian refugees, along with about 100,000	**SHOPPING**
(202) 966-2664	**TRAVEL DOCUMENTS FOR U.S. & U.K. CITIZENS**	**AVERAGE TRIP COST**	Bedouins and 20,000	Bedouin jewelry and
www.jordan embassyus.org	Passport and visa	$1,650/£1,050 for 9 days (Petra and hiking in Wadi Rum)	Kurdish Circassians. Capital: Amman	handmade glassware
www.visitjordan.com	**TRAVEL TIME TO DESTINATION & TIME DIFFERENCE**	**LANGUAGE & CURRENCY**	**RELIGION**	
Embassy of the Hashe-mite Kingdom of Jordan	New York to Amman:	Official language: Arabic; English is widely spoken	93 percent are Sunni Muslims	
6 Upper Phillimore	11 hours 35 minutes	Currency: Jordanian dinar		

What to See and Do in Jordan

▶ **MONUMENTS**

• Petra (temples and tombs)

• Jerash (Christian and Roman ruins), Al-Karak (crusader castle), "castles of the desert," ksurs

• Madaba (ruins), Qasr Amra Palace

• Bethabara (site of the baptism of Christ), Mount Nebo

▶ **LANDSCAPE**

• Desert of Wadi Rum

▶ **COAST**

• Beaches and diving in the Red Sea (Aqaba)

Advice

■ **Pros**

• Jordan offers cultural experiences, desert treks, and beach vacations all in one and has always managed to be open to visitors, despite its position in the heart of political tensions.

■ **Cons**

• Petra's rapid change from cultural highlight to mass tourism destination. Possible terrorism activity.

■ **Safety**

• Jordan is less safe than it used to be. Tourists are seldom a target, but there is some risk, as one attack in Amman showed in 2005.

■ **Recommendation**

• Jordan is a traditional Muslim country, and dressing for decency is important.

Monastery), as well as the High Place of Sacrifice and a Roman theater.

Perhaps the most famous structure is the magnificent al-Khazne, (the Treasury), which starred in Steven Spielberg's movie *Indiana Jones and the Last Crusade*. This is the most majestic spot in all of the Near East.

Jerash, the ancient Gerasa, is the second most important site in Jordan. This Roman settlement, often called the Jordanian Pompeii, preserves a theater, a forum, and two temples dedicated to Artemis and Zeus. The subsequent Christian overlords left various buildings and churches dedicated to John the Baptist, St. Christopher, St. Cosmas, and St. Damian.

The town of **Al-Karak,** surrounded by treacherous gorges, had its high period during the crusades. On a hillside stands the 12th-century crusader fortress, known then as Karak in Moab. The countryside is dotted with numerous hunting lodges, so-called desert castles, and *ksurs,* settlements of the Mamluk sultans, as well as ruins of sanctuaries and monasteries.

In **Madaba,** there are ancient Byzantine mosaics from the early high Christian era, and 22 miles outside the city in the Amman Desert is the eighth-century **Qasr Amra Palace,** one of the important examples of early Islamic art and architecture.

On the left bank of the Jordan River, near the north coast of the Dead Sea, is the region once called **Bethabara,** where John the Baptist baptized Jesus. From **Mount Nebo,** near the mouth of the Jordan, Moses is said to have looked down into the

Promised Land, and this is where he is said to have died.

▶ **LANDSCAPE AND WALKING TOURS**

The **Wadi Rum Desert,** also known as the Valley of the Moon, stretches far south. In 1917, T. E. Lawrence assembled warriors in Wadi Rum village to participate in the revolt against the Ottoman Empire. The film about his activities, *Lawrence of Arabia,* was made here as well. At the Seven Pillars of Wisdom Mountain, visitors will recognize sites that appeared in the film. Hikers may encounter Bedouins as they stride through the rocky and sandy terrain of this unique desert.

▶ **COAST**

Near **Aqaba,** the coast of the **Red Sea** invites vacationers with great beaches, coral reefs, and multicolored fish. Divers always come back with the most incredible images.

The Dead Sea also has a few beaches (Suweima) and scenic views.

When to Go		
	CLIMATE	HIKING IN WADI RUM
JANUARY		🚶
FEBRUARY		🚶
MARCH	☼	🚶
APRIL	☼	🚶
MAY	☼	
JUNE		
JULY		
AUGUST		
SEPTEMBER	☼	
OCTOBER	☼	🚶
NOVEMBER	☼	🚶
DECEMBER	☼	🚶

Kenya

Kenya is the place for a great safari adventure for photographers and observers alike, but it also has wonderful beaches and trekking opportunities in the north for encounters with the Maasai or other tribal peoples.

What to See and Do in Kenya

▶ WILDLIFE

- Maasai-Mara National Reserve and the big five (elephants, lions, leopards, rhinos, and cape buffalo), gnu and zebra migration, giraffes, hippopotamuses
- Lake Nakuru National Park (flamingos, pelicans)
- National parks and reserves: Amboseli, Tsavo, Samburo, Aberdare
- Lake Baringo, Lake Naivasha

▶ COAST

- Beaches of the Indian Ocean (Malindi, Mombasa, Lamu, Tiwi, Diani)

▶ LANDSCAPE AND TREKKING

- Mount Kenya, Lake Turkana

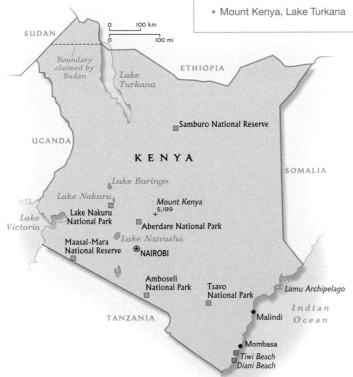

▶ WILDLIFE

Kenya's fauna is remarkable. The big five—elephants, lions, leopards, rhinos, and cape buffalo—can be found here and are the main attractions for a photo safari. Visitors watch the animals from open Land Rovers poised for the perfect angle and composition. The animal reserves are crowded with tourists in the summer and are more ideally visited in September or October, at the end of

For these "grand ladies" in the Maasai-Mara National Reserve, as well as for the other animals, tourists are part of everyday life.

the dry period, when the vegetation is getting skimpy and the animals move in herds in search of water.

The big five come together in **Maasai-Mara National Reserve,** the most interesting and best-known park. Hippopotamuses lounge in the Mara River and endless herds of gnus and zebras pass by in July and August during the great migration.

Lake Nakuru National Park harbors flamingo colonies and pelicans, side by side with giraffes, gazelles, and black rhinos.

Other stars among the reserves are **Amboseli National Park** with a view of Mount Kilimanjaro; **Tsavo National Park,** the largest one; **Samburo National Reserve;** and **Aberdare National Park.** Several hundred species of birds roost along

Lakes Baringo and **Naivasha.** On Mfangano Island in Lake Victoria, there is a chance to see fish eagles, ospreys, and cormorants.

▶ COAST

The Kenyan shores of the Indian Ocean have everything to offer: white sandy beaches, coconut palms, and above all, coral reefs where marine life can be studied at leisure. Diving,

Along Kenya's coast are many historic Muslim villages, as here on the Lamu Archipelago.

Traveler's Notebook

MAIN CONTACTS

Embassy of Kenya
2249 R Street, NW
Washington, DC 20008
(202) 387-6101
www.kenyaembassy.com
www.magicalkenya.com
www.tourism.go.ke

Kenya High Commission
45 Portland Place
London W1B 1AS, UK
+ 44 (0) 20 7636 2371
www.kenyahigh
commission.net

**TRAVEL DOCUMENTS FOR
U.S. & U.K. CITIZENS**

Passport and visa

HEALTH ISSUES

Vaccination against yellow fever is strongly advised for areas outside the cities. Malaria prophylaxis is important for areas below 6,000 feet, except in Nairobi.

**TRAVEL TIME TO
DESTINATION & TIME
DIFFERENCE**

New York to Nairobi:
16 hours 45 minutes
connecting flight; EST +8.
London to Nairobi:
8 hours 30 minutes
nonstop flight; GMT +3

AVERAGE TRIP COST

$1,550/£1,000 for a week on safari

LANGUAGE & CURRENCY

Official languages: Swahili and English
Currency: Kenyan shilling

POPULATION

Kenya's 36,914,000 inhabitants represent a high population density compared to other African countries. There are several ethnic groups, of which the Kikuyu, at 21 percent, are the most numerous.

Others include Asians (mostly Indians), Arabs, and Europeans. Capital: Nairobi

RELIGION

Catholics and Protestants are represented equally at 26 percent each. About 20 percent are animist and 6 percent Muslim (most of whom live on the Lamu Archipelago).

FESTIVALS

June 1: Madaraka Day (commemorating the day of attaining internal self-rule in 1963); July

or August (end of Ramadan): Eid al-Fitr; August: Maulidi Festival (birth of the Prophet) in Lamu; December 12: Independence Day

SHOPPING

Interesting purchases include wooden sculptures and masks, grass skirts, wicker ware, and Maasai jewelry. Bargaining is part of the game.

When to Go			
	CLIMATE	NATIONAL PARKS	INDIAN OCEAN
JANUARY		🐾	
FEBRUARY		🐾	
MARCH			
APRIL			
MAY			
JUNE	☼		
JULY	☼	🐾	
AUGUST	☼	🐾	☼
SEPTEMBER	☼	🐾	☼
OCTOBER	☼	🐾	☼
NOVEMBER			
DECEMBER			

windsurfing, and deep-sea fishing (especially from **Malindi** for barracuda, marlin, and tuna) are in fashion. Lodging is widely available in the beach towns north of **Mombasa** on the **Lamu** Archipelago or around Malindi, or south of Mombasa in **Tiwi** Beach or **Diani** Beach. So far, mass tourism hasn't reached these shores, but new beach resorts are springing up all over such areas as Galu Kinondo, Shanzu, and Chale Island.

▶ LANDSCAPE AND TREKKING

The three peaks that constitute **Mount Kenya** (17,057 feet) are the remains of an extinct volcano and are

sacred to the Kenyans. Climbing the mountain is good training for anyone wishing to scale Mount Kilimanjaro (in Tanzania). The other great trekking opportunities are around **Lake Turkana,** where hikers may encounter the El Molo fishermen or Turkana and Samburo peoples.

Kenya's mountains and lakes provide scenic views, dominated by the light yellow of the savanna. The volcanoes in the Great Rift Valley have created unusual rock formations such as the Elgon Caves and the Leviathan lava tubes.

Festive clothing and dances distinguish Kenyan ethnic groups, who greet visitors warmly.

The sculptures in Wat Xieng Khuan Park near Vientiane cannot compete with the beauty of Luang Prabang, but are still worth a detour.

Laos

Among many unusual destinations, Laos— "the country of a million elephants"—is a most surprising country in Southeast Asia. Besides its Buddhist heritage, especially in the ancient capital of Luang Prabang, visitors will discover a gracious and warmhearted people that have kept to their traditional way of life along the Mekong River.

Traveler's Notebook

MAIN CONTACTS
Embassy of the Lao People's Democratic Republic
2222 S Street, NW
Washington, DC 20008
(202) 328-9148
www.laoembassy.com
www.tourismlaos.org
Embassy of the Lao People's Democratic Republic
74, Ave. Raymond Poincaré
75116 Paris, France
+33 (0) 1 4553 0298
www.laoparis.com

TRAVEL DOCUMENTS FOR U.S. & U.K. CITIZENS
Passport and visa

HEALTH ISSUES
Malaria prophylaxis advised, except in Vientiane

TRAVEL TIME TO DESTINATION & TIME DIFFERENCE
New York to Bangkok-Vientiane: 22 hours 25 minutes connecting; EST +12. London to Bangkok-Vientiane: 15 hours 50 minutes connecting; GMT +7

AVERAGE TRIP COST
$2,550/£1,650 for a 15-day excursion (in combination with Cambodia)

LANGUAGE & CURRENCY
Official language: Lao, which is similar to Thai Currency: kip; Thai bahts are accepted, as are U.S. dollars

POPULATION
60 percent of the population of 6,522,000 is Lao, with a low population density overall compared to Laos's neighbors. Most Lao are farmers. Capital: Vientiane

RELIGION
The majority practices Theravada Buddhism; there are also animists.

FESTIVALS
May: Rocket Festival, a call for the monsoon

SHOPPING
Textiles are the thing, along with beautiful handwoven silks and cottons and silver jewelry.

What to See and Do in Laos

▶ **CITIES AND MONUMENTS**

- Buddhist monasteries and temples in Luang Prabang and Vientiane
- Statues of Pak Ou, Khmer temple ruins of Wat Phu

▶ **LANDSCAPE**

- Mekong River, mountains of the north, Bolaven Plateau

▶ CITIES AND MONUMENTS

Well tended and listed as a World Heritage site, the ancient city of **Luang Prabang** would be worth a trip by itself. Mount Phousi and its temple *(wat)* and stupa dominate the small town wedged along the confluence of the Nam Khane and Mekong Rivers. The many temples—first among them Wat Xieng Thong—the lively streets, and the monks in their saffron-yellow robes, all create a calm ambiance. The temples and the ancient royal palace are the town's major attraction.

In **Vientiane,** the temples play a major role as well, such as Wat Sisaket and Wat That Luang, the most important temple in the country. The peaceful capital has a major market (Talat Sao); the Victory Gate (Patuxai), a triumphal arch to celebrate independence from the French; and government buildings left over from the French colonial period.

But the country boasts many other unusual sites. In the west of Luang Prabang are the **Pak Ou** Caves, with more than 4,500 Buddha statues. In the east, scattered in the landscape of the Plain of Jars, are large megalithic containers that served as funerary urns 2,000 years ago.

In the south near the pretty village of Champasak, the Khmer site of **Wat Phu** (9th to 13th centuries) is related to Cambodia's Angkor Wat.

▶ LANDSCAPE

The **Mekong River** is the symbol of the country. Here, along the banks of the river, Lao farmers lead their traditional way of life.

In the north, the river narrows at times into rapids, and in the south, it changes into spectacular waterfalls in the Sipandone district; it's rarely calm and very often yellow or reddened by sediment. The Mekong is one of the great tourist destinations in Asia and must be traveled by slow

When to Go

	CLIMATE	MEKONG CRUISES	NORTHERN MOUNTAINS
JANUARY	☼	✔	☼
FEBRUARY	☼	✔	☼
MARCH	☼		☼
APRIL			☼
MAY			
JUNE			
JULY			
AUGUST			
SEPTEMBER			
OCTOBER			
NOVEMBER	☼	✔	
DECEMBER	☼	✔	

Advice

■ **Pros**

- The country shows the smiling face of Southeast Asia and traditional life along the banks of the Mekong River with many opportunities for river excursions. Costs for lodging and meals are relatively modest. Attempts at ecotourism are being made.

■ **Cons**

- A rainy, hot, and humid climate in the summer. Though still an authentic Southeast Asian country, increased tourism will soon change things.

■ **Safety**

- The Lao are a friendly, hospitable people. The past guerrilla war is really over. In the north, however, opium should be avoided at all costs.

boat—a shallow longboat, for example, sailing from the north between Houeisay and Luang Prabang.

But it's in the south of the country, where the Mekong begins to split into multiple arms around the Four Thousands Islands that it becomes the most interesting. A visitor could spend time on the very quiet island of Muang Khong and, during times of high water, travel by boat farther south. Or visitors could stay on the more often frequented islands of Don Khone and Don Det to watch for the rare river dolphins.

The Lantan and Mong hill tribes live in the mountains of the north and are getting used to seeing more and more foreign visitors. In the south, the hills of the **Bolaven Plateau** shelter other traditional villages where you can visit coffee plantations and waterfalls.

Between Luang Prabang and Vientiane, the town of Vangviang features undulating limestone formations along the Nam Song River.

What to See and Do in Madagascar

▶ **LANDSCAPE**

- Terraced rice fields, crater lakes, caves, mountain ranges
- High plateaus, limestone formations (Tsingy de Bemaraha), waterfalls, sandstone formations (Isalo National Park)

▶ **WILDLIFE**

- Lemurs, tortoises, lizards, chameleons, crocodiles, butterflies
- Black orchids, tropical pitcher plants, ylang-ylang trees, eucalyptus forests, traveler's palms, baobabs

▶ **COASTS**

- Indian Ocean beaches and diving (Bay of Antsiranana, Nosy Be Archipelago, Nosy Boraha, Toliara)

▶ **CITIES**

- Antananarivo, Antsirabe, Fianarantsoa

The characteristic Baobab Alley represents an iconic view of Madagascar.

Madagascar

If there is one reason to travel to Madagascar, it's to see the lemurs, a variety of rare animal species endemic to the island that are threatened by extinction. But there is much more: treks through the heart of the countryside, one of the most scenic in Africa; ecotourism; and a chance to relax on the beaches of the islands of the Nosy Be Archipelago or the Bay of Antsiranana.

Traveler's Notebook

MAIN CONTACTS
Embassy of the Republic of Madagascar
2374 Massachusetts Avenue, NW Washington, DC 20008
(202) 265-5525
www.madagascar-embassy.org
www.madagascar-tourisme.com
Embassy of the Republic of Madagascar
33 Stadium Street SW10 0PU London, UK
www.embassy-madagascar-uk.com

TRAVEL DOCUMENTS
For U.S. Citizens: Passport and visa

For U.K. Citizens: Passport and 90-day visa issued on arrival

HEALTH ISSUES
No vaccinations required; malaria prophylaxis advised, especially in coastal areas

TRAVEL TIME TO DESTINATION & TIME DIFFERENCE
New York to Antananarivo: 22 hours 45 minutes connecting flight; EST +8. London to Antananarivo: 13 hours 25 minutes connecting flight; GMT +3

AVERAGE TRIP COST
$2,540–$3,175/£1,640–£2,010 for 15 days of touring

LANGUAGE & CURRENCY
Official language: Malagasy; French and English are also common Currency: ariary

POPULATION
19,449,000 inhabitants (and steadily increasing) of Malaysian and African origin, forming an ethnic mosaic. Capital: Antananarivo

RELIGION
Nearly 50 percent of the population are animist, 23 percent

Protestant, 20 percent Catholic, and 2 percent Muslim

FESTIVALS
March: Malagasy New Year; May: Donia in Nosy Be (traditional music); June to September: Famadihana (Return of the Dead, a funerary tradition); June 26: Independence Day

SHOPPING
Wooden sculptures, embroidery, and spices are the typical items, but unusual toys made from various scrap materials are also attractive in the markets.

▶ LANDSCAPE

The natural features of Madagascar are some of the most unusual anywhere. In the north, in Amber Mountain National Park, grow tree ferns and epiphytes. This is also where the Andrafiabe Cave is located, the most spectacular among hundreds of other caves.

Moving south, the **Tsingy de Bemaraha** Plateau, which has been turned into a nature reserve, boasts some very strange, pointy limestone formations *(tsingy),* whose origin may be based on coral. In the south in Andringitra National Park, the limestone has created dramatic peaks, deep ridges, and waterfalls.

The high plateaus with terraced rice fields, the hills reddened by laterite, the rocks and sandstone basins in **Isalo National Park,** the famous Avenue of Baobabs in Morondava, and the crater lakes (such as Lake Tritriva)—all present different aspects of the country's interior and invite hikers for a trek.

Traveling the length of Highway 7 from Antananarivo to Ifaty, about 600 miles, or going by train from Antananarivo to Toamasina are the two best ways to explore the country.

▶ WILDLIFE

The lemurs (indri, aye-aye, and ring-tailed lemurs), which are endemic to Madagascar, can only be seen in their natural environment here. They live in the Isalo massif and in the Berenty private reserve, which is also home to tortoises, giant lizards, chameleons, and butterflies. The deforestation that has taken place, however, raises fears for the future of some of these species.

The isolation of Madagascar has favored expansion of a rich flora of at least 9,000 species. Some of the most exotic plants are the black

orchid, tropical pitcher plant (carnivorous), ylang-ylang tree (blossoms used in perfumes), eucalyptus, traveler's palms, and baobabs.

▶ COASTS

A number of small coves (Sakalava, Danas) extend along the 12 miles of the **Bay of Antsiranana.**

The islands of the **Nosy Be Archipelago** are abloom with flame trees and ylang-ylang trees and offer

When to Go			
	CENTRAL PLATEAU	WEST COAST	EAST COAST
JANUARY			
FEBRUARY			
MARCH			
APRIL	☆		
MAY	☆	☆	
JUNE	☆	☆	
JULY	☆	☆	
AUGUST	☆	☆	
SEPTEMBER	☆	☆	☆
OCTOBER	☆	☆	☆
NOVEMBER			
DECEMBER			

beaches and lagoons for diving and watching marine life, including whales, barracudas, groupers, manta rays, and whale sharks. Not far from the island of Nosy Be, the island of Nosy Komba features a lemur reserve, and Nosy Tanikely has a coral reef marine reserve allowing for snorkeling and diving.

On the east coast, the beaches and lagoons of **Nosy Boraha** offer snorkeling and diving, as well. On the west side, the town of **Toliara** and its neighbor Ifaty see few tourists.

▶ CITIES

The capital **Antananarivo,** with its attractive houses and red-tiled roofs, is built on a hill. Its Analekely quarter, the murals on the Silver Palace, the zoo, and especially the lower town with the big market (Zoma), which overflows with handicrafts and color, are the main attractions.

Two other towns bear mention: **Antsirabe,** for its colonial thermal baths (Hotel des Thermes), and **Fianarantsoa** for its position on the high plateau.

Kites in a workshop on the country's west side dazzle with all the colors of Asia.

What to See and Do in Mainland Malaysia

▶ **LANDSCAPE**
- Rain forest, mountains (Cameron Highlands)

▶ **CITIES AND MONUMENTS**
- Kuala Lumpur (mosque, palace, Petronas Towers)
- Vestiges of colonialism (Malacca)
- Temples, mosques, palaces, pagodas (Penang, Kuala Kangsar, Shah Alam)

▶ **COASTS**
- Penang, Langkawi, Tioman, Pangkor Island
- Giant leatherback turtles of Rantau Abang

Malaysia

Malaysia, the least known country in Southeast Asia, is split in two, as much by geography as by administration. Western Malaysia extends south of Thailand on the Malay Peninsula; eastern Malaysia is located on the north side of the island of Borneo. The western part offers a classic vacation in Southeast Asia, but the eastern part with its dense rain forests promises more of a tropical wilderness adventure.

Mainland Malaysia

▶ LANDSCAPE

From Penang Province toward the center of the peninsula, the landscape gets hilly, moving into the **Cameron Highlands** and changing from tea plantations to rain forest.

East of the Cameron Highlands ranges Taman Negara National Park (1,700 square miles) with one of the oldest rain forests in the world, which is home to some 8,000 species of plants, 800 of which are orchids, as well as waterfalls (Lata Berkoh) and caves (Gua Telinga, where frogs and bats will greet the visitor).

Farther to the east, tea plantations from the 19th century are still producing high-quality tea.

▶ CITIES AND MONUMENTS

In the capital **Kuala Lumpur,** the sites include the Grand Mosque, the Sultan Abdul Samad Palace, and the train station in Moorish Revival style, in contrast to the futuristic style of the **Petronas Towers,** which were the tallest buildings in

Although most Malaysians are Muslims, there is also room for Buddhist temples such as Sampoh Tong near Ipoh.

the world until Taipei and Dubai managed to build higher.

In **Malacca,** a Chinese imprint is clearly seen in its large cemetery and tombs of the Ming period, along with the diversity of building styles from the Dutch and Portuguese colonial periods.

In **Penang,** Burmese, Chinese, and Thai temples stand out, as well as mosques, pagodas, colonial house fronts, and Fort Cornwallis, a reminder of the British East India Company. Kota Baharu's highlights are the wooden houses and the sultan's palace, and in **Kuala Kangsar,** the palaces and a mosque.

In the Cameron Highlands, the caves of Batu shelter Hindu shrines. In **Shah Alam,** the very modern Sultan Salahuddin Abdul Aziz Mosque is the city's landmark.

▶ COASTS

The island of **Penang** was for a long time the destination in Malaysia for backpacking beach lovers in the 1970s. Today a different clientele demands more luxurious resorts. These tourists have been accommodated with excellent spa and health facilities.

Penang's success as a tourism center has helped other islands on the west coast to develop, as well. Increased tourism is seen in **Langkawi** (English style, excellent facilities, golf, diving, and, as a tax-free haven, intense shopping), **Tioman, Pangkor,** Redang, and Perhentian.

The beaches of the east coast are known as the most beautiful ones in Malaysia. From July to September, giant leatherback turtles lay their eggs on the beaches around Rantau Abang—albeit in much diminished numbers—and then drop back into the sea.

Sabah

▶ LANDSCAPE

Until recently **Mount Kinabalu** (13,455 feet) was barely known, but it has become a beloved trekking destination. The mountain is located in Kinabalu National Park, which is surrounded by rice fields and rubber plantations. From its peak, there is

Orangutans are learning to live in the wild again in the forests of Sabah.

What to See and Do in Eastern Malaysia (Borneo)

Sabah

▶ **LANDSCAPE**
- Mount Kinabalu (trekking)

▶ **COASTS**
- Beaches (islands of the Tunku Abdul Rahman National Park)
- Diving off Sipadan Island (barracudas, turtles, corals)

▶ **WILDLIFE**
- Orangutans, green turtles, rafflesia, rain forest

Sarawak

▶ **LANDSCAPE**
- Rain forest, dugout canoes, caves (Gunung Mulu National Park), Niah

▶ **COASTS**
- Beaches (Damai Beach)

a beautiful view over the rain forest and the Crocker Range.

On the northwest coast of Sabah, the beaches of the islands and the coral reefs that belong to **Tunku Abdul Rahman National Park** have become the trendy meeting place for beach vacationers in the South China Sea. Divers off the southern tip of **Sipadan Island** can watch for barracudas, manta rays, sharks, green turtles, and hawksbill turtles.

▶ **WILDLIFE**

Two species deserve special attention: Several thousand orangutans in the Sepilok Rehabilitation Center near Sandakan, where they are learning to return to the wild; and green turtles, which lay their eggs between July and September on the small islands of the Sulu Sea about three hours by boat from Sandakan.

The world's largest flowering plant, rafflesia, which produces a purplish blossom with a diameter of up to three feet, grows near Mount Kinabalu in the rain forests by the hot springs of Poring. It's a rare flower that wilts very quickly. The rain forest that extends throughout the south of Sabah is more than a 100 million years old and features numerous species of trees and other plants. Botanists find their Eden here and deplore the increasing deforestation.

Traveler's Notebook

MAIN CONTACTS

Embassy of Malaysia
3516 International Court, NW
Washington, DC 20008
(202) 572-9700
www.kln.gov.my/web/usa_washington/home
www.tourism.gov.my

High Commission of Malaysia
45–46 Belgrave Square
London SW1X 8QT, UK
+ 44 (0) 20 7235 8033
www.kln.gov.my/web/uki_london/home

TRAVEL DOCUMENTS FOR U.S. AND U.K. CITIZENS
Passport

HEALTH ISSUES
No vaccinations required; minor risk of malaria in the interior

TRAVEL TIME TO DESTINATION & TIME DIFFERENCE
New York to Kuala Lumpur: 20 hours 45 minutes connecting flight; EST +13. London to Kuala Lumpur: 11 hours 25 minutes nonstop; GMT +8

AVERAGE TRIP COST
$3,800/£2,450 for 15 days of touring

LANGUAGE & CURRENCY
Official language: Malay (Bahasi) is spoken by 50 percent of the population. Other languages are Chinese, Tamil, Punjabi, and Urdu; English is also widely spoken.

POPULATION
24,821,000 inhabitants; Malays (56 percent) are in the majority, followed by Chinese (33 percent) and Indians (10 percent). Capital: Kuala Lumpur

RELIGION
Many religions are represented, including Islam (53 percent), Buddhism (17 percent), Daoism (12 percent), Hinduism (7 percent), and Christianity (6 percent).

FESTIVALS
February: Chinese New Year; May 4: Wesak Day (Birth of Buddha); August 31: Independence Day; September to October: Deepavali (Hindu Festival of Lights)

SHOPPING
Batik textiles, silk, silver jewelry, Chinese porcelain, pearls

Bizarrely shaped sandstone pillars rise from Gunung Mulu National Park in the middle of the Sarawak jungle.

Sarawak

▶ LANDSCAPE

The rain forest of Sarawak is home to three million species of trees

When to Go			
	CLIMATE	PENANG AND WEST COAST	SABAH AND SARAWAK
JANUARY			
FEBRUARY		☼	
MARCH		☼	☼
APRIL			☼
MAY			☼
JUNE	☼	☼	☼
JULY	☼	☼	☼
AUGUST	☼		☼
SEPTEMBER	☼		☼
OCTOBER			
NOVEMBER			
DECEMBER	☼		

and 400 species of birds. Visitors can trek into the forest interior or travel by dugout canoe over the rapids.

Although there is much tourist activity, a tour up the Rajang River is still a solo adventure. Here visitors can see some of the longhouses of the Iban people, who are quite welcoming.

Near the borders of the Brunei sultanate, **Gunung Mulu National Park** features extraordinary caves: Deer Cave, Clearwater Cave, Wind Cave, and Wonder Cave.

South of Miri in the **Niah** caves, archaeologists have found evidence of a 40,000-year-old settlement.

▶ COASTS

Until recently, the north of Borneo was less well known for its beach resorts than for the *kampungs,* fishing villages built on pilings. But that has changed. Today hotels, golf

Advice

■ **Pros**

• The geographic as well as the human contrast between the two parts of the country make a trip to Malaysia tremendously interesting. During good weather periods, a fantastic vacation is guaranteed. The situation in the coastal regions of Sabah has stabilized.

■ **Cons**

• Costs are generally higher than in other regions of Southeast Asia. This long unknown destination is still trying to get international recognition.

■ **Safety**

• The danger of kidnapping in Sabah is a thing of the past, but travelers should proceed with the usual caution.

courses, and even luxury resorts are well established on the South China Sea coast. One of the famous resorts is **Damai Beach.**

The Maldives

The word atoll *comes from the Maldives, and that's understandable: A double chain of 26 atolls, with a total of 1,200 islands and islets, the archipelago extends from north to south over 500 miles of the Indian Ocean. The underwater ecosystem here is one of the most beautiful in the world and is protected by marine conservation laws. Divers keep coming back and are joined regularly by other fitness seekers.*

▶ DIVING

Whether beginners or pros, visitors will find that diving is the definitive activity in the Maldives, especially from January through April, which is a more enjoyable period than June to November. The clear water guarantees a full view of all the creatures in the reef. Divers find colorful coral reefs with a great variety of species: some 300 species of multicolored fish alone, along with manta rays, barracudas, hammerhead sharks, and turtles.

The tourism administration is a true guardian of the ecosystem: Collecting coral and spearfishing are not permitted, and only a dozen atolls are open to tourism, with a limited number of "island-hotels." These rules leave no alternatives, so it is not possible, for example, to spend a night on another island or in a fishing village.

▶ COASTS

What can you do if you're not a diver? You can enjoy the white sandy beaches and take advantage of the many water sports on offer (catamaran sailing, surfing, waterskiing) or tour the adjoining islands. Hand-line fishing and

What to See and Do in the Maldives
▶ **DIVING**
• Underwater flora and fauna (tropical fish, corals)
▶ **COASTS**
• Beaches, water sports, fishing

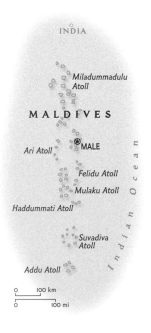

INDIA

Miladummadulu Atoll

MALDIVES

Ari Atoll · ⊕ MALE

Felidu Atoll

Mulaku Atoll

Haddummati Atoll

Suvadiva Atoll

Addu Atoll

Indian Ocean

0   100 km
0   100 mi

Traveler's Notebook				
MAIN CONTACTS *Embassy of the Republic of Maldives* 800 Second Avenue Suite 400 E New York, NY 10017 (212) 599-6195 www.maldives embassy.us www.visitmaldives.com *High Commission of the Republic of Maldives* 22 Nottingham Place London W1U 5NJ, UK + 44 (0) 20 7224 2135 www.maldiveshigh commission.org	**TRAVEL DOCUMENTS FOR U.S. & U.K. CITIZENS** Passport **HEALTH ISSUES** No vaccinations required. Any would-be diver must show a doctor's certificate attesting to fitness that is no more than six months old, as well as a valid diving permit. **TRAVEL TIME TO DESTINATION & TIME DIFFERENCE** New York to Male: 18 hours 5 minutes connecting flight; EST +10. London to Male: 12 hours 30 minutes connecting flight; GMT +5	**AVERAGE TRIP COST** $2,200/£1,400 for 15 days in combination with Sri Lanka **LANGUAGE & CURRENCY** Official language: Dhivehi (an Indo-European language); English is widely spoken **POPULATION** The population density is high for its 369,000 inhabitants. The earliest settlers came from Sri Lanka and India. Capital: Male, on the atoll of the same name **RELIGION** Islam is the state religion.	**FESTIVALS** July 26–27: Independence Day; July or August (end of Ramadan): Eid al-Fitr; November 3: Day of Victory; November: Islamic New Year **SHOPPING** Shells and items made of tortoise-shell are for sale everywhere. The village markets offer fabrics, lacquer-ware, and hand-made drums.	

Coral and multicolored fishes: The atolls of the Maldives offer limited choices, but the divers are happy.

deep-sea fishing (for tuna and bar-racuda) are other options. And, of course, this a good place to *learn* to dive.

Minicruises visiting one fishing atoll after the next are a new way to experience the Maldives. That is probably the best way to discover these islands that are strewn like confetti in the ocean.

In this smallest Asian nation and lowest country on the planet, one of the latest trends is to use the paradisiacal setting for weddings. After the festivities many newly-weds take part of their honeymoon here, then continue the celebration in Sri Lanka.

When to Go		
	CLIMATE	FEWER CROWDS
JANUARY	☼	
FEBRUARY	☼	
MARCH	☼	
APRIL	☼	
MAY		✔
JUNE		✔
JULY		✔
AUGUST		
SEPTEMBER		
OCTOBER		
NOVEMBER		✔
DECEMBER	☼	

Advice

■ Pros
• One of the world's most beau-tiful underwater environments. Excellent options: Besides activi-ties for experienced divers, there are countless diving courses for beginners, minicruises to other islands, wellness programs, and Asian-style spas.

■ Cons
• There are no alternatives to the water sports activities. Some restrictions: alcohol cannot be imported, and proper clothing—no nude thighs or shoulders in town—is required.

What to See and Do in Mali

▶ **LANDSCAPE**

• Bandiagara Escarpment (Dogon country)

• Niger River, Mandingo Mountains, Talary Gorges, Boucle du Baoulé National Park, Adrar des Ifoghas (sandstone plateau), camel treks

▶ **CITIES**

• Djenné, Mopti, Timbuktu, Gao, Bamako

The Bandiagara Escarpment, where Dogon farmers live, is no longer impassable.

■ *Most African countries attract vacationers with promises of treks through the savanna, but not through history. Mali can offer both: a long history, Dogon country and the Bandiagara Escarpment, and camel treks for adventure.*

Mali

▶ **LANDSCAPE**

Dogon country is not quite what it was at the time of anthropologist Marcel Griaule and his colleagues, who did groundbreaking studies into the complex religious beliefs of the Dogon and recorded life along the **Bandiagara Escarpment** from the 1930s to the 1960s. But today some 300,000 farmers still live in the simple villages at the foot of the cliffs and continue with their beliefs in a creator god, following ancient rituals. They watch

Traveler's Notebook

MAIN CONTACTS

Embassy of Mali
2130 R Street, NW
Washington, DC 20008
(202) 332-2249
www.maliembassy.us
www.officetourisme-
mali.com
Embassy of Mali
487 Avenue Molière
1050 Brussels, Belgium
(322) 345 74 32
www.amba-mali.be/en/
index.html

TRAVEL DOCUMENTS FOR U.S. & U.K. CITIZENS
Passport and visa

HEALTH ISSUES
Yellow fever immunization required; malaria prophylaxis necessary

TRAVEL TIME TO DESTINATION & TIME DIFFERENCE
New York to Bamako: 11 hours 35 minutes connecting flight; EST +5. London to Bamako: 8 hours 5 minutes connecting flight; GMT

AVERAGE TRIP COST
$2,000/£1,300 for 15 days in the Dogon area and on the Niger River

LANGUAGE & CURRENCY
Official language: French. The language heard most often in the streets, however, is the national language, Bambara; Malinke, Senufo, Soninke, and others are also heard. Currency: CFA-franc

POPULATION
11,995,000 inhabitants, divided among 23

ethnicities, with a majority of Fulani, Dogon, and Bambara. About 600,000 nomads (Tuaregs and Moors) also live in Mali. Capital: Bamako

RELIGION
90 percent Muslim; a minority of animists and Christians

FESTIVALS
January: Desert Festival in Essakane, and Saharan Nights Festival in Essouk (with dancing, poems, and camel races);

October or November: Tabaski Festival (Festival of Sacrifice)

SHOPPING
Djembe drums, wooden sculptures, leather goods; well-designed, artistic Tuareg gold jewelry—earrings, necklaces, pendants.

the steady trickle of tour groups with amusement.

The **Niger River** crosses the country in a wide arc, which gave it the nickname "camel's hump"; a second name, Djoliba, comes from a Bambara word meaning "blood." From Timbuktu to Gao, the river carries many traditions (Bozo fishermen—traditional, nomadic river dwellers—ferrymen, and dyers). The Fulani and Moors drive their herds along the riverbanks, thousands of birds can be heard in the reeds, and from time to time hippopotamuses raise their heads out of the water.

The **Mandingo Mountains** southwest of Bamako are amazing with their bizarrely eroded rocks and caves. Southeast of Kayes, the Senegal River drops into the **Talary Gorges.** Nearby, the national park and biosphere reserve of **Boucle du Baoulé** is worth a detour (prehistoric rock art, animals).

In the east rises the **Adrar des Ifoghas** sandstone massif, the historic gateway between the Maghreb and the Sahel region. Ruins of ancient cities (Essouk) can be found here, as well as rock drawings (war chariots of the Garamantes) near ancient Tuareg campsites.

The south of the Adrar des Ifoghas is a fairly unknown section of the Sahara, although the region is an important crossroads for caravans. When the situation allows, this is where tourists can join camel treks. This unusual tour, which requires a local guide and the latest safety information, begins in Timbuktu and ends in Taoudenni in the far north, on the route of the last salt caravans.

▶ CITIES

Djenné was a city long before the arrival of Islam, and its history makes the town particularly attractive. But the city's most imposing mud brick building is the Grand Mosque, a perfect example of Islamic art in Africa.

Mopti, known as Mali's Venice, is an important city on the Niger's five inland deltas. Its mosque, the river

When to Go			
	CLIMATE	DESERT	PHOTOGRAPHY IN THE SOUTH
JANUARY	☼		
FEBRUARY	☼		
MARCH			
APRIL			
MAY			
JUNE			
JULY			◁
AUGUST			◁
SEPTEMBER			◁
OCTOBER	☼		◁
NOVEMBER	☼	☼	
DECEMBER	☼	☼	

port, and the fish market are worth a detour.

Getting to **Timbuktu** means above all a challenge to survive the potholes in the road on the way there. The legendary desert city was known as a center of learning and commerce, but has lost much of its luster. The unusual architecture of its mosques, however, endures.

The city of **Gao,** strategically situated on the trans-Saharan trade routes, was the capital of the Songhai Empire at the end of the 15th and beginning of the 16th centuries. The tomb of its ruler Askia Mohammed dates to this period. The museum devoted to the Sahel is also worth seeing.

These cities are more original than the capital, **Bamako,** but its situation on the Niger, its markets, the House of Artisans, and the National Museum of Mali are highlights.

The walls of Valetta recall the power of the Maltese Order; today, the city is a tourist and beach paradise.

Malta

■ Despite its relative isolation between Sicily and Tunisia in the Mediterranean and its few sandy beaches, the Republic of Malta draws huge crowds every summer, ready for beachgoing and diving. The island's long history—going back to megalithic temple builders and, since the 16th century, the Knights Hospitaller—has left its stamp.

Traveler's Notebook

MAIN CONTACTS
Embassy of Malta
2017 Connecticut Avenue, NW
Washington, DC 20008
(202) 462-3611
www.mfa.gov.mt
www.visitmalta.com
Malta High Commission
Malta House
36–38 Piccadilly
London W1J 0LE, UK
+ 44 (0) 20 7734 1831
www.foreign.gov.mt

TRAVEL DOCUMENTS FOR U.S. & U.K. CITIZENS
Passport

TRAVEL TIME TO DESTINATION & TIME DIFFERENCE
New York to Valetta: 11 hours 55 minutes connecting flight; EST +6.
London to Valetta: 3 hours 10 minutes nonstop flight; GMT +1

AVERAGE TRIP COST
$625/£400 for a week's beach vacation

LANGUAGE & CURRENCY
Official languages: English and Malti (an Arabic dialect, written in the Latin alphabet)
Currency: euro

POPULATION
402,000 inhabitants, relatively densely populated. Capital: Valetta

RELIGION
Malta was the land of the first Christians in Europe; 97 percent are Catholic, with a small minority of Anglicans

FESTIVALS
February or March: Carnival; end of June: Imnarja (Harvest) Festival; June to September: *Festas* in the villages in honor of the patron saint of each; September: In-Guardia parade and festival in Mdina

SHOPPING
Traditional artisans still produce glass objects, model ships, and lace.

What to See and Do in Malta

▶ **COASTS**
- Malta, Gozo, and Comino
- Rocky beaches, sea caves, coves, fishing villages
- Diving, waterskiing, windsurfing

▶ **CITIES AND CULTURAL HERITAGE**
- Ggantija, Mdina, Valletta

▶ COASTS

The Mediterranean island group of Malta attracts vacationers from spring through summer despite its rocky beaches. True sand beaches exist only in Mellieha Bay in the northwest and Golden Bay in the west of the island of **Malta,** and Ramla Bay on **Gozo.** The sea caverns, however, make up for this lack, in particular the Blue Grotto on the south coast of Gozo, which should be part of every tourist itinerary for its shifting blue light. Water sports choices are endless, ranging from sea kayaking and diving to waterskiing, windsurfing, and (the trendiest choice) kitesurfing.

Tourists can stop in some of the fishing villages, like Marsaskala and Marsaxlokk, the latter especially on Sundays when the big fish market is on.

The islands of Gozo and car-free **Comino** are not as busy in the summer as Malta. They attract visitors with their quiet coves, water sports, and scenic landscapes. According to legend, there is a cave on Gozo where the nymph Calypso held Odysseus prisoner for seven years. Today it is the bathers and divers who make history on Gozo, particularly in the Bay of Xlendi

with its beautiful sandstone arch, the "azure window" above the blue water, which connects to Fungus Rock, rising for a steep 200 feet.

▶ CITIES AND CULTURAL HERITAGE

Megalithic tombs and temples erected some 5,000 years ago are one of the major attractions in Malta. They can still be found in **Ggantija** (Gozo), Hal Saflieni, and Tarxien. Equally interesting are St.

Paul Cathedral, the fortified walls, the citadel, and the narrow lanes of the old capital, **Mdina,** also called the "silent city."

In the capital, **Valletta,** baroque buildings stand next to fortified walls erected by the Maltese Knights to successfully withstand the Ottoman invasion of 1565. The National Museum of Fine Arts displays treasures from the Maltese Order and from the churches and Palace of the Grand Master (portraits, tapestries, medieval armor).

The 300 Knights Hospitaller who came from Rhodes in the 16th century settled in three adjacent cities, now known as Cottonera. These knights, a military religious order, are responsible for the military architecture on the island: fortifications; grand lodges such as the Auberge de Provence—today the National Museum of Archaeology; chapels; the Co-Cathedral of St. John; and marble tombstones of the grand masters.

When to Go		
	CLIMATE	CULTURAL VISITS FEWER CROWDS
JANUARY		
FEBRUARY		
MARCH		
APRIL	☼	
MAY	☼	✔
JUNE	☼	✔
JULY	☼	
AUGUST	☼	
SEPTEMBER	☼	✔
OCTOBER		✔
NOVEMBER		
DECEMBER		

Advice

■ **Pros**
- A nice mixture of beaches and cultural sights.

■ **Cons**
- A more expensive beach vacation than in other resorts along the Mediterranean.

■ **Special Tip**
- Malta is developing into a "long weekend" destination from other parts of Europe, with Valetta as a base for excursions into the surroundings.

🏴 *Martinique is a little bit of France in the Caribbean. The island is often called Flower Island, a hint that there is more to see than the beaches on the southwest and south coasts. Choices include walking tours in the north (tropical forest), trekking up Mount Pelée, and enjoying the turquoise waters.*

Martinique

What to See and Do in Martinique

▶ **COASTS**

- Beaches of the southwest coast (Anse-Noire, Anses-d'Arlets) and south coast (Le Diamant, Ste.-Luce)

- Yachting (Le Marin, Trois-Îlets)

- Bays of Le Robert and Le François (white sand bottoms)

▶ **LANDSCAPE**

- Forest and mountain treks (climbing Mount Pelée)

- Gardens and plantations

Traveler's Notebook

MAIN CONTACTS

Embassy of France
4101 Reservoir Road, NW
Washington, DC 20007
(202) 944-6000
www.ambafrance-us.org
www.martinique.org
Embassy of France
58 Knightsbridge
London SW1X 7JT, UK
+ 44 (0) 20 7073 1000
www.ambafrance-uk.org/-French-Embassy,2-.html

TRAVEL DOCUMENTS FOR U.S. & U.K. CITIZENS
Passport

TRAVEL TIME TO DESTINATION & TIME DIFFERENCE
New York to Fort-de-France: 7 hours 56 minutes connecting flight; EST +1. London to Fort-de-France: 17 hours 31 minutes connecting flight; GMT −4

AVERAGE TRIP COST
$775/£500 for a week's beach vacation

LANGUAGE & CURRENCY
Official language: French. People also speak Creole as a means of identity, as is apparent in the writings of novelists

Patrick Chamoiseau and Raphael Confiant.
Currency: euro

POPULATION
The population of 436,000 is largely of mixed ethnicity with a majority of Béké (Creoles of white European ancestry), along with people of European, Asian, African, and mixed descent. Capital: Fort-de-France

RELIGION
The majority are Catholics, with some Muslims and Hindus

FESTIVALS
February or March: Carnival; June: regattas (Le Marin); August: Tour de Martinique (bicycle race); December: Ste.-Marie rum festival; year-round: patron saint's days

SHOPPING
The much-praised island rum is a definite souvenir, but also objects made of precious woods, madras fabrics, silks, and a last bouquet of flowers before departure.

The 574-foot-high rock called the Diamond is home to colonies of birds.

▶ COASTS

The fishing villages and white Caribbean beaches of the southwest and south coasts are the main attraction for vacationers. The east coast, where the strong Atlantic waves crash ashore, draws the surfers. The small coves in the southwest—**Anse-Noire, Anses-d'Arlets,** and Trois-Îlets—and the beaches of the south coast—**Le Diamant, Ste.-Luce,** and Grande-Anse-des-Saline—invite sheer indolence.

Sailing, waterskiing, quad racing, kayaking, or riding Jet Skis are all possible activities. Sailors meet at **Le Marin** or **Trois-Îlets.** Along the southern coast and near the shipwrecks of St.-Pierre, much diving activity takes place. And the surfers and kitesurfers hang out on the east coast in the bays of **Le Robert** and **Le François,** which are particularly remarkable for their white sand bottoms—*fonds blanc*—islets,

and blue water. This is the place for a glass of rum punch.

The north and northeast coasts, not well known and rarely visited by tourists, have rugged cliffs and rocky shores (Basse-Pointe, Grand-Rivière).

▶ LANDSCAPE

The interior, especially the north with its mountains and tropical forests, is also intriguing. A particular achievement is a hike up **Mount Pelée** in a half-day or full day excursion. How much damage this mountain inflicted on the island in its 1902 eruption is well documented in the Volcano Museum of St.-Pierre.

The northern region has some 30 well-marked hiking trails through forests and past waterfalls, gardens, and plantations. The breathtaking variety of flowering plants (bougainvillea, cannas, hibiscus, anthurium) makes it a veritable Eden for botanists.

▶ CITIES

The island capital, **Fort-de-France,** exhibits a mixture of French culture and laid-back Caribbean lifestyle, whereas the small town of **Trois-Îlets** still basks in its fame as the birthplace of Empress Josephine, wife of Napoleon Bonaparte, nearly 250 years ago.

When to Go		
	CLIMATE	FLORA AND PHOTOGRAPHY
JANUARY		
FEBRUARY		
MARCH	☼	
APRIL	☼	
MAY		
JUNE		⟨
JULY		⟨
AUGUST		⟨
SEPTEMBER		⟨
OCTOBER		
NOVEMBER		
DECEMBER		

Mauritius

■ *The former French island of Mauritius, with its coconut palms and warm waters, attracts an upscale clientele to relax, play golf, honeymoon, or, the latest fashion, get married there in the first place. Ecotourism is expanding, with an emphasis on the country's rare landscape, abundant flora, and exceptional marine life. For architecture buffs, there are old Creole homes to see.*

▶ COASTS

Mauritius's beaches and lagoons, as well as the coral reef, give rise to all kinds of leisure activities at the sailing clubs, sportfishing (marlin, tuna) charter boats, and dive centers. The most fabulous beaches are on the wind-sheltered northwest coast: **Grand Bay,** Pointe aux Piments, Pointe aux Cannoniers, and Trou aux Biches. Farther south stretch other well-known beach resorts: Pointe Flic en Flac, Pointe Pecheurs, and Pointe Sud-Ouest.

Off the east coast, the **Île aux Cerfs** is an easily accessible island with beaches at Pointe des Puits, Pointe aux Boeufs, and, in the southeast, Pointe d'Esny and Pointe des Deux Cocos. The rocky south coast looks quite different.

Rodrigues Island, Robinson Crusoe's island, lies 350 miles to the east and is a one-and-a-half-hour commercial flight away. The island attracts ever more vacationers who dream of spending time on

What to See and Do in Mauritius

▶ **COASTS**
- Lagoon, coral reef
- Beaches (Grand Bay, Île aux Cerfs, Rodrigues Island)

▶ **LANDSCAPE AND FLORA**
- *Mornes* (hills), Trou aux Cerfs
- Pamplemousses Botanical Garden (giant water lilies, Talipot palms, flame trees, bougainvillea)

▶ **UNDERWATER WORLD**
- Catfish, doctor fish, zebra fish
- Big game fishing

▶ **CULTURAL HERITAGE**
- Old Creole homes, *sèga*

Traveler's Notebook

MAIN CONTACTS
Embassy of the Republic of Mauritius
1709 N Street, NW
Washington, DC 20036
(202) 244-1491
www.mauritius.net
www.tourism-mauritius.mu
Mauritius High Commission
32–33 Elvaston Place
London SW7 5NW, UK
+ 44 (0) 20 7581 0294/5

TRAVEL DOCUMENTS FOR U.S. & U.K. CITIZENS
Passport

HEALTH ISSUES
No problems

TRAVEL TIME TO DESTINATION & TIME DIFFERENCE
New York to Mauritius: 24 hours 10 minutes connecting flight; EST +9. London to Mauritius: 16 hours 30 minutes connecting flight; GMT +4

AVERAGE TRIP COST
$1,275/£825 for a week's beach vacation

LANGUAGE & CURRENCY
English is the official language, but French is more widely spoken. The language heard on the street is a French-based Creole.

Currency: Mauritian rupee

POPULATION
The 1,251,000 inhabitants represent a high population density on a small island with two dependencies. Indians are in the majority (70 percent); there are also Caucasians, Chinese, and Creoles. Capital: Port Louis

RELIGION
50 percent Hindu, 24 percent Catholic, lesser numbers of Muslims, Protestants, and Buddhists

FESTIVALS
January or February: Chinese Lantern Festival; February: Hindu Festivals at Lake Grand Bassin in honor of Shiva (Cavadee Festival, Maha Shivaratree Festival)

SHOPPING
Duty-free shops are on the increase, with clothing, photo equipment, and jewelry offered at reduced prices. Local artisans display elegant ships' models, basketware, and embroidery.

its beaches, in the fishing ports, and on its hills overgrown with casuarina trees.

▶ LANDSCAPE AND FLORA

Mauritius's interior consists of tropical forests and mornes, strangely formed hills (Morne Brabant). The state is committed to safeguarding its ecology.

The island has two natural lakes: Bassin Blanc and Grand Bassin, a crater lake. Its volcanic origin is also apparent in the 280-foot-deep crater **Trou aux Cerfs.** Examples of the dense vegetation of the island can be seen in detail in the **Pamplemousses Botanical Garden,** the oldest botanical garden in the Southern Hemisphere, famous for 500 species of plants such as the Talipot palm, which blooms only once every 60 years, and giant water lilies. The much-loved flame trees and bougainvillea are represented, as are 85 varieties of palm trees.

Other attractions are the Labourdonnais orchards (all kinds of tropical blooms and fruit); the adventure park Chamarel (featuring "colored

Blue ocean, red roofs, old Creole homes—Mauritius is a blended world.

earths"—volcanic rock that cooled at different temperatures, creating multicolored bands), Black River Gorges National Park, Vanille Reserve des Mascareignes (giant tortoises and crocodiles), the Club Domaine des Grand Bois, Le Val Nature Park, and Rochester Falls.

▶ FAUNA

Nondivers can observe the marine world (catfish, doctor fish, zebra fish) in the lagoon and the coral reef from a glass-bottom boat. Beyond the reef, swordfish, tuna, marlin, and barracuda can be spotted.

About 300 years ago, the island's legendary dodo bird, a large, flightless pigeonlike bird, became extinct. Sketches and skeletons of the legendary bird are showcased in the Natural History Museum of Port Louis.

▶ CULTURAL HERITAGE

The towns have intriguing names, such as Curepipe ("pipe-cleaner") and Poudre d'Or ("gold dust"). The markets (flowers, spices), the typical rectangular Creole homes with steep roofs, and colonial architecture are other things to see.

The sèga, the traditional dance of the former slaves, has become the national song and dance of Mauritius.

When to Go		
	CLIMATE	PHOTOGRAPHY
JANUARY		◅
FEBRUARY		◅
MARCH		◅
APRIL		◅
MAY		
JUNE	☼	
JULY	☼	
AUGUST	☼	
SEPTEMBER	☼	
OCTOBER	☼	
NOVEMBER	☼	
DECEMBER		

Mexico

🏳️ *Mexico is above all a classic destination for beaches and archaeological sites. And indeed, the ruins of the pre-Columbian civilizations are so extensive that they cannot be seen all in one trip. But there is so much more, ranging from timeworn Acapulco to the cactus forests and deserted beaches of Baja California.*

▶ ARCHAEOLOGICAL SITES AND CITIES

The ceremonial center of **Teotihuacan,** with its enormous Pyramids of the Sun and the Moon, temples, and palace, was an expression of a powerful culture whose influence reached far throughout Mesoamerica. No less impressive, the Zapotec civilization arose in **Monte Albán.** The Maya civilization, too, left countless temple sites spanning more than a thousand years; best known are **Uxmal** and **Palenque** with remnants of the classic Maya period (600–950), and **Chichén Itzá** and **Tulum** of the postclassic period (950–1500).

During the Spanish conquest, after having eliminated the Aztec in Tenochtitlán and founded **Mexico City** on its ruins, the Spaniards imposed a religious and urban

<table>
<tr><th colspan="2">What to See and Do in Mexico</th></tr>
<tr><td colspan="2">▶ ARCHAEOLOGICAL SITES AND CITIES</td></tr>
<tr><td colspan="2">• Teotihuacan (pre-Columbian ceremonial center), Monte Albán (Zapotec civilization), Uxmal, Palenque, Chichén Itzá, Tulum (Maya civilization)</td></tr>
<tr><td colspan="2">• Mexico City, San Cristóbal de las Casas, Oaxaca</td></tr>
<tr><td colspan="2">• Guanajuato, San Miguel de Allende, Morelia, Jalapa</td></tr>
<tr><td colspan="2">• Taxco, Puebla, Querétaro, Mérida</td></tr>
<tr><td colspan="2">▶ COASTS AND MARINE LIFE</td></tr>
<tr><td colspan="2">• Cancún, Playa del Carmen, Cozumel, Isla Mujeres (Riviera Maya in the Yucatán)</td></tr>
<tr><td colspan="2">• Acapulco, Ixtapa, Puerto Vallarta (Pacific beaches)</td></tr>
<tr><td colspan="2">• Baja California (gray whales)</td></tr>
<tr><td colspan="2">▶ LANDSCAPE</td></tr>
<tr><td colspan="2">• Paricutín, Popocatépetl (volcanoes)</td></tr>
<tr><td colspan="2">• Sierra Madre Occidental</td></tr>
<tr><td colspan="2">• Baja California (canyons and cactus)</td></tr>
</table>

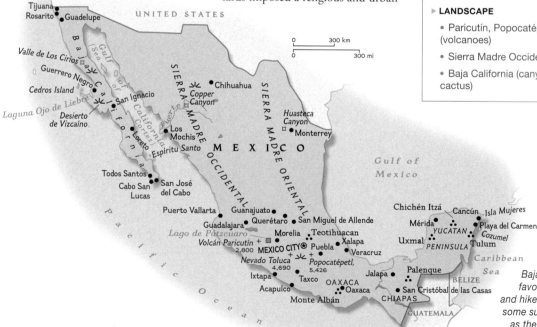

Baja California, a favorite of surfers and hikers, also holds some surprises, such as the 300-year-old San Ignacio Mission.

Chac Mool's statue watches over the Maya site of Chichén Itzá.

well as the Coyoacán district, where Leon Trotsky's house and Frida Kahlo's house-museum are open to visitors. The city's pride is the National Museum of Anthropology, one of the most important institutions because of its pre-Columbian collection, including the famous Aztec calendar, a massive stone disk weighing 24 tons.

San Cristóbal de las Casas in the state of Chiapas is one of those small towns where an authentic Indian market is still in full flow.

Oaxaca, founded by the Aztecs, stands out with its baroque cityscape, churches (Santo Domingo), and museums with treasures of Monte Albán in the Centro Cultural and pre-Hispanic art in the Museo Rufino Tamayo.

In **Guanajuato,** known for its silver mines, visitors admire the baroque churches that dominate the city. **San Miguel de Allende** has preserved its colonial character so well that it has been declared a national historic monument. In **Morelia,** the opulent flora (orchids, laurel) rivals the art (murals in the Governor's Palace). In **Jalapa,** not far from Veracruz, the Anthropological

(baroque) art on the country that remains in numerous churches, a cathedral, and a main square called the Zócalo in many of the cities.

Mexico City is often scorned as a polluted, overcrowded megalopolis, but endless treasures are to be found there: the cathedral, the Sagrario Metropolitano, the Basilica of Guadalupe, the Plaza de las Tres Culturas (Square of the Three Cultures), the Zócalo, monasteries, and palaces, as

Traveler's Notebook

MAIN CONTACTS

Embassy of Mexico
1911 Pennsylvania Avenue, NW
Washington, DC 20006
(202) 728-1600
http://portal.sre.gob
.mx/usa/
www.visitmexico.com
Embassy of Mexico
16 St. George Street
London W1S 1FD, UK
+ 44 (0) 20 7499 8586
portal.sre.gob.mx/
reinounidoeng/

TRAVEL DOCUMENTS FOR U.S. & U.K. CITIZENS
Passport

HEALTH ISSUES
No vaccinations necessary; malaria prophylaxis recommended in certain rural areas, particularly Oaxaca and Chiapas

TRAVEL TIME TO DESTINATION & TIME DIFFERENCE
New York to Mexico City: 5 hours 5 minutes nonstop flight; EST –1. London to Mexico City:

11 hours 40 minutes nonstop flight; GMT –6

AVERAGE TRIP COST
$1,275/£825 for a week's beach vacation at Riviera Maya

LANGUAGE & CURRENCY
Official language: Spanish; many people speak some English
Currency: peso

POPULATION
108,701,000 inhabitants. Indians make up 10 percent of the population

and live mostly in the mountains. Spanish descendants still make up 15 percent of the population, but the majority are mestizos. Capital: Mexico City (population more than 15 million)

RELIGION
The majority (93 percent) is Catholic; a minority is Protestant.

FESTIVALS
March or April: Holy Week, with a passion play in Ixtapalapa, a

suburb of Mexico; May 5: Cinco de Mayo (victory of Mexico's army against French forces); November 20: Revolution Day; December 12: Feast of Our Lady of Guadalupe

SHOPPING
Jewelry, pottery; from Yucatán: hammocks, embroidered clothing, sandals.

Uxmal forms a famous Maya triangle with Palenque and Chichén Itzá; the sites are located not far from one another.

Museum has the largest collection of artifacts from all pre-Columbian Gulf Coast cultures.

Other colonial cities that are worth a detour are: **Taxco** (baroque facades, *retablos*—devotional folk art paintings—in the Santa Prisca church); **Puebla** (baroque churches, Rosario Chapel of Santo Domingo); **Querétaro** (baroque cathedral); and **Mérida** (National Palace, city squares, Paseo de Montejo with important historic sites of the colonial period).

Tijuana, in Baja California, represents all the problems of a border town. A bit farther south in Rosarito, it's impossible to miss the Foxploration theme park with its movie sets for a behind-the-scenes look. In the southern part of Baja California, between Loreto and Cabo San Lucas, there are a number of old Spanish missions to explore.

▶ COASTS AND MARINE LIFE

Mexico's beaches are a pleasure all year round. Fringed by palm trees and coral reefs, they stretch for 6,000 miles on the Pacific and Atlantic coasts.

The coast of the Yucatán Peninsula, the **Riviera Maya,** is invaded by so many people that they risk endangering the marine life and coral reefs. From **Cancún** to Tulum,

When to Go			
	CLIMATE	NORTH AND BAJA CALIFORNIA	WHALE-WATCHING BAJA CALIFORNIA
JANUARY	☼		⋖
FEBRUARY	☼		⋖
MARCH	☼		⋖
APRIL	☼		⋖
MAY		☼	
JUNE		☼	
JULY			
AUGUST			
SEPTEMBER		☼	
OCTOBER	☼	☼	
NOVEMBER	☼		
DECEMBER	☼		

The pre-Columbian site of Tulum on the Riviera Maya draws visitors from around the world.

the beaches run on for 75 miles with the best section in **Playa del Carmen.** Divers prefer **Cozumel** to spot sponges, brain coral, barracudas, groupers, turtles, and an endless number of reef fish. **Isla Mujeres,** an old hippie hangout, is one of the more modestly priced resorts.

The Pacific coast attracts crowds of beach lovers to **Acapulco, Ixtapa,** and **Puerto Vallarta.** For something more unusual, the long peninsula of **Baja**

California offers resorts in San José del Cabo (quiet) or Cabo San Lucas (noisy). Surfers meet in Todos Santos.

Gray whales congregate in the warm waters off the coast of Baja California in February and March. The whales calve in the lagoon Ojo de Liebre ("jackrabbit's eye") in Guerrero Negro, a town also known for its saltworks.

The Sea of Cortez (Gulf of California) is one of the most

biologically diverse marine areas in the world. Depending on the season, you can find elephant seals (on Cedros Island), fin whales, dolphins, eared seals, fur seals, and sea lions (around Espíritu Santo Island), as well as a great variety of birds.

▶ **LANDSCAPE**

Between Guadalajara, a town with splendid colonial architecture in the

Popocatépetl looms above the church of Nuestra Señora de los Remedios.

western Pacific area, and Veracruz, the port city on the Gulf of Mexico, lie a series of volcanoes that shape Mexico's topography. In the west, **Paricutín** began as a fissure in a cornfield as witnessed by a farmer tilling this field in 1943.

Lake Patzcuaro, part of the Trans-Mexican Volcanic Belt, can best be surveyed from a hill on the island in the middle of the lake at the statue of revolutionary José María Morelos.

Nevado de Toluca has a wide summit caldera, and **Popocatépetl,** meaning "the smoking mountain" in the Aztec language, has a snowcapped cone 17,802 feet high, which can be climbed.

In the **Sierra Madre Occidental,** tributaries to the Río Fuerte have carved dozens of deep canyons, which can be studied at leisure from a train traveling from Chihuahua near the Copper Canyon to Los Mochis on the Pacific coast. There are other remarkable canyons such as Huasteca canyon and El Sumidero in Chiapas where the Río Chiapas cuts a 2,600-feet-deep trench and flows into the Gulf of Mexico.

The rugged interior of **Baja California** is not well known, but has found its niche among adventurers. The Vizcaino Desert shelters Baja elephant trees and giant *cardones,* and the gorges of the Sierras extend through the region to the southernmost point. The vineyards in the Valle de Guadalupe give way to the strange boojum trees that can get 80 feet high in the Valle de **Los Cirios.**

Advice

Pros
• Countless archaeological sites; only Peru has a comparable number of ancient ruins in Latin America. A landscape that is inviting to explore, combining beaches with cultural experiences, as in Yucatán.

Cons
• The tense political situation in some states, and the current problems in the northern border region because of drug trafficking. Rainy season from June to September.

Safety
• Political tensions continue in the states of Chiapas and Oaxaca. In addition, the U.S. State Department advises visitors to exercise extreme caution when traveling through the northern border regions. Beware of pickpockets in the larger cities and tourist sites.

Special Tip
• Tour organizers are slowly moving their focus from beaches and archaeological sites to cover the interior landscapes of the country, as well as Baja California.

What to See and Do in Mongolia

▶ **LANDSCAPE AND EXCURSIONS**

• Gobi desert, Orkhon Valley (horseback excursions), Altai Mountains

▶ **CULTURAL HERITAGE**

• Monasteries (Ulaanbaatar, Erdene Zuu), Karakorum ruins, temples

▶ **FESTIVALS**

• Naadam, New Year

 Genghis Khan and Ulaanbaatar are the names that immediately bring Mongolia to mind. In this large country where the steppes reach beyond the horizon, tourists enjoy excursions on horseback or by camel trek.

They say "the sky is higher" in this country, which is opening up to tourism.

Mongolia

Traveler's Notebook

MAIN CONTACTS

Embassy of Mongolia
2833 M Street, NW
Washington, DC 20007
(202) 333-7117
www.mongolian
embassy.us
www.mongoliatourism
.gov.mn
Embassy of Mongolia
7–8 Kensington Court
London W8 5DL, UK
+ 44 (0) 20 7937 0150
www.embassyof
mongolia.co.uk

TRAVEL DOCUMENTS

For U.S. Citizens:
Passport
For U.K. Citizens: Pass-port and visa

TRAVEL TIME TO DESTINATION & TIME DIFFERENCE

New York to Ulaanbaa-tar: 18 hours 40 minutes connecting flight; EST +13. London to Ulaan-baatar: 12 hours 30 minutes connecting flight; GMT +8;

AVERAGE TRIP COST

$3,175/£2,050 for 15 days of touring

LANGUAGE & CURRENCY

Official language: Khalkha Mongolian, spo-ken by three-quarters of the population (writ-ten in Cyrillic, although moves are under way to replace Cyrillic with the traditional Mongolian script). Several dialects are also spoken.
Currency: tögrög

POPULATION

2,952,000 inhabitants, half of whom live in the cities, with an over-all population density of 1 person per square mile. There are four eth-nic groups; the majo-rity is Khalkha. Capital: Ulaanbaatar

RELIGION

Besides shamanism, Tibetan Buddhism is gaining ground since the fall of the Soviet Union; Muslims form a minority.

FESTIVALS

Lunar New Year: Tsagaan Sar; May: White Flag Festival; July: Naadam Festival

SHOPPING

Great variety: cashmere sweaters, camel hair knit-wear, boots, saddles, belts, fur hats, and tradi-tional clothing

▶ **LANDSCAPE AND EXCURSIONS**

The Mongolian countryside seems unchanged over the millennia, but a steady influx of tourists into the region in hopes of finding untouched nature may endanger the nomadic pastoralism. Visitors can appreciate the beauty of the country, with the occasional yurt on the grazing land and the rather stony **Gobi desert,** from the window of a train traveling from Beijing to Ulaanbaatar.

The highlight of every trip to Mongolia—where riding is an old tradition—is an excursion on horseback. Such tours take place regularly in the **Orkhon Valley** and around the lakes and forests of the **Altai Mountains.**

▶ **CULTURAL HERITAGE**

Since the fall of the Soviet Union, Tibetan Buddhism has been reinvigorated, and the monasteries along with it. The monasteries in **Ulaanbaatar,** the Bogdo Gegeen Palace, and the Gandan monastery and its huge Buddha stand out from the rather drab architecture of the Mongolian capital.

The most visited monastery is Shar Süm in Hovd, which was rebuilt after its destruction under Stalin in 1937, and **Erdene Zuu,** which was constructed in part from the ruins of **Karakorum,** the ancient capital under Genghis Khan.

The Choijin Lama Temple Museum and the National Museum of Mongolian History in Ulaanbaatar are the important institutions where the country's cultural heritage is preserved.

▶ **FESTIVALS**

Mongolia has renewed one of its traditional festivals, Naadam, which is celebrated on the National Day in July and a few days before or after. The festival honors the three manly arts of wrestling, archery, and horse racing and takes place in Ulaanbaatar and all over the country.

The other important festival is Tsagaan Sar, the Lunar New Year, which is celebrated with traditional foods and rituals.

When to Go		
	CLIMATE	GOBI DESERT
JANUARY		
FEBRUARY		
MARCH		
APRIL		
MAY		
JUNE	☼	
JULY	☼	
AUGUST	☼	
SEPTEMBER		☼
OCTOBER		☼
NOVEMBER		
DECEMBER		

The Bay of Kotor is one of the most scenic coasts in all of Europe.

Montenegro

Independence in June 2006 was the "opening shot" and gave Montenegro a sudden stream of visitors over the following months. Thanks to its scenic coast and the Bay of Kotor, combined with its rugged, unexplored mountains, Montenegro—meaning "Black Mountain"—continues to be an enticing destination.

Traveler's Notebook

MAIN CONTACTS
Embassy of Montenegro
1610 New Hampshire Avenue, NW
Washington, DC 20009
(202) 234-6108
www.montenegro.travel/
Embassy of Montenegro
5th Floor, Trafalgar House
11–12 Waterloo Place
London SW1Y 4AU, UK
+ 44 (0) 20 7863 8806

TRAVEL DOCUMENTS FOR U.S. & U.K. CITIZENS
Passport

TRAVEL TIME TO DESTINATION & TIME DIFFERENCE
New York to Podgorica: 14 hours 10 minutes connecting; EST +6. London to Podgorica: 4 hours 35 minutes connecting; GMT +1

AVERAGE TRIP COST
$900/£575 for a week's beach vacation

LANGUAGE & CURRENCY
Official language: Montenegrin, a local variation of Serbo-Croatian; other languages: German, Italian, and English
Currency: euro

POPULATION
685,000 inhabitants. Besides Montenegrins, there are Albanians, Bosnians, Croats, and Serbs. Capital: Podgorica (formerly Titograd)

RELIGION
The majority are Orthodox; the rest are mostly Catholics and Muslims.

FESTIVALS
April: Orthodox Easter; May: Theater Festival in Podgorica

SHOPPING
Crafts, pottery, and carpets

► COAST

The coast of Montenegro is simply an ideal vacation spot and should be visited soon, before too many people discover the region. Many people compare it to the French Riviera.

Backed by breathtaking mountains, the coast runs for 185 miles and is dotted with fishing villages and small islands (Sveti Dorde).

Anyone nostalgic for Communist Yugoslavia should go to Sveti Stefan, where Joseph Broz Tito was born. Fans of the even older Yugoslavia go to Milocer, the former summer residence of the royal family.

What to See and Do in Montenegro

► COAST

- Bay of Kotor
- Beach resorts (Budva, Ulcinj, Sveti Stefan)

► LANDSCAPE

- National parks (Lovcen, Durmitor)

The **Bay of Kotor,** which resembles a fjord, is flanked by 5,000-foot-high mountains and the fortress of Sveti Ivan on a hill above the city of Kotor. Numerous small ports dot the shores, creating one of the most picturesque coastal backdrops in Europe. Cruise ships traveling from Italy to Greece or Turkey make regular stops in Kotor.

Farther south are the coastal resorts **Budva** and **Ulcinj,** and the island resort complex **Sveti Stefan.** These places have been favorite vacation spots for the locals for years, but are now being discovered by international tourism.

Advice

- **Pros**
  - A new country that has quickly joined international tourism, offering the gamut from beach vacations to mountain excursions.

- **Cons**
  - Some of the infrastructure still needs a bit of work.

- **Safety**
  - No major safety problems, but caution is advised if traveling in deserted border areas.

► LANDSCAPE

Montenegro's varied landscape holds scenic attractions such as **Lovcen National Park** near the Bay of Kotor and **Durmitor National Park,** with numerous mountain lakes at an altitude of 8,000 feet. The Tara River canyon, the longest in Europe, is suitable for rafting. Lake Skadar and Biogradska Gora National Park, with virgin forests and ski runs, complete the picture of the many excursions on offer.

When to Go

	COAST	HIKING
JANUARY		
FEBRUARY		
MARCH		
APRIL		
MAY		🚶
JUNE	☼	🚶
JULY	☼	
AUGUST	☼	
SEPTEMBER	☼	🚶
OCTOBER		🚶
NOVEMBER		
DECEMBER		

Morocco

Morocco is in competition with Egypt as the most interesting destination in North Africa. This country on the far western tip of the continent attracts ever more visitors because of its year-round sunshine, long beaches, Muslim architecture, royal cities, and tours in the High Atlas Mountains and the Sahara — all at reasonable prices.

▶ CITIES AND MONUMENTS

The four royal cities alone—Marrakech, Fez, Rabat, and Meknes—are worth a trip to Morocco.

Marrakech, where the Almohads, Almoravids, and Saadians ruled, has an elegant cityscape with fortified walls, lush gardens, the 12th-century minaret of the Koutoubia Mosque, the 16th-century Ben Yusef Madrassa, and traditional souks. The old town, the medina, is a jewel of Muslim architecture. Other sights include the remnants of the el-Badi Palace (end of the 16th century), the Jewish Quarter (the Mellah), the Saadian tombs, and the lively main square Djemaa el Fna. The city is the hub of Moroccan tourism, catering to an upscale clientele.

Fez, the first royal city, is the artistic and intellectual capital of

What to See and Do in Morocco

▶ CITIES AND MONUMENTS

- Royal cities: Marrakech, Fez, Rabat, and Meknes
- Safi, Casablanca, Tangier, Essaouira
- Moulay Idriss, Volubilis

▶ LANDSCAPE AND WALKING TOURS

- Rif Mountains
- High Atlas (Dades Valley), Middle Atlas Range, Anti-Atlas Range (Draa Valley)
- Great South: Casbahs, fortified villages, oases, palm forests, sub-Sahara

▶ COASTS

- Beaches on the Atlantic (Agadir, Essaouira, White Beach)
- Souss-Massa National Park

▶ FESTIVALS

- Moussem

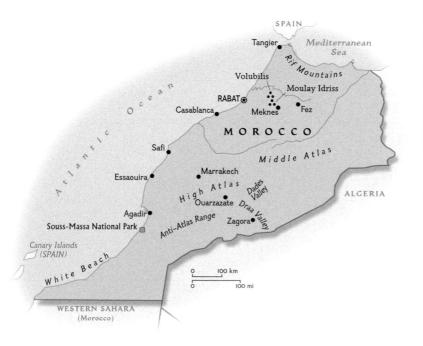

The Koutoubia Minaret dominates Marrakech's Djemaa el Fna square.

Home of aesthetes and intellectuals, Essaouira is known as the white city for its sun-bleached architecture.

Traveler's Notebook

MAIN CONTACTS
Embassy of the Kingdom of Morocco
1601 21st Street, NW
Washington, DC 20009
(202) 462-7979
http://dcusa.the
moroccanembassy
.com
www.visitmorocco
.com/index.php/eng/
Embassy of the Kingdom of Morocco
49 Queens Gate Gardens
London SW7 5NE, UK
+ 44 (0) 20 7581 5001/5004
www.moroccan

embassylondon
.org.uk

TRAVEL DOCUMENTS FOR U.S. & U.K. CITIZENS
Passport

HEALTH ISSUES
No vaccinations required

TRAVEL TIME TO DESTINATION & TIME DIFFERENCE
New York to Marrakech: 11 hours 10 minutes connecting flight; EST +5. London to Marrakech: 5 hours 40 minutes connecting flight; GMT

AVERAGE TRIP COST
$900/£575 for

a week's beach vacation

LANGUAGE & CURRENCY
Official language: Arabic; other languages: Berber. French is the primary language of commerce.

POPULATION
33,757,000 inhabitants, mostly of Arab, Berber, or Sudanese background. Capital: Rabat

RELIGION
Islam; there are Jewish and Christian minorities.

FESTIVALS
July or August (end of Ramadan): Eid al-Fitr; July 30: Feast of the Throne; after the harvest in summer: Moussems; October or November: Eid al-Adha; November 18: Independence Day

SHOPPING
The souks are filled with carpets, pottery, and basketware. Typical souvenirs are a pair of *baboushes* (leather slippers) or a *tagine* (covered ceramic pot).

the country. The city boasts a walled, large medina—the Fes el-Bali quarter—which surrounds the Zaouia Madrassa of its founder Moulay Idriss. It also has several other madrassas (Bou Inania, Al-Attarine) and the Karaouine Mosque, which holds 20,000 believers but is accessible only to Muslims. In this famous medina of nearly 2,000 streets and 200 mosques, the aromas of spices mingle with the smells of the henna souk and the stench of tanning hides in the leather souk.

Rabat, the capital city, features its monumental gateway to the Casbah of the Udayas, surrounded by a three-mile-long wall with five entry gates (constructed in the 12th century), which is simply an architectural masterpiece.

The Bou Inania Madrassa, the Ismail I Mausoleum, and the Bab Mansour gate are the major sites in **Meknes,** the least well known of the royal cities.

In the fishing port of **Safi,** the attractions include the *ribat* (a fortified monastery) and Portuguese-era fortifications. **Casablanca** shines with its old town, art deco houses, and the Hassan II Mosque, the largest in Africa. **Tangier** also stands out for its old town and casbah. The fortified, white port city of **Essaouira,** the former Mogador, designed in the 18th century in its current form, is a favorite enclave of artists and intellectuals today.

Moulay Idriss, the holy city with the mausoleum of Zaouia of the Idrisid dynasty (eighth century) is a pilgrimage site.

The nearby ruins of the Roman city of **Volubilis,** with columns and a triumphal arch of Emperor Caracalla (third century), are some of the best preserved in North Africa.

▶ LANDSCAPE AND WALKING TOURS

Walking tours in the Atlas Mountains are a new chapter in Morocco's organized tourism, but the country's landscapes, whether north or south, have always had a special attraction.

The scenic vistas begin on the limestone plateau of the **Rif Mountains** with the Kef Thogobeit, the deepest cave system in all of Africa, and the underground network of the Ouargha River cave, which swallows up a number of watercourses until they emerge as waterfalls from the Chiker grottoes. The three Atlas ranges, providing the most idyllic landscapes in Morocco, follow in succession.

Jbel Toubkal in the **High Atlas** reaches 13,700 feet; its majestic

The gate to the royal palace in Fez is a fine example of Muslim arts.

snowy peaks invite skiers. The Amesfrane cliff, called the "cathedral," is sculpted into an ornamented folded surface. In the **Dades Valley,** some of the red rock faces are cut into steep canyons. The region is famous for its thousand casbahs, palm forests, and rose gardens (El Kelaa, M'Goun),

When to Go				
	MARRAKECH AND ROYAL CITIES	BEACHES	ATLAS MOUNTAINS	DESERT
JANUARY			❄	☼
FEBRUARY			❄	☼
MARCH				☼
APRIL				
MAY	☼	☼		
JUNE	☼	☼	🚶	
JULY		☼	🚶	
AUGUST		☼	🚶	
SEPTEMBER	☼	☼		
OCTOBER	☼	☼		☼
NOVEMBER				☼
DECEMBER				☼

where Berber tradition reigns high (Ait Bou Goumez Valley) and religious festivals are important.

The **Middle Atlas** is appealing for its rivers, cedar and oak forests, and the hill stations of Ifrane and Midelt.

The **Anti-Atlas Range** cuts through the **Draa Valley**. In an excursion from Ouarzazate, the main attraction is the Taouirt Casbah, one of the most striking fortified homes of a local leader of old, followed by *ksurs* (fortified mud-brick villages), palm forests, rose gardens, gorges, and orchards with pomegranates, figs, and sea buckthorn. Once arrived in Zagora, a visitor can join a camel tour to ride into the first high dunes (*ergs*) of the **Sahara**.

The women of the Berber tribes wear colorful traditional clothes.

▶ COASTS

Tourists from all over beat a steady path to Morocco's white Atlantic beaches, where it's swimming season all year round. Most famous is the nearly six-mile-long beach of **Agadir,** which is blessed with sunny weather all winter. North of town is surfer territory (Anchor Point). South of Agadir, the **Souss-Massa National Park** of beaches, dunes, and wetlands is an important bird sanctuary.

The fishing port of **Essaouira** is not quite as famous for its beaches, but is concentrating on thalassotherapy in its resort hotels. Farther south, the towns of Tiznit and

Forests, canyons, valleys, wadis, and ocher-colored villages epitomize the Atlas Mountain scenery.

Tan-Tan are developing excellent new resorts.

From Agadir to Dakhla, some 30 miles of coastline, called the **White Beach** (Plage Blanche), merge directly with the desert, where anglers and surfers hold court. The town of Mirleft attracts more of the fishing enthusiasts.

Even the beaches of the western Sahara around the towns of Laayoune and Dakhla (for fishing) near the Mauritanian border are attracting more and more tourists.

The rugged Rif Mountains stretch nearly to the Mediterranean coast creating rocky rather than sandy beaches, but small fishing villages are hidden in some of the coves. The water here is warmer than in the Atlantic.

▶ FESTIVALS

After the harvest in July and August, Moussem, a festival to honor the *marabouts* (Islamic saints), is celebrated all over the country. The high point is the Fantasia, when riders in traditional dress charge in a straight line, firing guns into the air. The date of Moussem changes from year to year. The best-known festivals are held in Moulay Abdellah, south of Casablanca, and Moulay Idriss Zerhoun near Meknes.

Advice

■ **Pros**
- A wide variety of tour options, including cultural sites, walking tours into the mountains or the desert, and beaches.

■ **Cons**
- Morocco gets crowded in the summer months. Possible terror activity.

■ **Special Tip**
- Spending the night in a riad, a traditional house with a tiled courtyard and fountain, rather than in a hotel, is the latest trend. Marrakech was a pioneer in offering riads, and Essaouira has followed.

Bagan's many pagodas and temples reflect the country's Buddhist culture.

While keeping its doors closed to democracy, the government of Myanmar, the country formerly called Burma, has opened the doors to tourism. Whether visiting pagodas covered in gold leaf or coastal sites, a traveler will find much to see in this unusual country where Buddhism sets the tone for everyday life.

Myanmar

▶ MONUMENTS

Striking examples of world-class Buddhist art are found just about everywhere in Myanmar, in the form of pagodas as well as Buddha figures, standing or reclining, large or small. One important site is the **Shwedagon Pagoda** at Yangon, with a perimeter of more than 1,300 feet and a dome covered in gold leaf. Another is **Bagan,** site of 5,000 religious buildings, including more than 2,000 pagodas, as well as monasteries, temples (Ananda), and *zedis*—the equivalent of stupas—such as Shwezigon and Thatbyinnyu; these structures cover an area of 16 square miles, the most important ones dating to the 11th century.

In some places, **Yangon,** formerly Rangoon, recalls the charm of the British colonial period, but it is known above all for its market (Bogyoke) and its pagodas. In addition to Shwedagon, travelers should visit Botataung Pagoda, Kaba Aye Pagoda, and the most ancient shrine, the Sule Pagoda with its golden stupa.

Mandalay, a former capital and the second city of the country, is

Traveler's Notebook

MAIN CONTACTS

Embassy of the Union of Myanmar
2300 S Street, NW
Washington, DC 20008
(202) 332-3344
www.mewashingtondc
.com
www.myanmar-tourism
.com
Embassy of the Union of Myanmar
19A Charles Street
London W1J 5DX, UK
+ 44 (0) 20 7499 4340 or
7493 7397
http://www.mofa.gov.mm

TRAVEL DOCUMENTS FOR U.S. & U.K. CITIZENS
Passport and visa

HEALTH ISSUES
No vaccinations required; malaria prophylaxis strongly advised in areas below 3,000 feet

TRAVEL TIME TO DESTINATION & TIME DIFFERENCE
New York to Yangon: 15 hours 20 minutes connecting flight; EST +11:30. London to Yangon: 10 hours 9 minutes

nonstop flight; GMT +6:30

AVERAGE TRIP COST
$3,175/£2,050 for 15 days of touring, driver and guide included

LANGUAGE & CURRENCY
Official language: Birman; one in ten inhabitants speaks Karen, and there are numerous dialects. English is spoken in the cities and tourist places. Currency: kyat

POPULATION
69 percent of the 47,374,000 inhabitants are of Burmese ethnicity; the many different ethnic groups—Karen, Shan, Kachin, Mon, and others—are often at odds with the central government. Capital: Nay Pyi Taw has supplanted Yangon (Rangoon).

RELIGION
Buddhist: 87 percent; Christian: 5 percent; Muslim: 4 percent

FESTIVALS
August: holiday dedicated to *nats,* spirits devoted to both good and evil, on Mount Popa; October: feast of the pagoda at Phaung Daw U pagoda

SHOPPING
Local crafts include lacquer objects at Bagan, traditional *longuis* (a kind of wraparound skirt), sculpted wooden objects, and puppets; rubies are another possible purchase.

dominated by a hill charged with Buddhist symbolism. Like Yangon, the city is rich in pagodas and monasteries.

North of Mandalay, at **Mingun,** is the Pahtodawgyi, the remains of a massive unfinished Buddhist stupa meant to be the largest ever built. In 1838, an earthquake reduced the structure to rubble, but a gigantic bell weighing 87 tons stands unharmed near the ruins. West of Mandalay, the town of **Sagaing** shelters numerous temples and pagodas on its hill.

Besides some ancient pagodas, **Bago** features a 177-foot-long reclining Buddha (Shwethalyaung) from the tenth century, as well as four other giant Buddhas. The sites of the **Arakan Range** are less well known. At the foot of the mountains stand pagodas, monasteries, and the fortress temple of Shite-thaung of the 15th to 18th centuries.

▶ **LANDSCAPE AND EXCURSIONS**

A cruise on the **Ayeyarwady** (Irrawaddy) **River,** the main artery of the country and home to the rare freshwater dolphin, is very popular. Among the most beautiful sites are **Inle Lake** and its floating islets, the limestone caves of **Pindaya** with thousands of Buddha statues, and the **Salween (Thanlwin) gorge,** one of the biggest in the world.

To the north of Mandalay, the town of **Pyin-U-Lwin** (Maymyo) is of interest with its market and forest museum. Two other sites warrant detours: One is **Mount Popa,** not far from Bagan, and the other is **Mount Kyaikto** and its enormous golden rock, perched on the edge of a cliff, a pilgrimage destination.

Along the Mekong River at the frontier to Thailand at Tachilek and Mae Sai begins the infamous **Golden Triangle.**

When to Go		
	CLIMATE	LANDSCAPE PHOTOGRAPHY
JANUARY	☼	
FEBRUARY	☼	
MARCH	☼	
APRIL		
MAY		
JUNE		
JULY		
AUGUST		
SEPTEMBER		◅
OCTOBER		◅
NOVEMBER	☼	◅
DECEMBER	☼	

Advice

■ **Pros**

- Myanmar tourism combines a high level of cultural sites with beautiful landscapes while preserving its traditions.

■ **Cons**

- Serious issues over human rights and civil liberties. The cost of travel is higher than for other countries of Southeast Asia.

■ **Safety**

- Because of simmering conflicts, travelers are advised not to visit certain regions on the frontier with India and Thailand.

In the land of the Himba, the Epupa Falls interrupt the Kunene River.

What to See and Do in Namibia

▶ **LANDSCAPE**

• Dunes of the Namib Desert (Sossusvlei), Fish River Canyon

• Brandberg mountain and Waterberg Plateau (rock paintings)

• Kunene region, Hoba (meteorite crater)

▶ **COAST**

• Swakopmund, Lüderitz

▶ **WILDLIFE**

• Etosha National Park (the big five), Damaraland, and Waterberg National Park (elephants, giraffes, zebras, and more)

• Cape Cross (Cape fur seals, sea lions), Walvis Bay Lagoon (flamingos, pelicans)

• Rare plants: *Welwitschia,* kokerboom (Kokerboom Forest)

Namibia offers excursions into the desert to the highest dunes in the world and introduces travelers to unusual flora and fauna.

Namibia

▶ **LANDSCAPE**

The ancient **Namib Desert,** which follows the coast of Namibia along the Atlantic Ocean for some 1,300 miles and spans 30 to 60 miles in width, is in itself worth a detour. In the southern part, in the clay pan of the **Sossusvlei,** the desert harbors the highest dunes in the world—up to 1,000 feet tall; reshaped endlessly by the wind and sometimes blanketed by fog, the dunes rise and fall in fantastic formations and are a favorite destination for hikers. The Namib-Naukluft National Park in the

Traveler's Notebook

MAIN CONTACTS

Embassy of the Republic of Namibia

1605 New Hampshire Avenue, NW Washington, DC 20009 (202) 986-0540 www.namibian embassyusa.org www.namibiatourism .com.na

Namibia High Commission

6 Chandos Street London W1G 9LU, UK + 44 (0) 20 7636 6244 www.namibiahc.org.uk

TRAVEL DOCUMENTS FOR U.S. & U.K. CITIZENS

Passport

HEALTH ISSUES

No vaccinations required; malaria prophylaxis recommended in the northern regions from November to June, and all year along the Okavango and Kunene Rivers

TRAVEL TIME TO DESTINATION & TIME DIFFERENCE

New York to Windhoek: 19 hours 45 minutes connecting flight; EST +7. London to Windhoek: 12 hours 50 minutes

connecting flight; GMT +2

AVERAGE TRIP COST

$1,900/£1,230 for 12 days on safari

LANGUAGE & CURRENCY

Official language: English; other languages: Afrikaans is most widespread, along with dialects such as Kwanyama, used by one out of two inhabitants. German is spoken in the cities.
Currency: Namibian dollar, aligned with the South African

rand, which is equally accepted.

POPULATION

2,055,000 inhabitants, a modest figure for such a large country. The Herero and other African peoples are a large majority. Afrikaners and Germans represent 7.5 percent of the population. Capital: Windhoek

RELIGION

One out of two Namibians follows the Lutheran Church; 20 percent are Catholic; and others are Anglican or follow

the Dutch Calvinist Church.

FESTIVALS

March: Windhoek Art Festival; March 21: Independence Day; April to May: Windhoek Carnival; August and October: Mahereros, a traditional festival of Herero herders

SHOPPING

Precious or semiprecious stones (amethyst, topaz), leather goods, and basketry

When to Go		
	COAST	**NATIONAL PARKS**
JANUARY	☼	
FEBRUARY	☼	
MARCH	☼	
APRIL		🐾
MAY		🐾
JUNE		🐾
JULY		🐾
AUGUST		🐾
SEPTEMBER		🐾
OCTOBER		🐾
NOVEMBER	☼	
DECEMBER		

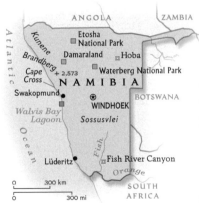

northern part is equally popular among hikers.

In the south, the dunes give way to the bare rock of the arid **Fish River Canyon;** at 1,800 feet deep, 100 miles long, and 17 miles wide, it is often compared to the Grand Canyon and increasingly attracts hiking tours.

The rock paintings in this region are among the most ancient yet found. The "White Lady" in the red granite massif of the **Brandberg** is attributed to the San (Bushman) tribes and dates from 3,500 years ago. Other rock carvings can be seen on the **Waterberg Plateau** at Twyfelfontein.

From there it is possible to go either to the **Kunene** region (formerly Kaokoland), where the semi-nomadic Himba tribe lives, or to **Hoba** to see the largest meteorite crater in the world. At the borders of the Angolan frontier are the strange Epupa Falls of the Kunene River.

The great variety in the landscape almost obscures any interest in Windhoek, the capital. Nevertheless the city has its highlights, among them the remains of the Alte Feste, a former German fortress.

▶ COAST

The coast is generally uninviting and overrun by fog caused by the collision between the heat of the Namib and the cold current of the Benguela Stream. The little towns of **Swakopmund** and **Lüderitz,** settled by Germans at the turn of the 20th century, are the most popular seaside resorts.

▶ WILDLIFE

The best time to visit the game parks is toward the end of the dry season (October), when many

watering holes dry up and the animals gather at the remaining ones. In the north, the 8,500-square-mile **Etosha National Park** is open from mid-March to the end of October. The park is home to the celebrated African "big five" (Cape buffalo, elephant, leopard, lion, rhinoceros) as well as antelopes, zebras, oryx, more than 300 species of birds, and 27 species of snakes.

Farther south are **Damaraland** and **Waterberg Plateau National Park.** Between the Namib Desert and the ocean, **Cape Cross** harbors a large colony of Cape fur seals and sea lions, and the **Walvis Bay Lagoon** has flocks of flamingos and pelicans.

The flora is rich in rare species endemic to the country, including the *Welwitschia mirabilis,* a living fossil classed among the oldest plants on Earth; the plant resembles an octopus, with extensions nearly six feet long, and may live for a thousand years or more. Another rarity is the koker-boom ("quiver tree"), a giant aloe tree that grows on the granite rocks of the **Kokerboom Forest.**

Advice

▪ Pros
• A unique kind of dune landscape. Remarkable diversity and uniqueness of fauna and flora. A mild winter so that the country can be visited year-round.

▪ Cons
• Relatively expensive. Most of the coast is inhospitable. Travel to the northern frontier is not advisable.

▪ Special Tip
• Meeting with the long isolated seminomadic Himba people is in style—perhaps too much so. That's a question for equitable tourism.

Nepal

Once one of the destinations on the "Passage to India," Nepal today is a paradise for hikers, who arrive in large numbers to scale the mountains of the Himalaya. The country is adapting to Western customs and mores, although the lifestyle of its people differs significantly. Recent political tensions have slowed down the tourist stream a bit.

What to See and Do in Nepal

▶ **LANDSCAPE AND TREKKING**

- Hikes in the Himalaya (Annapurna Circuit, Dhaulagiri, Everest)
- Dolpo, Mustang, Kangchenjunga
- Ama Dablam, Baruntse, Makalu

▶ **CITIES AND MONUMENTS**

- Kathmandu, Lalitpur, Bhaktapur
- Swayambhunath and Boudhanath (stupas), Pashupatinath (temple), Lumbini (Buddhist sacred sites)

▶ **WILDLIFE**

- Terai Plateau (Royal Chitwan and Royal Bardia National Parks): monkeys, buffaloes, rhinoceroses, elephants, crocodiles, tigers, river dolphins

▶ LANDSCAPE AND TREKS

The green terraced hills of the Kathmandu Valley are surrounded by the majestic snowy peaks of the **Himalaya,** which take on an orange glow at sunset. But for scenic beauty, the Pokhara Valley, with its lakes and gorges, and the canyons of the Karnali Valley can hold their own.

The terrain is ideal for all levels of trekking. The valleys and mountain trails in the Himalaya, the highest peaks in the world, are suitable for all kinds of hikers, from the most inexperienced to the hardiest. There are three kinds of treks: up to 3,000 meters (10,000 feet), up to 4,000 meters (13,000 feet), and up to 5,500 meters (18,000 feet). The requirements for good physical conditioning and a certain level of experience increase along with the altitude for a trek, which usually last about five hours per day. A modest, four-to-six-hour hike, from Kathmandu to Nagarkot, for example, is all that is needed to see the "Roof of the World." The average stay devoted to trekking is between 15 and 20 days.

Among the great classic treks are the **Annapurna Circuit,** which includes a fine view at Pokhara Lake; the **Dhaulagiri,** not far from the sacred Kali Gandaki River; and the **Everest** base camp via the Khumbu region. This area is home to the famous Sherpas, who have often exchanged their traditional occupations to become mountain guides. A hike starting from Kalapattar offers a marvelous view of the trio of Everest (29,035 feet),

Lhotse (27,940 feet), and Nuptse (25,801 feet).

Two areas influenced by Buddhist traditions include the **Dolpo** region and the former kingdom of **Mustang,** featuring monasteries, sacred caves, and splendid views of Annapurna. New routes are opening up in the far northeast, in the area of the **Kangchenjunga** (28,169 feet), the third highest mountain in the world. Other major peaks in the northeast include "seven thousands" (over 7,000 meters/23,000 feet: **Ama Dablam, Baruntse**) and "eight thousands" (over 8,000 meters/26,000 feet: **Makalu** and certain faces of Everest).

When to Go		
	TREKKING TERAI	FLORA
JANUARY	☼	
FEBRUARY	☼	
MARCH	☼	
APRIL		⚘
MAY		⚘
JUNE		⚘
JULY		
AUGUST		
SEPTEMBER		
OCTOBER	☼	
NOVEMBER	☼	
DECEMBER	☼	

The Buddha's all-seeing eyes watch from the Boudhanath stupa in Kathmandu.

▶ CITIES AND MONUMENTS

Since the 1970s, the mythic **Kathmandu** has changed its image a bit. The capital's old quarter, the Thamel, features artful gates and wooden sculpted balconies; a "living goddess," Kumari Devi (who regularly appears on her balcony on Durbar Square, the square of the former royal palace); market stalls; and Buddhist and Hindu temples. In the surrounding areas, **Lalitpur** retains its status as the center of Tantric Buddhism (Golden Temple, fountains), whereas **Bhaktapur** is a city of museums and has the magnificent Golden Spout and Gate. The two cities display the art of the Newar people, who formed the kingdoms around Kathmandu.

Other landmarks of the Kathmandu area are the stupas (domelike structures containing relics of the Buddha) of **Swayambhunath** and **Boudhanath,** and the Hindu **Pashupatinath** temple, a Shiva sanctuary with a two-level roof, covered in gold. **Lumbini,** near the border of India, is the holy site where Buddha was born six centuries before the Christian era, an important pilgrimage site.

▶ WILDLIFE

A great variety of animals live on the **Terai Plateau,** a tropical region on the Indian border. In **Royal Chitwan National Park,** visitors can spot monkeys, buffaloes, rhinoceroses, elephants, and crocodiles. At **Royal Bardia National Park,** elephants and monkeys can be found, as well as river dolphins in a tributary to the Ganges River.

Traveler's Notebook

MAIN CONTACTS
Embassy of Nepal
2131 Leroy Place, NW
Washington, DC 20008
(202) 667-4550
www.nepalembassyusa.org
www.tourism.gov.np
welcomenepal.com/promotional/
Embassy of Nepal
12A Kensington Palace Gardens
London W8 4QU, UK
+ 44 (0) 20 7229 1594
www.nepembassy.org.uk

TRAVEL DOCUMENTS FOR U.S. & U.K. CITIZENS
Passport and visa (issued on arrival)

HEALTH ISSUES
Malaria prophylaxis is recommended for travel in the Terai and to the borders of India.

TRAVEL TIME TO DESTINATION & TIME DIFFERENCE
New York to Kathmandu: 20 hours 8 minutes connecting flight; EST +5:45.
London to Kathmandu: 11 hours 13 minutes connecting flight; GMT +5:45

AVERAGE TRIP COST
$1,900/£1,230 for 15 days of trekking

LANGUAGE & CURRENCY
Official language: Nepali, which has some 60 dialects. In the cities and tourist centers, the main foreign language is English.
Currency: Nepalese rupee

POPULATION
The 28,902,000 inhabitants are of Mongolian, Tibetan, and Indo-Aryan origin. Capital: Kathmandu

RELIGION
Nine out of ten Nepalese practice Hinduism, once the state religion; minorities are Buddhist or Muslim.

FESTIVALS
Full moon in March or April: Holi Purnima and Nepalese New Year; October or November: Dasain and Tihar; November: Mani Rimdu at Tengboche monastery

SHOPPING
Local crafts such as cashmere sweaters and Tibetan or Indian silver jewelry; woolen handbags and *mandalas* (painted Buddhist images) are found in the Thamel quarter of Kathmandu.

Advice

■ Pros
• One of the most beautiful mountain ranges on the planet and the most esteemed place for trekking.

■ Cons
• In the high mountains, the local population has a hard time meeting all the needs of the tourists. The possible return of political tensions. May to September is monsoon season, bringing on high humidity and clouds, which conceal the peaks.

■ Safety
• Maoist guerrillas remain a threat, but do not focus on tourists. Nevertheless, it is important to get the latest information from the U.S. State Department or the embassy before traveling. Hikers and climbers should never strike out alone and should book through an established agency.

Hundreds of bridges and more than 150 canals give Amsterdam a romantic allure.

The Netherlands

Tulip fields as far as the eye can see in springtime; world-class museums; windmills, canals, and gabled houses; picturesque towns with harmonious architecture, energized by the hip, dynamic influence of Amsterdam—that's the Netherlands.

▶ **CITIES AND MUSEUMS**

Amsterdam lives up to its reputation as a young person's city: hip, cosmopolitan, and permissive. Thousands of visitors from around the world come to enjoy boat rides on the canals (most notably the Herengracht, Keizersgracht, and Prinsengracht) that crisscross the city, and from which one can see its 1,289 bridges and the gabled facades of its buildings.

The city boasts a number of outstanding museums, including the **Rijksmuseum,** which has an extensive collection of paintings from the 15th to 17th centuries—most importantly those by Rembrandt ("The Nightwatch"), Vermeer, and Frans Hals.

The **Van Gogh Museum** has 200 paintings and 500 sketches by the ill-fated artist. Also not to be missed are the Stedelijk Museum and the Hermitage Amsterdam, featuring a wing from the Hermitage in St. Petersburg.

▶ **CITIES AND MUSEUMS**

- Amsterdam (Rijksmuseum, Van Gogh Museum)
- Delft, The Hague (Mauritshuis)
- Rotterdam, Haarlem, Leiden, Utrecht, Maastricht

▶ **LANDSCAPE AND EXCURSIONS**

- Keukenhof Gardens
- Loosdrecht Lakes, Frisian Islands, Hoge Veluwe National Park
- Kinderdijk windmills, Flevoland polders, and Groote Peel marsh
- Beaches, bicycle tours

Rubens, Vermeer) and the Municipal Museum (Mondrian).

Rotterdam was largely destroyed in World War II and today is defined by the areas around two bustling main streets: Lijnbaan (shopping district) and Coolsingel (the Town Hall and Stock Exchange, miraculously spared from the war; the statue of Dutch Renaissance humanist Erasmus, and the futuristic bridge named after him). Of special interest are Rotterdam's surroundings, especially Delfshaven (former port of Delft, site of the Pilgrims' departure for England and later America) and Schiedam (windmills).

The port of Rotterdam, one of the largest in the world, is well worth the visit (boat tours available). Don't miss the Boijmans van Beuningen Museum and its

a former ducal palace, is very lively. There are two very different kinds of attractions: the Madurodam Park, a miniature replica of the major landmarks in the country; and the prestigious **Mauritshuis** Museum (Rembrandt,

Visits to the houses of Rembrandt and Anne Frank, the National Maritime Museum (exhibiting ships from the famous Dutch East India Company), and the narrow streets of the Jordaan neighborhood with its houses and courtyards make for a tour replete with the color and variety that is Amsterdam.

Delft boasts the charms of its canals, houses, churches, and Gothic bell tower and the home of its celebrated son, Vermeer.

The Hague, home to many international organizations, the royal court, and ample green space, has a sleepy reputation. But the heart of the city surrounding the Binnenhof,

Each spring, a million visitors come to see the symphony of colors in the tulip fields between Haarlem and Leiden.

Traveler's Notebook

MAIN CONTACTS
Royal Netherlands Embassy
4200 Linnean Avenue, NW
Washington, DC 20008
(877) 388-2443
www.netherlands-embassy.org
www.holland.com

Royal Netherlands Embassy
38 Hyde Park Gate
London SW7 5DP, UK
+ 44 (0) 20 7590 3200
www.netherlands-embassy.org.uk

TRAVEL DOCUMENTS FOR U.S. & U.K. CITIZENS
Passport

TRAVEL TIME TO DESTINATION & TIME DIFFERENCE
New York to Amsterdam: 7 hours 10 minutes nonstop flight; EST +6. London to Amsterdam: 1 hour 15 minutes nonstop flight; GMT +1

AVERAGE TRIP COST
$325/£200 for a 4-day weekend in Amsterdam

LANGUAGE & CURRENCY
Official language: Dutch; a separate dialect is spoken in the northern part of the country. The Dutch generally speak English, German, and French.

Currency: euro

POPULATION
16,571,000 people inhabit a relatively small area, resulting in a very high population density. Capital: Amsterdam was designated the capital in 1815, but the royal court and seat of government are located in The Hague.

RELIGION
Catholics (36 percent) outnumber Protestants (32 percent), who mostly belong to the Dutch Reformed Church; a third of the Dutch claim no religious affiliation

FESTIVALS
April 30: Queen's Day; June: Holland Festival in Amsterdam and The Hague; August: Gay Pride in Amsterdam; September: Bloemen Corso in Amsterdam

SHOPPING
Tulip bulbs, wooden shoes, Delft porcelain, Gouda cheese—all are perfect souvenirs from the Netherlands.

collection of paintings by Hieronymus Bosch, Van Eyck, Hals, Rembrandt, and Rubens.

Haarlem is a must-see for its Market Square bordered by beautiful buildings (church of St. Bavo, town hall, Meat Hall) and especially for the Frans Hals Museum.

Leiden is one of the most charming cities in the Netherlands, known for its gabled houses that line the Rapenburg Canal, windmill (De Valk), and prestigious university. Don't overlook the National Museum of Ethnology, Municipal Museum (decorative arts and the works of Lucas van Leyden), and National Museum of Antiquities.

Utrecht is captivating for its old town and canals, bell tower (Domtoren), Vredenburg Square, and progressive architecture of the Rietveld-Schröder House.

Kinderdijk, with two dozen well-maintained windmills, is a place captured in time.

Maastricht, renowned as the place where the landmark treaty creating the European Union was signed, also attracts visitors to its Basilica of St. Servatius, in the heart of the old city.

It is worth visiting any of these cities simply for their municipal museums. Add to the list of top museums the Kröller-Müller Museum (Mondrian, Van Gogh, Cubists, French Impressionists), located in Hoge Veluwe National Park.

▶ LANDSCAPE AND EXCURSIONS

The cultivation of flowering bulbs dates back more than four hundred years in the Netherlands. From the end of March to the end of May, the place to be is on the side roads between Haarlem and Leiden—where fields of blooming tulips, daffodils, and hyacinths form a geometric patchwork of purple, yellow, and white.

Near Lisse, the **Keukenhof Gardens,** with their magnificent landscape gardens and greenhouses, are the epicenter for tourism in the region (more than a million visitors annually).

Every ten years, from April to October, the Netherlands hosts Floriade, an international exhibition of flowers and gardening (next in 2012).

When to Go		
	CLIMATE	TULIP TIME
JANUARY		
FEBRUARY		
MARCH		
APRIL		☂
MAY		☂
JUNE	☼	
JULY	☼	
AUGUST	☼	
SEPTEMBER	☼	
OCTOBER		
NOVEMBER		
DECEMBER		

The country's flat terrain has its unique beauty. Some exemplary spots are **Loosdrecht Lakes,** near Utrecht, with their charming bridges, ports, and castles; the long beaches and bird sanctuaries of the **Frisian Islands; Hoge Veluwe National Park** (deer, birds); the marshes around **Kinderdijk,** which has an exceptional collection of well-maintained windmills; the dunes of Zealand Flanders; Lake Ijsselmeer, formed by the damming of the Zuider Zee, its shoreline dotted with villages (Volendam); the polders of **Flevoland,** land recently reclaimed from the sea; and the marshes of **Groote Peel** (birds and butterflies).

Although there are many beaches (Noordwijk, Scheveningen, Zandvoort, Katwijk), it may be warmer in the nearby casinos than on the sand.

The Netherlands has developed an entire industry of cycling tours, with over 6,000 miles of routes from the cities to the countryside and well-planned itineraries designed to leave the car behind.

New Caledonia offers an endless lagoon and sandy beaches.

What to See and Do in New Caledonia

▶ **COASTS**

- Coral reefs, white sandy beaches

- Diving and surfing around Grande-Terre, the Bélep Archipelago, the Isle of Pines, and the Loyalty Islands

▶ **LANDSCAPE AND CULTURAL HERITAGE**

- Grasslands, swamps, waterfalls, forests

- In the footsteps of "stockmen" and Kanak tribes

New Caledonia

▮ *The main island, Grande-Terre, is flanked by the Isle of Pines, the Bélep Archipelago, and the Loyalty Islands. With its beaches, the corals of its limitless lagoon—said to be the largest in the world—and the rich culture of its Kanak population, New Caledonia competes with French Polynesia as an ideal stopping point for French-speaking travelers in Oceania.*

Traveler's Notebook

MAIN CONTACTS
Embassy of France
4101 Reservoir Road, NW
Washington, DC 20007
(202) 944-6000
www.ambafrance-us.org
Embassy of France
58 Knightsbridge
London SW1X 7JT, UK
+ 44 (0) 20 7073 1000
www.ambafrance-uk.org

TRAVEL DOCUMENTS FOR U.S. & U.K. CITIZENS
Passport

TRAVEL TIME TO DESTINATION & TIME DIFFERENCE
New York to Nouméa: 25 hours 40 minutes connecting; EST + 16. London to Nouméa: 25 hours 30 minutes connecting; GMT +11

AVERAGE TRIP COST
$3,810/£2,460 for 15 days of cruising

LANGUAGE & CURRENCY
Official language: French; other languages: some 30 dialects of Melanesian origin
Currency: Pacific franc (CFP); euros are accepted, pending official adoption

POPULATION
Of the 221,900 inhabitants, 44 percent are Melanesian (Kanak) and 34 percent are European (called Caldoches); there are minorities of Wallisians, Futunians, Polynesians, Indonesians, and Vietnamese. Capital: Nouméa (population 91,000)

RELIGION
75 percent are Catholic; Protestants account for 16 percent and Muslims 4 percent.

FESTIVALS
February: Feast of the Igname; March: Festival of the Yam (Kanake holiday); May: Pacific Tempo Music Festival in Nouméa; August: Bourail Fair; September 24: National Day; October: Mwata Days (banana festival) in Pouébo

SHOPPING
Wooden sculptures from Pouébo, jewelry, basketware, woven textiles, necklaces, masks

Nouméa, the principal city of Grande-Terre, has splendid beaches not far from downtown on the twin bays of Vata Cove and the Bay of Citrons. Swimming, diving, and surfing are favorite activities. The **Bélep Archipelago** in the north, the **Isle of Pines** in the south, and **Loyalty Islands** in the east (Lifou, Maré, and Uvea) are similar to Grande-Terre. Besides beaches, these islands offer a range of water sports such as diving and windsurfing. On Lifou Island, the southern winter is whale-watching time, especially humpback whales. All of New Caledonia is considered an extraordinary bird area, rich in parakeet species.

▶ LANDSCAPE AND CULTURAL HERITAGE

The northern province is noted for its characteristic grasslands, niaoulis (endemic trees with white trunks), wetlands, mountains, rivers, and waterfalls. The forest with the "heart of Voh"—dense vegetation shaped like a heart, made famous by a photograph by Yann Arthus-Bertrand—is visible only from the sky.

The Hienghène region in the northeast offers swimming and diving and the opportunity to meet with native people. Tour operators can book lodging in traditional village homes, bringing visitors together with the locals to learn more about Melanesian culture.

The southern province is the land of "stockmen," who herd cattle on horseback. The area around Sarraméa is the land of Kanak tribes, and the forests there are perfect for walking tours. South of Nouméa is another remarkable region, with Lake Yaté, the falls of La Madeleine, and Mont-Dore. The rare kagu, an endemic bird of the archipelago, nests in the watershed zone of Rivière Bleue Provincial Park.

The Isle of Pines is noted for its beaches, but also for its extraordinary flora (the tall native pines, *Araucaria columnaris;* sandalwood trees; wild orchids) and the impressive Queen Hortense cave.

NEW CALEDONIA
(France)

Bélep Islands

Pacific Ocean

Loyalty Islands

Uvea
Lifou
Grande-Terre
Maré
NOUMÉA
Lake Yaté
Mont-Dore
Isle of Pines

0   100 km
0   100 mi

▶ COASTS

Grande-Terre, the main island of this French overseas territory in the Pacific Ocean, is surrounded by a 500-mile-long coral reef, which forms the longest lagoon in the world, rich in tropical fish. From the southern tip all the way to the bays of Poum in the north, sandy white beaches and rocky coves follow one after the other. The east coast is only slightly different because of its higher rainfall.

When to Go		
	CLIMATE	DIVING
JANUARY		
FEBRUARY		
MARCH		
APRIL	☼	
MAY	☼	
JUNE		
JULY		✔
AUGUST		✔
SEPTEMBER		
OCTOBER	☼	
NOVEMBER	☼	
DECEMBER		

New Zealand

The first Maori called these islands Aotearoa, the "land of the long white cloud." The country offers all kinds of activities, such as fishing, surfing, and above all hiking in unspoiled nature, where the white of the sheep's wool contrasts with the green of the forests at the foot of the mountains, and where glaciers, volcanoes, and geysers enliven the countryside.

▶ LANDSCAPE

In New Zealand, nature is the main attraction. Mountains, glaciers, forests, and lakes invite hiking, or skiing in winter, in an unspoiled landscape protected by strict laws. The North Island is also called "Smoking Island" because around **Rotorua,** a city marked by Maori culture, steam rises up from hot springs, the Waimangu "cauldron" (a boiling lake born of an eruption at the beginning of the 20th century), the Lady Knox Geyser at Waiotapu, and the Pohutu Geyser at Whakarewarewa, whose jet can rise to more than 100 feet. **Tongariro National Park**—with popular hiking routes and ski trails—is overshadowed by **Ruapehu,** the highest volcano in the country.

The South Island, also known as the Jade Island, is the larger of the two major islands. Its heart is

the Southern Alps, whose beautiful scenery includes glaciers (Franz Josef, Fox, Tasman) in **Westland National Park** near Mont Cook and waterfalls (Sutherland Falls, cascading in three levels for 1,900 feet, among the highest in the world). In addition, the South Island has **Nelson Lakes National Park** and **Paparoa National Park** with the Punakaiki Pancake Rocks. In the vicinity of Queenstown, skiing and rafting are popular.

▶ WILDLIFE

New Zealand is famous for the flightless kiwi, a protected species, and many other species of birds, particularly in Fiordland National Park. More prosaically, the country has a ratio of 20 sheep for every person.

Sperm whales, humpback whales, orcas, and dolphins frolic off the Kaikoura Peninsula.

Traveler's Notebook

MAIN CONTACTS
Embassy of New Zealand
37 Observatory Circle, NW
Washington, DC 20008
(202) 328-4800
www.nzembassy.com/usa/
www.tourism.govt.nz
New Zealand High Commission
New Zealand House
80 Haymarket
London SW1Y 4TQ, UK
+ 44 (0) 20 7930 8422
www.nzembassy.com/uk/

TRAVEL DOCUMENTS FOR U.S. & U.K. CITIZENS
Passport

TRAVEL TIME TO DESTINATION & TIME DIFFERENCE
New York to Auckland: 21 hours 5 minutes connecting flight; EST +17. London to Auckland: 23 hours 45 minutes connecting flight; GMT +12

AVERAGE TRIP COST
$3,810/£2,460 for 21 days of touring

LANGUAGE & CURRENCY
Maori has joined English as an official language. Currency: New Zealand dollar

POPULATION
4,115,800 inhabitants. One person in ten is Maori, descended from people coming from Polynesia. Capital: Wellington

RELIGION
Anglicans (24 percent), Presbyterians (18 percent), Catholics (15 percent), Methodists,

and Baptists are the largest denominations.

FESTIVALS
February 6: Waitangi Day; February: Wine festival at Waiheke Island; June: Matariki, in honor of kite fliers, on the occasion of the Maori New Year

SHOPPING
Sheepskin garments, pottery, basketry, and Maori objects

In New Zealand, nature harmoniously mixes tropical vegetation and volcanoes.

▶ COASTS

The coast of the Tasman Sea is carved out by fjords on the west side (Fiordland). **Milford Sound** is the most accessible and most beautiful one, extending for more than 12 miles into a landscape flanked by sheer rock faces that rise to 3,900 feet.

The country boasts more than 3,000 miles of coastline, with relatively cold waters. The **Coromandel Peninsula** on the North Island has the best beaches for swimming and surfing. Other good beaches are at Hawkes Bay and the port of **Napier.** On the South Island, the city of **Nelson**, on Tasman Bay, is also a popular beach resort. North of Christchurch, dolphins and whales can be seen, and fishing enjoys great popularity there.

Isolated **Tokelau** consists of three tiny atolls (less than 5 square miles) in the South Pacific Ocean, north of Samoa, with a population of 2,000. The people are of Polyncsian origin, but are British subjects and New Zealand citizens since 1948. Tourism has not really become established there, and the islands are little known except perhaps to coconut merchants.

▶ CITIES AND CULTURAL HERITAGE

Christchurch, the "garden city," looks very English; **Dunedin** has Scottish appeal; and **Wellington** boasts colonial houses, the Wellington City and Sea Museum with a reconstruction of Capt. James Cook's ship, and the new Museum of New Zealand Te Papa Tongarewa on the waterfront.

The city of **Auckland,** built on an isthmus, features a museum with important Maori exhibits. In the north as in the south, New Zealand is marked by Maori culture, which is being treated with new respect.

When to Go		
	CLIMATE	WINTER SPORTS SOUTH ISLAND
JANUARY	☼	
FEBRUARY	☼	
MARCH	☼	
APRIL		
MAY		
JUNE		
JULY		❄
AUGUST		❄
SEPTEMBER	☼	❄
OCTOBER	☼	❄
NOVEMBER	☼	
DECEMBER	☼	

Advice

▪ **Pros**

• Simply a hymn to nature, which, moreover, is respected and protected.

▪ **Cons**

• New Zealand is at the far end of the world. The country has a long rainy season, and it is winter during the Northern Hemisphere's prime vacation season. Between December and February, however, the sun makes itself felt.

What to See and Do in Niger

▶ **LANDSCAPE AND EXCURSIONS**

- Camel treks in the Aïr Mountains
- Crossing the Ténéré desert in an all-terrain vehicle
- Cruising down the Niger River

▶ **WILDLIFE**

- Elephants, lions, antelopes, baboons, hippos

▶ **PREHISTORIC SITES**

- Rock paintings in the Aïr Mountains and Djado Plateau

▶ **FESTIVALS**

- Festival of the Bororo tribe

This is the mythical Sahara, the desert of the Azalai trail and the Ténéré Tree.

Niger

Niger is where the Ténéré Desert spreads out, the most barren and most mythical region of the Sahara. But travelers find adventure and points of interest in the Aïr Mountains, where Neolithic rock engravings can be seen. In the far south, budding explorers can track wild animals or float down the Niger River.

Traveler's Notebook

MAIN CONTACTS

Embassy of Niger
2204 R Street, NW
Washington, DC
20008
(202) 483-4224
http://embassyof
niger.org
www.niger-
tourisme.com
*Embassy of the
Republic of Niger*
154, rue de
Longchamp
75116 Paris, France
+ 33 (0) 1 45 04
80 60
www.niger-
embassyuk.org

**TRAVEL DOCUMENTS
FOR U.S. & U.K.
CITIZENS**
Passport and visa

HEALTH ISSUES
Yellow fever
immunization is
required, and
malaria prophylaxis
is indispensable.

**TRAVEL TIME TO
DESTINATION & TIME
DIFFERENCE**
New York to Nia-
mey: 15 hours 30
minutes connec-
ting flight; EST +6.
London to Niamey:
8 hours connecting
flight; GMT +1

AVERAGE TRIP COST
$1,150/£750 for a
week in the desert

**LANGUAGE &
CURRENCY**
Official language:
French. Other

languages: Hausa,
which borrows
much from Ara-
bic, is widely spo-
ken; other dialects
include Songhai,
Fulfulde, Tamajeq,
and Kanuri.
Currency: CFA franc

POPULATION
Of the 12,895,000
inhabitants, a little
more than half are
Hausas; minority
groups include Zar-
mas, Songhais, Ful-
ani, Tuaregs, and
Kanuris. Capital:
Niamey

RELIGION
85 percent Muslim;
a minority of
animists

FESTIVALS
January: Tabaski
Sheep Festival;
mid-January: Hot-
tungo (Meeting
of Breeders); July
or August (end
of Ramadan): Eid
al-Fitr; Septem-
ber: Gerewol festi-
val; December 18:
National Holiday

SHOPPING
Tuareg silver
jewelry, wood car-
vings, leatherwork,
pearls, and semi-
precious stones

before the infinite desert expanse. Today—the political situation permitting—travelers can easily reenact this mythical trek in an all-terrain vehicle.

Another attraction is the **Niger River.** Traveling down the river in a motorized pinnace offers leisurely views of little islands populated only by birds, of the seasonal migration of herds led by Fula people, and of markets and fishermen's villages. Hippos deign to show themselves at times. Someone who has the time can visit the mud-brick villages by pirogue *(zirdji),* which serves as a water taxi.

Some three hours from Niamey, in Ayorou, the Sunday market with a great selection of goods is among the best in sub-Saharan Africa.

▶ LANDSCAPE AND EXCURSIONS

North of Agadez in the Sahara is the region favored by the Tuareg: the **Aïr Mountains** massif, with the Blue Mountains (the Bagzane Plateau with its 6,000-foot-high Mount Greboun), mountain oases, and the Arakao "crab claw" dunes. A camel trek—a *méharée*—or a hike in combination with an all-terrain-vehicle ride leads visitors past hot springs, lakes, granite peaks, and palm groves to villages nestled along the wadis.

At the foot of the Aïr Massif, the **Ténéré desert** spreads across several hundred miles. There was a time when, after many months of preparation, fans of desert travel would equip a small car and travel from Agadez to Dirkou, following the semiannual salt caravan route—the Azalai between the Aïr Mountains and Bilma Oasis, passing at the halfway mark the famous Ténéré Tree (now replaced by a metal sculpture) at the last well

▶ WILDLIFE

In the W National Park (or Tapoa), south of Niamey, where the Niger River meanders in a W-shape, visitors can go on safari to see elephants, lions, antelopes, giraffes, baboons, and hippopotamuses. The best months to go are from

When to Go			
	HIKING IN THE DESERT	WILDLIFE W NATIONAL PARK	PHOTOGRAPHY IN THE SOUTH
JANUARY	🚶		
FEBRUARY	🚶	🐾	
MARCH	🚶	🐾	
APRIL	🚶	🐾	
MAY			
JUNE			
JULY			
AUGUST			✇
SEPTEMBER			✇
OCTOBER	🚶		✇
NOVEMBER	🚶		
DECEMBER	🚶		

February to April, near the end of the dry season.

▶ PREHISTORIC SITES

The fascinating rock engravings and cave art in the **Aïr Mountains** and on the **Djado Plateau** are vestiges of the Neolithic age (many are of large mammals long since absent in the region). The National Museum of Niger in Niamey exhibits hundred-million-year-old fossils collected from all over Africa.

▶ FESTIVALS

The Bororo people, a subgroup of the Fulani, are herders who make their living from the cattle. In September, at the end of the rainy season, they honor the blessings of the season and celebrate the Gerewol, a festival with dances, parades in costumes, and ritualistic games of seduction between men and women.

In the Lofoten Islands near the Arctic Circle, life in the fishing villages is hardly touched by tourism.

Is it any surprise that the word fjord *is of Norwegian origin? These ancient glacial valleys, filled in by the sea, are what Norway is known for, with more than a thousand miles of them along the coast. But the fjords aren't the only attractions; the Lofoten Islands, the North Cape, and, of course, the midnight sun are serious competitors.*

Norway

▶ LANDSCAPE AND EXCURSIONS

Fjords are almost synonymous with Norway. These natural curiosities are long, narrow inlets between steep cliffs, repeated hundreds of times along the coast. The water shimmers alternately deep blue and soft green, sometimes with the reflection of a glacier.

The most famous fjords are in the south, in the vicinity of Bergen: the **Hardangerfjord**, the **Sognefjord** (the longest and deepest), and the **Nordfjord**. Also at the top of the list is the **Geirangerfjord**, a kind of glacial trough surrounded by snowcapped mountains, with long cascades falling from its steep walls.

Numerous lakes dot the interior, flanked by mountains reaching to more than 6,000 feet, which

Traveler's Notebook

MAIN CONTACTS *Royal Norwegian Embassy* 2720 34th Street, NW Washington, DC 20008 (202) 333-6000 www.norway.org *Royal Norwegian Embassy* 25 Belgrave Square London SW1X 8QD, UK + 44 (0) 20 7591 5500 www.norway.org.uk	**TRAVEL DOCUMENTS FOR U.S. & U.K. CITIZENS** Passport **TRAVEL TIME TO DESTINATION & TIME DIFFERENCE** New York to Oslo: 9 hours 5 minutes connecting flight; EST +6. London to Oslo: 2 hours 5 minutes nonstop flight; GMT +1	**AVERAGE TRIP COST** $2,540/£1,640 for 13 days of cruising **LANGUAGE & CURRENCY** Official languages: Norwegian and Sami; Bokmal and Nynorsk are the two variations of Norwegian. English is also widely used. Currency: Norwegian krone	**POPULATION** 4,628,000 inhabitants (including 20,000 Sami), with a low population density. Capital: Oslo **RELIGION** 90 percent Lutheran **FESTIVALS** April and May: Sami weddings; May 17: National Holiday; July 20: Olsok (Flag Day in honor of King	Olav); December 13: St. Lucia Day **SHOPPING** Painted wooden craft items, wool sweaters, and figurines of trolls—the goblins of Scandinavian stories—as well as Norwegian salmon

What to See and Do in Norway

▶ **LANDSCAPE AND EXCURSIONS**

- Fjords (Hardangerfjord, Sognefjord, Nordfjord, Geirangerfjord)
- National parks and winter sport areas (Jotunheimen, Rondane, Hardangervidda)
- Midnight sun, Northern Lights
- Lofoten Islands, Lapland, North Cape, Spitsbergen

▶ **CITIES AND MONUMENTS**

- Bergen, Oslo, Lillehammer
- Stave churches (Heddal, Lom, Ringebu, Røldal)

Advice

■ **Pros**

- Special attractions in majestic surroundings: fjords, midnight sun, Northern Lights. Thanks to the Gulf Stream, some of the finest cruising in northern Europe, not to mention access to Spitsbergen.

■ **Cons**

- Norway is expensive, reflecting a country with one of the highest standards of living in Europe.

■ **Special Tip**

- The "Coastal Express," which sails from Bergen to Kirkenes in six days, regardless of the season, long served strictly as the local postal package boat. But tourists are taking advantage of it and use it frequently during the summer.

can be admired in the **Jotunheimen, Rondane,** and **Hardangervidda** national parks, where all forms of skiing have a long tradition. In the summer tourists take long hikes or fish in the many rivers for trout or salmon.

Above the Arctic Circle, the midnight sun shines all night from mid-May to the end of June. In clear weather, the Northern Lights can be seen from November or December until February.

The **Lofoten Islands** are often compared to an Alpine massif plopped into the water. The islands are shaped by mountain peaks and basins, little fjords and gentle pastures, and the cod fishermen's colorful houses built on piles. Fulmars and puffins nest here, and in the fall, orcas swim through the Tysfjord.

Lapland (Finnmark County) is in the far north, where the Sami people and their customs are beginning to yield to modern ways. In the summer, reindeer graze on Ringvassoy Island. For tourists, there are snowmobile and dogsled excursions, and if you travel as far north as Kirkenes,

you can catch king crab and fish or even dive under the ice.

For a long time, the **North Cape** was considered the end of the world, but a flood of determined motorists has made it just another stop on the tour.

Even farther north, **Spitsbergen** is the largest island of the Svalbard archipelago. Here glaciers, icebergs, and black mountains make for dramatic scenery, amplified in spring by a brief but dazzling profusion of blooms. The marine life is a big attraction there.

When to Go			
	FJORDS AND CRUISES	WINTER SPORTS	MIDNIGHT SUN/AURORA BOREALIS
JANUARY		❄	⛷
FEBRUARY		❄	⛷
MARCH		❄	
APRIL		❄	
MAY			⛷
JUNE	⛷		⛷
JULY	⛷		
AUGUST	⛷		
SEPTEMBER			
OCTOBER			
NOVEMBER		❄	⛷
DECEMBER		❄	⛷

▶ **CITIES AND MONUMENTS**

In the 13th century, **Bergen** was an important trading post of the Hanseatic League. In Bryggen, the town's medieval quarter, vestiges of this era can still be found.

The capital, **Oslo,** is rich in museums: In addition to the Munch Museum with art by Edvard Munch, the Academy of Fine Arts has a large collection of Impressionists, and Frogner Park holds the Vigeland Sculpture Park featuring 212 bronze and granite sculptures representing the cycle of life by Gustav Vigeland. The Bigdoy neighborhood is located on a peninsula and features the Viking Ship Museum.

Lillehammer is known for its open-air museum Maihaugen, with some 200 Nordic dwellings.

Some villages still have their medieval wooden churches, called "stave churches," of post and beam construction with raised roofs. The finest examples standing are found in **Heddal, Lom, Ringebu,** and **Røldal.**

What to See and Do in Oman

▶ **LANDSCAPE AND WILDLIFE**

- Jebel Akhdar, Jebel Hajar, wadis

- Wahiba Desert (Arabian Oryx Sanctuary)

- Dhofar, Jebel al-Qamar (frank-incense and myrrh trees), Rub al-Khali

▶ **COASTS**

- Beaches, fishing villages, div-ing (coral)

- Musandam Peninsula, Ras al-Hadd (sea turtles)

▶ **CITIES AND MONUMENTS**

- Muscat, Nizwa, Sur, Rustaq
- Salalah, Sumhuram, Ubar
- Ksurs, forts

Muscat, Oman's capital and port city, extends along the cliff road to Muttrah.

Oman

The rich Sultanate of Oman adheres to a tourism policy that is careful to preserve its authenticity. So far, that has been possible because tourists have been few. But following in the footsteps of the United Arab Emirates, Oman is slowly opening up some of its attractions: its jebels, wadis, shorelines, deserts, and legendary incense trees.

Traveler's Notebook

MAIN CONTACTS
Embassy of the Sultanate of Oman
2535 Belmont Road, NW
Washington, DC 20008
(202) 387-1980
www.oman embassy.net
www.omantourism .gov.om
Embassy of the Sultanate of Oman
167 Queen's Gate
London SW7 5HE, UK
+ 44 (0) 20 7225 0001
www.oman embassy.org.uk

TRAVEL DOCUMENTS FOR U.S. & U.K. CITIZENS
Passport and visa

(issued on arrival)

HEALTH ISSUES
No immunizations required; minor malaria risk in Musandam

TRAVEL TIME TO DESTINATION & TIME DIFFERENCE
New York to Mus-cat: 14 hours 45 minutes connec-ting flight; EST +9.
London to Muscat: 8 hours 45 minutes connecting flight; GMT +4

AVERAGE TRIP COST
$2,540/£1,640 for a 10-day all-terrain excursion

LANGUAGE & CURRENCY
Official language: Arabic; other lan-guages: Baluchi, Mehri, Persian, Urdu, Swahili, and, in the cities, English.
Currency: rail

POPULATION
3,205,000 inhab-itants; foreign workers, mainly Indians, make up 15 percent of the population. Capital: Muscat

RELIGION
75 percent Muslim (with a large major-ity of Ibadites), 13 percent Hindu,

and a minority of Christians

FESTIVALS
January or February: Festi-val of Muscat; July or August (end of Ramadan): Eid al-Fitr, and Khareef in Salalah; Novem-ber 18: National holiday

SHOPPING
The souks offer artisanal goods, gold and silver jewelry, carpets, fabrics, perfumes, and frankincense and myrrh.

▶ LANDSCAPE AND WILDLIFE

Two words characterize the Omani landscape: *jebel* (mountain chain) and wadi (riverbed). West of the capital city Muscat, the **Jebel Akhdar** features canyons, cliffs, fortified mountain villages, and oases (Hamz); to the east, the **Jebel Hajar** has deep canyons alternating with palm groves. At the bottom of these canyons, the riverbeds often feature waterholes; the best known of these is the Wadi Bani Auf with its many oases.

Along the east coast, the ocher and reddish dunes of the **Wahiba Desert** stretch for some 50 miles and are still populated by the Wahabi tribe. Here, the Arabian Oryx Sanctuary is a reserve for the Arabian oryx, the first since these gazelles' extinction in the wild in 1972 and the reintroduction of the species in 1982. Other species in the park are ibex, Arabian wolves, lynx, honey badgers, and caracals.

In the south, the **Dhofar** region is crossed by dizzying canyons. On **Jebel al-Qamar** and Wadi Dawkah grow the rare and legendary frankincense and myrrh trees. Some excursions lead to the edge of the great Saudi desert, the **Rub al-Khali.**

▶ COASTS

The shores see few visitors, and beach tourism remains modest. On the north coast, in the villages, fishermen have preserved their traditional lifestyle. However, the ocean floor and its corals are attracting diving fans. Between the Persian Gulf and the Gulf of Oman, the **Musandam Peninsula**—including the United Arab Emirates—is becoming a tourist hub. Along the coastal road from Muscat to Sur lie many wadis and breeding places for sea turtles, such as **Ras al-Hadd.**

▶ CITIES AND MONUMENTS

Muscat, a capital with many small neighborhoods, extends for 25 miles along the coast. For centuries, this was the center of the frankincense trade. The city is noted for its souks (Muttrah), the two fortress castles (Mirani and Jalali) left from Portuguese colonial times, and the sultan's palace (al-Alam).

Nizwa attracts visitors to its fort and cattle auctions. The city is located in a pretty palm grove near the spectacular Wadi Bani Auf. The historic port of **Sur** was known for the building of wooden dhows, boats used for pearl fishing. **Rustaq** experienced its greatest period during the 17th and 18th centuries under the Yaruba dynasty, when it was the capital city.

Salalah, the capital of Dhofar, is famous for its souks, where the trade in little pebbles of incense resin has flourished for a long time. In the nearby village of **Sumhuram,** where the incense was collected before being sent off in bulk, there are still ruins of a fortress. **Ubar** was once an important center of the Incense Route.

Omani architecture can boast of about a hundred ancient *ksurs* (fortified mud-brick villages), which the government has decided to restore. Many forts are emblematic of the area; the route of the citadels, at the foot of the Jebel Akhdar, passes three of them: Bahla (walls and towers of brick), Birket el-Mouz, and Nizwa.

When to Go			
	CLIMATE	OASES	DIVING
JANUARY	☼		
FEBRUARY	☼		
MARCH	☼		✔
APRIL			✔
MAY			✔
JUNE		✔	
JULY		✔	
AUGUST		✔	
SEPTEMBER		✔	✔
OCTOBER			✔
NOVEMBER	☼		
DECEMBER	☼		

Peru

▶ ARCHAEOLOGICAL SITES

The Inca Empire flourished for half a millennium before falling to the Spanish conquistador Pizarro. Yet the memory of the Inca remains in their majestic ruins, of which the most spectacular is **Machu Picchu,** at 7,972 feet high.

The best way to reach Machu Picchu is by walking the Inca Trail; a faster way is by taking the Andes train from Cusco to Machu Picchu Pueblo (Aguas Calientes). Along the way, visit the sacred valley of Urubamba, with its imposing ruins (Pisac, Ollantaytambo).

Other civilizations predating the Inca have left their mark and can be visited at the archaeological sites of Túcume and Sipán (pyramids) and the small town of **Lambayeque,** where the Archaeological Museum contains a royal tomb (the only one of its kind); the ceremonial center of **Pachacámac,** south of Lima; the ten walled citadels of **Chan Chan,** ancient capital of the Chimu civilization (near Trujillo, on the northern coast); and Chavín de Huántar, a religious center with monumental sculptures (north of Lima, in the Cordillera Blanca). Particularly notable are the **Nasca lines,** the work of an artistically rich culture dating from A.D. 450 to 650; these mysterious soil designs (geoglyphs) of geometric shapes and animals measure up to several miles long and attract countless tourists and scientists trying to decipher their meaning.

▶ LANDSCAPE AND EXCURSIONS

The majority of tourist activities involve exploring archaeological sites, the most popular being the **Inca Trail.** Hikers (who should always be with a guide) leave from the outskirts of Cusco and descend stone steps to the trail, which passes through various ancient sites

---

What to See and Do in Peru

▶ **ARCHAEOLOGICAL SITES**
- Inca ruins (Machu Picchu, Cusco)
- Ruins from other civilizations (Lambayeque, Pachacámac, Chan Chan, Chavín de Huántar)
- Nasca lines

▶ **LANDSCAPE AND EXCURSIONS**
- Inca Trail, the Altiplano, Lake Titicaca
- Cordillera Blanca, Huarón, Cordillera Vilcanota, Misti volcano, Maras salt pans
- Ballestas Islands, Amazon rain forest, rafting

▶ **FESTIVALS AND MARKETS**
- Religious festivals, Lima Festival, markets

▶ **CITIES**
- Cusco, Lima, Arequipa, Iquitos

Machu Picchu is seen here in full glory—but this world-famous destination has yet to reveal all its secrets.

(Ollantaytambo), culminating at the zenith, Machu Picchu.

The **Altiplano** offers spectacular views of the valleys and snow-covered peaks surrounding **Lake Titicaca**—the highest navigable lake in the world (12,500 feet), said to be the birthplace of the "children of the sun," the Inca. Boat tours visit the Uros community (Indians who live on floating islands made of reeds) and Taquile Island.

Northwest of Lima is the **Cordillera Blanca**, with 125 miles of glaciers and 30 peaks above 19,000 feet. An equally beautiful destination lies in the lowlands to the south: the rock formations of **Huarón,** which were carved by ice flows after volcanic eruptions.

East of Cusco is the **Cordillera Vilcanota,** its highest peaks reaching about 16,000 feet. To the south, in the Arequipa region, are volcanoes (**Misti**) and canyons (Colca) where lucky tourists may see rare condors. Not far from the Sacred Valley of the Inca are the salt pans of **Maras.**

The cold currents off the Peruvian coastline do not make for ideal

A giant candelabra design is etched on a hill of the Ballestas Islands.

beachgoing. However, there are several interesting beaches and fishing villages near Chiclayo. The **Ballestas Islands** are also home to a wide variety of birds and marine life (whales, sea lions, seals, manta rays). The islands' dark, fertile soil is enriched with guano.

Traveler's Notebook

MAIN CONTACTS

Embassy of Peru
1700 Massachusetts Avenue, NW
Washington, DC 20036
(202) 833-9860
www.peruvianembassy.us
www.peru.info
www.visitperu.com

Embassy of Peru
52 Sloane Street
London SW1X 9SP, UK
+ 44 (0) 20 7235 1917/2545
www.peruembassy-uk.com

TRAVEL DOCUMENTS

For U.S. Citizens: Passport

For U.K. Citizens: Passport and visa

HEALTH ISSUES

No vaccinations are required, but yellow fever vaccine is recommended for travelers to areas of the Amazon below an altitude of 7,500 feet and malaria prophylaxis for areas below 5,000 feet—especially in the Amazon Basin—and the Andean and coastal valleys. In the Altiplano, travelers are advised to take it slowly to adjust to the high elevation and avoid altitude sickness *(soroche).*

TRAVEL TIME TO DESTINATION & TIME DIFFERENCE

New York to Lima: 7 hours 55 minutes nonstop flight; Same as EST. London to Lima: 15 hours 50 minutes connecting flight; GMT –5

AVERAGE TRIP COST

$3,175/£2,050 for 15 days of hiking on the Inca Trail

LANGUAGE & CURRENCY

Official languages: Aymara, Spanish, and Quechua (the Inca language spoken by 40 percent of the population); some English is spoken

Currency: nuevo sol; U.S. dollars preferred in small denominations of cash or travelers' checks

POPULATION

28,675,000 inhabitants, of which almost half are Indian, one out of five living on less than one U.S. dollar per day; the other half are of European, African, or Asian descent. Capital: Lima

RELIGION

92 percent Catholic

FESTIVALS

February: Virgin of Candelaria in Puno; May: Qoyllur Rit'i pilgrimage in Quispicanchis; June: Inti Raymi in Sacsayhuamán; July: Independence Day; October to November: Lima Festival

SHOPPING

Alpaca sweaters, Andean hats, ponchos, pan flutes, and Indian crafts (figurines, mobiles)

Adventure lovers may opt to raft down the sacred Urubamba River, but all visitors to Peru must experience a trip into the **Amazon** rain forest. Long canoes, or *peque-peques,* lead travelers into the "Green Hell," stopping at Puerto Maldonado, Madre de Dios River, and the town of Iquitos.

▶ FESTIVALS AND MARKETS

Atop the tourist's to-do list in South America are the Indian markets and festivals: In Sacsayhuamán, the Inti Raymi (Festival of the Sun) is an Inca ceremony celebrating the winter solstice (June), replete with sacrificial rituals and dances pleading for the return of the sun.

Also in June, in Quispicanchis (a seven-hour bus ride from Cusco), 50,000 faithful make an annual pilgrimage to the shrine of Qoyllur Rit'i, a sacred place, where local legend and Christian beliefs mix.

Not to be missed are the **Lima Festival** (October–November) and the ceremonial dances in Puno honoring the city's patron, the Virgin of Candelaria (February).

▶ CITIES

Cusco (elevation 10,800 feet) was the ancient capital of the Inca Empire and later a colonial city. Cusco's architecture is a combination of Inca ruins and colonial-style structures, which tells the story of a city with two cultures: indigenous and foreign, and the threat to all traces of the former (for example, the Convent of Santo Domingo, built on the remains of the Temple of the Sun). Perhaps the most beautiful city in Peru, Cusco includes such highlights as the Incan stone-masonry of Hatumrumiyoc and the Palace of Inca Roca, with its 12-angled stones; the popular San Blas neighborhood; and the Plaza de Armas. In the distance, the imposing walls of Sacsayhuamán, a former fortress, keep watch over the city.

	When to Go		
	MACHU PICCHU AND ALTIPLANO	LIMA AND COAST	AMAZON REGION
JANUARY		☼	
FEBRUARY		☼	
MARCH		☼	
APRIL			
MAY	☼		
JUNE	☼		
JULY	☼		☼
AUGUST	☼		☼
SEPTEMBER	☼		
OCTOBER			
NOVEMBER			
DECEMBER			

The capital city, **Lima** boasts numerous tourist attractions, including its baroque cathedral, the Church of San Francisco (catacombs and *azulejos,* or tile work), and colonial buildings with their wooden balconies—all in Lima's historical center. The National Archaeological Museum, Gold Museum, and Lorca Museum are also well worth visiting.

In the shadow of the beautiful Misti Volcano, **Arequipa** draws visitors to its churches, the Convent of Santa Catalina, and the Museum of Andean Sanctuaries, whose famous mummy—Juanita the "Ice Maiden"—was discovered intact in 1975.

Lastly, on the edge of the rain forest lies the town of **Iquitos.** Originally an Indian village made rich in modern times from the cultivation of rubber, it is now the departure point for Amazon tours.

The terraced rice fields of Banaue on Luzon are some of the most beautiful in the world.

The Philippines

An archipelago counting more than 7,000 islands and 11,000 miles of coastline, the Philippines is a land of endless beaches and coral reefs.

▶ LANDSCAPE

The terraced rice fields in the mountainous region of **Banaue** on Luzon were established by the ancestors of the Ifugao people and are considered among the most beautiful in the world. The road between Baguio and Bontoc, known as the Mountain Trail, is the highest in the country and offers spectacular panoramic views of the surrounding mountains.

There are 30 volcanoes scattered throughout the Philippines. In 1991, **Mount Pinatubo,** northwest of

---

Traveler's Notebook

MAIN CONTACTS

Embassy of the Philippines
1600 Massachusetts Avenue, NW
Washington, DC 20036
(202) 467-9300
www.philippineembassy-usa.org
www.philtourism.com
www.tourism.gov.ph
Embassy of the Philippines
6–8 Suffolk Street
London SW1Y 4HG, UK
+ 44 (0) 20 7451 1800
www.philembassy-uk.org

TRAVEL DOCUMENTS FOR U.S. & U.K. CITIZENS
Passport

HEALTH ISSUES
No vaccinations required. Malaria prophylaxis necessary for travel to areas below 1,800 feet.

TRAVEL TIME TO DESTINATION & TIME DIFFERENCE
New York to Manila: 20 hours 35 minutes connecting flight; EST +13. London to Manila: 14 hours 25 minutes connecting flight; GMT +8

AVERAGE TRIP COST
$3,175/£2,050 for 15 days of excursions

LANGUAGE & CURRENCY
Official language: Tagalog, also known as Filipino, which has evolved from nearly 100 languages and dialects; other languages: English, some Spanish
Currency: Philippine peso

POPULATION
91,077,000 inhabitants (high density), the majority of Malayan origin, with approximately 20 significant minorities. Capital: Manila

RELIGION
85 percent Catholic; the largest minorities are Aglipayan (members of the Independent Philippine Church), Muslim (of whom 6 million live in Mindanao), and Protestant.

FESTIVALS
January 9: Black Nazarene Festival (Manila); January: Ati-Atihan Festival; February: Chinese New Year; June 12: Independence Day; July or August (end of Ramadan): Eid al-Fitr; August 31: National Heroes Day

SHOPPING
Porcelain, textiles, bamboo and rattan products, and mother-of-pearl items made by local artisans

What to See and Do in the Philippines

▶ **LANDSCAPE**

- Terraced rice fields of Banaue, volcanoes (Pinatubo, Taal, Mayon)
- Chocolate Hills, Pagsanjan Falls, Mindanao (grotto, terraces, Mount Apo)

▶ **COASTS**

- Visayas and Palawan
- Scuba diving at Mindoro and Palawan

▶ **CITIES AND MONUMENTS**

- Manila, Zamboanga, Cebu (churches, forts)

Advice

■ **Pros**

- World-class beaches and a wide variety of water sports for the seasoned traveler, the allure of the islands, a rich cultural life, and reasonable rates.

■ **Cons**

- Airfares are consistently high. Seasonal weather can be problematic for some travelers.

■ **Safety**

- Check in advance for travel advisories to the Sulu Archipelago, Zamboanga Peninsula, and the region west of Mindanao.

Manila, experienced a massive eruption, leaving behind a desert of ash that has since been reshaped by the effects of rain and typhoons. Today hikers enjoy surveying this volcanic landscape. Southwest of the capital, the **Taal Volcano** rises from the lake of the same name. Its beautiful, pure lines are rivaled only by the temperamental **Mount Mayon,** the most active volcano in the Philippines.

On the island of Bohol are the **Chocolate Hills,** the unusual rolling hills that turn dark brown during the rainy season. About 60 miles southeast of Manila are the **Pagsanjan Falls,** where the movie *Apocalypse Now* was filmed.

On **Mindanao,** the main places of interest are the Davao Grotto, Lake Sebu, and terraced rice fields near the village of Bangaan.

Palawan Island deserves a visit to its beaches as well as its interior. North of Palawan, the Calamian Islands are famous for their forests, hot springs, and mangrove swamp; the islands of Busuanga and Coron are known for their coral reefs.

▶ COASTS

The coasts are lined with numerous fine sand beaches and coral beds that are home to a wide variety of tropical fish. Tourists flock to the islands of **Visayas** (Cebu, Bohol, Panay, Boracay) for water sports activities.

The nearby island of **Palawan** is considered one of the most

When to Go		
	CLIMATE	RICE FIELDS ON LUZON
JANUARY	☼	
FEBRUARY	☼	
MARCH	☼	⋞
APRIL	☼	⋞
MAY	☼	
JUNE		
JULY		
AUGUST		
SEPTEMBER		
OCTOBER		
NOVEMBER	☼	⋞
DECEMBER	☼	⋞

beautiful islands of the Far East. Its distinctive black cliffs are dotted with swallows' nests (El Nido region). Zamboanga, with its white sand beaches and coral reefs, is another popular destination.

The Philippines are a well-kept secret among Westerners who enjoy scuba diving (particularly in the Visayas) and other water sports. Aficionados prefer the areas around the island of **Mindoro** (Puerto Galera), at Palawan, at Batangas on Luzon, and in the Mindoro and Bohol straits.

▶ CITIES AND MONUMENTS

Manila lives up to its reputation as an overpopulated, sprawling city. However, its several cultures (predominantly Spanish and American) make it well worth visiting. Spain's long presence in the Philippines left its architectural impact on countless churches and forts. Don't miss the 16th-century intramuros (the old town inside fortified walls), churches, palace, market (Quinto), and Chinatown. In **Zamboanga** and **Cebu,** the architecture reflects these cities' Spanish and Muslim past.

What to See and Do in Poland

▸ **CITIES AND MONUMENTS**

- Krakow, Gdansk, Warsaw
- Malbork, Sandomierz, Szczecin, Torun, Wroclaw, Poznan, Zakopane

▸ **LANDSCAPE AND WILDLIFE**

- Mazury Lakes, Warmia, Pomeranian lakes and waterways
- Sudetes Mountains, High Tatra Mountains (woodworking tradition)
- Bialowieza Forest, Beskidy Mountains (national park)

▸ **COAST**

- Northwest beaches (Sopot, Leba)

Sophisticated Krakow acts as a bridge between the Poland of yesterday and today.

Poland is steadily becoming one of Europe's top tourist destinations—thanks to the enormous appeal of beautiful Krakow, the lakes and forests of the Mazury region, and year-round sports on the High Tatra Mountains.

Poland

▸ **CITIES AND MONUMENTS**

Krakow, considered the most beautiful city in Poland, is also the country's center for arts, culture, and education. Not to be missed are the Grand Place (Rynkek Glowny); Hall of Flags; Gothic, baroque, and Renaissance palaces; 24 churches; Jewish neighborhood of Kazimierz; Wawel Royal Castle; old university; and literary cafés.

Not far from the city are three places of particular interest: the village of Wadowice (birthplace

Traveler's Notebook

MAIN CONTACTS	+ 44 (0) 20 7291 3520	2 hours 25 minutes nonstop flight; GMT +1	**POPULATION**	**FESTIVALS**
Embassy of the Republic of Poland 2640 16th Street, NW Washington, DC 20009 (202) 234-3800 www.washington .polemb.net www.poland.travel/ *Embassy of the Republic of Poland* 47 Portland Place London W1B 1JH, UK	www.london.polemb.net **TRAVEL DOCUMENTS FOR U.S. & U.K. CITIZENS** Passport **TRAVEL TIME TO DESTINATION & TIME DIFFERENCE** New York to Warsaw: 10 hours 45 minutes connecting flight; EST +6. London to Warsaw:	**AVERAGE TRIP COST** $500/£325 for a 4-day weekend in Krakow and Warsaw **LANGUAGE & CURRENCY** Official Language: Polish; other language: English Currency: zloty	38,518,000 inhabitants— a relatively high number considering the 15 million Poles who emigrated (two-thirds to the U.S.) in the 20th century. Capital: Warsaw **RELIGION** 95 percent Catholic	May 3: Constitution Day; July: Chopin Festival in Warsaw; August: Music Festival in Old Town Krakow; November 11: Independence Day **SHOPPING** Jewelry (Baltic amber), hand-painted ceramics, embroidered tablecloths, and fabrics

of Pope John Paul II); the enormous salt mine at Wieliczka; and the infamous Auschwitz concentration camp.

Gdansk, formerly known as Danzig and part of the Hanseatic League, suffered extensive damage in World War II. Visit the Town Hall, St. Mary's Church, half-timbered houses, and mansions of the bourgeoisie (Golden House).

In **Warsaw,** the drab boulevards of the Soviet era are now lined with trendy bars, restaurants, and boutiques. The city's reconstructed center dates back to the Middle Ages and is rich in national heritage, with its Monument to the Heroes of the Warsaw Ghetto Uprising, royal castle and art collection, St. John's Cathedral, baroque palaces (Lazienki and its surrounding park), and 40 museums. Very little remains of the Jewish ghetto, but visitors can follow remembrance tours of former landmarks.

About 30 miles away is the village of Zelazowa Wola, birthplace of Chopin. Visitors can tour the composer's manor house—now a museum—and surrounding park.

Also worth adding to the itinerary are **Malbork** (13th and 14th-century castle), **Sandomierz** (town hall, cathedral, museums), **Szczecin** (Pomeranian Dukes' Castle), **Torun** (Copernicus's birthplace), **Wroclaw** (market square), and **Poznan** (Old Town).

To the south lies **Zakopane,** Poland's largest winter sports area. The region is also famous for its village houses and churches built of the distinctive larch wood.

Advice

- **Pros**
  - Cultural, architectural, and natural points of interest. The tourist infrastructure is steadily improving.

- **Cons**
  - High incidence of theft of foreign cars. Tourist attractions outside the major cities are underpromoted.

- **Special Tip**
  - Beautiful, sophisticated Krakow is a first choice for travelers who want to experience the youthful energy of the new Poland; many choose a combined trip to Krakow and Warsaw.

▶ LANDSCAPE AND WILDLIFE

The **Mazury** region, known as the "Land of a Thousand Lakes," comprises a series of lakes connected by rivers and canals and is the perfect destination for boating, kayaking, fishing, and bird-watching (Pomeranian and white-tailed eagles, black storks). West of Mazury lie the beautiful lakes and forests of the **Warmia** region, near Olsztyn.

Pomerania extends inland from the coast and attracts kayakers and trout fishermen to its numerous lakes and waterways.

To the southwest, the rugged peaks and sheltered valleys of the **Sudetes** and **High Tatra Mountains** are a popular area for hiking, skiing, and thermal spas.

Farther east is the **Bialowieza Forest.** Europe's oldest natural forest, it protects 5,000 species of plants, 12,000 species of birds, wolves, and the last remaining bison on the continent. The **Beskidy Range** also attracts enthusiasts for hiking its mountain and forest trails and viewing wildlife (eagles, bears, bison).

▶ COAST

In spite of the Baltic Sea's chilly temperatures, there are several beach resorts on the coast, including Swinoujscie, Miedzyzdroje (national park on Wolin Island), Kolobrzeg, and most notably **Sopot,** popular for its white sand, long pier, and adjoining forest.

The shores are dotted with natural reserves in which rare flora and birds flourish. Tourists can see an unusual natural phenomenon in **Leba,** where hundreds of sand dunes shift an average of 30 feet every year.

When to Go		
	CLIMATE	FLORA AND BALTIC COAST
JANUARY		
FEBRUARY		
MARCH		
APRIL		
MAY	☼	⋦
JUNE	☼	⋦
JULY	☼	
AUGUST		
SEPTEMBER	☼	⋦
OCTOBER		⋦
NOVEMBER		
DECEMBER		

Portugal

Portugal's many tourist attractions are scattered throughout the country. Visitors are drawn to its unique late Gothic, or Manueline, architecture and the charm of its cities and coasts. Others prefer the isolation of the islands of Madeira and the Azores in the Atlantic. Portugal protects its cultural heritage by emphasizing the importance of the azulejos (tilework) and fados (folk songs) in the Alfama district of Lisbon—one of Europe's most captivating cities.

Lisbon's Belém Tower was built almost 500 years ago, during the reign of King Manuel I.

Mainland Portugal

▶ MONUMENTS

Encouraged by his conquistadores' colonial successes in the late 15th and early 16th centuries, King Manuel I promoted the development of a particular Gothic style of architecture, which became known as Manueline. The most beautiful examples of this period can be found in **Lisbon** (Belém Tower, Jeronimos Monastery), **Tomar** (headquarters of the Order of the Knights Templar; stained-glass window in the Convent of the Order of Christ), **Coimbra** (university chapel gates), and **Batalha** (statuary in Santa Maria da Vitoria Monastery).

Other great architectural sites include **Alcobaça** (Cistercian monastery; tombs of Pedro and Inês,

the "Dead Queen," made famous by novelist Henry de Montherlant) and **Fatima** (pilgrimage site, sanctuary). Throughout the country, baroque art is represented in the gilded wood sculptures and azulejos (colorful ceramic tiles).

There are beautiful azulejos in the **Sintra Palace** (King Ferdinand II's summer residence), which combines Gothic, Egyptian, Moorish, and Renaissance styles. Surrounding the sumptuous palace are lovely

What to See and Do in Mainland Portugal

▶ MONUMENTS
- Manueline architecture (Lisbon, Tomar, Coimbra, Batalha)
- Alcobaça, Fatima
- Sintra Palace (baroque art, azulejos)

▶ CITIES
- Lisbon, Porto, Evora, Coimbra,
- Braga, Guimarães, Lamego, Obidos, Viana do Castelo

▶ COASTS
- Algarve, Nazaré, Peniche
- Berlengas Islands
- Arrábida Mountains

▶ LANDSCAPE AND FLORA
- Algarve, Douro Valley

Sintra Palace, the former residence of Ferdinand II, combines many architectural styles.

gardens and churches, which complete the tour of this must-see town near Lisbon.

▶ CITIES

Built on seven hills, each with its own neighborhood, **Lisbon** is one of the most beautifully situated cities in Europe. Numerous viewpoints and funicular rides offer travelers ample opportunities for stunning panoramas of the city. Lisbon has seen many changes in the past several years, the most important being the transformation of the docks *(docas)* into a trendy bar and nightclub area.

In addition to visiting the Manueline-style monuments, tourists should not miss Rossio and Commerce Squares, Saint George's Castle, the churches (baroque Madre de Deus Church; Carmo Church, its nave destroyed by an earthquake in 1755), the museums (Chiado Contemporary Art Museum, National Tile Museum, Calouste Gulbenkian Museum), the palaces (Queluz National Palace, Fronteira Palace), the botanical gardens at the Polytechnical Institute, the Monument to the Discoveries with Henry the Navigator

Traveler's Notebook

MAIN CONTACTS

Embassy of Portugal
2012 Massachusetts Avenue, NW
Washington, DC 20008
(202) 328-8610
www.visitportugal.com
Embassy of Portugal
11 Belgrave Square
London SW1X 8PP, UK
+ 44 (0) 20 7235 5331

TRAVEL DOCUMENTS FOR U.S. & U.K. CITIZENS

Passport

TRAVEL TIME TO DESTINATION & TIME DIFFERENCE

New York to Lisbon: 7 hours 50 minutes nonstop flight; EST +5. London to Lisbon: 2 hours 30 minutes nonstop flight; GMT

AVERAGE TRIP COST

$1,150/£750 for a week's beach vacation in the Algarve

LANGUAGE & CURRENCY

Official language:

Portuguese; other languages: English, French Currency: euro

POPULATION

10,643,000 inhabitants, in a relatively homogeneous populace; 252,000 live in the Azores, and 267,400 in Madeira (one-third of whom live in Funchal, the capital of the island). Capital: Lisbon

RELIGION

Nine out of ten

Portuguese are Catholic, and there are Jewish and Muslim minorities.

FESTIVALS

February: Fado Festival in Lisbon; May: Festival of Roses in Minho; June 10: Portugal Day; August 15: Processions in Viana do Castelo in honor of Nossa Senhora de Agonia

SHOPPING

Among the original souvenirs are ceramic

roosters from Barcelos, azulejo-painted ceramic tiles from the markets of Alfama, and Port wine from Porto (after visiting the wine cellars there); other choices include jewelry (gold), leather goods, porcelain, lace, and pottery from the Algarve.

Water, boats, and hillside houses create a charming setting for Porto, the home of port wine.

at the prow, Monsanto Castle and park, Santa Clara flea market, the old streets of the Bairro Alto, and especially the Alfama neighborhood, where an experienced traveler can hear the music of real fados performed in clubs. Visitors can get a feel for modern-day Lisbon in the Park of Nations, with its Oceanarium—the largest oceanic exhibit in the world and site of Expo 1998.

Porto is not as famous as Lisbon, but is perhaps more typically Portuguese. Traditional sites include the old town, where terraced houses line the Douro River; Oporto Cathedral and cloister (azulejos, mosaics); the baroque Saõ Francisco church; the magnificent Stock Exchange Palace and its Arab Room; Serra do Pilar Monastery; Torre dos Clerigos (views of

the city); and on the other side of Maria Pia Bridge, the Nova de Gaia wine lodges, where a Port wine tasting can make a traveler happy.

Evora, with its Moorish architecture, stands at the edge of the Alentejo region. Farther north is **Coimbra** and its three main attractions: the 12th-century Romanesque cathedral, 11th-century university (Manueline chapel with azulejos, baroque library), and the Queima das Fitas student festival in May.

Other interesting cities to add to the itinerary are: **Braga** (Bom Jesus do Monte shrine, where pilgrims climb the baroque stairs on their knees); **Guimarães** (fortified castle with unusual facades and tilework, belonging to the Dukes of Braganza); **Lamego** (entrance

to the Douro Valley, sanctuary of Nossa Senhora dos Remedios); **Obidos** (medieval town surrounded by

When to Go			
	MAINLAND	MADEIRA	AZORES WHALES-WATCHING
JANUARY			
FEBRUARY			
MARCH			
APRIL	☼	⋖	✔
MAY	☼	⋖	✔
JUNE	☼	☼	✔
JULY	☼	☼	✔
AUGUST	☼	☼	✔
SEPTEMBER	☼	☼	✔
OCTOBER	☼		
NOVEMBER			
DECEMBER			

crenellated ramparts); and **Viana do Castelo** (grand parade of flower-bedecked floats during the August 15 festival).

▶ COASTS

The **Algarve** and its many coastal sites (Portimão, Albufeira, Faro, and especially Praia da Rocha) extend far to the south along a hundred miles of shoreline with beaches, inlets, and some of the best golf courses in Europe. To the west rise the great promontories of Sagres and Cape St.

such as **Nazaré,** where the old tradition of fishermen using oxen to pull their brightly colored boats from the sea has become a popular tourist attraction.

Add to the itinerary the Aveiro Lagoon; **Peniche** and its citadel; the **Berlengas Islands,** where the underwater tunnels and caves create the perfect place for underwater fishing; and the **Arrábida Mountains** (near Setúbal), where the sea has carved inlets and caves into the white cliffs.

azulejos and mosaics (Tavira), and Moorish architecture (Silvès Cathedral). In short, the Algarve is a year-round destination.

To the north are the plains of the Alentejo—a great, rolling expanse of wheat fields, punctuated by cork oak and olive trees. Opposite the Alentejo, the **Douro Valley** displays its terraced vineyards and farms *(quintas),* which have rebounded in recent years, thanks to the popularity of river cruises in the region.

A tranquil scene in the Aveiro and Beira Alta neighborhood, in the south of Porto

Vincent—the westernmost point in Europe, where travelers can watch spectacularly fierce waves crashing into the rocks.

The Atlantic coast does not get very hot in summer (several degrees cooler than the Mediterranean in the same season). The coastal resorts distinguish themselves by their activities: Cascais is ideal for surfing, Estoril for golf. There are other interesting spots,

▶ LANDSCAPE AND FLORA

Portugal is never as beautiful as in springtime, when the abundant flowers are in bloom. In the **Algarve,** the churches with their colorful azulejos are surrounded by flowering almond and mimosa trees. The Algarve is much more than a beach destination. The region is famous for a special quality of light, unique vegetation, whitewashed villages, baroque churches adorned with

The Azores

▶ LANDSCAPE AND HIKES

Located 750 miles from Lisbon and 1,250 miles from the United States, the Azores can boast of a number of tourist attractions besides their clear skies. Travelers will be delighted by the beautiful landscape—shaped by the islands' volcanic origins—and unique flora (including hydrangeas, which carpet the islands with color by the end of June). Roads and trails cross the hilly, lush terrain and offer hikers a wide variety of interesting sights, such as Faial Island (Capelhinos Point, Caldeira) and São Jorge Island (central peaks, Pico da Esperança Natural Forest Reserve). The islands' picturesque parishes *(fajãs)* comprise fields and meadows dotted with white cottages along the ocean.

On Pico Island, hikers will find their calves put to the test on the ascent of the legendary **Ponta do**

The Algarve is famous for its beaches, such as this one in Lagos, but its villages—with their white walls and blue window shutters—are also charming.

Hydrangeas, the emblematic flowers of the Azores, bloom in late June and July.

Pico, the country's highest peak (7,713 feet). There are splendid and unforgettable views of the Grupo Central from the summit.

The birds (seagulls, chaffinches) may be shy, but the flora is a riot of color: hydrangeas and special varieties of heather and knotweed (polygonum).

A curiosity: The reputed center of high atmospheric pressure above the Azores is over the westernmost Florès Islands, where it's usually rainy, but nature is always in bloom.

▶ **COASTS**

The islands' relatively cool climate and rocky beaches do not make for a premier beach destination: Sand is nonexistent, and good weather is never guaranteed. However, sailing and scuba diving are popular activities near **Horta,** the main town in the Faial Islands and a port of call for sailors en route to the Antilles. Whale-watching (blues, humpbacks, sperms, rorquals, dolphins)

is a highlight in this region of the Atlantic. In 1987, a law was passed banning sperm whale hunting; their teeth and bones were coveted for making the engravings called scrimshaw. Excursions by Zodiacs are worthwhile, especially from Pico Island and its small coastal town, **Lajes do Pico,** where there is an interesting Whaling Museum.

Madeira

Off the coast of Morocco and approximately 600 miles southwest of Lisbon is the archipelago of Madeira. Formed by volcanic eruptions, these islands are a favorite spot for nature lovers and hikers. Thanks to the Gulf Stream, Madeira benefits from a consistently temperate climate (between 65 and 77 degrees Fahrenheit) and is the most lush of all the Atlantic islands. It is called the "Island of Eternal Spring" and has become an alternative to the more crowded

What to See and Do on Portugal's Islands

The Azores

▶ **LANDSCAPE AND HIKES**

• Lava fields, volcanoes, Ponta do Pico

▶ **COASTS**

• Sailing, scuba diving (Horta), whale-watching (Lajes do Pico)

Madeira

▶ **LANDSCAPE AND HIKES**

• Volcanic landscape, canals, trails

▶ **COASTS**

• Fishing

A typical view of the "eternal spring" in Funchal on Madeira

Spanish Canary Islands (especially in summer).

▶ LANDSCAPE AND HIKES

Madeira is also called the "Garden of the Atlantic." Springtime brings forth a burst of flowers (amaryllis, azaleas, bougainvillea, camellias) on the terraces of Monte Palace Tropical Gardens in Funchal, with its superb panoramic views.

The volcanic landscape lends itself to walking tours—often along cliffs. Nearly 1,200 miles of trails along irrigation canals *(levadas)* provide countless itineraries for serious hikes, for example, from Santana to the summit of Ruivo Peak—a difficult hike, but the spectacular view from the top is a just reward.

▶ COASTS

Madeira's picturesque and rugged coastline does not have sandy beaches; nevertheless visitors can still swim and enjoy many water sports year round on the southern coast. Some 25 miles from Madeira, the small island of Porto Santo boasts nearly six miles of fine sand beaches and is said to be the place where Christopher Columbus landed.

Deep-sea fishing is popular, as is golf—in particular on the sloping greens near Funchal.

Advice

■ **Pros**
  • A country that combines many assets: beautiful scenery, typical villages, important monuments, and beaches that are not overcrowded.

■ **Cons**
  • The Atlantic Ocean is chilly, even in summer.

■ **Safety**
  • No particular risks

■ **Special Tip**
  • Take a weeklong cruise on the Douro River, where the steep hills are covered in vineyards and travelers can taste fine-quality port in the local wine cellars.

The small village of Hell-Bourg, in the heart of Réunion's Cirque de Salazie, is an adventurer's dream destination.

Réunion

Réunion in the Indian Ocean, nicknamed the "Intense Island," was born from a volcanic eruption that created its unusual landscape of valleys, waterfalls, calderas, and volcanic terrain. Thanks to an extensive network of trails, an adventurous traveler can experience all that this lush and verdant island offers—well beyond its beaches.

Traveler's Notebook

MAIN CONTACTS
Embassy of France
4101 Reservoir Road, NW
Washington, DC 20007
(202) 944-6000
www.ambafrance-us.org
www.reunion.fr
Embassy of France
58 Knightsbridge
London SW1X 7JT, UK
+ 44 (0) 20 7073 1000
www.ambafrance-uk.org

TRAVEL DOCUMENTS FOR U.S. & U.K. CITIZENS
Passport

HEALTH ISSUES
No vaccinations required

TRAVEL TIME TO DESTINATION & TIME DIFFERENCE
New York to St.-Denis: 22 hours 20 minutes connecting; EST +9. London to St.-Denis: 17 hours 45 minutes connecting; GMT +4

AVERAGE TRIP COST
$1,900/£1,230 for 10 days of excursions

LANGUAGE & CURRENCY
Official languages: Réunion Creole and French
Currency: euro

POPULATION
784,000 inhabitants. The majority of the population is young and of mixed race (Cafres), Malabars (Indians), Zarabes, and Malagasy peoples. There are approximately 20,000 mainland French citizens (called Z'oreilles, meaning "ears," for frequently asking Creole speakers to repeat themselves). Capital: St.-Denis

RELIGION
The majority (90 percent) of the population are Catholic; Muslims, Hindus, and Buddhists make up the remainder.

FESTIVALS
January: Cavadee (Tamil festival), and the Honey Festival in Tampon; October: Diwali (Festival of Lights); December: firewalking in St.-Paul; December 20: Abolition of Slavery Festival

SHOPPING
Lace and embroidery from Cilaos

What to See and Do in Réunion

▶ **LANDSCAPE AND HIKES**

- Calderas (Cirques de Mafate, Salazie, Cilaos), Piton des Neiges, Piton de la Fournaise
- Hiking trails, horseback riding, motorcycle and 4x4 riding, golfing

▶ **COASTS**

- St.-Gilles, Boucan-Canot St.-Leu (scuba diving),
- Deep-sea fishing, surfing

▶ **FLORA**

- A wide variety of trees and flowers

▶ LANDSCAPE AND HIKES

Three of the most unusual sites on the island are the volcanic calderas **Cirques de Mafate** (the most remote), **Salazie,** and **Cilaos** (impressive "Marvelous Rock"). These are best seen by helicopter to appreciate their dramatic beauty. Explore the region's waterfalls, forests, moonlike volcanic terrain, and isolated villages *(îlets)* for an unforgettable experience.

Looming over the calderas are the **Piton des Neiges** (Snow Peak) and **Piton de la Fournaise** (Peak of the Furnace). Their trails are relatively easy for the average hiker and offer panoramic views. The volcano is no longer dormant and periodically spews lava. Witnessing the spectacle of lava flowing into the sea has become the ultimate tourist attraction.

A network of 500 miles of trails extends throughout the island, inviting tourists to explore the abundant valleys and rivers on horseback, motorcycle, or four-wheel-drive vehicles. The

ST.-DENIS
Boucan-Canot
Cirque de Mafate
Cirque de Salazie
St.-Benoît
St.-Gilles-les-Bains
Piton des Neiges 3,069
St. Leu
Cirque de Cilaos
RÉUNION (France)
St.-Louis
Piton de la Fournaise 2,631
St.-Joseph
Indian Ocean
0 15 km
0 15 mi

mountainous terrain attracts more adventurous travelers for paragliding, rock climbing, mountain biking, and rafting. Golf is also available.

▶ COASTS

The beaches are not the primary attraction on Réunion. Volcanic eruptions have left only about 18 miles of open beaches on the western and southern coasts, where a lagoon protects the land from dangerously high tides. The most popular beaches are around **St.-Gilles** and the Bay of **Boucan-Canot.** The main water sports are scuba diving, surfing (both at **St.-Leu**), and windsurfing. The ports of St.-Gilles and St.-Pierre offer deep-sea fishing (high season in October and May).

When to Go

	CLIMATE	FLORA
JANUARY		✿
FEBRUARY		✿
MARCH		
APRIL		
MAY	☼	
JUNE	☼	
JULY	☼	
AUGUST	☼	
SEPTEMBER	☼	✿
OCTOBER	☼	✿
NOVEMBER	☼	✿
DECEMBER		✿

Advice

Pros

- A good variety of sports and leisure activities, and favorable weather year-round. The threat from the Chikungunya epidemic has ended.

Cons

- Few sites of architectural interest. Beaches are not a high point. Airfares spike in the high season.

Safety

- No major security problems

Special Tips

- Book a seven-day car rental when purchasing a round-trip airline ticket. For local flavor, stay at the island's charming inns or bed-and-breakfasts. Combined trips to Réunion and Mauritius are very popular.

▶ FLORA

Réunion's tropical environment produces abundant flora, including 600 species of trees and 800 species of flowers, many of which are orchids. The region of Les Hauts is famous for its flowers (vetiver, ylang-ylang, cardamom, flamboyant tree, bougainvillea, azalea), which were an important commodity on the Spice Route. The island's passion for plants and flowers is evident in its numerous botanical gardens and museums: the Garden of Eden (L'Hermitage-les-Bains), Vanilla House (St.-André), and Stella-Matutina Agriculture Museum (near St.-Leu) devoted to Réunion's botanical history.

The Bucovina region is famous for its painted monasteries.

■■ *The Black Sea may be Romania's primary tourist attraction, but visits to the lesser known highlights of the Bucovina monasteries, Danube Delta, Bucharest, and Sibiu complement the tour.*

Romania

What to See and Do in Romania

▶ **MONUMENTS**

- Monasteries (Bucovina, Bucharest, Iasi)
- Transylvania (Dracula legend)

▶ **COAST**

- Black Sea (Neptun, Olimp)

▶ **LANDSCAPE AND HIKES**

- Carpathian, Maramures, Apuseni, and Bucegi Mountains (hiking, skiing)

▶ **WILDLIFE**

- Danube Delta Biosphere Reserve (birds, fish, plants)

▶ **MONUMENTS**

The northern region of **Bucovina** is famous for five 16th-century monasteries (Voronet, Moldovita, Humor, Sucevita, and Arbore) that are part of the country's architectural heritage.

Bucharest is perhaps best known for its enormous Palace of the Parliament (also known as the Palace of the People), which was built during the infamous Ceausescu regime—tragically at the expense of the most beautiful old neighborhoods and

Traveler's Notebook

MAIN CONTACTS

Embassy of Romania
1607 23rd Street, NW
Washington, DC 20008
(202) 332-4846
http://washington.mae.ro
www.romaniatourism.com
Embassy of Romania
4 Palace Green
London W8 4QD, UK
+ 44 (0) 20 7937 9666
http://londra.mae.ro

TRAVEL DOCUMENTS FOR U.S. & U.K. CITIZENS
Passport

HEALTH ISSUES
No problems

TRAVEL TIME TO DESTINATION & TIME DIFFERENCE
New York to Bucharest: 11 hours 35 minutes connecting flight; EST +7. London to Bucharest: 3 hours 15 minutes nonstop flight; GMT +2

AVERAGE TRIP COST
$750/£500 for a week's beach vacation on the Black Sea

LANGUAGE & CURRENCY
Official language: Romanian (derived from Latin); other languages: primarily German
Currency: leu or lev

POPULATION
22,276,000 inhabitants, including Hungarian,

German, and Serbian minorities. Capital: Bucharest

RELIGION
70 percent are Eastern Orthodox; minorities are Greek Orthodox or Muslim

FESTIVALS
July: Medieval Days in Sighisoara; August: Hora de la Prislop dance festival in Prislop Pass;

September: Sambra Oilor (festival celebrating the return of the sheep herds from the mountains) in the Bran area

SHOPPING
Embroidery, painted eggs, icons, pottery

churches in the city. Northeast of the palace is the Lipscani neighborhood, once the economic heart of the city; Stavropoleos Street and its church (arcades and balustrades in the Brancovan style—named after the former governor of Wallachia); University Square (Piata Universitatii), site of a 1990 student protest; and the Romanian Athenaeum, with its delicate staircases of Carrara marble. The city also boasts several large and popular parks, including Cismigiu and Herastrau (Village Museum).

Not far from the capital, the Mogosoaia Palace typifies the Brancovan style with its arcades, loggias, and balustrades.

It is worth the detour to **Iasi** to see the Golia Church and the Church of the Three Hierarchs, along with the Cetatuia Monastery outside the city.

Transylvania is a popular destination for those interested in the story of Count Dracula. English author Bram Stoker chose Transylvania as the setting for his book, which is based on the real-life story of Vlad the Impaler—a Wallachian prince and cruel (though nonetheless respected) national hero. Although Romanians dispute Stoker's version of the story, tourists can follow a circuit of its important places: Sighisoara, Vlad's birthplace; Sibiu, the historic Saxon city where he supposedly lived for a year; and Bran Castle, his reputed lair.

▶ COAST

The most popular resorts on the **Black Sea** coast are concentrated along approximately 30 miles of fine sand beaches from Constanta to the Bulgarian border. Their myth-inspired names (**Neptun, Olimp,** Saturn) contrast with the

somber architecture of the communist era.

The spa resorts of Eforie, Neptun, and Mangalia are renowned internationally for their therapeutic cures derived from the combined effects of the sea, salt, mud, and aerosol inhalations (sodium or chlorine). The rates are very reasonable.

▶ LANDSCAPE AND HIKES

In the **Carpathian Mountains,** summer hikers and winter skiers can enjoy good, inexpensive accommodations year-round. The **Maramures Mountains** are particularly

When to Go		
	BLACK SEA	INTERIOR AND DANUBE DELTA
JANUARY		
FEBRUARY		
MARCH		
APRIL		☼
MAY		☼
JUNE	☼	☼
JULY	☼	
AUGUST	☼	☼
SEPTEMBER	☼	☼
OCTOBER		☼
NOVEMBER		
DECEMBER		

Advice

■ Pros

• A good balance of cultural and resort tourism. The Black Sea resorts are more affordable than those of the Mediterranean and have more spas.

■ Cons

• The Dracula legend is somewhat exploitative of tourists.

■ Safety

• The country is generally safe, but one should be careful in certain tourist sites and the large cities.

■ Special Tips

• The Black Sea coastline is inexpensive and continues to attract new tourists. Nature enthusiasts will not be disappointed by the amazing flora and fauna of the Danube Delta. The historic city of Sibiu, named Europe's City of Culture in 2007, is now a popular destination.

interesting for their dense forests, while the **Apuseni Mountains** offer many natural wonders (caves, waterfalls, sinkholes or dolines). The region of the **Bucegi Mountains** is known for its sandstone walls, ski slopes, and abundant fauna and flora.

Romania's 168 spa resorts account for a significant part of the country's tourism. The majority of the spas are situated on the Black Sea coast; some are in the Carpathians.

▶ WILDLIFE

The Danube River ends its long course in an expansive delta that is the largest natural reserve in Europe. Designated a biosphere reserve by UNESCO, the **Danube Delta** is home to 300 bird species (pelicans, spoonbills, ibis, common shelducks), 60 fish species, and 1,100 plant varieties. The region is fairly isolated and not yet overrun with tourists. The country's mountainous interior boasts another 70 natural reserves.

Russia

Two world-famous jewels—impressive St. Petersburg, celebrated as the "Land of White Nights," and Moscow, the capital city—highlight any visit to Russia. Here, too, visitors can enjoy cruises on the Volga River, hikes around Lake Baikal and on the Kamchatka Peninsula, the medieval towns of the "Golden Ring" near Moscow, and much more.

▶ CITIES AND MONUMENTS

Moscow is a city of culture (with 150 museums, among them the Pushkin Museum with works by Rubens, Rembrandt, and the Impressionists) and art (with 40 theaters and concert halls, among them the Bolshoi Theater). The city features the Kremlin, which lies on some 70 acres of land rich with palaces, cathedrals, and churches, some of which are up to a thousand years old.

One side of the **Kremlin** opens up to the famous Red Square, flanked by the Lenin Mausoleum and **St. Basil's Cathedral** with its splendid onion domes. The palaces (Ostankino, Kuskovo), the baroque churches (Kadashi and its green onion domes), and the Novodevichi Convent (where writers Gogol

What to See and Do in Russia

▶ **CITIES AND MONUMENTS**

- Moscow (Kremlin, St. Basil's Cathedral)
- St. Petersburg (Nevsky Prospekt, Hermitage Museum)
- The Golden Ring (Sudzal, Vladimir, Sergiyev Possad)

▶ **LANDSCAPE**

- West: Volga River (Moscow–St. Petersburg cruises), Lakes Ladoga and Onega, Karelian Forest
- South: Caucasus Mountains
- Siberia: Lake Baikal; Amur, Lena, and Ob Rivers
- Kamchatka Peninsula

▶ **COASTS**

- Black Sea beaches (Sochi), Black Sea cruises

In Moscow, the unusual beauty of St. Basil's Cathedral, with its onion domes, draws the attention of any visitor to Red Square.

The Dormition Cathedral in Moscow is the site where the tsars were crowned.

and Chekhov and former Soviet leader Khrushchev, among others, are buried) are must-see attractions. The city wants to make people forget its Communist past, both in its architecture (rehabilitation or renovation of churches and religious buildings) and its economy (neocapitalism generating new inequalities).

St. Petersburg, known as Leningrad for most of the last century, is also called the "Venice of the North" because it is built on dozens of small islands on the Neva River and along canals. You can ride a boat to view the baroque palace facades that made the city famous. This is the most beautiful city in the country, thanks to Peter the Great, who, at the beginning of the 18th century, built it as a showcase of the powerful Russia of the tsars. In June, when the daylight lingers until dawn, the city reaches its high point in beauty and charm; during the "white nights" celebration, ballets and concerts are performed all over.

Nevsky Prospekt, bordered by palaces and theaters, is St.

Traveler's Notebook

MAIN CONTACTS

Embassy of the Russian Federation
2650 Wisconsin Avenue, NW
Washington, DC 20007
(202) 298-5700
www.russianembassy.org
www.visitrussia.org.uk
Embassy of the Russian Federation
6–7 Kensington Palace Gardens
London W8 4QP, UK
+ 44 (0) 20 7229 6412/7281
www.rusemb.org.uk

TRAVEL DOCUMENTS FOR U.S. & U.K. CITIZENS
Passport and visa

TRAVEL TIME TO DESTINATION & TIME DIFFERENCE
New York to Moscow: 9 hours 15 minutes nonstop; New York to St. Petersburg: 10 hours 5 minutes connecting; EST +8. London to Moscow: 3 hours 45 minutes nonstop; from London to St. Petersburg: 3 hours 20 minutes nonstop; GMT +3

AVERAGE TRIP COST
$1,650/£1,050 for 12 days of cruising on the Volga, Moscow to St. Petersburg

LANGUAGE & CURRENCY
Official language: Russian, spoken by four-fifths of the population. Other languages: There are a hundred other languages and dialects spoken in the country. English is sometimes spoken, especially in the cities.
Currency: ruble

POPULATION
Of 141,378,000 inhabitants, four-fifths are Russian. Since the fall of the Iron Curtain, many among the non-Russian one-fifth of the population have increasingly

pushed to be autonomous (in some cases violently, as in Chechnya).
Capital: Moscow

RELIGION
Mostly Russian Orthodox; some ethnic minorities are Muslim, and there are also congregations of Jews and Protestants.

FESTIVALS
January 7: Orthodox Christmas; February 7: Feast of the Walrus; April 12: Cosmonauts Day; June: White Nights in St. Petersburg; December:

Russian Winter Festival in Moscow and St. Petersburg

SHOPPING
The four musts: caviar, a *chapka* (fur hat), matryoshkas (the famous nesting dolls), and vodka; for something extra, add a balalaika (a three-string guitar).

The Catherine Palace in Tsarskoje Selo, south of St. Petersburg, was built in neoclassical and baroque style.

Petersburg's equivalent of the Champs Elysées in Paris. SS. Peter and Paul Cathedral (where the Romanovs, including Nicholas II, are buried), St. Isaac's Cathedral, the Church of the Resurrection, the Smolny Institute, St. Nicholas of the Sailors Church, the Admiralty and its gold weathercock, Pushkin's house, the icons in St. Sophia Cathedral, and the Piskarevo Cemetery are some of the major attractions of a city that is proud of its great cultural reputation.

The **Hermitage Museum** consists of the Winter Palace, the former residence of the Russian tsars, and several auxiliary buildings. Four and a half million visitors a year come here to see some of the greatest masterpieces by such artists as Renoir, Van Gogh, Rembrandt, Raphael, Pissarro, Matisse, and Leonardo da Vinci, as well as the treasures of the Scythians. The Hermitage is the second largest art museum in the world, after the Metropolitan Museum of Art in New York.

Other cultural attractions are the Pushkin Theater, the Mariinsky Theater (formerly the Kirov), the Russian Museum, and the Pushkin Monument. There are also house museums devoted to the famous writers Dostoevsky, Gorki, Pushkin, and Tolstoy.

No doubt, St. Petersburg and Moscow have the most famous landmarks, but the historic cities of the so-called Golden Ring, mostly dating from the 12th century, are no less important. **Sudzal** has a *kremlin* (meaning "fortress"), the Cathedral of the Nativity, abbeys, and wooden churches. **Vladimir** has its Golden Door and **Sergiyev Possad** (formerly Zagorsk) its Trinity Lavra of St. Sergius Monastery. Yaroslavl, Kostroma, and Rostov are also worth seeing. It is here, in the crucible of Holy Russia, that the tsars established their power as manifested in architecture.

Peter the Great similarly highlighted his power by building a palace in Petrodvorets, near St. Petersburg, equivalent in splendor to Versailles.

When to Go		
	WEST (MOSCOW)	EAST (SIBERIA)
JANUARY		
FEBRUARY		
MARCH		
APRIL		☼
MAY	☼	☼
JUNE	☼	☼
JULY	☼	☼
AUGUST	☼	☼
SEPTEMBER		☼
OCTOBER		
NOVEMBER		
DECEMBER		

Floating houses on the Volga, the longest river in Europe, exude a special charm.

Other important monuments are: the kremlin of **Kazan,** the Tartar capital; the icons of St. Sophia Cathedral, the citadel, and medieval churches of **Novgorod;** the citadels, churches, and monasteries of **Pskov;** the opera house of **Novosibirsk,** a town that is also an important stop on the Trans-Siberian Railway; the old kremlin in **Astrakhan,** a city that once was a stop along the Silk Road, close to the Volga Delta; and the two wooden churches of the **Kizhi Island** national open-air museum in Lake Onega.

▶ LANDSCAPE

The West

The easiest way to see Moscow and St. Petersburg is to take a cruise on the **Volga River,** leaving from either city, a 1,200-mile-trip through the Volga-Baltic Waterway and its locks. Other Volga cruises travel from Kazan to Astrakhan. The delta of

the great river where it flows into the Caspian Sea is a paradise for beavers, otters, sea lions, and anglers.

Typical wooden houses flank the shores of **Lakes Ladoga** and **Onega** north of St. Petersburg. The nearby **Karelian Forest** is not much frequented by humans as by deer and occasionally wolves. The countryside is at its most brilliant when the birch, elm, and poplar trees turn colors during the *babje leto,* the Russian version of Indian summer.

The South

The **Caucasus** is a massive mountain range that divides Europe from Asia. The highest peak, Mount Elbrus, rising to 18,510 feet and covered with glaciers, attracts mountain climbers and skiers to the winter sport resorts on the slopes. On the north slope, around the towns of Ordzhonikidze and Nalchik, there are many forests, glaciers, and waterfalls.

Siberia

The wide horizons travelers discover looking at the landscape through the window of the Trans-Siberian Railway are beautiful, if sometimes monotonous, on the six-day journey of nearly 5,000 miles from Moscow to Beijing via Mongolia. Fortunately, after the first 24 hours of travel, **Lake Baikal** appears out of nowhere in the middle of the tundra. With its very special flora and fauna (dolphins and freshwater seals on the Ushkani Islands), this lake is the world's largest freshwater reservoir, 370 miles long and 30 miles wide. The lake is always beautiful, even in the dead of winter, when people can walk across it on a three-foot-thick layer of ice or go cross-country skiing around its banks.

One day, when Siberia attracts more tourists, visitors may enact their own version of the *Dersu Uzala* story filmed here by Japanese director Akira Kurosawa, exploring the region's primitive natural beauty

The Cathedral of the Assumption in Sergiyev Possad

with the aid of a local guide. In the meantime, tourists can try a cruise on the **Amur** or **Lena Rivers** and enjoy the landmarks and countryside. Another great Siberian river, not much traveled, is the **Ob,** with clear waters and its banks bordered by weeping willows.

Tourism is spreading ever farther into Siberia. Travelers can be found as far as Krasnoyarsk and Norilsk, at the mouth of the Yenisei, a river

that can be navigated by boat during the summer.

The **Kamchatka Peninsula** is of interest to fans of volcanology, with more than two hundred craters between the Bering Sea and the Sea of Okhotsk. It is the most active volcanic region in the world and features a "valley of the geysers" with scalding hot-water springs.

Other attractions in this region are the Franz Josef Land

Archipelago, north of Novaya Zemlya, where some privileged tourists have already trod the pristine Arctic soil. Northeast of the Bering Strait is Wrangel Island and the habitat of the Chukchi people to explore.

▶ **COASTS**

The **Black Sea** is the only place in the country that is suitable for swimming. The most famous resort is **Sochi,** where celebrities meet and from where the Black Sea cruises depart—and the site of the 2014 Winter Olympic Games.

Senegal is the "Land of Teranga," meaning hospitality. Beyond its beautiful coast, the Casamance region and the Saloum River Delta happily unite views of small settlements, palm groves, and aquatic fauna. The historic cities of St.-Louis and Gorée have their own stories to tell.

The banks of the Saloum River Delta are as attractive as the Atlantic beaches.

Senegal

▶ COAST

Senegal's fine sandy beaches are extensive, well tended, and bordered with palms and casuarina trees. The sun shines year-round, and the coast is refreshed by the trade winds. The resorts of the **Petite Côte** south of Dakar are the most popular. In addition to its beaches, **Saly** offers deep-sea fishing, golf, and a lively nightlife scene. **Nianing** and **La Somone** are more reserved. Each resort seeks to provide an ecotourist alternative to the beach-life atmosphere.

Cap Skirring, on the coast of the Basse-Casamance (Ziguinchor), is the other favorite seaside resort. The waters of the Atlantic abound in

fish, lending themselves to big-game fishing. Red carp, barracuda, marlin, and yellowtail scad await lovers of deep-sea fishing. Visitors can travel by pirogue (dugout canoe) through the **Saloum Delta** and its mangrove swamps.

▶ LANDSCAPE AND WILDLIFE

The **Casamance** and Basse-Casamance National Park are among the most beautiful landscapes of Senegal. The park consists of savanna woodlands and mangroves, casuarinas, baobabs, and

---

Traveler's Notebook

MAIN CONTACTS
Embassy of the Republic of Senegal
2112 Wyoming Avenue, NW
Washington, DC 20008
(202) 234-0540
www.ambasenegal-us.org
Embassy of the Republic of Senegal
39 Marloes Road
London W8 6LA, UK
+ 44 (0) 20 7938 4048 or

7937 7237
www.senegalembassy.co.uk

TRAVEL DOCUMENTS
U.S. Citizens: Passport
U.K. Citizens: Passport and visa (for stays of more than 3 months)

HEALTH ISSUES
Yellow fever immunization is mandatory; malaria prophylaxis is advised

TRAVEL TIME TO DESTINATION & TIME DIFFERENCE
New York to Dakar: 11 hours 10 minutes connecting flight; EST +5.
London to Dakar: 7 hours 25 minutes connecting flight; GMT

AVERAGE TRIP COST
$1,000/£650 for a week's beach vacation

LANGUAGE & CURRENCY
Official language: French; some 20 other languages are spoken, including the predominant Wolof
Currency: CFA Franc

POPULATION
12,522,000 inhabitants; 40 percent Wolof, with sizable minorities of Fulfulbe, Serer, and Jola peoples. Capital: Dakar

RELIGION
91 percent Muslim; some Catholics and animists

FESTIVALS
January: Taabasids (festival of the sheep): April 4: Independence Day; May: St.-Louis Jazz festival; July or August (end of Ramadan): Eid al-Fitr; October: St.-Louis regattas

What to See and Do in Senegal		

▶ COAST

• Beaches of the Petite Côte (Saly, Nianing, La Somone) and the Casamance (Cap Skirring)

• Ecotourism, deep-sea fishing, diving

• Saloum Delta

▶ LANDSCAPE AND WILDLIFE

• Casamance, Lake Rose

• Djoudj (birds), Saloum Delta (birds, aquatic fauna), and Niokolo-Koba National Parks

▶ CITIES AND MEMORIALS

• Island of Gorée

• St.-Louis, Dakar, Ziguinchor

Advice

■ **Pros**

• A country with varied choices for travelers, agreeable beaches during most of the year, and affordable prices.

■ **Cons**

• Weather in the south is sometimes iffy between April and October.

■ **Safety**

• The regions near the southern frontier of Gambia and Guinea-Bissau remain unsafe. Consulates can provide up-to-date information to any traveler to these areas.

■ **Special Tip**

• St.-Louis, a former French trading post has undergone a renewal three and a half centuries after the construction of its first fort. The *Bou-el-Mogdad,* a historic former ship of the Messageries du Senegal company offers cruises on the Senegal River.

poincianas, but the park is currently closed because of political conflicts. The estuaries of the Casamance River where habitat and traditions are well preserved add to the interest of the place. Near Dakar, **Lake Rose** (Retba) owes its name and color to the cyanobacteria in the water. Not far from La Somone is the Bandia Wildlife Reserve.

Birds are king in Senegal. **Djoudj National Park** is home to flamingos, cormorants, and terns. **Saloum Delta National Park** harbors pelicans, flamingos, terns, spoonbills, grey herons, and ibis. Besides birds, **Niokolo-Koba National Park** shelters hippos, elephants, elands, lions, chimpanzees, and colobus monkeys.

▶ **CITIES AND MEMORIALS**

Off the coast of Dakar, the island of **Gorée** was a slave-trading center for the Americas until 1848. Today it serves as a memorial; its historic colonial houses, the House of Slaves, and a history museum are reminders of this period. Three cities merit a visit:

• **St.-Louis** was West Africa's first European settlement. Built on an island, the town is noted for its Faidherbe Bridge, fishermen's quarters, colonial architecture, and Airmail Museum.

• **Dakar** on the Cap-Vert Peninsula has the Grand Mosque, a cathedral, numerous markets, and the IFAN Museum of West African Culture.

• **Ziguinchor,** a pleasant fishing port, is also the port of entry to the Casamance region.

When to Go		
	CLIMATE	PHOTOGRAPHY
JANUARY	☼	
FEBRUARY	☼	
MARCH	☼	
APRIL	☼	
MAY	☼	⋞
JUNE		⋞
JULY		⋞
AUGUST		⋞
SEPTEMBER		⋞
OCTOBER	☼	⋞
NOVEMBER	☼	
DECEMBER	☼	

What to See and Do in the Seychelles

▶ **COASTS**

- Islands: Mahé, Praslin, La Digue, Silhouette
- Beaches: diving, waterskiing, cruising, windsurfing, deep-sea fishing

▶ **LANDSCAPE**

- Vallée de Mai Nature Preserve (palm trees and coconut trees)
- Morne Seychellois National Park (hiking)

▶ **WILDLIFE**

- Giant tortoises, birds, tropical fish in dazzling colors, poinciana trees, red latan palms, coco de mer palms, and vanilla trees

Pink granite cliffs edge La Digue's soft sand beaches.

The Seychelles

Turquoise water, white sand, and blue sky: It does not get better than this! The beach resorts in this archipelago of 115 islands spread out over 750 miles.

▶ **COASTS**

The beaches of the Seychelles deserve to be called "heavenly." Turquoise water, very fine white sand, and rows of palms and casuarina trees in the background define the coasts of these granite islands, 30 of which are inhabited. **Mahé,** the largest island, has some 65 beaches; **Praslin** is popular for its secluded coves; and **La Digue** is famous for its pink granite blocks. Tourism here is subject to strict ecological regulations:

Traveler's Notebook

MAIN CONTACTS

Embassy of Seychelles
800 Second Avenue,
Suite 400C
New York, NY 10017
(212) 972-1785
www.seychelles.com
Republic of Seychelles Consulate
111 Baker Street
London W1U 6RR, UK
+ 44 (0) 207 935 7770
www.freewebs.consulate

TRAVEL DOCUMENTS FOR U.S. & U.K. CITIZENS
Passport

HEALTH ISSUES
No immunizations required

TRAVEL TIME TO DESTINATION & TIME DIFFERENCE
New York to Victoria: 18 hours 5 minutes connecting flight; EST +9. London to Victoria: 11 hours 15 minutes

connecting flight; GMT +4

AVERAGE TRIP COST
$2,800/£1,800 for a week of beach and diving

LANGUAGE & CURRENCY
Official language: Creole; other languages: French and English
Currency: Seychelles rupee

POPULATION
The majority of the islands' 81,900 inhabitants live on the island of Mahé, where the capital, Victoria, is located.

RELIGION
90 percent Catholic; most of the others are Anglican

FESTIVALS
January: Kavardi procession; May 29:

Independence Day; October: Creole Festival (music, poetry reading, theater)

SHOPPING
Among the local products: objects made from exotic woods, shell jewelry, batiks, *pareos*, and *coco de mer* (double coconut)

No more than one hotel per island is allowed, except for the main islands, and no building may be higher than the coconut trees.

Silhouette Island and its rain forest promise a relaxing, quiet time and so do the atolls and coral reefs in the west, such as Amirante Islands and Aldabra Atoll. In the south, the Farquhar Islands are almost deserted. A few of the islands, such as Fregate, are expensive and quite upscale.

Excursions on local sailboats and catamarans leave mostly from the many docks on Mahé or Praslin. Active vacationers can go snorkeling or scuba diving. There are numerous dive spots, and the underwater world is beautiful and interesting. Waterskiing, windsurfing, sailing, catamaran cruising, and deep-sea fishing (marlin, tuna, barracuda, swordfish) are also available.

▶ LANDSCAPE

The beaches are the main attractions in the Seychelles, but they are not the only reason for traveling there, especially in the southern part of the archipelago. The interior of the islands, endowed with luxurious vegetation, can be compared to French Polynesia. Hiking is most pleasant on Praslin, which is proud of its national symbol, the coco de mer, commonly referred to as coco-fesse for its seductive feminine curves. The coco de mer, or double-coconut tree, grows only on Praslin in the **Vallée de Mai Nature Preserve,** which features a palm forest.

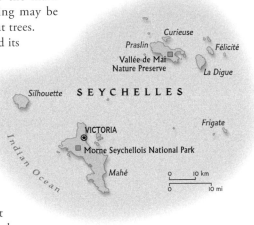

On Mahé Island, in the **Morne Seychellois National Park**, tourists are inspired to climb the park's nearly 3,000-foot mountain for an amazing view of the coast.

The architecture of the Creole houses in the small capital city of Victoria is admirable, especially the verandas, called *varangues* here. The Creole Festival at the end of October is a participatory event.

When to Go		
	CLIMATE	CALM SEAS, FEWER CROWDS
JANUARY		
FEBRUARY		
MARCH		
APRIL	☼	✔
MAY	☼	✔
JUNE	☼	
JULY		
AUGUST		
SEPTEMBER	☼	✔
OCTOBER	☼	
NOVEMBER	☼	
DECEMBER		

▶ WILDLIFE

The giant tortoises live in the wild on Cousin Island and the Aldabra Atoll, the world's largest raised coral atoll and a wildlife sanctuary, listed as a World Heritage site. The tortoises share their ecosystem with exotic birds (black parrots, terns, frigatebirds, tropicbirds) that can be found in great numbers there, but also on Bird and Denis Islands, where they come to nest between May and November.

Tropical fish can be observed in the coral reefs, either by diving, snorkeling, or watching them from a glass-bottom boat.

The flora is rich with more than 80 species, among them flame trees, red latan palms, casuarina trees, and vanilla trees. Local tour companies take visitors on special hikes to look for and identify wildlife and plants, especially on Cousin Island.

* In Singapore—the "City of the Lion" founded by Sir Stamford Raffles in the 19th century—the atmosphere alternates between easygoing living and frenetic commerce. This ministate, with its contrasting architecture and ethnic communities, is a good starting point for visiting Malaysia or Indonesia.*

▶ CITY AND MONUMENTS

"Asia's Manhattan" is characterized by trade. Thanks to its status as a free port, the city is brimming over with all kinds of high-tech products. Shopping in style—including for high fashion—is especially active on **Orchard Road,** but it is also possible to find some "buys" in **Chinatown.** No matter the neighborhood and the nature of shopping, though, visitors must look carefully, as the good deals are more elusive than they were 20 years ago.

European influence can still be found in Singapore's heart.

Singapore

Traveler's Notebook

MAIN CONTACTS
Singapore Embassy
3501 International Place, NW
Washington, DC 20008
(202) 537-3100
www.mfa.gov.sg
Singaporean Embassy
9 Wilton Crescent
Belgravia
London SW1X 8SP, UK
+44 (0) 20 7235 8315
www.singapore.embassy
homepage.com/

TRAVEL DOCUMENTS FOR U.S. & U.K. CITIZENS
Passport

HEALTH ISSUES
No immunizations required

TRAVEL TIME TO DESTINATION & TIME DIFFERENCE
New York to Singapore: 20 hours 40 minutes connecting flight; EST –13. London to Singapore: 12 hours 35 minutes connecting flight; GMT +8

AVERAGE TRIP COST
$1,000/£650 for a 4-day/3-night weekend

LANGUAGE & CURRENCY
Official languages: English, Malay, Mandarin, and Tamil
Currency: Singapore dollar

POPULATION
4,553,000 inhabitants, with a very high population density; 75 percent are Chinese, and others include Malays, Indians, and Tamils. The city of Singapore proper

has about one million inhabitants.

RELIGION
28 percent Buddhist, 19 percent Christian, 16 percent Muslim, 13 percent Taoist, and 5 percent Hindu, plus Sikhs and others

FESTIVALS
February: Chinese New Year, and Festival of the Dragon Boats; August 9: Independence Day; October: Thimiti (walking on embers); November:

Deepavali

SHOPPING
Crafts and textiles have a hard time competing with electronics, cameras, videos, stereos, computers, and other high-tech products.

What to See and Do in Singapore

▶ **CITY AND MONUMENTS**

• Orchard Road and Chinatown shopping (trade and tax-free items; high-tech camera, video, stereo, and computer products)

• Little India

▶ **MUSEUMS, TEMPLES, MOSQUES**

• Raffles Hotel, Har Par Villa

• Jurong Bird Park, Van Kleef Aquarium, Bukit Timah Nature Reserve

Outside of business, this rich and prosperous city-state thrives in an atmosphere where classicism and extravagance go hand in hand. The different communities have created some typical neighborhoods, such as Chinatown (with its Chinatown Heritage Center) and **Little India.** The varied customs find expression in four different kinds of cuisine: Chinese, Indian, Malay, and Peranakan, a Sino-Malay mixture.

It's calmer in the museums (National Museum of Singapore, History Museum, Asian Civilizations Museum) or a few miles away on the pleasant beaches of Sentosa Island or nearby Bintan Island, a fashionable resort that belongs to Indonesia. The presence of four national cultures produced

an amazingly rich architecture: The Hindu Sri Mariammam temple sits next to the Buddhist Temple of a Thousand Lights and the Sultan Mosque. As for Western architecture, the **Raffles Hotel,** a national monument restored in 1991, is one of the most prestigious establishments of the colonial era.

An interesting park to visit is the **Har Par Villa** (formerly called Tiger Balm Gardens, after a famous ointment invented in Singapore),

a Chinese mythological theme park where characters carved in the rock tell Chinese legends.

It is hard to avoid the *wayangs* (street opera shows), karaoke places, and amusement parks.

There are several places of interest for nature lovers: the **Jurong Bird Park, Van Kleef Aquarium,** Japanese gardens, botanical garden, and zoo are open until late at night. A good place for a walk is the **Bukit Timah Nature Reserve.**

When to Go

	CLIMATE	SHOPPING
JANUARY	☼	
FEBRUARY	☼	
MARCH		
APRIL		
MAY		
JUNE		
JULY	☼	✔
AUGUST	☼	
SEPTEMBER	☼	
OCTOBER		
NOVEMBER	☼	
DECEMBER	☼	

Advice

■ **Pros**

• A microcosm of all the contrasts found in Asia. Advantageous shopping.

■ **Cons**

• Travel is more expensive than in the neighboring Southeast Asian countries.

■ **Safety**

• Singapore has always been a safe place for tourists, but they may be surprised or even disappointed by the political-correctness rules enforced in the country, which clearly contribute to its safety.

The High Tatras, known as the "smallest high mountains in the world," have ten peaks rising to more than 8,000 feet.

Slovakia

Even before separating from the Czech Republic, Slovakia focused its tourist industry on attracting hikers to the peaks of the High Tatras and Malá Fatra (in the Eastern Beskids). Visits to the capital Bratislava and other medieval cities add cultural attractions to the itinerary.

Traveler's Notebook

MAIN CONTACTS
Embassy of the Slovak Republic
3523 International Court, NW Washington, DC 20008
(202) 237-1054
www.slovak embassy-us.org/
Embassy of Slovakia
25, Kensington Palace Gardens London W8 4QY, UK
+ 44 (0) 207 3136470
www.slovak embassy.co.uk

TRAVEL DOCUMENTS FOR U.S. & U.K. CITIZENS
Passport

TRAVEL TIME TO DESTINATION & TIME DIFFERENCE
New York to Bratislava: 10 hours 50 minutes connecting flight; EST +6. London to Bratislava: 4 hours connecting flight; GMT +1

AVERAGE TRIP COST
$1,150/£750 for a week of hiking

LANGUAGE & CURRENCY
Official language: Slovakian; other languages: German Currency: koruna (cannot be converted outside the country)

POPULATION
5,448,000 inhabitants; larger minorities include Hungarians (11 percent) and Roma (8 percent). Capital: Bratislava

RELIGION
60 percent Catholic; minority of Protestants

FESTIVALS
May: Bratislava Music Festival; June: pop-rock festival in Bratislava; July to August: Summer Cultural Festival in Bratislava; September 1: Day of the Constitution

SHOPPING
Ceramics, embroidery, basketware

▶ LANDSCAPE AND HIKES

The **High Tatras** define the border with Poland and comprise the country's highest and most interesting region. Hikers can enjoy views of valleys, glacial lakes, rocky peaks, animals (golden eagles, wolves, bears, chamois, marmots), and plants from trails leading to the summit or, far below, from the Magistrala Trail (approximately 30 miles long). Other sites in the High Tatras include the Roháce Valley (four lakes), the Ziar Valley, and the town of Zverovka. In winter, skiers can choose from many excellent ski resorts in areas such as Stary Smokovec, Strbské Pleso, and the outskirts of Tatranska Lomnica.

The **Low Tatras** (Donovaly, Certovica, Tále) are steadily becoming as popular as their big brothers, thanks to the beautiful scenery in Slovensky Raj National Park. Located between the Hornad and Hnilec Rivers, this "Slovakian Paradise" is replete with forests, waterfalls, cliffs, giant sinkholes, and ice caves (Dobsinska). Add the **Malá Fatra** mountains (west), **Eastern Beskids** (between Poland and Ukraine), and **Slovak Karst National Park** (forests, sinkholes) and you have a complete tour of some of the most interesting places in Central Europe.

▶ CITIES

Located on the banks of the Danube River, **Bratislava** does not quite shine like Prague, but a visit to the old town is worthwhile. The castle—once a royal residence—overlooks the Danube and is now the National Museum. The main attractions of this quiet, intellectual city are St. Martin Cathedral, Mirbach Palace (rococo style), Primatial Palace, the opera house, and Napoleon Hill (beautiful views). The Austrian capital Vienna is only 35 miles from Bratislava.

Not far from the city, yet less visited by tourists, are the ruins of Devin Castle overlooking the confluence of the Morava and Danube Rivers.

It is worth making a detour to **Trnava** to see the castle ruins and fine examples of baroque (St. John the Baptist Church, facades of old houses) and Gothic (St. Nicholas Church) architecture. The sites in **Levoca** include St. Jacob's Church (main altarpiece) and Gothic-style houses; in **Trencín**, the 18th-century royal castle; and in **Spis** (Spissky hrad), the largest castle in Central Europe. In the east, many villages have wooden churches typical of the region.

In a land of castles and fortresses, some cities are known for their Gothic and Renaissance styles, such as **Bardejov** (altarpieces of St. Egide Church) and **Banska Stiavnica.** Slovakia also has several thermal spas, for example, Piestany.

When to Go		
	CLIMATE	WINTER SPORTS IN THE HIGH TATRAS
JANUARY		❄
FEBRUARY		❄
MARCH		❄
APRIL		
MAY	☼	
JUNE	☼	
JULY	☼	
AUGUST	☼	
SEPTEMBER	☼	
OCTOBER		
NOVEMBER		❄
DECEMBER		❄

What to See and Do in Slovenia

▶ **LANDSCAPE AND EXCURSIONS**

- Julian Alps resorts (hiking, skiing), Bled, Postojna (caves)
- Thermal spas, Lipizzan horses, brown bears

▶ **CITIES**

- Ljubljana, Maribor

▶ **COAST**

- Koper, Portoroz, Piran

In the shadow of the Alps, Slovenia is as pleasant a place to visit as to live. Tourism is on the rise since the end of the conflicts within the former Yugoslavia. In addition to its small but inviting coastline, the country boasts forests and high mountain pastures, the enchanting Bled region, the Postojna Caves, and Ljubljana monuments.

The fishing port of Piran reflects the country's tranquil spirit.

Slovenia

▶ **LANDSCAPE AND EXCURSIONS**

In summer, the forest-covered **Julian Alps** beckon hikers to their peaks, which reach to nearly 6,000 feet. The Alps are best viewed from Triglav National Park and the

Traveler's Notebook

MAIN CONTACTS

Embassy of the Republic of Slovenia
2410 California Street, NW
Washington, DC 20008
(202) 386-6633
http://washington
.embassy.si/en
Embassy of the Republic of Slovenia
10 Little College Street
London SW1P 3SH, UK

+ 44 (0) 207 222 5700
http://london.embassy
.si/en

TRAVEL DOCUMENTS FOR U.S. & U.K. CITIZENS
Passport

TRAVEL TIME TO DESTINATION & TIME DIFFERENCE
New York to Ljubljana: 10 hours connecting; EST +6. London to Ljubljana:

3 hours 20 minutes connecting; GMT +1

AVERAGE TRIP COST
$1,270/£820 for a week on the coast

LANGUAGE & CURRENCY
Official language: Slovenian, a cousin to Serbo-Croatian; German is also commonly spoken
Currency: euro

POPULATION
2,009,000 inhabitants
Capital: Ljubljana

RELIGION
Catholicism is the predominant religion, but Protestantism has remained significant since the Reformation.

FESTIVALS
February 8: Slovenian Cultural Festival;

February or March: Carnival; June to July: Maribor Festival and Ljubljana Music Festival

SHOPPING
Local artisanal products: Idrija lace, woodcarvings, black pottery, hand-painted Easter eggs

With the exception of the Alpine region, Slovenia has several areas where, over time, karst formations have left their mark on the landscape: in **Postojna** (12-mile-long caves, the largest in Europe); Skocjan, near the Rak River; and Rakov Skocjan National Park (small enclosed canyon).

Other attractions include the 20 thermal spas, Lipizzan horses, and brown bears in the southeast region.

▶ CITIES

In addition to its baroque and art nouveau architecture, the capital city **Ljubljana** boasts two points of interest: the town square and the central marketplace. The most beautiful views can be had from the city's 12th-century castle. Its cathedrals, churches (Annunciation, St. Nicholas, Knights Templar, Franciscan), and fine museums prove that Ljubljana is the heartbeat of the country.

Maribor is second to Ljubljana on the tourist circuit, with its Romanesque and baroque cathedral, 15th-century castle, and fortress ruins.

▶ COAST

On the narrow Adriatic coastline (24 miles) is the city of **Koper**, less than 18 miles from Trieste in Italy and known for its historical ties to Venice. The city is embellished with palaces in the Venetian-Gothic style, most notably Taco Palace (large collection of Italian paintings).

The beach and spa resort at **Portoroz** is the largest and most popular in the country. Casinos, restaurants, and lovely beaches only enhance its reputation. On the other end of the spectrum is the medieval fishing village of **Piran,** where salt reclamation from the local marshes has brought prosperity to the region.

resorts that surround it: Bohinj and its lake; Kranjskagora; Bovec; and especially **Bled**—which is nestled next to a peaceful lake in a lovely setting that once hosted the members of the Austrian and Hungarian aristocracies.

When to Go		
	CLIMATE	WINTER SPORTS
JANUARY		❄
FEBRUARY		❄
MARCH		
APRIL		
MAY		
JUNE	☼	
JULY	☼	
AUGUST	☼	
SEPTEMBER	☼	
OCTOBER		
NOVEMBER		
DECEMBER		❄

AUSTRIA

Triglav National Park
Bled

HUNGARY

Maribor

ITALY

SLOVENIA

Postojna

LJUBLJANA

Julian Alps

Piran Koper
Portoroz

Adriatic Sea

CROATIA

0   30 km
0   30 mi

South Africa

What to See and Do in South Africa

▶ WILDLIFE

• Kruger National Park and Hluhluwe-Umfolozi Reserve (Cape buffaloes, elephants, leopards, lions, rhinos)

• iSimangaliso Wetland Park (crocodiles, hippos)

• Game reserves in the Karoo (springboks), Addo (elephants), and Pilanesberg (giraffes, white rhinos, zebras)

• Kalahari Gemsbok National Park (springboks, cheetahs, gnus, meerkats, martial eagles)

• Oudtshoorn (ostrich farms)

▶ LANDSCAPE

• Drakensberg (Blyde River Canyon)

• Cango Caverns

• KwaZulu-Natal (rock art), Augrabies Falls, Kimberley diamond mines

▶ COASTS

• Durban, Wild Coast

• Garden Route, Peninsula Coast

▶ CITIES

• Cape Town, Johannesburg, Pretoria, Sun City

▰ *Although travel to South Africa is rather expensive and security problems in the towns continue to some extent, tourism is booming. The wildlife reserves and excellent facilities to welcome travelers make the journey worthwhile, and there are numerous other attractions.*

▶ WILDLIFE

Traveling from the northeast to the southwest of South Africa, you will find some of the greatest animal diversity on the continent: the big five—Cape buffaloes, elephants, leopards, lions, and rhinoceros—are present, as well as giraffes and cheetahs in the largest and best known of the 22 national parks, **Kruger National Park** (217 miles long by 34 miles wide). The bush vegetation, the rare animals (African wild dog, black rhino), and comfortable,

In addition to the famous national parks, South Africa's game parks include private reserves such as Singita.

luxurious lodges make a stay in this well-organized park a pleasure.

In the south of Swaziland, the **Hluhluwe-Umfolozi Reserve** also has the big five, including the white rhinoceros, a rare species that is close to extinction. The marshes of the **iSimangaliso Wetland Park** in KwaZulu-Natal shelter hippopotamuses, crocodiles, and a great number of bird species. In the north, in Bophuthatswana, **Pilanesberg National Park** harbors white rhinos, zebras, buffaloes, and giraffes.

Not far from the Cape are the wild bird sanctuaries of the Langebaan Lagoon and Lambert's Bay. Between the Cape and Port Elizabeth around **Oudtshoorn,** travelers can visit ostrich farms. North of Port Elizabeth, the **Addo Elephant National Park** is famous for its elephants. Graceful springboks frolic across the savanna of the **Karoo.**

Springboks can also be seen in the **Kalahari Gemsbok National Park** on the borders with Namibia and Botswana, where lions, cheetahs, zebras, gnus, meerkats, and numerous bird species, including the martial eagle, make their home. Best times to visit are the months of June and July.

▶ **LANDSCAPE**

The South African landscape ends in a long mountain chain, the **Drakensberg** range, running from Mozambique south to Eastern Cape Province. The Drakensberg area in the Transvaal harbors some 4,500 animal species, and the **Cango Caverns** are famous for their San (Bushman) rock art. Other rock art can be found in **KwaZulu-Natal** along the border of Lesotho (Royal Natal National Park, Giant's Castle), where you can also observe some Zulu customs.

The Orange River region features two remarkable sights: **Augrabies**

Along Cape Town's beaches, visitors can hike with a view of Table Mountain and the Twelve Apostles range.

When to Go		
	CLIMATE	NATIONAL PARKS
JANUARY	☼	
FEBRUARY	☼	
MARCH	☼	
APRIL		
MAY		🐾
JUNE		🐾
JULY	☼	🐾
AUGUST	☼	🐾
SEPTEMBER		🐾
OCTOBER		🐾
NOVEMBER		
DECEMBER	☼	

Falls, cascading 480 feet, and the **Kimberley** diamond mines.

Most of these sights have the benefit of excellent tourist infrastructure and a national network of roads.

▶ COASTS

The Indian Ocean coast is hot: **Durban,** where Mahatma Gandhi lived, is a popular stop for visitors all year round and is ideal for surfers.

Traveling eastward, you come to the **Wild Coast:** some 180 miles of windy hills, sloping down to a coast that is still free of tourist crowds and interspersed by traditional Xhosa homes. This region is also the birthplace of Nelson Mandela, whose museum is located in Umtata.

Between Mossel Bay (great white sharks) and Storms River stretches the very busy **Garden Route,** meandering along forests, lakes, estuaries, and beaches.

The Atlantic and Indian Oceans meet at the **Peninsula Coast** of the Cape, which is dotted with myriad seaside resorts. The water is colder here.

▶ CITIES

Above all, **Cape Town** is known for its striking Table Mountain (which can be reached by cable car or a

Traveler's Notebook

MAIN CONTACTS *Embassy of the Republic of South Africa* 3051 Massachusetts Avenue, NW Washington, DC 20008 (202) 232-4400 www.saembassy.org www.southafrica.net *South African High Commission* South Africa House Trafalgar Square London WC2N 5DP, UK + 44 (0) 20 7451 7299 www.southafricahouse.com **TRAVEL DOCUMENTS FOR U.S. & U.K. CITIZENS** Passport	**HEALTH ISSUES** No vaccinations required. Malaria prophylaxis is advised, especially from October to May for areas of low altitude in the northern provinces, in Mpumalanga province (including Kruger Park), and in the northeast in KwaZulu-Natal. The country has a high rate of HIV/AIDS infection. **TRAVEL TIME TO DESTINATION & TIME DIFFERENCE** New York to Johannesburg: 15 hours 10 minutes nonstop flight; EST +7. London to Johannesburg: 10 hours 50 minutes	nonstop flight: GMT +2 **AVERAGE TRIP COST** $3,175/£2,050 for 15 days **LANGUAGE & CURRENCY** Official languages: Afrikaans, English, and nine other languages (especially Xhosa and Zulu) Currency: rand **POPULATION** 43,998,000 inhabitants. Three-quarters of the population is black; 5 million people are Caucasian, and 3 million are of mixed race. Capital: Pretoria is the seat of government, Cape Town the seat of parliament.	**RELIGION** Christians are in the majority, divided into Anglicans, Methodists, Catholics, and independent black churches. **FESTIVALS** January 2: Big Carnival parade in Cape Town; March 21: Human Rights Day; June 16: Youth Day; September 24: Heritage Day **SHOPPING** Diamonds, precious gems, leather, crocodile-skin purses, and excellent wines

circuit hike). Dutch colonial architecture (Koopmans-de Wet House) is one of the attractions, along with the old docks of the Waterfront (the busiest artery). Off the Cape, Robben Island, where Mandela was imprisoned, has become a museum for tolerance and human rights.

Johannesburg was established during the gold rush at the end of the 19th century. Its history is the theme of the Gold Reef City amusement park. Other attractions include the Newton Cultural Precinct, once known as the most violent suburb; now rehabilitated, it is a vibrant cultural hub, with the African ethnology museum, the FUBA (Federated Union of Black

Artists) Gallery displaying native arts, Constitution Hill, and the Apartheid Museum, along with musical traditions (jazz). Hot-air balloon rides over the city are available, as are guided tours of the former black township of Soweto, a crucible of the anti-apartheid movement. Visitors are invited nowadays to visit the once ignored townships and discover traditions of all kinds (art, dance, healers). Several miles north of Johannesburg, **Pretoria,** the city founded by the Boers, spreads out from it central Church Square.

One curiosity is in Bophuthatswana: The new town of **Sun City** sees itself as a small Las Vegas; it features a casino and famous golf courses, as well as a crocodile museum and the extravagant Palace of the Lost City hotel complex, complete with jungle and artificial beach.

Advice

▪ Pros

• The greatest diversity of animal species in Africa. The quality of the tourism infrastructure and management in the wildlife parks and other sites throughout the entire country.

▪ Cons

• The overall high cost of travel and still some security risks

▪ Safety

• South Africa is one of those countries where tourists are cautioned to always keep the windows of the rental car closed and never to wander alone into the townships. Everyone should be careful, but not to the point of paranoia.

▪ Recommendation

• Although apartheid no longer exists, significant tensions are still apparent. It is important to show respect for the customs of the San and Zulus.

What to See and Do in South Korea

▶ **LANDSCAPE**

- Taebaek Mountains (hiking, skiing)
- National parks (Seorak Mountain National Park, Hallyeo Marine National Park)
- Jeju Island

▶ **CITIES AND MONUMENTS**

- Kyongju, Buyeo, Seoul, temples and Buddhist statues

▶ **COASTS**

- Beaches of the east and west coasts, Jeju Island

 The "land of the clear morning" is not a well-known tourist destination. But the country has much to offer: Buddhist temples and statues and palaces of the old kingdom, beaches, and scenic mountains.

Wherever there is a mountain, there is a rock-cut Buddha, as above in Naksan.

South Korea

▶ **LANDSCAPE**

On the east coast, the **Taebaek Mountains** plunge into the Sea of Japan, creating a beautiful landscape and inviting backpackers for hikes. Skiing is also becoming popular in the new resorts of the Yongpyong Valley.

South Korea has a number of national parks. Among the best

Traveler's Notebook

MAIN CONTACTS

Embassy of the Republic of Korea
2450 Massachusetts Avenue, NW
Washington, DC 20008
(202) 939-5600
www.koreaembassyusa.org
Embassy of the Republic of Korea
60 Buckingham Gate
London SW1E 6AJ, UK
+ 44 (0) 20 7227 5500
http://gbr.mofat.go.kr/eng

TRAVEL DOCUMENTS FOR U.S. & U.K. CITIZENS
Passport

HEALTH ISSUES
No immunizations necessary. A low malaria risk exists in the north in the province of Kyunggi Do.

TRAVEL TIME TO DESTINATION & TIME DIFFERENCE
New York to Seoul: 14 hours nonstop flight; EST +14. London to Seoul: 10 hours 50

minutes nonstop flight; GMT +9

AVERAGE TRIP COST
$3,175/£2,050 for 12 days

LANGUAGE & CURRENCY
Official language: Korean
Currency: won

POPULATION
49,044,800 inhabitants, a quarter of whom live in metropolitan Seoul. Capital: Seoul

RELIGION
Buddhists and Protestants predominate, a minority of Catholics and Confucians

FESTIVALS
January or February: Lunar New Year; April: Cherry blossom festival on Mount Maisan; May 1: Lotus Lantern Festival (Buddha's birthday); fifth day of the fifth month of the lunar calendar: Dano Festival in Gangneung; July 17: Constitution

Day; October: Harvest Festival (Chusok), and festival to honor the Silla dynasty in Gyeongju

SHOPPING
You can shop for clothing, electronics, and silver and gold jewelry.

known are **Seorak Mountain National Park,** with its excellent trail system, and, not far from Pusan, the **Hallyeo Marine National Park** and its many islands. Spring flowering is a special time in Korea, particularly for viewing the celebrated cherry blossoms near Pusan. In the south, **Jeju Island,** the "island of the gods," is a favorite among young couples who flock there on their honeymoon. It has beaches and cratered mountains, dominated by Mount Halla, with a trail system that leads to the summit.

▶ CITIES AND MONUMENTS

Among the historic towns, **Kyongju** (Gyeongju), the ancient royal capital, is architecturally rich with royal tombs, an observatory, square pagodas, stone Buddhas, and the Bulguksa Monastery, with its great terraces and the seated Buddha in the Sokkuran grotto. **Buyeo** is home to an unusual construction from the sixth century, a five-story stone pagoda.

In **Seoul,** the ancient capital of the Joseon dynasty, three of its five Grand Palaces—the 14th-century Gyeongbokgung, Changdeokgung, and Deoksugung, are open as museums today. The capital is also full of sanctuaries (Jongmyo Shrine),

When to Go		
	INTERIOR	COASTS
JANUARY	☼	☼
FEBRUARY	☼	
MARCH	☼	
APRIL		
MAY		
JUNE		
JULY		☼
AUGUST		☼
SEPTEMBER	☼	☼
OCTOBER	☼	☼
NOVEMBER	☼	
DECEMBER	☼	

temples (Jogyesa), traditional markets, and a national museum with vast collections of exquisite pottery and Buddhist sculptures. Modern Seoul's shopping venues are constantly expanding, and the Olympic Park has become one of its main tourist sites.

Buddhist temples and statues are everywhere: Beopjusa temple and its 55-foot-high Buddha; Kwanch'oksa, with the largest stone Buddha in all of Asia; Yakcheonsa on Jeju Island; Jung-Hwa-sea; Hwaom, one of the oldest temples; Haiensa in the Gaya Mountains, the depository of thousands of the Tripitaka Koreana woodblocks; and Songqwongsa, the most important of the temples that are open to foreigners who want an initiation into Buddhist culture and traditions.

▶ COASTS

Beaches are not the main reason for coming to South Korea, although they are as beautiful and numerous on the east coast (Hwajinpo, Naksan, Gyeongpo, Haeundae) as on the west coast (Songdo, Mallipo, Taechon, Byeonsan). The beaches on Jeju Island, especially Jungmun, are particular favorites.

Spain

Mainland Spain

▶ COASTS

The Mediterranean shores continue to be a preferred destination thanks to their long beaches and sunny weather. From Catalonia to Andalusia stretch the *costas:* **Costa Brava** (Cadaqués, Rosas), **Costa Dorada** (Sitges, Salou, and Port Aventura Park), **Costa del Azahar, Costa Blanca** (Benidorm), and **Costa del Sol** (Marbella, Torremolinos).

The Atlantic beaches have more variety to offer. From west to east, the north (Cantabrian) coast is split into the **Costa Verde,** near Santander, and the Basque coast.

The southeast coast, called **Costa de la Luz,** with the towns of Cádiz

What to See and Do in Mainland Spain

▶ COASTS

- Costa Brava, Costa Dorada, Costa del Azahar, Costa Blanca, Costa del Sol, Costa Verde, Costa de la Luz

▶ CITIES AND MONUMENTS

- In the north: Santiago de Compostela, León, Zaragoza, Valladolid, Barcelona, Salamanca, Segovia, Ávila, Madrid
- In the south: Cuenca, Aranjuez, Toledo, Almagro, Valencia, Trujillo, Cáceres, Mérida, Córdoba, Seville, Granada, Almería, Cádiz

▶ LANDSCAPE

- Aragón and the Pyrenees
- Picos de Europa, Andalusian peaks, Guadalquivir River

▶ CULTURAL HERITAGE

- Corridas, pilgrimages, Don Quixote (La Mancha)

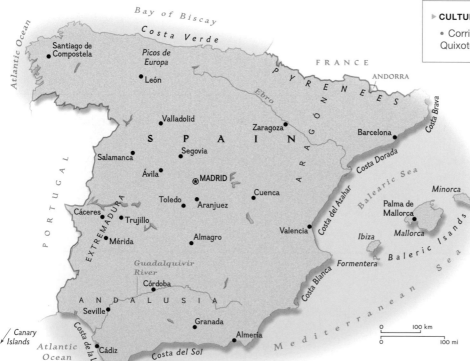

Casa Batllo in Barcelona is an example of Antoni Gaudí's extravagant architecture.

A statue of Philip III occupies the center of the imposing Plaza Mayor in Madrid.

and Caleta, is one of the rare sites international beach tourism has not overwhelmed.

▶ CITIES AND MONUMENTS

Most of the large cities have a monument and a historic section around their Plaza Mayor. The country's urban highlights are listed below, from north to south.

In Bilbao, the Guggenheim Museum built by Frank Gehry is admired as much for its collection of contemporary art as for its architecture. The Romanesque cathedral of **Santiago de Compostela,** the age-old pilgrimage destination, continues to draw a steady stream of pilgrims and tourists. The cathedral of **León** also deserves a visit for its splendid stained-glass windows.

In **Zaragoza,** the Basilica of Our Lady of the Pillar and the Aljaferia Palace, the ancient palace of Muslim rulers and later the residence of the Catholic kings of Aragón, are witnesses to Spain's turbulent history.

The altarpieces and colorful sculptures in the San Gregorio College of **Valladolid;** the Black Madonna of Montserrat, "mother of the

Traveler's Notebook

MAIN CONTACTS
Embassy of Spain
2375 Pennsylvania Avenue, NW
Washington, DC 20037
(202) 452-0100
www.spainemb.org
www.spain.info
Spanish Consulate General
20 Draycott Place
London SW3 2RZ, UK
+ 44 (0) 20 7589 8989
www.conspalon.org

TRAVEL DOCUMENTS FOR U.S. & U.K. CITIZENS
Passport

HEALTH ISSUES
No problems, other than staying in the sun too long

TRAVEL TIME TO DESTINATION & TIME DIFFERENCE
New York to Barcelona: 7 hours 35 minute nonstop flight; EST +6. London to Barcelona: 2 hours nonstop flight; GMT +1

AVERAGE TRIP COST
$2,540/£1,650 for a classic 15-day stay

LANGUAGE & CURRENCY
Official languages: Spanish; Basque in Basque Country; and Catalan in Catalonia and on the Balearic Islands
Currency: euro

POPULATION
40,448,000 inhabitants in 15 provinces that show distinct

regional differences.
Capital: Madrid

RELIGION
Mostly Catholic

FESTIVALS
January 6: Three Kings Day; February or March: Carnival in Cádiz; middle of March: *fallas* to honor St. Joseph in Valencia; March or April: Holy Week (procession of the penitents in Seville); beginning of July: St.

Fermín's Day in Pamplona; end of July: Feast of St. James; September 24: Festa de la Mercè in Barcelona

SHOPPING
Classical guitars from Andalusian craftsmen, painted fans, castanets

The Tagus River flows around Toledo, a city whose Moorish heritage found expression in its architecture.

Catalans"; and the clock towers and portals of the small Romanesque churches are some of the treasures of Catalonia. Figueres features the extravagant Dalí Museum, and nearby the house where Dalí lived in Port Lligat and the house-museum Gala Dalí—the villa he dedicated to his wife Gala—in the village of Púbol are both open for visitors.

In **Barcelona,** architect Antoni Gaudí left a legacy with the fantastic buildings of the Sagrada Familia, Park Güell, Casa Mila, and Casa Batllo. Here visitors rub shoulders with a multiethnic citizenry in the historic, Gothic neighborhoods, in the Plaça Reial and Ribera, the Chinese *barrio,* and in the *bodegas* (bars) and restaurants. The Catalan capital is also home to the Miró Foundation, Picasso Museum, and Maritime Museum.

Salamanca is famous for the 13th-century university and its plateresque facade, the Vieja and Nueva Cathedral, and the Museum of Modern Art. The Alcázar and aqueduct of **Segovia** and the ramparts, churches, and mysticism of St. Teresa enliven Ávila.

Madrid's sites include the Plaza Mayor; the royal palace; baroque monuments and churches; the Prado, featuring works by Goya, Rubens, Velazquez, Titian, and El Greco, among many others; the Thyssen-Bornemisza Foundation and its Impressionist art; and the Reina Sofia Center, with art by Dalí, Miró, and Picasso (among them his famous *Guernica*). Madrid is also known for its nightlife in the historic quarter around Plaza Santa Ana or the scene in the popular quarter of Lavapiés.

Northeast of Madrid, El Escorial, the large royal necropolis of the 16th century, where paintings by Titian,

When to Go			
	MAINLAND BEACHES	CANARY ISLANDS	BALEARIC ISLANDS
JANUARY			
FEBRUARY			
MARCH			
APRIL			☼
MAY		☼	☼
JUNE	☼	☼	☼
JULY	☼	☼	
AUGUST	☼	☼	
SEPTEMBER	☼	☼	☼
OCTOBER		☼	☼
NOVEMBER			
DECEMBER			

The picturesque Alhambra with the artful gardens of the Palacio de Generalife are the main attraction in Granada.

El Greco, and early Flemish masters are on view, should not be forgotten.

Other worthwhile destinations include the "hanging" houses of **Cuenca** and the royal palace and splendid gardens of **Aranjuez. Toledo,** the city of El Greco (home and museum), built on a promontory and encircled by the Tagus River, displays historic Moorish architecture, a cathedral, and the Judería quarter with the Synagogue de el Transito. The wooden galleries of the Corral de Comedias theater in **Almagro** are in a league by themselves.

Valencia is known as much for its public monuments (Lonja de la Seda, the silk exchange market, Dos Aguas Palace) as for its religious buildings (cathedral and numerous Gothic structures). The beautiful facades of the palaces of the marquis and the dukes and a statue of Pizarro make **Trujillo** stand out.

Cáceres is inscribed on the UNESCO World Heritage list for its mixture of Roman, Muslim, and Christian architecture. A Roman amphitheater and aqueduct are also highlights in **Mérida.** The towns of Guadalupe, Jerez de los Caballeros, and Zafra in **Extremadura** are known for the religious monuments.

The eighth-century Great Mosque with double arches in **Córdoba** was transformed into the Cathedral of our Lady of Assumption.

Seville offers an immense 15th-century cathedral, flanked by the bell tower and ancient minaret called the Giralda; the 16th-century Alcázar (Moorish architecture); the

historic Santa Cruz and Macarena districts; and in the provincial fine arts museum, works by Zurbaran and Murillo.

In **Granada,** the gems are the Alhambra—a Moorish palace and fortress complex, complete with baths and mosques—and the accompanying Generalife Gardens.

The Alcazaba, an ancient Moorish fort in **Almería;** the two hundred works by native son Pablo Picasso in the Museo Picasso in Málaga; the white houses and Hospital de Nuestra Señora del Carmen, and art in the

Toward Galicia, the **Picos de Europa** mountains (Cantabrian Cordillera), Sierra de Montserrat, Guadarrama, Gredos, and Cazorla define the landscape.

Visitors lament the closing of the Altamira cave, located between the northwest coast and the Cantabrian Cordillera, where Paleolithic rock paintings show prehistoric bison and other animals; however, a visitor center does its best to reproduce the experience. Other area caves include the Torca del Carlista, the largest cavern in Europe, and the Ojo Guarena.

The Picos de Europa in the Cantabrian Mountains attract hikers and climbers.

churches—such as the Oratorio de la Santa Cueva, with three altarpieces by Goya—in **Cádiz** complete the list.

▶ LANDSCAPE

In **Aragón,** the Pyrenees are best visited in the National Park of Ordesa at the foot of Monte Perdido (Mascun River, Gallego River). This nature reserve of the Sierra de Guara is a favorite of canyoneers. Southeast of Andorra, the **Pyrenees** attract hikers on little-known trails in the Cadi-Moixero reserve and the volcanic region of Garrotxa.

Between Madrid and Valencia, it's worthwhile to make a detour to the Ciudad Encantada (Enchanted City) with its amazing rock formations. North of Málaga, a similar strange karst formation occurs at the Torcal de Antequera.

In the south, dominated by the Sierra Nevada, sun-blazed **Andalusia** offers a succession of interesting panoramas: olive groves and haciendas in the Jaen region; arid plains in Almería; semidesert country and a mini-Hollywood in Tabernas, where "spaghetti Westerns" are filmed (for example, *Once upon a Time in the West* with Henry Fonda); and the white villages, such as Arcos de la Frontera and Ronda. The mighty **Guadalquivir River** is best seen in spring when the fields are covered with flowers and the cork oak forests harbor varied wildlife.

▶ CULTURAL HERITAGE

Spaniards flock to their local Plaza de Toros arena for the beginning of the corrida—bullfighting—on Sundays at 5 p.m. The San Fermín festival in Pamplona at the beginning of July is not so punctual; that's when the bulls run down the streets and people try to outrun them.

The pilgrimages to the Virgin, processions during Holy Week (Seville has the most famous one), the *ferias* (fairs), and the Cavalcade of the Magi on January 6 make for a year of rituals. During the *fallas* in Valencia, imposing papier-mâché statues are paraded through town and burned on St. Joseph's Day. The Festa de la Mercè in Barcelona on September 24, Carnival

in Cádiz in the Vina neighborhood, and of course, the flamenco shows in Andalusia all draw the crowds.

In New Castile, the country's heart, the La Mancha plateau compensates for its monotonous landscape with picturesque, fortified villages and is well known thanks to Cervantes. Indeed, there is the Don Quixote Route that passes through the locations where the hero was knighted (an inn in Puerto Lapice), the windmills of Consuegra or Quintanar de la Orden,

What to See and Do in the Balearic Islands
▶ **COASTS** • Beaches of Mallorca, Minorca, and Ibiza
▶ **LANDSCAPE AND HIKES** • Caves of Drach, Mallorca
▶ **MONUMENTS AND MUSEUMS** • Palma de Mallorca (La Seu cathedral, royal palace, Miró Foundation)

the homeland of Dulcinea at El Tobosco, and the castles of Belmonte and Guadamur.

Balearic Islands

▶ COASTS

The names Mallorca, Minorca, Ibiza, and to a lesser degree Formentera are practically synonyms for European beach vacations. And there is much more available, especially for those who are fans of sailing, diving, and windsurfing.

In **Mallorca,** the long beaches around Palma are often crowded. It's quieter along the riverbanks and coves of the north coast.

Minorca has some 120 miles of coast, with favorite beaches at Cala Pregonda and La Vall. Fewer people visit the coves.

As to **Ibiza,** the beaches near the city are always crowded, whereas

A festival in Seville never goes without colorful demonstrations.

The Balearic Islands with their charming villages bask in the warm sun.

the deep coves in the north offer a calmer scene.

▶ LANDSCAPE AND HIKES
Mallorca offers hiking trails that lead up to 4,900-foot-high peaks and to the Caves of Drach, site of an underground lake, near Porto Cristo. At Formentera, the sandstone cliffs, deep coves, and pines lend variety to the otherwise flat landscape.

▶ MONUMENTS AND MUSEUMS
Art is all around in **Palma de Mallorca.** La Seu cathedral has one of the highest naves in the world, and the Arab baths and royal palace of La Almudaina are a few remnants of the island's Moorish past.

The Miró Foundation holds a permanent collection of the namesake painter's works, and the Es Baluard Museum of contemporary art exhibits works by Miró, Dalí, Picasso, and Barceló.

Canary Islands

▶ COASTS
The water in the Canaries is not as warm as in the Balearics despite the latitude. But the hotels along the beaches are just as plentiful, especially on the south coast of **Gran Canaria.**

What to See and Do in the Canary Islands

▶ COASTS
• Beaches of Gran Canaria, Tenerife, Lanzarote, Fuerteventura, El Hierro

▶ LANDSCAPE AND HIKES
• Volcanoes (Pico de Teide), La Gomera

Favorite beaches on **Tenerife** are Los Cristianos and Playa de las Américas in the south. **Lanzarote** and **Fuerteventura** have kept their typical Spanish character. The strong waves off the beaches of Tenerife, Lanzarote, and Fuerteventura attract funboard surfers. **El Hierro,** the westernmost island, is not yet known as a strong tourist draw.

▶ LANDSCAPE AND HIKES
More than in the Balearics, the fascinating volcanic landscape of the Canary Islands invites hikers and trekkers to explore the volcanoes of La Palma Island, the violet-colored cone of **Pico de Teide** on Tenerife, the peaks on Gran Canaria, and the craters of the Montanas del Fuego on Lanzarote.

The small island of **La Gomera** can be reached only by boat from Tenerife and offers hikers a subtropical laurel forest to explore. El Hierro has a similar landscape and trails that lead up to the 4,900-foot-high Malpaso.

The famous sleeping Buddha bestows an enigmatic smile on its visitors.

Sri Lanka

📷 *Tourists enjoy this island of myriad attractions, where a day's tour can start with a visit to Buddhist ruins and end with relaxation on white sandy beaches.*

What to See and Do in Sri Lanka

▶ **MONUMENTS**
- Anuradhapura, Polonnaruwa, Dambulla
- Medirigiriya, Aukana, Sigiriya, Kandy

▶ **COASTS**
- Southwest and northwest coasts (beaches, surfing, scuba diving)

▶ **FESTIVALS**
- Esala Perahera Festival (Kandy)
- Pilgrimage to Adam's Peak

▶ **FAUNA AND FLORA**
- National parks (elephants)
- Botanical gardens (Peradeniya), tea plantations (Nuwara Eliya), spice gardens

▶ MONUMENTS

Sri Lanka boasts numerous architectural landmarks, the majority of which are Buddhist shrines and annual pilgrimage sites. The former capital, **Anuradhapura,** is home to monasteries, stupas (Jetavanarama, Thuparama, Ruvanvaliseya), and ruins of palaces and pools. It is also famous for its sacred Bodhi tree, an offshoot of the *Ficus religiosa* tree in Bodh Gaya (India) under which the Buddha attained enlightenment.

Polonnaruwa offers stupas, temples, relics, and imposing Buddha

Traveler's Notebook

MAIN CONTACTS
Embassy of Sri Lanka
2148 Wyoming Avenue, NW
Washington, DC 20008
(202) 483-4025
www.slembassyusa.org
Sri Lanka High Commission
13, Hyde Park Gardens
London W2 2LU, UK
+ 44 (0) 207 262 1841
www.srilanka
.embassyhomepage.com

TRAVEL DOCUMENTS FOR U.S. & U.K. CITIZENS
Passport
30-day landing visa issued on arrival

HEALTH ISSUES
Malaria prophylaxis is recommended for travel to all areas except Colombo, Kalutara, and Nuwara Eliya.

TRAVEL TIME TO DESTINATION & TIME DIFFERENCE
New York to Colombo: 18 hours connecting

flight; EST +10:30. London to Colombo: 9 hours 45 minutes nonstop flight; GMT +5:30

AVERAGE TRIP COST
$1,775/£1,150 for a week at a beach resort

LANGUAGE & CURRENCY
Official languages: Sinhalese (spoken by three out of four people) and Tamil; English is widely spoken
Currency: Sri Lankan rupee; U.S. dollars accepted

POPULATION
Of the 20,926,000 inhabitants, 70 percent are Sinhalese; the restive Tamil minority (20 percent) live in the north of the country.
Capital: Colombo is the seat of government, Sri Jayewardenepura Kotte the seat of parliament

RELIGION
Sinhalese are predominantly Buddhist, and Tamils are Hindu; 7.5 percent of the population is

Muslim, and another 7.5 percent is Christian.

FESTIVALS
June: Poson Poya, Buddhist pilgrimage celebrated on the full moon in Anuradhapura; August: Esala Perahera procession in Kandy; December to April: Pilgrimage to Adam's Peak

SHOPPING
Tea, precious stones, textiles (saris), batik, woodcarvings

states, especially the Sleeping Buddha in the Gal Vihara rock temple. The city of **Dambulla** completes this "cultural triangle," with its 48 Buddhas guarding the rock temples. Other important sites include **Medirigiriya,** where 68 stone pillars form a pattern of three concentric circles, and the giant Buddha at **Aukana.**

Representative of a different architectural style, the fortress of King Kassapa I in **Sigiriya** is decorated with frescos of young women, known as the "maidens of Sigiriya." In the center of the island, the town of **Kandy** is famous for its temples, notably Dalada Maligawa, where within its pink walls visitors can see the relic of the tooth of the Buddha.

▶ COASTS

A tropical destination, Sri Lanka has some 1,000 miles of coastline dotted with beaches. The southwest coast is lined with fishing villages and long beaches and is home to the most popular resorts (Negombo, Kalutara, Bentota, Mount Lavinia). Other areas in the south (Galle, Hikkaduwa, Weligama) are trying to reestablish tourism after the destruction from the tsunami. Batticaloa and Trincomalee are the most popular spots for snorkeling on the northeast coast. Conditions for surfing and scuba diving are ideal around the island.

▶ FESTIVALS

The Esala Perahera Procession takes place in Kandy at the full moon in August. It is the most spectacular festival on the island. Pilgrims give homage to the relic of the tooth of the Buddha, carried on a sacred elephant.

During the full moon from December to April, the pilgrimage

to Adam's Peak attracts Christians, Muslims, Hindus, and Buddhists.

▶ FAUNA AND FLORA

Elephants abound in the parks, the most famous being Gal Oya National Park, Wilpattu National Wildlife Park, and Yala National Park. In Pinnawela (about 60 miles

	COLOMBO AND WEST COAST	EAST COAST	INTERIOR
When to Go			
JANUARY	☼		
FEBRUARY	☼		☼
MARCH	☼	☼	☼
APRIL		☼	☼
MAY		☼	
JUNE		☼	
JULY		☼	
AUGUST		☼	
SEPTEMBER		☼	
OCTOBER			
NOVEMBER			
DECEMBER			

Advice

■ **Pros**
• A diverse itinerary highlighting beach and cultural attractions. The climate differs from east to west, which extends the favorable travel season.

■ **Cons**
• The country's struggle for a lasting peace.

■ **Safety**
• Travel to the northern and northeastern regions (Jaffna, Trincomalee, Batticaloa, and Ampara Provinces) is not advised.

■ **Special Tip**
• Visitors increasingly come to Sri Lanka to experience Ayurvedic medicine, a Hindu practice known as "veda of life."

from Colombo), tourists flock to the elephant "orphanage," home to elephants unable to survive in the wild. Near Kandy are three botanical gardens, of which **Peradeniya** is the most famous and elaborate, with its thousands of trees, bamboo forests, and 150 species of orchids. In the south, the Sinharaja Forest Reserve is also worth visiting.

In the south, the Sinharaja Forest Reserve has been designated a Biosphere Reserve and World Heritage site for its rain forest eco-region with a wealth of endemic species and rare species of birds.

Tea plantations surround the **Nuwara Eliya** weather station and date back to the British era. Visitors can tour the Lipton and Dilman factories, where tradition and expertise have nurtured two of the world's best known tea companies.

Spices are also abundant on Sri Lanka (cinnamon, ginger, vanilla). Touring spice gardens is becoming increasingly popular, especially in the area between Dambulla and Kandy.

What to See and Do in Sweden

▶ **OUTDOOR AND LEISURE ACTIVITIES**

- Hiking in national parks and in Lapland (midnight sun, northern lights)
- Lakes (fishing), Göta Canal (cruising), Tyresta National Park
- Gotland Island, Gotska Sandön

▶ **WINTER SPORTS**

- Downhill and cross-country skiing

▶ **CITIES AND MONUMENTS**

- Malmö, Uppsala, Göteborg
- Stockholm (old town, museums, castles)
- Sigtuna, Scania (manors, castles, medieval churches, Kalmar Castle)

The "multiactivity trip" has drastically changed tourism in Lapland.

Sweden

Tourism in Sweden focuses on its large forests and lakes, as well as an invigorating climate, ideal for all kinds of hiking or multiactivity trips to Lapland, land of the midnight sun and the northern lights.

▶ **OUTDOOR AND LEISURE ACTIVITIES**

Lakes, rivers, and forests are the main attractions for hiking in the national parks of Abisko, Muddus, Padjelanta, Peljekaise, Sarek, and Stora Sjöfallet. Around Vänern Lake, the Kinnekulle lava plateau is by far the most beautiful place in southern Sweden.

The most tiring but also most interesting walking tours, however, lead through **Lapland.** In addition to the unique sight of the midnight sun in summer or the northern lights in winter, visitors can meet with the Sami people and discover their traditions, besides encountering reindeer, beavers, lynx, and, in summer, mosquitoes.

A cruise on the **Göta Canal,** which connects Stockholm with Göteborg, is a pleasant experience as the boat passes by islands, lakes, and locks. Not far from Stockholm, **Tyresta**

Traveler's Notebook

MAIN CONTACTS

Embassy of Sweden
2900 K Street, NW
Washington, DC 20007
(202) 467-2600
http://www.sweden
abroad.com
Embassy of Sweden
11 Montagu Place
London W1H 2AL, UK
+44 (0) 207 917 6400
http://www.sweden
abroad.com/

TRAVEL DOCUMENTS FOR U.S. & U.K. CITIZENS
Passport

TRAVEL TIME TO DESTINATION & TIME DIFFERENCE
New York to Stockholm: 8 hours 10 minutes nonstop; EST +7. London to Stockholm: 2 hours 30 minutes nonstop; GMT +2

AVERAGE TRIP COST
$1,775/£1,150 for 10 days of winter sports in Lapland

LANGUAGE & CURRENCY
Official language: Swedish; English
Currency: Swedish krona

POPULATION
9,031,000 inhabitants, concentrated in the south; about 10,000 are Sami people and immigrants from Mediterranean countries
Capital: Stockholm

RELIGION
The majority of the population is Protestant (Lutheran), the state religion until 1983; minority of Catholics, Pentecostals, Greek Orthodox, Muslims, and Jews are also present.

FESTIVALS
March: Vasaloppet Race; June 24–26: Midsomman (midsummer night) celebrations; December 13: crowning of St. Lucia

SHOPPING
Glass objects, wooden clogs, and the famous little horses carved of pinewood

Advice

■ **Pros**
- Well-organized excursions for visitors focused on nature. Tourism for all seasons.

■ **Cons**
- Expensive.

■ **Safety**
- Like other Nordic countries, this is a quiet place for visitors. No major problems.

■ **Trends**
- Activities such as dogsledding or snowmobiling at Jukksjärvi in Lapland are becoming increasingly popular.

National Park protects a primeval forest of huge pine trees, where deer, elk, and a multitude of birds dwell. The southwestern coast is sunny and endowed with a mild climate, and the beaches between Halstad and Strömstad invite visitors to swim.

Gotland Island in the Baltic Sea is famous for its prehistoric ruins and unique limestone peaks, which also occur on nearby Fårö Island. **Gotska Sandön,** another neighbor island, is a national park with pine forests, dunes, and a variety of flowers, including—amazingly—orchids.

▶ WINTER SPORTS

Skiing (both downhill and cross-country) is very popular in Sweden. Some people would never miss the 90-kilometer Vasaloppet cross-country race, made famous by the future king of Sweden, Gustav Vasa I, when he skied it in 1521 while escaping Danish troops.

▶ CITIES AND MONUMENTS

Malmö (St. Peter's Church, town hall, fortress), **Uppsala** (ancient university, Gothic cathedral, castle, burial place of the heathen kings),

and **Göteborg** are attractive cities.

The Swedish capital, **Stockholm,** also called the "Scandinavian Venice," is built on 14 islands, along canals and bridges. To the east extend the islands and peninsulas of the Skärgard archipelago, dubbed the "Welcome Garden."

The attractions in Stockholm include the old town (Gamla Stan with its art nouveau–style facades, cobblestone streets, and baroque royal palace), its museums (Modern Art Museum; Vasa Museum, housing the wreck of a 17th-century ship by the same name; and especially the Skansen Museum, an open-air museum, exhibiting more than 100 historic buildings from all over the country), and the royal castles of Drottningholm and Gripsholm. The Christmas Markets in the Skansen Park and Stortorget, which take place during the first three weeks in December, are winter highlights, as is the crowning of St. Lucia on December 13.

Visitors should not miss some Swedish cultural monuments such

as the rune stones found at several locations between Stockholm and Malmö, the ruins of 12th-century churches, and the ancient streets of **Sigtuna,** as well as the medieval manors, castles, and churches in the south (**Kalmar Castle** in the province of **Scania**).

The small towns of Arvidsjaur, Jokkmokk, and Östersund are worth seeing for their wooden houses typical of the Sami people in Lapland.

When to Go			
	CLIMATE	WINTER SPORTS	MIDNIGHT SUN AND AURORA BOREALIS
JANUARY		❄	✔
FEBRUARY		❄	✔
MARCH		❄	
APRIL		❄	
MAY			✔
JUNE	☼		✔
JULY	☼		
AUGUST	☼		
SEPTEMBER			
OCTOBER			
NOVEMBER			✔
DECEMBER			✔

✚ *If you travel across Switzerland from Basel to Lugano, you will find the ideal setting for an exceptional film documentary that includes the most majestic peaks, the widest lakes, and the longest tunnels. If you let Switzerland seduce you, you'll come back in the summer for hiking and in winter for downhill and cross-country skiing.*

▶ LANDSCAPE, HIKES, AND WINTER SPORTS

Hiking is a staple of Swiss tourism, especially in the **Engadine** (canton of Graubünden), **Valais** (where the mountains rise above 13,000 feet), and **Ticino.** But the most diverse countryside is found in the **Bernese Oberland.** The cliffs bordering the Aar River are 160 feet high in some places, leaving only a narrow riverbed. The Interlaken region has many waterfalls, including the Giessbach, Reichenbach, Staubbach, and Trummelbach. On the southern slopes of the Bernese Mountains, mountain climbers as well as skiers and hikers appreciate the 15-mile-long Great Aletsch Glacier.

The Alpine resorts are geared to all kinds of winter sports; some of the most famous towns are **Zermatt** (between Monte Rosa, the Matterhorn, and the Weisshorn), **Davos** and **St. Moritz** (in Graubünden), **Gstaad** (in the canton of Bern), and **Crans-Montana** (in the Valais). The **Swiss National Park** in the Engadine is home to a great variety of wildlife.

The scenic lakes are also a big attraction, ranging from Lakes

Chillon Castle on Lake Geneva is one of Switzerland's romantic settings.

Switzerland

Traveler's Notebook

MAIN CONTACTS
Embassy of Switzerland
2900 Cathedral Avenue, NW Washington, DC 20008
(202) 745-7900
www.swissemb.org
www.my switzerland.com
Embassy of Switzerland
16–18 Montagu Place
London W1H 2BQ, UK
+ 44 (0) 20 7616 6000
www.swiss embassy.org.uk

TRAVEL DOCUMENTS FOR U.S. & U.K. CITIZENS
Passport

TRAVEL TIME TO DESTINATION & TIME DIFFERENCE
New York to Geneva: 7 hours 55 minutes nonstop flight; EST +6. London to Geneva: 1 hour 35 minutes nonstop flight; GMT +1

AVERAGE TRIP COST
$750/£500 for a week of hiking in the Alps

LANGUAGE & CURRENCY
Official languages: German (spoken by 75 percent), French, Italian, and Romansh. Currency: Swiss franc

POPULATION
7,555,000 inhabitants, distributed around 23 cantons; about one million are foreign born. Capital: Bern.

RELIGION
Catholics (47 percent) slightly out-

number Protestants (44 percent).

FESTIVALS
February or March: Carnival in Basel; July: Jazz Festival in Montreux; early October: grape harvest in Lugano; December 6: Fête de l'Escalade in Geneva

SHOPPING
A winning combination: knives, watches, and chocolate

Geneva and Neuchâtel to Lakes Constance, Lugano, Maggiore, and Lucerne.

▶ CITIES AND MONUMENTS

Geneva deserves a visit for its location on the lake and its *jet d'eau* fountain, but also for its old town (ancient cathedral, medieval houses, palaces, town hall, and Madeleine Church), its trendy neighborhoods (Carouge, Les Pâquis), and its botanical garden and many museums, such as the Ariana Museum (china and porcelain), Watch Museum, and Museum of Jean-Jacques Rousseau. On December 6, there is an event called Fête de l'Escalade, when the city celebrates its victory over the Savoyards four centuries ago.

Lausanne is worth seeing for its 13th-century cathedral and museums. **Montreux,** famous for its jazz music festival, also claims a milder

---

What to See and Do in Switzerland

▶ **LANDSCAPE, HIKES, AND WINTER SPORTS**

- Engadine, Valais, Ticino, Bernese Oberland (hiking)
- Zermatt, Davos, St. Moritz, Gstaad, Crans-Montana (winter sports)
- Swiss National Park, lakes

▶ **CITIES AND MONUMENTS**

- Geneva, Lausanne, Montreux, Basel, Lugano, Zürich
- Medieval towns

---

climate and is known as the "Vaud Riviera." Sion is visited for its fortified church, Notre Dame de Valère. **Basel's** Carnival is one of the best of its kind in Europe, but the town also has several good museums (Schaulager, Tinguely, and Vitra Design Museums, and the Beyeler Foundation). Beautiful gardens flank the shores of the

lake in **Lugano,** and the Villa Favorita holds the private collection of the Thyssen Bornemisza Foundation.

Three medieval towns in eastern Switzerland should be on any traveler's itinerary: Schaffhausen, with 12 of the former guildhalls still intact; Stein am Rhein, for its frescoed facades; and St. Gall, for its abbey and the two thousand early medieval books—handwritten—kept in the library.

Zürich, favorably situated on the Limmat River, features its Romanesque cathedral (Grossmünster) and the Frauenmünster, an old convent church adorned with stained-glass windows by Giacometti and Chagall, besides many important museums.

When to Go		
	CLIMATE	WINTER SPORTS
JANUARY		❄
FEBRUARY		❄
MARCH		❄
APRIL		❄
MAY	☼	
JUNE	☼	
JULY	☼	
AUGUST	☼	
SEPTEMBER	☼	
OCTOBER		
NOVEMBER		❄
DECEMBER		❄

Advice

■ **Pros**
- Ideal for winter sports and hiking in the most beautiful mountains of Europe. Great roads, railways, and high mountain trains.

■ **Cons**
- Expensive.

■ **Special Tip**
- Hiking and winter sports are the main attraction, but excursions by small panoramic train, such as the Bernina, the Wilhelm Tell, and especially the Jungfrau railway are appealing to ever more tourists and are no longer a secret.

An Arab fortress overlooks the ruins of the ancient Aramaic city of Palmyra, now listed as a World Heritage site.

Syria

Syria's history begins with some of the world's earliest civilizations, and its cultural heritage includes the ruins of ancient cities such as Palmyra, Apamea, and Ugarit, as well as the crusader fortress Krak des Chevaliers. As to other interests, the seaport of Latakia has first-class beach resorts.

Traveler's Notebook

MAIN CONTACTS
Embassy of Syria
2215 Wyoming Avenue, NW
Washington, DC 20008
(202) 232-6316
www.syrian embassy.us
www.syria tourism.org
Embassy of Syria
8 Belgrave Square
London SW1X 8PH, UK
+ 44 (0) 20 7245 9012
http://syremb.com

TRAVEL DOCUMENTS FOR U.S. & U.K. CITIZENS
Passport and visa

HEALTH ISSUES
Malaria prophylaxis is recommended between May and October for the northeast of the country and a few regions along the northern frontier (however, the risk is low).

TRAVEL TIME TO DESTINATION & TIME DIFFERENCE
New York to Damascus: 12 hours 30 minutes connecting flight; EST +7. London to Damascus: 5 hours 10 minutes nonstop flight; GMT +2

AVERAGE TRIP COST
An automobile tour of one week (flight; automobile with chauffeur and hotel at the stopover point) will be around $1,500/£970. An accompanied trip of Syria and Jordan of 15 days, everything included, comes to $1,900/£1,230.

LANGUAGE & CURRENCY
Official language: Arabic; other languages: French and English, and Aramaic is still spoken in a few areas
Currency: Syrian pound

POPULATION
19,315,000 inhabitants, 90 percent Arab with numerous minorities of Kurds, Armenians, Circassians, Jews, and others. Capital: Damascus

RELIGION
Islam is the primary religion; Christians make up 9 percent of the population.

FESTIVALS
April 17: National Holiday; July or August (end of Ramadan): Eid al-Fitr; September: Cotton Festival in Aleppo

SHOPPING
The broad selection of goods—including brocades, embroideries, hookahs, handblown glass, copper, silver, and handmade Aleppo soap—is enhanced by the atmosphere of the souks.

What to See and Do in Syria

▶ **RUINS**

- Palmyra, Hama, Apamea-on-Orontes, Doura-Europos
- Ras Shamra
- Bosra, Mari, Ebla, Krak des Chevaliers, Tell Mozan

▶ **CITIES**

- Damascus, Aleppo

▶ **COAST**

- Beaches near Latakia

▶ RUINS

Syria is one of the oldest countries of the Middle East, and its important civilizations have left behind great archaeological riches through the ages.

Palmyra (second and third centuries B.C.), Queen Zenobia's city, presents a vast group of ruins: a great temple of Baal, an agora, a Roman theater, and above all, imposing funerary monuments with towers, vaults, busts, and chambers.

Sculptures from the time of a neo-Hittite kingdom, established in the ninth century B.C., are preserved in **Hama.** Here, great wooden wheels called *norias* raised water from the Orontes River to route it into canals for irrigation.

In **Apamea-on-Orontes,** the main thoroughfare flanked by columns—the Cardo Maximus—was once one of the most beautiful streets in the Roman Empire; many of its ruins (temples, fortress) are still standing. On the site of **Doura-Europos,** archaeologists found the sanctuary of a synagogue from the third century, as well as a Christian house with a baptistery.

North of Latakia, **Ras Shamra** was the crucible of the Ugarit kingdom (second millennium B.C.). In 1929, archaeologists discovered at this site some clay tablets in alphabetical cuneiform, traces of the oldest alphabet in the world (some 3,600 years old).

Bosra is rich in monuments of several periods (Roman theater, cathedral, Umayyad mosque, fortifications, madrassas). The remains of the ancient royal palaces of **Mari** and **Ebla** are other sites that merit a visit. The fortresses on the hills were built much later by the crusaders. Between the towns of Tartus and Homs, the **Krak des Chevaliers** (Qala'at al-Husn) is one of the most beautiful fortresses in the Middle East.

The site of **Tell Mozan,** located about 400 miles northeast of Damascus, will perhaps become a new tourist center. In 1995, archaeologists uncovered the remains of the ancient capital Urkesh there. A temple erected around the 20th century B.C. by the Hurrians is one of the first traces discovered of these people.

▶ CITIES

Damascus takes pride in the prestige of its great Umayyad mosque

(begun in 706), one of the oldest and largest mosques and a true masterpiece. Other attractions are the citadel, the city ramparts, Saladin's tomb, the old Christian quarter, and the convent of Our Lady, Seidnaya. The archaeological museum presents a good survey of all the different epochs.

Damascus is currently undergoing some change. Many historic wood and mud-brick houses are being restored and turned into hotels, while every attempt is made to preserve the original architectural style.

Aleppo has its own Umayyad-period mosque (715) and a citadel, begun in the 12th century. Between these two points spreads a warren of little streets and shops. The souks of Aleppo are among the best in the Middle East. One specialty here is handmade laurel soap. The Ottomans left the city a number of other mosques and caravanserai.

▶ COAST

Syria has some 120 miles of coastline on the Mediterranean. But the cultural attractions eclipse interest in the beach resorts, the best of which are around **Latakia.**

When to Go		
	INTERIOR	COAST
JANUARY		
FEBRUARY		
MARCH		
APRIL	☼	
MAY	☼	
JUNE	☼	☼
JULY		☼
AUGUST		
SEPTEMBER	☼	☼
OCTOBER	☼	☼
NOVEMBER		
DECEMBER		

Taiwan

What to See and Do in Taiwan

▶ **CITIES AND MONUMENTS**

• Taipei (228 Peace Memorial Park, Longshan Temple, National Palace Museum)

• Taichung, Tainan (Sacrificial Rites Martial Temple, Confucius Temple), Kaohsiung

▶ **LANDSCAPE**

• Central Mountains (Yu Shan), Taroko National Park

▶ **COASTS**

• Baishawan Beach, Fulong Beach

• Kenting National Park

• Jibei Island, Green Island

Portuguese explorers called it Ilha Formosa, the "beautiful island," when they discovered Taiwan's pristine tropical coast. Today, the independent Republic of China is a country of 23 million people, a vibrant mixture of cultures and ethnicities, crowded on 14,015 square miles. However, the interior—with its lush mountains, soaring cliffs, and tropical beaches in the south—still sum up the old name perfectly.

▶ **CITIES AND MONUMENTS**

Taipei, the capital of Taiwan, is a modern and lively city of three million people. Visitors can tour the 228 Peace Memorial Park and Chiang Kai-shek Memorial Hall for a glimpse of incredible revival architecture or visit Longshan Temple, famous for the exquisite detail of its stone sculptures, woodcarvings, and bronze work. The National Palace Museum holds a large collection of Chinese artifacts. For an excursion from the hectic capital, Muzha's tea plantations in the hills and Yangmingshan National Park offer a respite. The Taipei night markets usually open around 6 p.m.

While **Taichung** is known for its vibrant nightlife, Taiwan's third largest city is also renowned as an educational and cultural center, thanks

Traveler's Notebook

MAIN CONTACTS
Taipei Economic and Cultural Representative Office
4201 Wisconsin Avenue, NW Washington, DC 20016
(202) 895-1800
www.taiwan embassy.org/US/ http://eng.taiwan .net.tw
Taipei Representative Office
50 Grosvenor Gardens London, SW1W 0EB, UK
+ 44 (0) 20 7881 2650
www.roc-taiwan .org/uk/

TRAVEL DOCUMENTS FOR U.S. & U.K. CITIZENS
Passport and visa (if staying for more than 30 days)

HEALTH ISSUES
No problems

TRAVEL TIME TO DESTINATION & TIME DIFFERENCE
New York to Taipei: 18 hours 35 minutes connecting flight; EST +13. London to Taipei: 13 hours 35 minutes nonstop flight; GMT +8

AVERAGE TRIP COST
$80–$250/£50–£165 per night at a three-star (or better) hotel

LANGUAGE & CURRENCY
Official language: Mandarin Chinese; other languages: Taiwanese and Hakka dialects
Currency: yuan (new Taiwan dollar)

POPULATION
23,024,956 inhabitants; 84 percent are Taiwanese, 14 percent mainland Chinese, and 2 percent ethnic minorities. Capital: Taipei

RELIGION
93 percent of the population is a mix of Buddhist and Taoist; 4.5 percent are Christians,

and the rest follow other religions

FESTIVALS
January 1: Founding Day; February 4: Farmers' Day; 15th day of the first month in the lunar calendar: Lantern Festival; first day of the seventh lunar month: Ghost Festival

SHOPPING
Jade from one of the jade markets, other precious stones, oolong tea, and electronics

Matsu
East China Sea
CHINA
Baishawan Beach
TAIPEI
Fulong Beach
Taiwan Strait
Quemoy
Jibei Island
TAIWAN
Taichung
Taroko National Park
Central Mountains
Pescadores
Philippine Sea
South China Sea
Tainan
Kaohsiung
Green Island
Kenting National Park

0 60 km
0 60 mi

to its National Museum of Natural Sciences, Botanical Gardens, and National Taiwan Museum of Fine Arts. Here visitors can explore the different calligraphic styles from imperial China as well as other Chinese art and antiquities. Northeast of the city, the 74-acre Encore Garden is a patchwork of European- and Japanese-style landscape gardens with models of famous European statuary. The pedestrian-only Jingming 1st Street is for boutique browsing and a cup of famous Taiwanese tea.

Tainan was Taiwan's political and military center from 1624 to 1885 and its capital from 1683 to 1885. The city holds nearly a quarter of the country's nationally listed cultural sites, mainly ancient temples, shrines, and forts. The western district features the Eternal Fortress, complete with moat, and the Old Fort at Anping; the central district has the Sacrificial Rites Martial Temple, one of the oldest Taoist temples in Taiwan, and the Confucius Temple of 1665.

Kaohsiung is Taiwan's second city, largest port, and major industrial center. It also boasts a wealth of

The gate to the Chiang Kai-shek Memorial in Taipei

museums and historical buildings, such as the former British Consulate, built in 1858, and the Kaohsiung Museum of History. The National Science and Technology Museum offers information on everything from the food industry to petrochemical products.

Other cities worth a visit are Banciao and Hualieu.

▶ LANDSCAPE

The rugged and largely unspoiled east coast is locked between Taiwan's **Central Mountains** (tallest mountain: Yu Shan) and the Pacific Ocean with towering sea cliffs along the shore. Erosion has carved spectacular gorges and expansive valleys throughout.

Broad, fertile plains extend over the west and northwest. **Taroko National Park** holds the famous Taroko Gorge, a top tourist destination for hiking through its marble-walled canyons. Hot springs dot the landscape throughout Taiwan and many have been developed as spas and resorts.

▶ COASTS

Taiwan's northern **Baishawan** and **Fulong** beaches are not well

developed, but the southern tip of the island, with **Kenting National Park** and beautiful beaches, is Taiwan's tropical playground. **Jibei Island** and **Green Island** are the other great beach destinations, complete with white sand, green mountains, and blue sea, including a seawater hot springs.

Advice

■ **Pros**
• Preserved Chinese culture, a center of Chinese pop culture, and impressive scenic sites.

■ **Cons**
• Crowded and congested city streets.

■ **Safety**
• The country is considered fairly safe from petty crime, but typhoons and tropical storms between May and November pose a different kind of threat.

■ **Special Tip**
• For traveling efficiently and with minimal hassle, use Taipei's modern, stylish, and convenient Mass Rapid Transit system, the most extensive of any in Asia.

When to Go		
	CLIMATE	KENTING NATIONAL PARK
JANUARY		
FEBRUARY		
MARCH		✔
APRIL		✔
MAY		✔
JUNE		
JULY		
AUGUST		
SEPTEMBER	☼	
OCTOBER	☼	
NOVEMBER	☼	
DECEMBER		

Tanzania

Tanzania is the worthy companion to Kenya for a safari, and in addition has the attraction of the snows of Kilimanjaro. The proximity of their national parks allows for an easy visit to both countries on the same trip. As an alternative, many travelers choose the hot sands of the Indian Ocean beaches, such as on Zanzibar, where old coastal towns and the scent of spices abound.

▶ WILDLIFE

As long as there are wild animals in East Africa, there will be crowds of visitors and cameras, but the numbers of animals are being reduced because of poaching and loss of habitat.

The **Serengeti** is the biggest natural zoo in the world with more than 3,600,000 acres of savanna, interspersed by granite islets, where 35 species of large mammals are living in the wild, including lions, giraffes, impalas, elephants, and gnus. The gnus undertake enormous migrations, at times with as many as a million animals, trekking from the Serengeti in Tanzania to the Maasai-Mara in Kenya. During the migration, they must cross the Grumeti River and survive its dangers (crocodiles, jackals).

The Serengeti is extended southwestward by the ancient volcanic **Ngorongoro Crater.** About 20,000 animals (lions, zebras, antelopes, cheetahs) roam in this caldera, including those that were hunted for a long time: elephants (only about 500 left, compared with 2,500 animals 20 years ago) and black rhinoceroses (on the brink of extinction with no more than 500 remaining). On the lakes along the rim of the volcano, there are great numbers of pink flamingos and hippopotamuses.

Nearby at **Lake Manyara,** visitors can spot lions, elephants, and some 400 species of birds. On the other side of the lake is the famous **Tarangire National Park.**

To the east and the southeast of Dar es Salaam, two parks are getting more attention: **Ruaha National Park** (and its 10,000 elephants) and the Selous Game Reserve, which includes the national parks of **Mikumi** (elephants, giraffes, gnus, lions) and **Udzungwa** with its primeval forest riches of birds and colobus monkeys.

What to See and Do in Tanzania

▶ **WILDLIFE**
- Elephants, flamingos, giraffes, gnus, hippopotamus, lions, rhinoceroses, zebras
- Serengeti, Ngorongoro Crater, Lake Manyara
- Other national parks (Tarangire, Ruaha, Mikumi, Udzungwa)

▶ **LANDSCAPE AND EXCURSIONS**
- Ascent of Mount Kilimanjaro
- Rift Valley, Ol Doinyo Lengai, Lake Tanganyika, Lake Malawi
- Spice Route to Zanzibar

▶ **PREHISTORIC AND HISTORIC SITES**
- Olduvai Gorge, Zanzibar

▶ **COASTS**
- Beaches on Zanzibar and Mafia Island

Animal lovers the world over are attracted to the national parks of Tanzania, where elephants still rule.

An iconic view in Tanzania: giraffes and Mount Kilimanjaro

Off the coast on the island of Zanzibar, the Jozani Forest harbors rare red colobus monkeys. Dolphins can also be seen along the coast playfully flipping and diving.

▶ **LANDSCAPE AND EXCURSIONS**
Mount Kilimanjaro, Africa's highest summit, is an iconic sight, but its legendary snows may be melted by 2020. Scaling the mountain involves a trek

of five to ten days, depending on the difficulty of the climb. It's a rather easy trek by the most common route (Marangu), but more tiring and more scenic by the steeper route (Machame). The landscape is majestic, but on some days, the number of visitors makes it seem like one endless crowd.

Kilimanjaro's fame has a tendency to mask the three other grand attractions of the country:

• The **Rift Valley** and its 9,442-foot-high **Ol Doinyo Lengai,** a sacred volcano of the Maasai, which offers an incomparable view of Lake Natron.
• **Lake Tanganyika**—two-thirds of which belongs to Tanzania— offers spectacular views of the highlands in the west, which plunge so steeply and abruptly that water pours down in a high, thin cascade (Kalambo Falls).
• **Lake Malawi,** the former Lake Nyasa, offers the most beautiful panoramas on the Tanzanian side of the high escarpment of the Livingstone Mountain Forests.

Ever since the Sultan of Oman had the idea of planting clove trees in Zanzibar a few centuries ago, the island has become famous for its spices. The Spice Route offers cloves, anise, bergamot, cinnamon, vanilla, and a veritable cornucopia of tropical fruits.

▶ **PREHISTORIC AND HISTORIC SITES**
A stop to see the two-million-year-old footsteps of *Australopithecus* and other more "recent" remains of

Traveler's Notebook

MAIN CONTACTS
Embassy of the United Republic of Tanzania
1232 22nd Street, NW
Washington, DC 20037
(202) 884-1080
www.tanzaniaembassy-us.org
http://tanzaniatourist board.com
Tanzania High Commission
3 Stratford Place
London W1C 1AS, UK
+ 44 (0) 20 7569 1470
www.tanzania-online .gov.uk

TRAVEL DOCUMENTS FOR U.S. & U.K. CITIZENS
Passport and visa

HEALTH ISSUES
Vaccination against yellow fever is strongly recommended outside urban zones. Malaria prophylaxis is indispensable as well in areas below 4,600 feet. A medical examination is advised for those intending to climb Mount Kilimanjaro.

TRAVEL TIME TO DESTINATION & TIME DIFFERENCE
New York to Dar es

Salaam: 19 hours connecting flight; EST +8. London to Dar es-Salaam: 9 hours 35 minutes nonstop flight; GMT +3 /

AVERAGE TRIP COST
$3,175/£2,050 for 15 days on safari, including Zanzibar

LANGUAGE & CURRENCY
Official languages: English and Swahili; the latter's principal dialect originated in Zanzibar and on the continental coast, but there are numerous other dialects.

Currency: Tanzanian shilling (U.S. dollars widely accepted)

POPULATION
39,384,000 inhabitants, 95 percent of whom are Bantu; principal minorities include Maasai, Sukuma, and Chaga. Capital: Dar es Salaam is the seat of government, Dodoma the seat of parliament

RELIGION
34 percent Christian (both Catholic and Protestant); 3 percent Muslim; and a large contingent of animists

FESTIVALS
January 12: Anniversary of the Revolution; July: Festival of Mwaka Kongwa and Tomasha in Zanzibar; December 9: Independence Day

SHOPPING
Maasai crafts dominate; also textiles with batik designs, rugs, coffee, and spices from Zanzibar

The beaches of Zanzibar offer a welcome respite after a safari trek.

Homo habilis and *Homo erectus* in the **Olduvai Gorge** is a must for students of anthropology.

When to Go

	CLIMATE	WILDLIFE	MOUNT KILIMANJARO
JANUARY			🚶
FEBRUARY			🚶
MARCH			🚶
APRIL			
MAY		🐾	
JUNE	☼	🐾	
JULY	☼	🐾	🚶
AUGUST	☼	🐾	🚶
SEPTEMBER	☼	🐾	
OCTOBER	☼	🐾	🚶
NOVEMBER			
DECEMBER			

The city of **Zanzibar** has several surprising historic sites to offer. Stone Town, built of black coral, is a fine example of a Swahili coastal trading town, but unhappily some of the old quarters are beginning to deteriorate.

Other sites in Zanzibar include the high houses with sculpted wooden doors, and the old Arab fortress Beit el-Ajaib, the "House of Wonders."

▶ COASTS

Zanzibar's white sandy beaches are very popular, especially those in the north and increasingly in the east. The beaches of **Mafia Island,** south of Zanzibar, are quieter, but the island's coral reefs and palm trees will soon attract more of an international clientele.

Advice

■ **Pros**
• Tanzania is one of the last paradises for large game animals living in the wild. Nowhere else but in Tanzania and Kenya are they as plentiful and as varied. The animals can best be seen in the period between July and October during the dry season, when the water holes are becoming scarce.

■ **Cons**
• A trip that needs to be planned long in advance because safaris are often booked up

■ **Safety**
• Travel in the frontier zones of Rwanda and Burundi, as well as to the northern part of Lake Tanganyika, is strongly discouraged.

Thailand

Thailand has mostly recovered from the tragedy of the tsunami of December 2004 and has regained its reputation as a sought-after, inexpensive tourist destination in Southeast Asia. The former Siam has much more to offer than beaches on the Andaman Sea and the Gulf of Thailand, namely, a strong Buddhist culture, Khmer architecture, pleasant countryside with orchids and rice fields, and, in the north, a chance to meet members of the hill tribes.

What to See and Do in Thailand

▶ **CITIES AND MONUMENTS**

• Bangkok, Nakhon Pathom

• Former royal cities of Ayutthaya, Lopburi, and Sukhothai

• Prasat Hin Phimai, Prasat Muang Tam (Khmer temples), Surin

• Chiang Mai, Lampang

• Bridge on the River Kwai

▶ **COASTS**

• Phuket, Krabi (west coast)

• Pattaya, Songkhla, Rayong (east coast)

• Cruising, diving (Similan Islands)

▶ **LANDSCAPE AND EXCURSIONS**

• Golden Triangle

• Highlands (long-necked Burmese women, hill tribes)

▶ CITIES AND MONUMENTS

Crisscrossed by endless traffic dominated by its noisy *tuk-tuks*, **Bangkok** presents a hectic image, but its 350 temples—including the Wat Phra Keaew (Temple of the Emerald Buddha), Wat Arun (18th century) and its iridescent tower, Wat Phutthaisawan, and Wat Benchamabophit—impart a calmer, devotional side. What adds to the city's attractions is the boats on the Chao Phraya River; the floating markets and the canals *(khlongs)* of another time; the food of street vendors and in the markets; and its futuristic elevated Skytrain. The Thonburi district, on the west side of the Chao Phraya River, holds numerous Buddhist temples.

Beyond Bangkok's *wats,* there are a number of nearby sites that

should be included in any itinerary, such as the stupa at **Nakhon Pathom,** which readily shows why it is the most sacred site for Buddhists in the country. The best known floating market in the country is held in a khlong of the Damnoen Saduak district.

Ayutthaya, the former capital, can be reached from Bangkok by boat on a 60-mile cruise on the Chao Phraya River. The city is noteworthy for its many temples, well-restored stupas, and an important collection in the Chao

An intriguing combination in Bangkok: the red roofs of the temples and blue water of the Chao Phraya River

Sam Phraya National Museum.

In the ancient city of **Lopburi,** the extravagance of King Narai's palace reveals some of the refinements of the old kingdom of Siam.

Sukhothai was the center of Thailand's first independent kingdom, established in 1238. The city flourished until the rise of Ayutthaya in 1378. The city's historic park holds a great seated Buddha and the ruins of the Wat Mahathat temple (13th and 14th centuries) and its stupas.

Near the border of Cambodia are the well-restored temples of **Prasat Hin Phimai** (eighth century), **Prasat Muang Tam,** and Prasat Phanom Rung with impressive Khmer architecture in **Surin.**

Despite the heavy tourist presence, the atmosphere is peaceful in **Chiang Mai,** the "rose of the north." The city's markets, festivals, and craftsmen (lacquer, silk, cotton) and the sacred temple of Prasat Doi Sutep are some of the highlights. Not far from there, in **Lampang,** the

Lampang Luang monastery is considered one of the most interesting and most beautiful of the country.

One unforgettable site is the Kwai River bridge built by Allied prisoners during World War II by order of the Japanese and at the price of thousands of human lives—an event dramatized in the film *The Bridge on the River Kwai.*

▶ COASTS

Although some 75 miles of the west coast were struck by the 2004

Koh Phi Phi, off the west coast, together with Phuket, possess some of Thailand's most coveted beaches.

Traveler's Notebook

MAIN CONTACTS

Royal Thai Embassy
1024 Wisconsin
Avenue, NW
Washington, DC
20007
(202) 944-3600
www.thaiembdc.org
www.tourism
thailand.org
Royal Thai Embassy
29–30 Queen's Gate
London SW7 5JB,
UK
+ 44 (0) 20 7589
2944
www.thai
embassyuk.org.uk

**TRAVEL DOCUMENTS
FOR U.S. & U.K.
CITIZENS**
Passport

HEALTH ISSUES
Malaria prophylaxis
is recommended in
the rural zones and
regions near Cam-
bodia and Myanmar.
However, there is no

risk in Bangkok and
in the principal tou-
rist areas.

**TRAVEL TIME TO
DESTINATION & TIME
DIFFERENCE**
New York to Bang-
kok: 19 hours 55
minutes connec-
ting flight; EST +12.
London to Bangkok:
11 hours 5 minutes
nonstop flight;
GMT +7

AVERAGE TRIP COST
A stay of about
ten days, includ-
ing Bangkok and
a beach extension
to Phuket, will run
about $1,270/£820
for the flight and
lodging. An excur-
sion to the eth-
nic groups of the
Golden Triangle
costs around
$2,100/£1,300
for 15 days.

**LANGUAGE &
CURRENCY**
Official language:
Thai; other lan-
guages: Chinese
and Malay, and
English in the cities
and tourist centers
Money: baht

POPULATION
65,068,000 inhab-
itants, divided into
numerous ethnic
groups. Capital:
Bangkok

RELIGION
Buddhism so per-
meates life in the
country that each
Thai is said to
spend at least three
months of his life
in a monk's habit.
The 6 percent of the
population that is
not Buddhist com-
prises Muslims and
Christians.

FESTIVALS
January or
February: Chinese
New Year; February
or March: Feast
of the Flowers
in Chiang Mai;
November:
Elephant roundup in
Surin, the Full Moon
Festival with flowers
and incense in the
boats in Sukhothai,
and the Feast of
Lights in Bangkok;
December 5:
national holiday

SHOPPING
Wood carvings,
silk, silver jewelry,
purses, sculptures,
handwoven textiles,
fashionable silk
clothes

tsunami, especially around Khao Lak and Koh Phi Phi, all the sites of the region have fully recovered. The much-loved beach resorts on the Andaman Sea, which had seen such boom years during the last several decades thanks to their rea-sonable prices, are restored to their old luster.

In **Phuket,** visitors must choose between a stylish atmosphere (Patong beach) or peaceful shores. Elsewhere, certain resorts have long been crowded, while others are tranquil escapes such as **Krabi,** Koh Samui, and Trang, the newest resort area, bordered in the east by numer-ous islets still free from the great tourist trade.

Koh Lanta and its two islets in the Andaman Sea are also very pop-ular and cash in on their renown as one location of the television series *Survivor.*

On the Gulf of Thailand, noisy **Pattaya,** the beach where Bangkok's

In Ayutthaya, a seated Buddha watches over the temples of the ancient capital of Siam.

When to Go

	CLIMATE	BEACHES IN THE SOUTH	DIVING
JANUARY	☼	☼	
FEBRUARY	☼	☼	
MARCH		☼	
APRIL			
MAY			✔
JUNE			✔
JULY			✔
AUGUST			✔
SEPTEMBER			
OCTOBER			
NOVEMBER	☼		
DECEMBER	☼	☼	

youth hangs out, is the veteran of Thai beach tourism. **Rayong,** east of Pattaya, is one of the newer beach meccas.

Divers congregate near the **Similan Islands** and Mu Koh Surin Island (sea turtles), not far from the coast of Myanmar, exploring the coral reefs and underwater grottoes for whale sharks, leopard sharks, barracudas, and groupers.

▶ LANDSCAPE AND EXCURSIONS

The hill tribes and their villages are situated in more isolated regions, with thick green forests to inspire an interest in hiking. The border region near Laos and Myanmar, known as the **Golden Triangle,** is infamous for its opium production. Some travel agents take advantage of this shady reputation to invite tourists to discover the authentic and just a bit mysterious atmosphere of the place.

In the mountains of the northwest, near Mae Hong Son, travelers may encounter the long-necked "giraffe-women." They are of Burmese origin, wearing traditional coils of brass rings that excessively elongate their neck.

Over the last few years, tourism in Thailand has embraced ecotourism. Long-established national parks are being discovered as worthwhile attractions, such as the Khao Yai National Park, southwest of Bangkok, and the caves of Tham Le Khaokob, not far from Krabi.

Tunisia

Tunisia is above all one of the great beach destinations on the Mediterranean. But more and more visitors come to join one of the méharées, *the camel riding excursions through the Grand Erg Oriental, or Great Eastern Sand Sea, in the Sahara. Other reasons for going include a hospitable population, northern regions that are as unknown as they are untouched by modern life, and a considerable architectural heritage.*

▶ COAST

Tunisia's many well-equipped beaches, offering everything imaginable for water sports, spread along 800 miles of shoreline. The beaches have star billing above other attractions because it is on the beaches that Tunisia built its reputation as a tourist destination, and this is where most tourists stay. The beaches get ever more crowded toward the south.

The dream of a vacation of sun, blue ocean, R&R, and spa services (thalassotherapy) can be fulfilled on the Jasmine Coast near **Nabeul** and **Hammamet.** The new and imposing

Jasmine Hammamet resort offers 40-odd hotels, a new medina (old town), an amusement park (Carthageland), and a marina—simply everything for an indolent vacation devoted to idleness, spa treatments, and water sports.

Other beaches along the coast are at **Port el-Kantaoui, Sousse, Monastir,** and **Zarzis,** ending with **Djerba Island,** where, according to Homer, Ulysses once stayed; that most legendary of travelers would be seriously challenged today by the crowds.

For divers, the seabed of the **Tabarka** peninsula, off the Coral Coast, is the best place to see red coral. Golfers can also enjoy their game in Tabarka.

▶ LANDSCAPE AND VILLAGES

The landscape in Tunisia's interior is quite varied and most pleasant in the south. The **Tozeur Oasis,** for example, is said to be the most beautiful in Africa, covering 2,500 acres with 400,000 palm trees. The ecological balance, however, is somewhat upset because of the presence of so many tourists and the construction of golf courses.

A few miles to the north lie the mountain oases of Chebika, Mides, and Tamerza. Moving farther south, visitors will travel one of the most unusual routes in existence, crossing the vast expanse of the **Chott**

What to See and Do in Tunisia

▶ **COAST**
- Nabeul, Hammamet
- Port el-Kantaoui, Sousse, Monastir, Zarzis, Djerba Island (beaches)
- Tabarka (diving)

▶ **LANDSCAPE AND VILLAGES**
- Tozeur Oasis, Chott el-Djerid, Nefta
- Matmata, Route of the Ksars, Berber villages (Chenini)
- Kroumirie Massif

▶ **DESERT**
- Grand Erg Oriental (*méharées*)

▶ **CITIES AND MONUMENTS**
- Tunis, Sousse, Monastir, Mahdia, Kairouan
- Ancient ruins (Carthage, el-Djem, Bulla Regia, Sbeïtla, Dougga)
- Mosques, synagogue

The way to al-Zaytuna Mosque leads uphill along the little shops and restaurants of the medina in Tunis.

Map labels: Tabarka, Bulla Regia, Carthage, TUNIS, Nabeul, Kroumirie Massif, Dougga, Hammamet, Port el-Kantaoui, Sousse, Monastir, Kairouan, Mahdia, Sbeïtla, el-Djem, TUNISIA, Mediterranean Sea, Djerba Island, Nefta, Tozeur Oasis, Matmata, Zarzis, Chott el-Djerid, Chenini, ALGERIA, LIBYA, Grand Erg Oriental

0 80 km
0 80 mi

Hammamet is a classic Tunisian beach resort, with its port and beautiful medina right on the shore.

el-Djerid salt lake, where mirages are guaranteed. **Nefta,** another famous oasis, lies west of the lake.

Farther east are the underground "troglodyte" settlements of **Matmata.** The **Route of the Ksars** is dotted with ancient Berber fortresses and their *ghorfas,* multi-level wheat storage houses; these include Ksar Ouled Soltane, Ksar Ouled Debbab, Ksar Hadada, Ksar Ghilane, and especially **Chenini,** a veritable eagle's nest, the most typical of the Berber villages.

Four top destinations in the north are: Jugurtha's Table, a curious isolated mound; the steep slope of Djebel Zaghouan; the cliffs of

Traveler's Notebook

MAIN CONTACTS

Embassy of Tunisia
1515 Massachusetts
Avenue, NW
Washington, DC 20005
(202) 862-1850
www.tconsulate.com
Embassy of Tunisia
29 Prince's Gate
London SW7 1QG, UK
+ 44 (0) 20 7584 8117

TRAVEL DOCUMENTS FOR U.S. & U.K. CITIZENS
Passport

HEALTH ISSUES
No vaccinations
required

TRAVEL TIME TO DESTINATION & TIME DIFFERENCE
New York to Houmt
Souk: 14 hours 10
minutes connecting
flight; New York to Tunis:
11 hours 20 minutes
connecting flight; EST
+6. London to Houmt
Souk: 6 hours 35 minutes
connecting flight; London

to Tunis: 4 hours 35
minutes connecting
flight; GMT +1

AVERAGE TRIP COST
$900/£575 per week
for a beach vacation
during the low season,
$1,000/£640 during high
season, not including
excursions; a camel trip
(méharée) in the Grand
Erg Oriental can some-
times be found for less
than $1,300/£840.

LANGUAGE & CURRENCY
Official language: Arabic,
though French is known
practically everywhere
Currency: dinar

POPULATION
10,270,000 inhabitants,
one-fifth of whom live
in Tunis, the capital,
and its suburbs

RELIGION
Islam is predominant;
minority of Catholics and
Jews

FESTIVALS
March: Festival of Car-
thage; July: Festival of
Jazz in Tabarka, and
symphonic music festi-
val in el-Djem; December:
Festival of Douz

SHOPPING
Pottery, Berber rugs,
carpets from Kairouan,
leather goods

Dougga features second-century ruins of the Roman Capitoline temple.

Cape Blanc, accessible near Bizerta by a cliff road along the Mediterranean with vertical drop of about 300 feet; and the **Kroumirie Massif,** not far from Tabarka, suitable for some fine hiking excursions.

▶ DESERT

The Sahara begins by way of the Grand Erg Oriental. At the end of December, the little town of Douz holds a festival celebrating traditional desert culture. Douz is also the gateway to the Sahara and the departure point for méharées. Tourists can join a one-week tour, alternatly traveling by camel or on foot, and gain an understanding of the desert life of the camel drivers. This may turn into a great adventure and yet is not terribly exhausting. The traditional itinerary goes from Douz to Ksar Ghilane, but tour operators keep finding variations, including a stop at the hot spring of Haouïdet.

▶ CITIES AND MONUMENTS

It's a pleasure to visit the capital city **Tunis** and the nearby villages of Sidi Bou Saïd and La Marsa. In the city, Bourguiba Avenue seems rather European, but the large attractive medina bursts with traditional architecture, especially around al-Zaytuna Mosque, the most famous one in Tunisia. The Bardo Museum holds a collection of some of the most beautiful mosaics in the world.

When to Go			
	CLIMATE	COAST	DESERT
JANUARY			☼
FEBRUARY			☼
MARCH	☼		☼
APRIL	☼		☼
MAY	☼	☼	
JUNE		☼	
JULY		☼	
AUGUST		☼	
SEPTEMBER	☼	☼	
OCTOBER	☼	☼	
NOVEMBER			
DECEMBER			

The town of **Sousse** also has an interesting medina, a grand mosque, and an important *ribat* (fortified convent). The ancient Punic city of **Monastir** boasts ramparts, its own ribat, and a mosque with pink marble columns. **Mahdia,** with its Great Mosque and sailors' cemetery, is also worth a detour.

Kairouan, the fourth most holy city of the Muslim world (Great Mosque of Sidi Oqba, Mosque of the Barber, Mosque of the Three Gates), is also known for the quality of its artisanship (carpets) and its Museum of Muslim Art.

Only a few walls remain of ancient **Carthage,** and the few artifacts that were found are exhibited in museums. But the amphitheater of **el-Djem,** the ruins of **Bulla Regia** (thermal baths, amphitheater, mosaics), the temples of **Sbeïtla,** and the impressive ruins of **Dougga** recall the Roman era. El Ghriba synagogue on Djerba Island is the oldest one in Tunisia.

Turkey

Turkey as a travel destination has come a long way from the 1970s, when tourists mostly stopped en route to other destinations. Today Turkey attracts visitors with great prices for trips to its premier beach resorts on the western and southern coasts, culture-rich Istanbul, and its exceptional landmarks at Pamukkale and Cappadocia.

▶ COAST

The development of beach resorts over the past 30 years has transformed the Turkish coasts—more than 5,000 miles of shoreline on four seas—into a destination that rivals other Mediterranean countries. Travel costs and accommodation choices (hotels, resort clubs) are comparable with rivieras farther west, and the favorable travel season extends to November.

While the Aegean coast (Kusadasi, Bodrum) is the most popular, the **Turquoise Coast** near Antalya in the south is the most inviting. This landscape features blue-green inlets with the peaks of the Bolkar and Taurus Mountains looming in the distance. The Turkish coasts are a favorite destination of cruise tour operators, as they welcome all kinds of vessels—from traditional wooden fishing boats to ocean liners. Cruising by schooner is very popular in the **Aegean Sea** (Bodrum, Gulf of Gökova, Dalyan) and off the southern coast.

More and more visitors come to Turkey to play golf, especially in the Beke-Antalya region.

What to See and Do in Turkey

▶ **COASTS**
- Turquoise Coast, Aegean Sea

▶ **LANDSCAPE AND HIKES**
- Cappadocia, Pamukkale
- Mount Nemrut, Mount Ararat
- Bolkar, Taurus, and Kaçkar Mountains (hiking)

▶ **CITIES, RUINS, AND MONUMENTS**
- Istanbul, Ankara
- Troy, Pergamum, Bursa, Ephesus, Aphrodisias
- Antalya, Aspendos, Side, Myra
- Konya, Göreme Valley (rock churches)
- Trabzon, Sümela Monastery, Ishak Pasha Palace

The coast around Bodrum, with its crusader castle, is a popular beach resort area on the Aegean Sea.

▶ LANDSCAPES AND HIKES

Turkey boasts two natural wonders: Cappadocia and Pamukkale. In the valleys of **Cappadocia**, centuries of volcanic eruptions produced lava flows that deposited a tufa ash. The best examples of these unusual formations are in the Göreme Valley with fairy chimneys and caves, which allowed for the construction of dwellings, resulting in veritable underground cities at Derinkuyu, Kaymakli, and Özkonak.

Pamukkale, meaning "Cotton Castle," is famous for its white rock terraces, which were created from the constant flow of hot, calcified water along rock walls where stalactites eventually formed.

In the interior, atop **Mount Nemrut** in the Munzur Range, is the tomb-sanctuary of Antiochus I Theos of Commagene (first century B.C.). This magnificent site, with its colossal statues and bas-reliefs, is rich in ancient history.

Far to the east is **Mount Ararat,** the long-inaccessible sacred peak where, according to the Bible, Noah's Ark ran aground after the Flood. The mountain attracts climbers to enjoy the summit's panoramic views, but the three-day trek can end in disappointment due to the persistent cloud layer.

To the south, in the **Bolkar** and **Taurus** mountain ranges, summer hikers can climb as high as 12,139 feet (Mount Embler), along the way encountering seminomadic people

Cappadocia owes its fame to the region's unusual rock formations and dwellings made of soft volcanic rock, or tufa.

grazing their sheep. To the north, the **Kaçkar Mountains** hover along the length of the Black Sea coastline and, although they are less well known, offer similar opportunities for hiking and climbing.

▶ CITIES, RUINS, AND MONUMENTS

First Byzantium, then Constantinople during the Roman Empire, and finally **Istanbul** during the Ottoman Empire—the names of the city may have changed over the centuries, but its allure and strategic importance astride the Bosporus strait have never waned. The jewel of Islamic art, its most famous highlights are the Galata Bridge over the Golden Horn; swarming crowds at the Grand Bazaar; the prestigious Süleymaniye Mosque; the rare elegance of the 17th-century Sultan Ahmed Mosque (Blue Mosque), adorned with blue mosaics; the Hagia Sophia, a fourth-century church transformed into a mosque (15th century) and later a museum (1935); the Topkapi Palace, the former sultans' residence and now a museum of Islamic art; other great museums devoted to ceramics, antiquities, and mosaics; and palaces, villages,

Traveler's Notebook

MAIN CONTACTS

Embassy of the Republic of Turkey
2525 Massachusetts Avenue, NW
Washington, DC 20008
(202) 612-6700
www.turkishembassy.org
Embassy of the Republic of Turkey
43 Belgrave Square
London SW1X 8PA, UK
+ 44 (0) 20 7393 0202

TRAVEL DOCUMENTS FOR U.S. & U.K. CITIZENS
Passport and visa

HEALTH ISSUES
No vaccinations

required. Malaria prophylaxis is recommended in the southeastern regions of Çukurova and Amikova from May to October.

TRAVEL TIME TO DESTINATION & TIME DIFFERENCE
New York to Istanbul: 10 hours nonstop flight; EST 7+. London to Istanbul: 4 hours nonstop flight; GMT +2

AVERAGE TRIP COST
$750/£500 for a week on the Aegean Coast, a little more on the Turkish Riviera, and

$1,000/£640 for a week in Cappadocia

LANGUAGE & CURRENCY
Official languages: Turkish (part of the Altay branch of the Ural-Altaic linguistic family, which used Ottoman script until 1928) and Kurdish (spoken by one out of five people, long ignored but now taught in schools); English is frequently spoken in cities and tourist areas
Currency: lira

POPULATION
71,159,000 inhabitants,

the majority descendants of Turkish nomadic tribes whose origins date back a thousand years; large minorities include Armenians, Greeks, and, in the southeast, Kurds (17 percent). Istanbul is the largest city with 7,500,000 inhabitants. Capital: Ankara

RELIGION
98 percent of the population is Muslim; however, Islam is not the state religion, and Turkey is officially a secular state.

FESTIVALS
January: Camel Wrestling Festival in Selçuk (Kusadasi region); June to July: Izmir Festival, Bursa Festival; September: Grape Harvest Festival in Urgüp; December: Ceremony for Mevlana in Konya

SHOPPING
Rugs, silver and gold jewelry, tea, and Turkish delight *(lokum)*—especially in the Grand Bazaar, where bargaining is a way of life.

Istanbul's Blue Mosque represents the epitome of Ottoman art.

and wooden houses (*yalis*) along the Bosporus. Istanbul has another beautiful but less familiar face: the art deco facades of the renovated and Westernized Beyoglu district. The beaches and fragrant vegetation of the nearby Princes' Islands (Prens Adalar) beckon those who want a brief escape from the city.

The capital, **Ankara,** pales in comparison to Istanbul, in spite of its citadel, old neighborhoods (Ulus, Samanpazan), Museum of Anatolian Civilizations, and Atatürk Mausoleum.

The country is astonishingly rich in archaeological sites. The ruins discovered at the site that was once **Troy** have only a distant tie to the legendary stories by Homer. Other ancient cities to add to the itinerary are: **Pergamum** (Greek ruins); **Bursa** (Ottoman influence); **Ephesus** (Greco-Roman city and former site of the Temple of Artemis, one of the Seven Wonders of the World); and **Aphrodisias** (Greco-Roman auditorium and stadium).

Along the southern coast, there are many interesting attractions, including **Antalya** (Roman and Islamic monuments), **Aspendos** (arguably the most beautiful Roman theater in antiquity), **Side** (variety of Roman ruins), and **Myra** (theater, Lycian necropolis, Church of St. Nicholas).

In the heart of the country, the city of **Konya** is home to the "whirling dervishes," an order of Sufi-Muslim ascetics. The order was founded

When to Go		
	CLIMATE	ISTANBUL AND INTERIOR
JANUARY		
FEBRUARY		
MARCH		
APRIL		☼
MAY	☼	☼
JUNE	☼	☼
JULY	☼	
AUGUST	☼	
SEPTEMBER	☼	☼
OCTOBER	☼	☼
NOVEMBER		
DECEMBER		

in the 13th century by Mevlana, whose birthday is celebrated every year in December, particularly in Konya. The **Göreme Valley** is noted for its churches hewn from soft volcanic rock and adorned with beautiful painted murals (Carikli, Elmati, Karanlik).

On the Black Sea coast, **Trabzon** (Trebizond) boasts many Byzantine and Byzantine-inspired churches (St. Sophia) and is surrounded by a rampart and ruins of a fortress dating back to the Greek period.

Traveling to the south from Trabzon, there are several sites worth visiting: the **Sümela Monastery,** founded in the fourth century, destroyed and later rebuilt; **Ishak Pasha Palace,** a former caravanserai on the Silk Road, near Mount Ararat; and the Armenian Cathedral Church of the Holy Cross, located on Akhtamar Island in Lake Van.

In Dubai, tourism is concentrating on the sea, as is evident in the offshore Burj al-Arab Hotel.

United Arab Emirates

Can it be true that after the black gold comes tourist gold? Dubai has forged an image as a paragon of extravagance with its hotels and shopping arcades—very luxurious, rarely affordable— and at the same time setting the trend in the recent, booming beach scene. Other pastimes include visits to the neighboring emirates, such as Abu Dhabi and, to a lesser degree, Sharjah and Ras al-Khaimah.

Traveler's Notebook

MAIN CONTACTS
Embassy of the UAE
3522 International Court, NW
Suite 400
Washington, DC 20008
(202) 243-2400
www.uae-embassy.org
Embassy of the UAE
30 Princes Gate
London SW7 1PT, UK
+ 44 (0) 20 7581 1281
www.uae embassyuk.net

TRAVEL DOCUMENTS FOR U.S. & U.K. CITIZENS
Passport

HEALTH ISSUES
No problems, except for extreme heat in the summer

TRAVEL TIME TO DESTINATION & TIME DIFFERENCE
New York to Dubai: 12 hours 30 minutes nonstop flight; EST +9. London to Dubai: 6 hours 45 minutes nonstop flight; GMT +4

AVERAGE TRIP COST
$900/£575 for a weekend in Dubai

LANGUAGE & CURRENCY
Official language: Arabic
Currency: dirham

POPULATION
4,444,000 inhabitants are spread over seven emirates: Abu Dhabi, Dubai, Sharjah, Fujairah, Ajman, Umm al-Qaiwain, and Ras al-Khaimah. The emirates count 850,000 foreigners among them (Arabs from various countries, but also Iranians, Indians, and Pakistanis). Capital: Abu Dhabi

RELIGION
80 percent of the population follows Sunni Islam, 16 percent Shiite Islam

FESTIVALS
January 12: Dubai marathon; March: Jazz Festival of Dubai; July or August (end of Ramadan): Eid al-Fitr; December 2: National Day; mid-December to beginning of February: Dubai Shopping Festival

SHOPPING
In the local souks, gold and oriental carpets are widely available.

What to See and Do in the United Arab Emirates

▸ **CITIES**
- Dubai, Abu Dhabi, Sharjah, Ras al-Khaimah

▸ **COAST**
- Beaches around Abu Dhabi

▸ **LANDSCAPE**
- Al Ain oasis, Ras al-Khaimah

▸ CITIES

Within a few years, thanks to a tourism marketing wizard, **Dubai** has become an obligatory stop for world travelers, a place where the West had an influence.

The modernist architecture and daring constructions—such as the Ski Dubai Dome, where you can ski on real snow—are extravagances that still do not obscure the old Dubai. The souks, the gold market, and the neighborhoods such as Bastakiya try to preserve their authenticity near the 18th-century Al-Fahidi Fort (which is now the Dubai Museum), Sheikh Said's palace, and the ancient port at Dubai Creek, where old dhows slumber, except for

a few wooden boats that are used for excursions.

Every year from mid-December to the beginning of February, the city holds a shopping festival with heavy promotions, when gold, oriental carpets, and all other sorts of fashionable things are sold at reduced prices.

Abu Dhabi should be visited for its mosques, palaces, gardens, souks, museum explaining the history of the discovery of oil, and the wharf where wooden boats are still made by hand.

The most interesting souks in the Emirates are in **Sharjah.** In **Ras al-Khaimah,** you can visit the fort and the archaeological site of Shimal with pre-Islamic tombs and a settlement from the third millennium B.C.

▸ COAST

Gone are the pirate coves, pearl fishers, and smugglers—today the fine, sandy beaches are in demand. The most visited beaches are around **Abu Dhabi, Dubai** (Jumeirah), and **Ras al-Khaimah,** and they may all experience a major tourist boom in the future, as scuba diving (at Fujairah), deep-sea fishing (barracudas, swordfish, yellowfin tuna), and golf (around Dubai) will be added to the attractions.

Actually, the traditional dhows and pearl fishers are still for real and contrast sharply with the Palm Jumeirah, a recently constructed palm-shaped artificial island with luxury villas and the Atlantis resort hotel.

▸ LANDSCAPE

Al Ain is the most spectacular oasis thanks to its camel

markets, whereas the regions of the northern point and those of **Ras al-Khaimah** have only a hilly terrain to offer. There are no great expanses of desert for trekking, but you can ski on sand dunes, watch trainers practice the art of falconry, or go on excursions by all-terrain vehicle.

When to Go		
	CLIMATE	BUDGET TRAVEL
JANUARY	☼	
FEBRUARY	☼	
MARCH	☼	
APRIL	☼	
MAY		✔
JUNE		✔
JULY		
AUGUST		
SEPTEMBER		
OCTOBER		
NOVEMBER	☼	
DECEMBER	☼	

United Kingdom

When you leave the suburbs of London behind, you'll realize how much the heart of the United Kingdom deserves to be explored. Scotland and its lakes, castles, and islands; the legendary land of King Arthur; the elegant gardens and manor houses; Wales and Northern Ireland—they are all so close and easy to visit.

England

▶ CITIES AND MONUMENTS

One of the first things tourists want to see in **London** is the Changing of the Guard at **Buckingham Palace** (every day from April to the end of July, and every other day during the rest of the year). Travelers can visit the rooms of the palace in August and September and see the Royal Collection (Rembrandt, Rubens) and the Queen's Gallery.

What to See and Do in the United Kingdom

▶ **CITIES AND MONUMENTS**

• London (Buckingham Palace, Westminster Abbey, St. Paul's Cathedral, Tower of London, museums)

• York, Bath, Bristol, Derby, Liverpool, Oxford, Cambridge, Stratford-upon-Avon

• Windsor Castle, Canterbury Cathedral, Stonehenge

• Tintagel, Glastonbury (King Arthur's legend)

▶ **LANDSCAPE**

• Cotswolds, Thames Valley, Cornwall, Peak District, Lake District

▶ **COASTS**

• Brighton, beaches of Kent, Isle of Wight, Cornwall, Beachy Head

---

Medieval Arundel Castle in Sussex is one of the many stately homes typical of the English countryside.

The British Museum is one of the largest and richest museums in the world.

One of the world's largest cities, London has a great deal to offer outside the palace gates:

• **Westminster Abbey,** a building close to the hearts of the English because it is there that all kings and queens are crowned

• Westminster Palace, the seat of Parliament, with its emblematic tower, Big Ben

• **St. Paul's Cathedral,** famous for its dome and its baroque architecture, overlooking the city's business district

• The **Tower of London,** a fortress known for the role it played in the past when it was used as a prison, but also as the place where the Crown Jewels are kept

• Tower Bridge, with its Gothic towers and its drawbridge system that was operational until 1976

• The British Museum, one of the world's great museums, free of charge by tradition, with rich collections of Egyptian, Greek, Roman, and Middle Eastern antiquities

• The British Library, with its famous books, manuscripts, and musical transcriptions

• The National Gallery, which displays famous works of art from the Italian, Flemish, and Dutch Schools

• Tate Britain (formerly Tate Gallery) with works of Turner and the Pre-Raphaelite painters

• Tate Modern, which provides London with the great modern art museum it lacked

• Victoria and Albert Museum, a decorative arts museum (famous chests, beds, china)

• Madame Tussaud's wax museum, as well as the Sherlock Holmes, Charles Dickens, and Geffrye museums

• Pubs in famous neighborhoods and squares (Soho, Trafalgar Square, Piccadilly Circus)

• Parks (Hyde Park, Kensington) and gardens (the Royal Botanical Kew Gardens)

The places on this list, together with the city's nightlife, and

Traveler's Notebook

MAIN CONTACTS
British Embassy
3100 Massachusetts Avenue, NW
Washington, DC 20008
(202) 588-6500
http://ukinusa.fco.gov
.uk/en/
www.visitbritain.com/
en/US/
www.enjoyengland.com

TRAVEL DOCUMENTS FOR U.S. CITIZENS
Passport

HEALTH ISSUES
No problems

TRAVEL TIME TO DESTINATION & TIME DIFFERENCE
New York to London:
6 hours 45 minutes
nonstop flight; EST +5

AVERAGE TRIP COST
$500/£320 for a weekend in London

LANGUAGE & CURRENCY
Official language: English, for the past six hundred years; other regional languages: Gaelic (western Scotland, Hebrides Islands, part of Northern Ireland),

Welsh (one fifth of the Welsh population), Manx (Isle of Man), and a distant French dialect (Channel Islands)

POPULATION
England: 60,776,000 inhabitants; Scotland: 5,200,000 inhabitants; Wales: 2,800,000 inhabitants; Northern Ireland: 1,600,000 inhabitants. Capital: London (city population 7 million; greater London 12 million)

RELIGION
Protestant majority: 57 percent belong to the official Church of England (Anglican) and Church of Scotland (Presbyterian); 13 percent are Catholic. In Northern Ireland, 54 percent of the population are Protestant, 42 percent Catholic.

FESTIVALS
May: Music and Arts Festival in Glastonbury; June: Tourist Trophy on the Isle of Man; summer: Fringe Festival

(arts festival) and Military Tattoo in Edinburgh; last weekend of August: Notting Hill Carnival in London

SHOPPING
London: classic styles at Harrods, hip styles on Carnaby Street, everything on Oxford Street; weekend flea markets in Camden Town, Portobello, and Covent Garden; post-Christmas sales Scotland: Shetland and tweed clothing, whiskey, ales

London shines with its famous Big Ben and the Great Wheel of the Millennium Dome.

shopping options—on Oxford Street and Regent Street, famous stores such as Harrods and Selfridges, Covent Garden and Camden Town markets, Notting Hill Carnival (with a distinct Jamaican flavor), Portobello Road Market, and the post-Christmas sales—and a privileged position on the Thames make London one of the great urban destinations in the world.

Moreover, London is constantly changing and at times turns things upside down. Places that once were forgotten or unimportant have now become trendy, such as the East End, Canary Wharf, and the Docklands. The Design Museum, Wine Museum, and Football Museum are also popular. Less successful has been the Millennium Dome near Greenwich, inaugurated in 2000.

York is the English city that has best kept its medieval heritage: its cathedral, York Minster, a Gothic masterpiece; its narrow streets, called "snickelways"; and its half timbered houses. **Bath,** an ancient hot springs spa from Roman times, was frequented by the aristocracy in the 18th century and boasts a neo-classical architecture like none other (Royal Crescent).

Bristol is a dynamic town, thanks to its university and its harbor with two legendary ships, the *Great Britain* and the *Mathew*, and water taxis. The city also features a Perpendicular Gothic church, St. Mary Redcliffe, and the Clifton Bridge—an amazing suspension bridge over the Avon Valley.

Derby, with its ancient cathedral dating from 943, is famous for its ale, the most symbolic of all beers. It is also the place where fine bone china used in the tragically famous *Titanic* was manufactured. Dishes in the pattern are on

When to Go		
	CLIMATE	FLORA
JANUARY		
FEBRUARY		
MARCH		
APRIL		
MAY	☼	✦
JUNE	☼	✦
JULY	☼	
AUGUST	☼	
SEPTEMBER	☼	✦
OCTOBER		✦
NOVEMBER		
DECEMBER		

display at the Royal Crown Derby Visitor Centre.

Liverpool—despite the reputation of its architecture, red sandstone cathedral, and museum (Walker Art Gallery, rich in British works by several Pre-Raphaelite painters)—is identified with the Beatles to such an extent that it is almost impossible not to visit the museum that tells their story (Britannia Pavilion). **Manchester** is changing its industrial image and becoming a pilgrimage destination for Manchester United fans.

Oxford and **Cambridge** are famous for their architecture and academic atmosphere, as well as for the quality of their museums (Ashmolean Museum in Oxford, Fitzwilliam Museum in Cambridge). In **Stratford-upon-Avon,** the memory of Shakespeare lives on with sites such as the home where he is said to

Tiny Mousehole Harbor in Cornwall

have been born, his tomb in Holy Trinity Church, and the Shakespeare Memorial.

Although the most famous monuments can be found in London, many others are no less important, such as the following:

• **Windsor Castle,** not far from London—a royal residence and the largest castle in the country—is famous for the beauty of Saint George's Chapel.

• **Canterbury Cathedral** dates from the 12th century and is famous for its delicate Gothic architecture and stained-glass windows.

• Durham Cathedral represents one of the finest examples of Norman architecture; and the city of Wells is proud of the early Gothic Wells Cathedral.

• Castles (Howard Castle, Harewood House) define the landscape in the Harrogate region north of Leeds.

• In Wiltshire, not far from Southampton, the **Stonehenge** megaliths—dating in their early stage from the end of the Neolithic—keep the secret of their origins, in spite of the efforts of archaeologists and "neodruids."

King Arthur's legend provides an unusual itinerary that leads from **Tintagel Castle** in Cornwall, where the famous king was said to have been born, to a site in Glastonbury that is the location of his supposed tomb. The Holy Grail, the object of the search by the Knights of the Round Table, is also supposed to be hidden there.

Another famous region is the moors near the village of Haworth, where the Brontë sisters lived and worked.

▶ **LANDSCAPE**

England's lack of high mountains is compensated for by the charm

of its countryside and the care the English lavish on their gardens, especially in Kent, Surrey, and Sussex. Other areas of interest are the **Cotswolds** and the **Thames Valley** between Windsor and Oxford, with a mandatory stop at Eton College; **Cornwall,** with its mild climate; and North York Moors and Yorkshire Dales national parks.

In the center of the country, the Dovedale Valley in **Peak District National Park,** featuring moors, rocks, and glens, is also worth seeing. Farther north, near the Scottish border, the **Lake District** is dotted with 17 lakes set among rolling hills and all of England's mountains higher than 3,000 feet.

Eilean Donan Castle in Loch Duig is one of Scotland's many medieval strongholds.

What to See and Do in Scotland

▶ **LANDSCAPE**

- Scottish Borders, lochs (Loch Ness)
- Archipelagos (Hebrides, Orkneys, Shetlands)

▶ **MONUMENTS**

- Castles and manors

▶ **CITIES**

- Glasgow, Edinburgh

▶ **WILDLIFE**

- Puffins, cormorants, snow owls, fish eagles.

▶ COASTS

The long beach at **Brighton** and the coasts of **Kent** are appreciated for their sophistication. The Yorkshire coast (Filey, Bridlington, Whitby), the resort areas of the **Isle of Wight,** and the **Cornwall** shoreline—where surfing is sometimes possible (Torquay)—are preferred by tourists, who go as far as the Isles of Scilly to see puffins and seals.

If travelers find the English Channel a little too chilly for swimming, they may warm up in the pubs of the fishermen's villages, for example, in Leigh-on-Sea, or visit the majestic white cliffs overlooking the Channel around **Beachy Head.**

Scotland

▶ LANDSCAPE

Scotland offers a great variety of landscapes, especially in the Highlands of the north. The moors are never more beautiful than in the fall when the heather blooms, contrasting with the green of the hills and the yellow of the broom.

Traveling from England, visitors discover the **Scottish Borders** region and are charmed by the castles, manor houses, and scenery (such as the Tweed River) described by Sir Walter Scott.

The trip north leads to the famous Scottish lakes (lochs). There are hundreds of them, but the most famous and most visited of all is **Loch Ness,** where the legendary monster supposedly lives, yet continues to elude searchers. Just as spectacular are Loch Morar and the high hills of the Loch Assynt region.

On a clear day, most of the lochs can be seen from Ben Nevis, the highest peak in the United Kingdom. Its peak can be easily climbed in the summer, as can its "rival," Ben Macdui, in Cairngorms National Park.

A popular alternative to the road to the lochs is the Whisky Road along the Spey Valley. It is a way of discovering the beauty of the landscape together with some traditions, visiting the older distilleries of the kingdom (dating from as early as the ninth century) with such famous names as Chivas and Glenfiddich.

Just as distinctive as the Highlands are the three archipelagos of the **Hebrides,** the **Orkneys** (with the Ring of Brodgar stone circle), and the **Shetlands,** marked by jagged cliffs, where in the open sea dolphins and whales frolic about. The

Edinburgh Castle in Scotland is a fortress built on a volcanic rock.

mild microclimate engendered by the Gulf Stream in the Inner Hebrides may even allow forget-me-nots, eucalyptus, and palm trees to grow in places like Gruinard Bay. The most beautiful grotto in the United Kingdom, Fingal's Cave, is found here, with its basalt columns reminiscent of organ pipes. The Isle of Skye is quite impressive for the shape of its cliffs ending with a 450-foot-high stone peak, the "Old Man of Hoy," a lighthouse made by nature.

▶ MONUMENTS

There are a great number of castles and manors in Scotland. The most famous are Tantallon Castle and Hopetoun House in the Lothian region; Floors Castle, Mellerstain House, Traquair House, and Abbotsford House in the Scottish Borders; Castle Campbell and Doune Castle in the central region; Glamis, where Shakespeare set *Macbeth,* and Dunnottar Castle on the northeast coast, sitting high on a headland above the sea; and finally the Dee Valley castles, including Balmoral.

The most romantic of the Hebrides Islands is Iona, mentioned by Jules Verne, Robert Louis Stevenson, and Sir Walter Scott, but it is cursed by 300 days of rain a year. The island hosts among its churches the burial places of several kings of Scotland, including Macbeth. The Orkneys harbor Neolithic sites of the Celts and Vikings, which can be found on an easy hike.

▶ CITIES

Glasgow carries the mark of Charles Mackintosh, an architect who, in the early 20th century, established his famous art school at 167 Renfrew Square. This school is an absolute must for any visitor, as well as the city's museums (Burrell Collection, National Galleries of Scotland, Kelvingrove Art Gallery, Hunterian Museum and Art Gallery).

Edinburgh divides into a modern town (Georgian facades on private homes) and an old town (citadel, royal treasures, Palace of Holyroodhouse) with a beautiful view of the Firth of Forth estuary. Leith Harbor to the north is steadily becoming a trendy neighborhood. At the end of the Royal Mile is a whisky museum.

▶ WILDLIFE

The archipelagos and northern islands are of special interest to ornithologists and bird-watchers, who can find cormorants, puffins, snow owls, and fish eagles.

What to See and Do in Wales
▶ LANDSCAPE
• Snowdonia National Park, Lake Vyrnwy
• South coast, Brecon Beacons National Park
▶ CITIES AND MONUMENTS
• Cardiff
• Castles (Caernarfon), Porthmadog

Wales

▶ LANDSCAPE

Wales boasts many beautiful natural sites, such as **Snowdonia National Park,** which offers hiking and climbing expeditions to the top of Snowdon (only 3,560 feet high, but hard to climb). You can reach the area by a 100-year-old steam train and come across sheep, heaths, and ferns in great quantity; the village of Portmeirion (with its amazing architecture), the Isle of Anglesey, the Lleyn Peninsula, and **Lake Vyrnwy** Nature Reserve and Estate are also among the region's attractions.

The south coast, between Cardiff and Swansea, is appreciated by the English, who like to spend the summer in quiet sea resorts with long beaches and many walking

South Stack, on the coast of Welsh Anglesey, features steep cliffs beaten by the waves.

In Northern Ireland, the Giant's Causeway flaunts its basalt columns.

and hiking destinations, such as the village of Mumbles on the Gower Peninsula. Going west to Pembrokeshire, there are several pleasant towns and seaports (Saint Davids and especially Tenby). Not far from Tenby, the Pembrokeshire Islands, especially Skomer Island, shelter many sea birds and seals.

Brecon Beacons National Park is another place where one can escape and enjoy nature.

▶ CITIES AND MONUMENTS

Cardiff has renovated its waterfront area at Cardiff Bay docks, which gave the city a needed facelift and has become a lively neighborhood. The same thing happened when the Millennium Stadium was built, which has relegated the legendary Arm's Park to a lesser venue. Cardiff Castle curbs this futuristic trend, as well as the unchanged National Museum and Gallery, whose collection of Impressionists is worth seeing.

At the end of the 13th century, King Edward I built about 20 castles throughout Wales to preserve England's dominance. The castles in Beaumaris, Conwy, Harlech, and especially **Caernarfon** are the best preserved of these.

Another interesting place to visit is **Porthmadog** in Gwynedd, the site of the world's oldest train company and the 13.5-mile-long Rheilfford Pfestiniog Railway.

Northern Ireland

▶ LANDSCAPE

Northern Ireland's main attraction is the **Giant's Causeway,** on the northern coast in County Antrim. Thousands of interlocking basalt columns, one after the other, create an unusual musical instrument played by the wind on stormy nights. The area is surrounded by cliffs and bays that contribute to the uniqueness of the landscape.

South of Belfast, in County Down, the **Mourne Mountains** are perfect for hiking and fishing.

▶ CITIES

Belfast, the capital and a major seaport, remembers the time when the *Titanic* was launched from its harbor with a museum and a spring festival.

Two other towns deserve a visit: **Armagh** (with a church built by St. Patrick in the fifth century) and **Derry** (an old fortified town of the 17th century).

The Channel Islands

▶ LANDSCAPE

The Channel Islands—Guernsey, Jersey, and Sark—are great for shopping and famous for the beauty of their countryside in bloom, their cliffs, seabird nesting sites, beaches and coves, little harbors, megalithic ruins, manor houses, museums, and castles. **Guernsey** still evokes the presence of Victor Hugo (Hauteville House is open to visitors from April to the end of September). The solitude-loving romantic will enjoy visiting Herm Island, East of Guernsey, in the low season.

Jersey, often considered one of the best hiking places in the United Kingdom, also enjoys an excellent reputation for its cuisine. On scenic **Sark,** cars are not allowed—a fact that draws many tourists.

Advice

■ **Pros**

• London is one of the world's great urban destinations. The countryside and cultural attractions (gardens, castles, lochs) from northern Scotland to Kent offer tourists a wide choice of vacations.

■ **Cons**

• The cost of a visit to London is very high.

■ **Safety**

• Getting used to driving on the left—a skill that can be acquired quickly enough. Latent terrorism.

■ **Special Tip**

• London, full of youthful energy, never stops attracting visitors. There is plenty going on—the end-of-the-year sales and the Notting Hill Carnival are just two examples. The evolution of new trendy neighborhoods continues, and special offers by travel agencies change with the times.

The Seigneurie on Sark, one of the Channel Islands, displays its roses in bloom.

United States

Many of the most *spectacular sites in the United States are not in the cities, but in the wide-open spaces of the countryside, where more than 50 national parks have been set aside for their unique natural features and great beauty.*

District of Columbia

▶ CITY

Washington, D.C., is a scene of celebrations and protests, of extensive green spaces and marble monuments, and of power and politics. The attractions of the capital city bring crowds year-round. First among the sites are the White House, the Lincoln Memorial, and the Capitol.

The museums on the National Mall cover a vast area of knowledge and popular culture and include the National Museum of Natural History, National Gallery of Art (Miró, Raphael, Rembrandt, Rubens, Van Gogh, Velasquez, Vermeer), National Museum of the American Indian, and the National Air and Space Museum with exhibits including the *Apollo 11* spacecraft.

Across the Potomac River at Arlington National Cemetery, alongside military veterans lie the gravesites of John F. Kennedy, Robert Kennedy, Edward Kennedy, and Jacqueline Kennedy Onassis.

Abraham Lincoln, who stood up against slavery and could not avoid a civil war, is memorialized with the Lincoln Memorial.

New York

▶ **CITY**

New York City, "the city that never sleeps," tries to justify this nickname without letup. Initially overwhelmed by the tragedy of the destruction of the Twin Towers of the World Trade Center on September 11, 2001, the city is recovering. Ground Zero will reopen as a memorial in 2014 with five new towers, the main building to be called One World Trade Center.

New York continues to show off its numerous attractions in lively city neighborhoods (SoHo, TriBeCa, the East Village, Columbus Circle) and offers culture in some 40 museums (Metropolitan Museum of Art, MoMA, the Guggenheim, the American Museum of Natural History), and music

What to See and Do in the East
District of Columbia
▶ **CITY**
• Washington
New York
▶ **CITY**
• New York City
▶ **LANDSCAPE**
• Hudson River Valley, Finger Lakes
Massachusetts
▶ **CITIES**
• Boston, Cambridge, Salem
▶ **LANDSCAPE**
• Berkshires
▶ **COAST**
• Cape Cod (whale-watching), Martha's Vineyard, Plymouth
Pennsylvania
▶ **CITIES**
• Philadelphia, Pittsburgh
▶ **CULTURAL HERITAGE**
• Amish communities

venues (Lincoln Center, Broadway theaters, jazz in the nightclubs and churches of Harlem).

The 1886 Statue of Liberty and Ellis Island signaled arrival in the New World to some 17 million European immigrants who entered New York between 1890 and 1920. The old Ellis Island buildings house the Immigration Museum today.

▶ **LANDSCAPE**

Upstate New York has many scenic byways along the **Hudson River Valley** and the **Finger Lakes.** The state's beaches dot the coast of Long Island; from Montauk at the eastern tip, visitors can book four-hour-long whale-watching cruises.

Fast-paced New York City steadily reinvents itself.

Boston's modern skyline contrasts sharply with its old neighborhoods that have kept their European flair.

Massachusetts

▶ CITIES

Boston is one of the oldest cities in the United States, founded in 1630 by English colonists. A whiff of England still pervades the city with its brick row house neighborhoods on Beacon Hill and renowned Museum of Fine Arts and Isabella Stewart Gardner Museum. A visitor can get an insight into Boston's history by following the red line of bricks indicating the Freedom Trail (American Revolution), Beacon Hill Walk, and Black Heritage Trail.

Across the Charles River in **Cambridge,** Harvard, the nation's oldest university and one of the most prestigious, spreads out along the riverbank.

About a dozen miles from Boston and more than three hundred years since their alleged misdeeds, the witches of **Salem** have become a tourist drawing card (museums, historic houses, shops) for this small coastal town.

▶ LANDSCAPE

Here and in the other New England states, Indian summer is cause for celebration. In the **Berkshires** of western Massachusetts and elsewhere, the leaves of the sugar maples turn red and other trees flame bright orange and yellow. Peak color usually runs from the end of September to mid-October.

▶ COAST

Cape Cod is a favorite destination for beachcombers. Many of the wide, sandy beaches are protected as Cape Cod National Seashore. The small island of **Martha's Vineyard** is famous for its gingerbread cottages and jet-set cachet.

The Pilgrims from the *Mayflower* landed at **Plymouth** in 1620. A living

When to Go				
	EAST	WEST	SOUTH	MIDWEST
JANUARY			☼	
FEBRUARY			☼	
MARCH			☼	
APRIL		☼	☼	☼
MAY	☼	☼		☼
JUNE	☼	☼		☼
JULY		☼		
AUGUST		☼		
SEPTEMBER	☼	☼		☼
OCTOBER	☼			☼
NOVEMBER				
DECEMBER				

Pennsylvania's Amish communities reject the modern ways of their surroundings.

history museum, Plimoth Plantation, re-creates the early setting.

Between April and October, visitors have opportunities to go on whale-watching cruises from Plymouth, Boston, or ports on Cape Cod.

Pennsylvania

▶ CITIES

Philadelphia recalls its early history as the social and geographical center of the 13 American colonies at Independence National Historical Park in the old city, site of the Liberty Bell and Independence Hall, where the Declaration of Independence was signed in 1776. The Society Hill area preserves many gracious colonial and Georgian homes. The city also has important museums such as the Philadelphia Museum of Art (Asian and European collections, works by Léger and Picasso), the Barnes Foundation (Impressionist and cubist art), the Rodin Museum, and the Franklin Institute.

If **Pittsburgh** was once largely known as the Steel City, today it looks renewed with its high-rise downtown and Victorian neighborhoods. This is the birthplace of

Andy Warhol, the pop art painter, who endowed the city with the Warhol Museum, one of the four Carnegie Museums of Pittsburgh.

▶ CULTURAL HERITAGE

The traditions of the Old Order Amish, a subdivision of the Mennonite church, originally from Switzerland and Germany, whose communities are founded on austerity and a rejection of modern ways, always cause curious glances. Their lifestyle, use of horse-drawn buggies, and dress- and quiltmaking, have changed little since the 17th century, as seen in the 1985 movie *Witness.*

Virginia

▶ CULTURAL HERITAGE

In 1607, the first Europeans settled permanently in Virginia at **Jamestown.** A short distance away, **Williamsburg,** the old state capital, has been restored to its colonial splendor.

Charlottesville is the location of the University of Virginia and Monticello, Thomas Jefferson's mansion, which attracts as many visitors as George Washington's Mount Vernon plantation near Alexandria.

What to See and Do in the South

Virginia

▶ **CULTURAL HERITAGE**
- Williamsburg, Charlottesville

▶ **LANDSCAPE**
- Shenandoah National Park, Blue Ridge Mountains, Chesapeake Bay

Tennessee

▶ **CULTURAL HERITAGE**
- Country music (Nashville), rock and blues (Memphis), tribute to Elvis

Georgia

▶ **CITIES AND LANDSCAPE**
- Savannah, Atlanta
- Stone Mountain

Florida

▶ **COASTS**
- Suncoast (beach resorts), the Florida Keys (diving at Key Largo), Miami Beach

▶ **ATTRACTIONS**
- Disney World, Cape Canaveral

▶ **WILDLIFE**
- Everglades (alligators, panthers, lynx)

Mississippi

▶ **CULTURAL HERITAGE**
- Route 61, blues (Clarksdale), Coca-Cola Museum (Vicksburg), colonial mansions (Natchez)

Louisiana

▶ **CULTURAL HERITAGE**
- French Quarter of New Orleans (Dixieland jazz), Cajun culture, plantations

▶ **CITIES**
- New Orleans, Baton Rouge, Lafayette, Natchitoches

▶ **LANDSCAPE**
- Mississippi River (river cruises)

▶ LANDSCAPE

In western Virginia, **Shenandoah National Park** is the gateway to the **Blue Ridge** Parkway, leading through the hills and forests of the Appalachian Mountains. Along the coast, **Chesapeake Bay** invites with beaches and small fishing villages.

Tennessee

▶ CULTURAL HERITAGE

The highway interchanges surrounding **Nashville** are said to look like guitars to announce the importance of the city's passion for country music.

Nashville has the Country Music Hall of Fame, some 200 recording studios, and Studio B of RCA, where the music—with roots in traditional folk music—is king. One curiosity among many is Elvis Presley's solid gold Cadillac and record player. Each year in June, the Country Music Fan Fair takes place here.

Memphis, home of the blues, still celebrates the music in the clubs of historic Beale Street. The blues, a mixture of work songs, spirituals, and field hollers, made their way up along Route 61 from the Mississippi Delta; its history is documented in the Rock 'n' Soul Museum. Elvis's spirit lives on at Graceland, at Sun Studios, and in the souvenir shops, filled with trinkets to remember him by. Paddle wheelers ply the Mississippi for sightseeing cruises.

Georgia

▶ CITIES AND LANDSCAPE

Beyond modern cityscapes, historic architecture defines many city centers, as in **Savannah,** with typical colonial-style houses around the squares and churches dating back to 1733.

Not far from ultramodern **Atlanta,** with the State Museum of

The Tennessee River unwinds below Lookout Mountain near the borders of Tennessee, Georgia, and Alabama.

Art and the World of Coca-Cola museum, rises **Stone Mountain.** Carved on the side of this 1,686-foot-high granite rock is a bas-relief showing Confederate heroes Stonewall Jackson, Robert E. Lee, and Jefferson Davis.

Florida

▶ COASTS

Florida's Gulf coast is a popular tourist destination, particularly the **Suncoast** from Tampa to the state's southern tip, where sun worshippers, often of an older generation, enjoy beaches at Naples, Sarasota, and St. Petersburg. Here you can find the Ringling Museum of Art and the Salvador Dalí Museum or enjoy playing on one of the many golf courses. Sanibel Island is acclaimed for its beaches, its many shells, and Ding Darling National Wildlife Refuge, which protects a large mangrove ecosystem and is a refuge for migratory birds.

At the southernmost point of the United States, the **Florida Keys** form a chain of 42 islands, immortalized by Humphrey Bogart in the movie *Key Largo* and by Ernest Hemingway, who arrived in Key West in 1931 and stayed for nine years. Hemingway described the scene as the homeport of writers among the smugglers. **Key Largo's** John Pennekamp Coral Reef State Park is a paradise for snorkeling fans and scuba divers.

On the Atlantic coast, Miami stretches along Biscayne Bay; its Little Havana neighborhood gives visitors a taste of Cuba. Across the bay, **Miami Beach** boasts Millionaire's Row with glamorous mansions in gated communities, scenic Ocean Drive, an Art Deco historic district, and South Beach. To the south of Miami, lies Coral Gables, a planned city known for its Mediterranean-style architecture. Other famous resorts along the east coast are Daytona Beach and West Palm Beach.

▶ ATTRACTIONS

Larger than its forerunner Disneyland, Florida's **Walt Disney World Resort** (25,000 acres) near Orlando has four main parks: the Magic Kingdom, Epcot, Disney's Hollywood Studios, and Disney's Animal Kingdom. In addition to

The Art Deco neighborhood of Miami Beach is a historic district.

Disney World, Orlando has numerous other attractions, including Universal Orlando Resort.

Miami has the interesting Dolphin Harbor Miami Seaquarium. Halfway between Daytona Beach and West Palm Beach lies **Cape Canaveral,** home of the Kennedy Space Center.

▶ WILDLIFE

Visiting the wetlands of the **Everglades,** a national park, is a good alternative to beach life. You can hike, bicycle, or tour by airboat, observe a great variety of birds, and reliably spot alligators. With some luck, you may also catch a glimpse of a panther, lynx, or other wildcat.

Mississippi

▶ CULTURAL HERITAGE

Route 61, the Blues Trail, meanders along the Mississippi River, past cotton fields where slaves labored and expressed their sorrows in the blues, past the crossroads in **Clarksdale,** where Robert Johnson "sold his soul to the devil to master the blues," and past small African-American communities where Muddy Waters and Bessie Smith are remembered. The Delta Blues Museum tells their stories.

Native writers Tennessee Williams and William Faulkner set many of their plays and novels in this region.

During the Civil War, the surrender of the city of **Vicksburg** to the Union Army marked a turning point in the war. On a happier note, Coca-Cola was invented here in 1894, and the inventor's candy store has been turned into a museum. **Natchez,** at the starting point of the Natchez Trace, the Native American Trail to Nashville, boasts romantic antebellum houses,

Old-fashioned paddle steamers offer river cruises on the Mississippi.

many of which have been turned into hotels.

Louisiana

▶ CULTURAL HERITAGE

Dixieland, the most traditional form of jazz, was born in the South and is still popular in the clubs and cafés of New Orleans's **French Quarter** and Bourbon Street; the presence of strip clubs and rowdy bars has lost the quarter some of its appeal. The sound is still true at Preservation Hall and the city's annual Jazz and Heritage Festival, as well as during Mardi Gras.

In some of the small towns, for example, St. Martinville, near Lafayette, you can still hear some French spoken, reminders of the

French-speaking Acadians who were exiled from Canada in 1755 and settled in the Mississippi Delta as "Cajuns." Visitors can join in local festivities with Saturday-night dances accompanied by zydeco music, crawfish trapping, and spicy cuisine.

Many historic mansions on former cotton and sugarcane plantations grace the riverbanks, illustrating the antebellum lifestyle. Best known in Vacherie are Oak Alley, flanked by magnificent live oaks, and the elegant Laura Plantation, as well as Loyd Hall Plantation in Cheneyville.

▶ CITIES

Deluged by Hurricane Katrina in August 2005, **New Orleans** has slowly been rebuilt. The city's multi-ethnic roots go deep: It was founded by the French in 1718, ceded to Spain in 1763, then returned to France before being sold by Napoleon in the Louisiana Purchase of 1803 to the United States for $15 million. The French Quarter bears the distinctive character of its heritage with St. Louis Cathedral, Ursuline Convent—the oldest building in the Mississippi Valley—and town houses with Spanish accents, such as iron-rail balconies. Paddle wheelers offer numerous boat tours.

Other cities of note are **Baton Rouge, Lafayette,** and in the northwest, **Natchitoches,** named for the Indian tribe of the same name and the first permanent settlement of the Louisiana Purchase (historic quarter, Cane River).

▶ LANDSCAPE
Tourists can watch it all glide by from paddle wheelers cruising on the **Mississippi River** accompanied by jazz tunes, or take a swamp tour of Cajun country by airboat or canoe into the bayous and backwaters of the Delta to see alligators, ospreys, egrets, and herons.

A Dixieland band goes full blast in New Orleans.

Illinois

▶ CITIES
Chicago has long lost its reputation as the city of Al Capone and organized crime. Founded in the 18th century, the city is known as much for its pioneer spirit as for its innovations (Frank Lloyd Wright architecture). Numerous parks and museums dot the city, among them the Chicago Art Institute with Impressionist art (Degas, Manet, Monet, Pissarro, Renoir) and the Museum of Contemporary Art (Bacon, Calder, Klee, Picasso). Situated on Lake Michigan, Chicago is proud of having one of the tallest buildings in the world—Willis Tower (formerly called Sears Tower) at 1,451 feet and 110 stories high.

Chicago is also a hotbed of blues and jazz. Here, too, begins the famous Route 66, the pioneering highway leading for nearly 2,500 miles to Los Angeles. The route is no longer an official U.S. highway, but travelers are often invited to follow this Mother Road that once was a major route for migrants to the west.

Although less imposing than Chicago, the state capital of **Springfield** highlights Abraham Lincoln's rise in politics and remembers him at the Lincoln Home National Historic Site.

What to See and Do in the Midwest
Illinois
▶ CITIES
• Chicago, Springfield
Michigan
▶ CITY
• Detroit
▶ LANDSCAPE
• Great Lakes (Superior, Michigan, Huron, Erie)
South Dakota
▶ LANDSCAPE
• Jewel Cave, Wind Cave, Badlands, Mount Rushmore

South Dakota

▶ **LANDSCAPE**

There is only one rival to the 150 miles of caves in **Jewel Cave** National Monument, and that is **Wind Cave** National Park, with 119 miles of caves. The cave's name came from wind gusts escaping along the cave's crevices, depending on atmospheric pressure, and the cave is notable for its calcite "boxwork" formations. These two cave systems are located where the grasslands plateau meets the pinnacles and buttes of **Badlands** National Park.

In the Black Hills, southwest of Rapid City, the sculpted heads of presidents George Washington, Thomas Jefferson, Theodore Roosevelt, and Abraham Lincoln grace the side of **Mount Rushmore.** South of Mount Rushmore, the Pine Ridge Indian Reservation of the Oglala Sioux is one of the largest reservations in the United States.

Four presidents at Mount Rushmore

Oregon

▶ **LANDSCAPE**

A volcano that blew its top and collapsed created the landscape of the vast **Crater Lake.** The lake is now part of the national park in the middle of the Cascade Range.

▶ **COAST**

Oregon's coast is not well known, but its 370 miles are a treasure to behold. Alongside the coast runs scenic Highway 101, framed by cliffs, estuaries, bays (Depoe Bay), and capes (Cape Foulweather) and passing by lighthouses, dunes, wide beaches (Gold Beach), and diverse marine wildlife (whales, sea lions, otters).

Michigan

▶ **CITY**

Michigan's largest city, **Detroit,** stands out with the Henry Ford Museum and the Detroit Art Institute. Along its waterfront loom Art Deco and modernist skyscrapers.

▶ **LANDSCAPE**

Bounded by four of the five **Great Lakes**—Superior to the north, Michigan to the west, Huron to the east, and Erie to the southeast, Lake Michigan has the longest freshwater shoreline in the United States. It offers plenty of opportunities for swimming, fishing, and boating.

Washington

▶ **LANDSCAPE AND WILDLIFE**

Washington lies in the northwest, cut by the Cascade Range, which is spiked with volcanoes that are covered by glaciers.

The most famous peaks are **Mount St. Helens,** which violently erupted in 1980, and **Mount Rainier,** known for its white cone above the pines. The steep Willis Wall, the Cascades, and Douglas fir forests contribute to the beauty of the state that has become a favorite of backpackers.

Whale-watching cruises depart Everett for the San Juan Islands.

Le Conte is one of Alaska's thousands of glaciers.

What to See and Do in the Northwest

Washington

▶ **LANDSCAPE AND WILDLIFE**

• Mount St. Helens, Mount Rainier

• Whales, Orcas

Oregon

▶ **LANDSCAPE**

• Crater Lake

▶ **COAST**

• Beaches, cliffs, marine life

Montana

▶ **LANDSCAPE AND WILDLIFE**

• National Bison Range

• Glacier National Park

Wyoming

▶ **LANDSCAPE**

• Yellowstone National Park, Grand Tetons, Devils Tower

▶ **CULTURAL HERITAGE**

• Dude ranches

Alaska

▶ **LANDSCAPE**

• Glaciers, mountains, fjords, hot springs

▶ **WILDLIFE**

• Caribou, grizzlies, beavers, whales

▶ **CULTURAL HERITAGE**

• Inuit culture

Montana

▶ LANDSCAPE AND WILDLIFE

Over the centuries, Indians and buffalo have traveled the same route. Today buffalo are protected in some 20 parks and reserves in Montana, with a few more in Idaho. The **National Bison Range** at Moiese is one example. A side trip to the Museum of the Plains Indians in Browning helps understand the region's history. North of Browning, the 130 lakes in **Glacier National Park** hold hundreds of aquatic species.

Wyoming

▶ CULTURAL HERITAGE

Wyoming is a state of the western plains that features ranches, horses, and cowboys. Visitors can spend a week as a cowboy at one of many dude ranches. For more casual tourists, there is Cody, the city of Buffalo Bill, with a museum of popular arts and traditions. Wyoming's winter sports attractions include Jackson Hole for skiing and snowmobiling.

▶ LANDSCAPE

Yellowstone National Park, the largest and most prestigious of the national parks in the United States, is open in summer for hiking and in winter for snowmobiling. The forests harbor Douglas firs, some up to 500 years old, and lodgepole pines, preferred material for Indian tepees. The park, after being ravaged by fire in 1988, has rebounded remarkably fast. The hot springs and geysers, especially Old Faithful, and wildlife ranging from grizzly bears to elk, wolves, and buffalo are popular attractions.

Yellowstone is surrounded by mountains, the most famous of all being the **Grand Tetons.** A geological curiosity, **Devils Tower,** a granite spire 1,267 feet high, rises at the other end of the state and is a favorite of mountaineers.

Alaska

▶ LANDSCAPE

Alaska, the "Last Frontier," owes much of its beauty to thousands of glaciers; Columbia, Portage, and especially Malaspina and Nabesna glaciers are among the most famous. Visitors can best observe them from a tour boat, all the while enjoying the antics of whales, dolphins, and seals in the ocean.

Every September before the big frosts, the landscape comes alive in fall colors. The state is dominated by 20,320-foot-high Mount McKinley, in Denali National Park, and the peaks of the Wrangell Mountains. Mount McKinley is the highest peak in North America and was one of the destinations of gold prospectors in the 1890s, although areas near Fairbanks, Juneau, and Nome held most of the gold.

The fjords of Kenai National Park along the peninsula, the lower portion of the Yukon River, and the many hot springs are favorite attractions. Rivers, lakes, and waterfalls, in addition, invite kayakers and fishers to indulge in their pastimes. Charters along the Yukon and Tanana Rivers, as well as the Lynn Canal, offer short cruises.

▶ WILDLIFE
Denali National Park is rich with elk, caribou, grizzly bears, beavers,

and eagles. Seals, porpoises, and whales can be seen in Glacier Bay.

▶ CULTURAL HERITAGE
The Inuit, Inupiaq, and Yupik, whose villages can be visited, try to preserve their Native way of life, which is amply described in the Anchorage Museum of History and Art.

The narrow-gauge railway linking Skagway, Alaska, to Whitehorse, Canada, built during the gold rush of 1897, is in operation again during the summer months.

California

▶ LANDSCAPE
Several large national parks are in California, including **Kings Canyon, Sequoia,** and **Yosemite,** with lakes, giant redwoods, and geological features such as the 4,737-foot-high Half Dome. Unique bristlecone pines are nearby in the Sierra Nevada.

The **Mojave Desert** boasts the driest, hottest, and lowest location in North America, **Death Valley**

What to See and Do in the Far West & Pacific

California
▶ LANDSCAPE
- National parks (Kings Canyon, Sequoia National Park, Yosemite National Park, Death Valley), Napa Valley, Mojave Desert
▶ CITIES
- Los Angeles, San Francisco, San Diego
▶ COAST
- Beaches of the southern coast, Monterey Bay

Nevada
▶ CITY
- Las Vegas
▶ FESTIVALS
- National Finals Rodeo

Hawaii
▶ COASTS
- Beaches, surfing, fun boards
▶ LANDSCAPE
- Volcanoes

The Golden Gate Bridge is San Francisco's landmark.

(282 feet below sea level at its lowest point). Farther to the southeast is Joshua Tree National Park, named for its unusual desert plants. Palm Springs stands out as an oasis.

Along the California coast, the Pacific Coast Highway (Route 1) presents one of the most spectacular drives. You can observe ocean life along the way, ranging from elephant seals to sea otters, and in November and spring, gray whales on their migration.

If you are interested in the mysteries of earthquakes, you can search for the San Andreas Fault between Point Arenas and the Mexican border.

▶ CITIES

Los Angeles stretches for some 80 miles along the ocean in Southern California. This is where the famous and the wannabes make their home: Hollywood, Beverly Hills, and Santa Monica. On Hollywood Boulevard, Grauman's Chinese Theatre preserves the handprints, footprints, and signatures of the great stars of earlier decades embedded in concrete, and brass-edged stars set into the sidewalk feature the names of celebrities from the entertainment world in the Hollywood Walk of Fame. A few blocks away, Melrose Avenue awaits with its funky boutiques and upscale restaurants.

A visit to Disneyland in Anaheim is still every child's dream, while Universal Studios brings movies to life. For the adults, a number of museums are worth a visit, including the Getty Center, Los Angeles County Museum of Art, and Pasadena's Huntington Library.

San Diego is noted for its year-round comfortable climate, its museums (Maritime Museum, San Diego Art Museum), its old town neighborhood of the Spanish period, and its SeaWorld Oceanarium with exhibits and shows.

Another sort of oceanic display takes place off the coast between mid-December and mid-February, when gray whales migrate from Alaska to Baja California. Stargazers will want to visit Palomar Observatory a couple of hours north to see the 200-inch Hale telescope.

Finally, a place that is more myth than reality: the Bagdad Café of movie fame is located at Newberry Springs, ten miles east of Barstow.

Along its renowned bay, **San Francisco** charms visitors with such attractive sites as the Golden Gate Bridge, cable cars, Telegraph Hill, Chinatown, Alcatraz, and the San Francisco Museum of Modern Art, along with an air of permissive freedom that once made its reputation. But times are changing; Jack Kerouac and the Beat Generation are long past, and the hippies of Haight-Ashbury share the streets with yuppies. The formerly rebellious Mission District is now undergoing an invasion of startup companies.

On the other side of the Golden Gate Bridge is Sausalito, where boutiques and tourists have succeeded the fishermen. Not far away, **Napa Valley** invites wine lovers to taste California vintages. Continuing northeast, travelers in search of more unusual activities can explore Sutter's Mill, where the 1849 gold rush began, and mountain lakes and rivers for kayaking and rafting.

▶ COAST

Some of the most famous beaches are around Los Angeles (Santa Monica, Malibu, Venice, and for the surfers Huntington Beach) or north of there (around Santa Barbara). Less crowded are the cooler beaches along **Monterey Bay** (aquarium). The rugged California coast can be seen on the 17-mile scenic road from Pacific Grove to Carmel and in the **Big Sur** area, known for its artists' colony.

Traveler's Notebook			
MAIN CONTACT *Embassy of the United States* 24 Grosvenor Square London W1A 1AE, UK + 44 (0)20 7499-9000 www.London .usembassy.gov **TRAVEL DOCUMENTS FOR U.K. CITIZENS** Passport **TRAVEL TIME TO DESTINATION & TIME DIFFERENCE** London to New York: 7 hours nonstop flight; EST +5	**AVERAGE TRIP COST** £400 for a four-day weekend in New York **LANGUAGE & CURRENCY** Official language: English Currency: dollar **POPULATION** 50 states and 301,140,000 inhabitants; 75 percent of the population lives in cities (200 cities have more than 100,000 inhabitants); among minorities 12 percent of	the population is African American, others include Hispanics, Asians, and Indians Capital: Washington, DC **RELIGION** 50 percent are Protestant, 30 percent Catholic; other world religions **FESTIVALS** December 31: New Year's Eve in New York (Times Square); July 4: Independence Day; October	31: Halloween; fourth Thursday in November: Thanksgiving **SHOPPING** Indian crafts and jewelry. In the cities, bargains can be found in textiles, shoes, blue jeans, T-shirts, and electronics.

Lumahai Beach on Kauai, far from Hawaii's active volcanoes

Nevada

▶ CITY

Las Vegas in the heart of the desert is a major gambling resort, with dozens of casinos and 300,000 slot machines. The light shows and extravagance of the Strip are without equal. Over the last few years, the city has multiplied its follies with re-creations of Manhattan, Egypt, Venice, and Paris.

▶ FESTIVALS

Each year at the beginning of December, the **National Finals Rodeo** is celebrated here for ten days. This popular sport of the West was invented at the end of the 19th century. True cowboys—and cowgirls, as well—show off their skills riding horses and bulls.

Hawaii

▶ COASTS

The exotic appeal of this archipelago of seven major islands and many islets, with its tropical climate in the heart of the Pacific Ocean, is hard to match: fine, white sandy beaches, coconut palms, and coral reefs. The greatest surfing competitions in the world take place on the island of Maui. Windsurfing and funboarding are enjoyed here, too.

▶ LANDSCAPE

Lava flows often from the volcanoes on the Big Island of Hawaii and makes the landscape look otherworldly. All around Mauna Kea and Mauna Loa, hiking trails invite visitors to wander among hibiscus flowers.

What to See and Do in the Southwest

Arizona

▶ **LANDSCAPE**
- Grand Canyon, Monument Valley, Meteor Crater, Petrified Forest, Canyon de Chelly

▶ **CITIES**
- Tucson, Phoenix

Colorado

▶ **LANDSCAPE**
- Mesa Verde, Black Canyon, Summit County (ski resorts)

New Mexico

▶ **CULTURAL HERITAGE**
- American Indians, Santa Fe

▶ **LANDSCAPE**
- White Sands, Carlsbad Caverns

Texas

▶ **CULTURAL HERITAGE**
- Ranches, missions (Kingsville, the Alamo), country music (Austin)

▶ **CITIES**
- Dallas, Fort Worth, Houston

Utah

▶ **LANDSCAPE**
- Bryce Canyon, Great Salt Lake, Rainbow Bridge, Lake Powell, Arches National Park, Cataract Canyon, Capitol Reef National Park, Salt Lake City (surrounding ski resorts)

Arizona

▶ LANDSCAPE

The **Grand Canyon** in Arizona is one of the world's greatest natural wonders. The steep-sided, red-colored gorge carved by the Colorado River ranges in width from four to eighteen miles, with depths of more than a mile, for a length of 277 miles. Visitors can fly over the terrain by

In Organ Pipe Cactus National Monument in Arizona, the cacti can grow to 16 feet.

Colorado

▶ LANDSCAPE

Colorado diverges from its neighbor Arizona at **Mesa Verde,** a large limestone plateau cut by dozens of canyons. In these pockmarked cliffs, Indians took refuge and built stone villages between the 11th and 14th centuries. Today these cliff dwellings—some several stories high—can be visited at Cliff Palace and Sun Point Pueblo.

The **Black Canyon** on the Gunnison River seems more savage than the Grand Canyon, with its narrow openings and sheer walls.

Summit County, not far from the city of Denver, is an elegant skiing mecca: Vail, Beaver Creek, Breckenridge, Aspen, and Keystone are here.

New Mexico

▶ CULTURAL HERITAGE

Adobe houses and remains of pre-Columbian villages mark New Mexico. Moreover, the state's population includes the largest proportion of Native Americans. A number of museums in Santa Fe and Albuquerque honor their history.

Santa Fe was the gateway to the American Southwest via the Santa Fe Trail, Old Spanish Trail, and El Camino Real. Tourists enjoy visits to the popular Indian communities of Acoma, Taos and other pueblos, and the ancient ruins of Chaco Canyon.

▶ LANDSCAPE

With its open desert, red sandstone cliffs, mountain lakes, and forests, New Mexico has an ever changing landscape. In the center of the Tularosa Basin, between the Sacramento Mountains and San Andres,

helicopter or small airplane or travel by mule or on foot to the bottom.

At the border region between Arizona and Utah, on the huge Navajo Reservation, rise the pillars of **Monument Valley,** which have been standard background scenery for filmmakers of westerns. Also within the reservation are the 1,200-year-old cliff dwellings of **Canyon de Chelly.**

Just to the south, the colorful **Petrified Forest** National Park features wood that became fossilized millions of years ago. **Meteor Crater** near Flagstaff, created by a meteorite impact some 50,000 years ago,

is a hole about 4,000 feet in diameter and 570 feet deep.

Cacti take over with dense stands of giant saguaro in Saguaro National Park at the border with Mexico and organ pipe cactus in the park of the same name in the Little Ajo Mountains.

▶ CITIES

West of **Tucson** is Old Tucson Studios, a theme park and old movie set where the first western, the movie *Arizona,* was filmed in 1939. The city of **Phoenix** is no less spectacular than its many statewide attractions.

The red rocks of Utah's Bryce Canyon National Park

lies **White Sands National Monument,** with its vast dunes composed of white gypsum crystals. Only a few yucca and cactus plants grow there.

In the east, **Carlsbad Caverns National Park,** with large underground chambers, presents immense stalactite and stalagmite pillars.

Texas

▶ CULTURAL HERITAGE

If they were granted a last refuge, cowboys would choose Texas, for its grazing land, ranches, and rodeos. They would go perhaps to **Kingsville,** site of the largest ranch in the world. They might pay tribute to Davy Crockett, who was killed in 1836 at the **Alamo,** and listen to country music from the capital city of Austin.

▶ CITIES

Dallas, Fort Worth, and **Houston** each have important museums.

Houston has the additional attraction of the Lyndon B. Johnson Space Center, with exhibits of space exploration artifacts, especially of the Apollo moon landings.

Utah

▶ LANDSCAPE

Utah boasts several national parks. **Bryce Canyon,** one of the famous attractions of the West, shows off geological oddities in stone reddened by iron oxide. Not far from there is **Zion Canyon,** reminiscent of California's Yosemite. **Arches** features numerous sandstone arches sculpted by wind, such as Landscape Arch, a thin, 300-foot-long blade of rock above a limestone amphitheater. Less visited are **Canyonlands,** at the confluence of the Colorado and Green Rivers, and the red cliffs of **Capitol Reef.**

The **Great Salt Lake** is the residue of a larger lake that dried up in the course of time. The area represents the entrance to ski resorts in the surroundings of Salt Lake City. Other sites include **Rainbow Bridge** National Monument at the foot of Navajo Mountain, a pink sandstone natural arch more than 240 feet high and nearly as wide, and the vast reservoir **Lake Powell.**

Chor Minor in Bukhara with its blue-domed minarets is an example of Uzbekistan's varied architecture.

Uzbekistan

Uzbekistan's brilliant architecture of palaces, mosques, and madrassas in Samarkand, Bukhara, and Khiva began during the 14th-century empire of Tartar conqueror Tamerlane. Enhanced by a landscape of mountains, deserts, and oases, the country combines the attractions of North and Central Asia in one.

Traveler's Notebook

MAIN CONTACTS
Embassy of the Republic of Uzbekistan
1746 Massachusetts Avenue, NW
Washington, DC 20036
(202) 887-5300
www.uzbekistan.org
www.uzbek
tourism.uz
Embassy of the Republic of Uzbekistan
41 Holland Park
London W11 3RP, UK
+ 44 (0) 20 7229 7679
www.uzbek
embassy.org

TRAVEL DOCUMENTS FOR U.S. & U.K. CITIZENS
Passport and visa

HEALTH ISSUES
No vaccinations required

TRAVEL TIME TO DESTINATION & TIME DIFFERENCE
New York to Tashkent: 15 hours 55 minutes connecting flight; EST +10. London to Tashkent: 8 hours 10 minutes connecting flight; GMT +5

AVERAGE TRIP COST
$1,775/£1,150 for a week's excursions

LANGUAGE & CURRENCY
Official language: Uzbek, spoken by 80 percent of the population; other languages: Dari and Russian; Western languages are little known
Money: som

POPULATION
27,780,000 inhabitants; 80 percent are Uzbek and minorities include Russians, Tajiks, Tatars, and Kazakhs. Capital: Tashkent

RELIGION
Islam is predominant; Russian

Orthodox is the largest minority

FESTIVALS
February: Navruz (Zoroastrian New Year); September 1: Independence Day; September: "Golden Autumn" in Tashkent, and Pakhta-Bairam (harvest festival)

SHOPPING
The carpets sold in the markets of Bukhara (but sometimes made in Turkmenistan) dominate the crafts. Also, cotton and silk fabrics, ceramics, decorated knives, and wood sculptures.

▶ CITIES

Seven centuries before Tamerlane, Samarkand had known its first hour of glory under the Sogdians; it was then the most important crossroads of the Silk Route between China and India. When Tamerlane decided to make **Samarkand** the capital of his empire in the 14th century, he enhanced the city with prestigious buildings. Today, the necropolis of Shahi Zindah (group of mausoleums and mosques decorated with blue ceramic tiles), the Gur Emir (Tamerlane's mausoleum with blue and gold ceramic tiles), the enormous Registan madrassas (Islamic schools), and the Bibi Khanum Mosque with its blue dome are first-class tourist attractions. The easygoing atmosphere in the colorful bazaars adds to the allure.

Bukhara is an important center of Islamic art. The massive *ark* (fortress)—seat of the emir's court—Samanid mausoleum, Kalyan minaret, mosques, and madrassas bear witness to that. Another historic city, surrounded by fortified walls and a former stop on the Silk Road, is **Khiva.** Its sights include a Great Mosque and freestanding minaret, mausoleums of Sayid Alauddin and Pahlavan Mahmud, and madrassas.

In the Fergana Valley, the cities of **Kokand, Rishton,** and **Fergana** showcase their mausoleums and mosques and the Khudayar Khan palace in Kokand.

The capital, **Tashkent,** is a noteworthy cultural center; its oriental quarter showcases madrassas, the mausoleum of Kaffal Chachi, the Museum of Applied Arts, and a Romanov palace.

▶ LANDSCAPE AND EXCURSIONS

The rocky plateaus and desert dunes of the **Kyzyl Kum** (meaning "red sand"), along with the **Fergana Valley,** are some of the beautiful regions of Central Asia that the tourism industry has barely begun to touch. During the Han dynasty, the famous "Heavenly Fergana horses" were exchanged for silk coming from China.

In the west, two sites attract attention: the very long Aydar Lake and the region of Ayaktchi, whose rivers and falls are fed by the high Pamirs.

More and more active travelers are alternating visits between cultural attractions and hiking tours in these steppe landscapes and along the ancient caravan trails, especially because this type of travel allows for personal contact with people.

Elsewhere, the landscape consists of large cotton fields, but irrigation required the diversion of two rivers, which has caused the Aral Sea to nearly dry up.

When to Go	CLIMATE	HIKING
JANUARY		
FEBRUARY		
MARCH		
APRIL	☼	🚶
MAY	☼	🚶
JUNE	☼	
JULY		
AUGUST		
SEPTEMBER	☼	🚶
OCTOBER	☼	🚶
NOVEMBER		
DECEMBER		

Venezuela

Venezuela, "little Venice," reminded the first Europeans of the famous Italian city when they saw houses on stilts on the coast. Since then, Venezuela has developed into an attractive tourist destination. The country has plenty of sunshine and beaches to offer, Caribbean islands, and the highlands of the Guiana Massif with its strange tabletop mountains. If only Venezuela had important pre-Columbian ruins to show, it would be overrun with tourists.

What to See and Do in Venezuela

▶ **COAST**

- Margarita Island, Los Roques and Las Aves Archipelagos, Paria Peninsula

▶ **LANDSCAPE AND EXCURSIONS**

- Guiana Massif (*tepuis,* cataracts), dugout canoes on the Orinoco River
- Llanos (fauna), Cordillera de Mérida

▶ **MONUMENTS**

- Spanish heritage at Caracas, Barcelona, Ciudad Bolívar, Coro
- Pre-Columbian rock art

▶ **COAST**

The beautiful Caribbean shores and the quality of the coral reefs are what is making Venezuela more and more prominent a destination among the world's great beach resorts. The islands—in particular **Margarita Island** with 75 beaches, mountains, and rather reasonable prices—lend themselves to a premier vacation.

The archipelago of **Los Roques,** as tropical as one could wish (corals, multicolored fish), in the Caribbean Sea, is also expanding its tourism venues. Sailboat cruises let vacationers explore the

Margarita Island and its 75 beaches are catching up little by little with the great beach resorts of the Caribbean.

archipelago. These islets still offer a good number of deserted beaches and the option of deep-sea fishing (blue marlin, swordfish). **Las Aves Archipelago,** where colonies of pink flamingos roost, is another favorite attraction.

On the continental coast, the Paraguaná Peninsula and the region of Chichiriviche alternate fine sand beaches with fishing villages. Beach and rain forest harmoniously succeed each other on the **Paria Peninsula,** fed by rivers suitable for swimming, whereas the swamps harbor caimans.

▶ LANDSCAPE AND EXCURSIONS

The **Guiana Massif,** scattered with Indian villages and interspersed by numerous rivers, has become a popular destination in recent years. In the region of the Gran Sabana rise the tepuis, strange sandstone "table-top" plateaus, surrounded by tropical forest, both feared and venerated by the Pemon Indians. The tepuis lend themselves to great hiking tours. The highlight of every tour is the ascension of Mount Roraima, at 9,219 feet the highest tepui of all.

This region was settled by the conquistadores in search of El Dorado hoping to find large quantities of gold. Here travelers can explore the rivers by pirogues—dugout canoes—or visit the falls (*saltos,* "leaps") of the Río Carrao. The best known of these, though difficult to access, is Angel Falls, the world's highest waterfall at 3,212 feet.

The Guiana Massif and the area around Roraima represent the most picturesque region on the Atlantic coast in South America, with additional waterfalls and breathtaking views.

Farther westward rises the **Orinoco River.** The river's mangrove

Warao Indians travel in a dugout canoe on the Orinoco, one of the legendary rivers of South America.

forest can best be explored by pirogue with a Warao guide. Rapids, crocodiles, and freshwater dolphins make this a lively excursion. The region of the upper Orinoco is the homeland of the Yanomami Indians.

Not far from there, nature has produced two imposing sinkholes: the Sima Humboldt, with a depth of more than a thousand feet, and the nearby Sima Martel; it's not possible to visit them, however,

because they are difficult to access, and the geology seems unstable around them.

On the way to the border of Colombia, there is a sanctuary for endangered animal and plant species

Traveler's Notebook

MAIN CONTACTS
Embassy of the Bolivarian Republic of Venezuela
1099 30th Street, NW
Washington, DC 20007
(202) 342-2214
http://venezuela-us.org
www.mintur.gob.ve
Embassy of the Bolivarian Republic of Venezuela
1 Cromwell Road
London SW7 2HW, UK
+ 44 (0) 20 7584 4206 or
7581 2776
www.embavenez-uk.org

TRAVEL DOCUMENTS FOR U.S. & U.K. CITIZENS
Passport and tourist card issued on arrival

HEALTH ISSUES
Vaccination strongly recommended against yellow fever outside urban zones; Malaria prophylaxis advised in certain rural zones and the Amazon jungle

TRAVEL TIME TO DESTINATION & TIME DIFFERENCE
New York to Caracas: 7 hours 55 minutes

connecting flight; EST +0:30. London to Caracas: 13 hours connecting flight; GMT −4:30

AVERAGE TRIP COST
One week "all inclusive" on Margarita Island begins at $1,500/£960. Count on at least $3,175/£2,050 for a 15-day guided tour that includes the Guiana Massif, the Orinoco Delta, and Los Roques Archipelago.

LANGUAGE & CURRENCY
Official language:

Spanish; other language: English
Currency: bolivar fuerte

POPULATION
26,024,000 inhabitants, concentrated in the mountain ranges and on the Caribbean coast (and experiencing a strong population increase). Capital: Caracas (home to one out of six Venezuelans)

RELIGION
92 percent of Venezuelans are Catholic

FESTIVALS
February: Feria del Sol (Bullfighting Carnival) in Mérida; July 5: Independence Day; July 24: Simon Bolivar's Birthday

SHOPPING
Two Venezuelan specialties go hand in hand: a hammock and rum. There are also wood carvings, leather goods, pottery, and colorful blankets.

Angel Falls plunges into the depth of the bizarre landscape of the Guiana Massif.

Coro was the first capital during colonial times and is a showcase of the most attractive historic buildings in the country.

The Piedras Pintadas and Cerro Pintado national parks are located near Valencia, west of Caracas. The parks have pre-Columbian pictographs and drawings.

near the city of Puerto Ayacucho, in the state of Amazonas. Farther north extend the **llanos,** the great grassy plains where *llaneros*—cowboys—herd zebu cattle. This area is home to exotic wildlife like anacondas and iguanas and more than 300 species of birds, which can be spotted and identified during a fascinating guided tour.

The highest peak in the **Cordillera de Mérida** is Mount Bolívar at 16,427 feet. The landscape here, called Páramo, is a tropical ecosystem of lakes, peat bogs, wet grasslands, and well-preserved colonial villages.

▶ MONUMENTS

The Spanish era has left a colonial heritage in the form of churches, cathedrals, and old-town sections, as in **Caracas** (Capitol building), **Barcelona** (Museum of Tradition's regional history collection), **Ciudad Bolívar,** and **Coro.** The city of

When to Go		
	CLIMATE	FLORA GUIANA MASSIF
JANUARY	☼	
FEBRUARY	☼	
MARCH	☼	
APRIL	☼	
MAY		
JUNE		
JULY		
AUGUST		⋵
SEPTEMBER		⋵
OCTOBER		⋵
NOVEMBER		
DECEMBER	☼	

Vietnam

What to See and Do in Vietnam

▶ **LANDSCAPE**

- Northern mountains
- Red River, Black River, Hai Van Pass, Da Lat and Central Highlands
- Mekong Delta, Mandarin Road

▶ **CITIES AND MONUMENTS**

- Ho Chi Minh City, Hanoi, Hue, Da Nang, Hoi An

▶ **COAST**

- Halong Bay
- Vung Tau, Phan Thiet, Nha Trang, Phu Quoc Island (beaches)
- Floating markets

★ *Vietnam has become a favorite destination for its cultural sites as well as its natural beauty: unexpected, lovely views of Halong Bay; the imperial city of Hue; pagodas, forests, and rice fields; and hill tribe communities (montagnards) in the north.*

▶ LANDSCAPE

The landscape is simply seductive thanks to the brilliant green rice fields. The mountains of the north, which are getting ever more popular with hikers, are home to many minorities, including the Hmong, Nung, and Dao. In the plains, the cultural aspect of the region is shaped more by the Yao and Tày people. Some travel agencies can arrange for tourists to meet with different minority groups in an attempt to offer something new and rewarding.

The coastal road, also called the **Mandarin Road,** is the itinerary most frequently suggested by travel agents.

From north to south, the sites worth a visit come in quick succession: the **Red River** and **Black River** valleys, the latter embellished by gorges (Lai Chau Canyon); the road from Da Nang to Hue (**Hai**

Van Pass, or "Pass of the Clouds"), **Da Lat,** and the **Central Highlands.**

The endless rice fields and gardens along the canals in the **Mekong Delta** can be visited by sampan (small boat) excursion. These days, it's even possible to take a cruise from Ho Chi Minh City to Phnom Penh in Cambodia.

▶ CITIES AND MONUMENTS

Ho Chi Minh City (formerly Saigon) was the capital of the former

Scenic Halong Bay, with its nearly 3,000 rocky islands, is reason enough to visit Vietnam.

French Cochinchina, "the Pearl of the Far East," with its wide avenues and European villas in the suburbs. Today it is the youngest and most dynamic city in the country. Most interesting is the area around the docks, the Ben Thanh market, and the Chinese quarter of Cholon, where a jumble of commerce and motorcycles keeps things moving. Political and economic changes are helping to slowly return the metropolis to its former status as one of the most envied cities in Southeast Asia. The main cultural attractions of Ho Chi Minh City are the History Museum's Champa sculptures and artifacts from the times of Angkor Wat, as well as the Thien-Hau Pagoda.

Hanoi lies around Hoan Kiem lake on the Red River Delta. The city's sites include pagodas (One Pillar Pagoda) and historic houses at the edge of the old town. The 11th-century Temple of Literature is dedicated to Confucius, whose statue is surrounded by gardens, ponds, and the steles of 82 scholars. The mausoleum of Ho Chi Minh, the palace of former French governor Doumer, and the Ethnographic Museum are on most tour itineraries.

Hue, the old imperial city, is divided into an old town and a colonial city, which can be easily

In Hanoi, Confucius (Temple of Literature) and Ho Chi Minh (mausoleum) are honored separately.

explored by boat on the Perfume River. The star attractions are the architectural legacy of the Thien Mu Pagoda, the royal tombs of the Nguyen dynasty, and the park of Emperor Tu Duc.

Da Nang has two great attractions: its celebrated collection of Champa sculptures, and the grotto-pagodas of the "Marble Mountains," excavated in white marble. South of Da Nang, the old port of **Hoi An**

Traveler's Notebook

MAIN CONTACTS
Embassy of the Socialist Republic of Vietnam
1233 20th Street, NW
Suite 400
Washington, DC 20036
(202) 861-0737
www.vietnamembassy-usa.org
www.vietnamtourism.com
Embassy of the Socialist Republic of Vietnam
12–14 Victoria Road
London W8 5RD, UK
+ 44 (0) 20 7937 1912
www.vietnamembassy.org.uk

TRAVEL DOCUMENTS FOR U.S. & U.K. CITIZENS
Passport and visa

HEALTH ISSUES
No vaccinations are required, but malaria prophylaxis is recommended for travel in the villages, Red River Delta, and coastal plains north of Nha Trang. The greatest risks are in the south (Ca Mau and Bac Lieu Provinces) and in the highlands below 4,500 feet.

TRAVEL TIME TO DESTINATION & TIME DIFFERENCE
New York to Ho Chi Minh City: 20 hours 35 minutes connecting; EST +12. London to Ho Chi Minh City: 13 hours 40 minutes connecting; GMT +7

AVERAGE TRIP COST
Guided tour of 15 days costs about $2,540/£1,640; a trip of two weeks of excursions combined with Cambodia could amount to $2,600/£1,700.

LANGUAGE & CURRENCY
Official language: Vietnamese
Currency: dông; U.S. dollars widely accepted

POPULATION
85,262,000 inhabitants, densely populated; ethnic Vietnamese are in the majority, with 53 minority groups. Capital: Hanoi

RELIGION
55 percent Buddhist, 7 percent Catholic, 1 percent Muslim

FESTIVALS
End of January to beginning of February: Tet festival, celebrating the Lunar New Year; April 30: anniversary of the liberation of the South; September 2: Independence Day

SHOPPING
Lacquer objects inlaid with mother-of-pearl, paintings on silk, Vietnamese bamboo hats

The Perfume Pagoda near Hanoi is a well-known pilgrimage site.

When to Go			
	NORTH	CENTER	SOUTH
JANUARY			☼
FEBRUARY		☼	☼
MARCH		☼	☼
APRIL	☼	☼	☼
MAY	☼	☼	
JUNE		☼	
JULY			
AUGUST			
SEPTEMBER			
OCTOBER			
NOVEMBER	☼		
DECEMBER	☼		☼

once exported spices and silk, is today visited for its temples and pagodas, old merchant houses, and a covered bridge.

In the region of Qui Nhon, the ancient towers of the Champa temples, the legacy of a Malayo-Polynesian civilization, reveal their delicate contours.

▶ COAST

One of the most scenic destinations in Vietnam is **Halong Bay,** a labyrinth of some 3,000 rocky islets in bizarre shapes, often with large caves and grottoes, spread out over 600 square miles. Travelers can cruise the bay on traditional junks and spend the night.

Toward the south stretch 1,800 miles of coast, which are largely still untouched by tourists and have beautiful beaches to offer, in the image of *China Beach*. Not far from Ho Chi Minh City is the **Vung Tau** resort (during French colonial times famous as Cap St. Jacques), and farther north **Phan Thiet** and **Nha Trang** with its coral reefs are the most popular beaches. The latest "in" resort is the mountainous **Phu Quoc Island** in the far south. Its white sandy beaches will soon be crowded with exclusive, luxury resorts.

South of Ho Chi Minh City, the canals and the port of Can Tho are booming with activity, especially near the floating markets of Cai Rang, Phong Vien, and Phung Hiep. Cruises along the South China Sea coast are experiencing a boom. The coastal cities on this route include some of the most interesting sites in Vietnam, representing several cultural eras.

What to See and Do in Zimbabwe

▶ **LANDSCAPE**

- Victoria Falls, Lake Kariba (canoeing, fishing)
- Matobo National Park, Balancing Rocks, Chinhoyi Caves

▶ **WILDLIFE**

- Matusadona National Park, Hwange National Park (elephants, crocodiles, birds)

▶ **MONUMENTS**

- Great Zimbabwe, Khami

Zimbabwe shares with Zambia the seething Victoria Falls.

Zimbabwe

Explorer David Livingstone was the first white person to discover the Zambezi Falls and was honored with a statue. Today's "explorers" enjoy the exceptional panorama, the amazing wildlife, and unique archaeological sites of Zimbabwe.

Traveler's Notebook

MAIN CONTACTS
Embassy of the Republic of Zimbabwe
1608 New Hampshire Avenue, NW
Washington, DC 20009
(202) 332-7100
www.zimbabwe-embassy.us
Embassy of the Republic of Zimbabwe
Zimbabwe House
429 The Strand
London WC2R 0JR, UK
+ 44 (0) 20 7836 7755

TRAVEL DOCUMENTS FOR U.S. & U.K. CITIZENS
Passport and visa

HEALTH ISSUES
Malaria prophylaxis is recommended for the whole year in the Zambezi Valley, and from November to the end of July for other areas below 3,600 feet; risk is minimal in Bulawayo and Harare.

TRAVEL TIME TO DESTINATION & TIME DIFFERENCE
New York to Harare: 19 hours 40 minutes connecting flight; EST +7. London to Harare: 13 hours 35 minutes connecting flight; GMT +2

AVERAGE TRIP COST
Victoria Falls and the national parks are the stopping points of a guided tour, often in addition to Botswana and Namibia. Plan on at least $3,175/£2,050 for 18 days, more during holidays and school vacations.

LANGUAGE & CURRENCY
Official language: English; Shona is the local language most used. Currency: Zimbabwe dollar

POPULATION
12,311,000 inhabitants, with Shonas in the majority and minorities of Caucasians, Indians, and people of mixed race. Capital: Harare (formerly Salisbury)

RELIGION
Primarily Christian (Protestant, Catholic, and African variants); 40 percent animist

FESTIVALS
April 18: Independence Day; end of May: Africa Days; important festivities at Harare, the House of Stone Music Festival (dates variable).

SHOPPING
Craft items such as textiles, sculptured objects in wood, and above all, masks

ways. One-third of the 5,677-foot width of the falls lies in Zimbabwe; the other two-thirds belong to Zambia. Nearby, **Lake Kariba,** born of a dam on the Zambezi, makes a pretty site, where people are swimming, canoeing, and fishing.

But there are other attractions:
• **Matobo National Park** features giant blocks of stone and has numerous San rock paintings. Cecil Rhodes, the founder of Zimbabwe (formerly Rhodesia), is buried there.
• The **Balancing Rocks** of Epworth, near Harare, are perfectly balanced without support.
• The **Chinhoyi Caves** hold a pool of cobalt-blue water, ever changing in intensity in its depths.

▶ LANDSCAPE

The Zambezi River suddenly plunges into a 354-foot-deep abyss for the biggest of its five falls. The fury of the water creates an intense fog that takes on all the colors of the rainbow. Mosi-oa-Tunya—the "fog that thunders and groans"—is as fascinating as the other great falls like Niagara and Iguaçu.

Listed as a World Heritage site, **Victoria Falls,** so named by Livingstone in honor of the Queen of England, can be viewed in a thousand

▶ WILDLIFE

In **Matusadona National Park** around Lake Kariba, elephants drink side by side with herons and crocodiles. **Hwange National Park,** the largest of Zimbabwe's parks, has several elephant herds of up to a hundred animals; there are more than a hundred different species of mammals and about four hundred species of birds.

In these two parks, as elsewhere in Africa, the animals can be most easily watched near the end of the dry season when they gather at the few remaining watering holes.

▶ MONUMENTS

Near Lake Mutirikwi are the vast stone ruins of **Great Zimbabwe,** one of the capitals of the ancient Bantu kingdom of Monomotapa, with remains of a palace, 30-foot-high ramparts, and a granite tower. The ruins merit a visit all the more as sub-Saharan Africa possesses few architectural ruins of this kind. The site of this hillside city was first explored only in the 1870s; some

of the remarkable finds are unusual bird-shaped monoliths cut straight from the rock.

Near Bulawayo, the ruins of **Khami** are of lesser importance, but are witness to the time when the city was the capital of the Torwa dynasty, between the 15th and 17th centuries.

When to Go		
	CLIMATE	VICTORIA FALLS FLORA
JANUARY		⚜
FEBRUARY		⚜
MARCH		⚜
APRIL	☼	
MAY	☼	
JUNE	☼	
JULY	☼	
AUGUST	☼	
SEPTEMBER	☼	
OCTOBER	☼	
NOVEMBER		⚜
DECEMBER		⚜

APPENDIX

The Right Trip for Your Interests

Whether you are interested in archaeology or strenuous hikes, beach vacations or nights in the desert, the reasons for travel are wide-ranging. The chart below presents destinations and their various offerings for the traveler, weighted by significance.

	LANDSCAPE	OCEAN	SNOW	DESERT	WILDLIFE	MARINE LIFE	HISTORIC STRUCTURES	CITIES	MUSEUMS & MONUMENTS	FESTIVALS & TRADITIONS
Antarctica	•••					•••				
Argentina	••					••	•			
Armenia	•						•			
Australia	••	•••		•	••	•				
Austria	•		•••				•	•	••	•
Baltic Countries	••							••		
Belgium	•						•	••		
Bolivia	•••						•			
Botswana	••				•••					
Brazil	•	•••			•		•	••		•••
Bulgaria	••	•	••				••	•		
Cambodia							•••	•		
Canada	•••		•••		•••			•		
Cape Verde Islands	••	••								••
Chile	•••	•		•	•••	•••	••			
China	•••			•			•••	•		
Costa Rica	•••	••								
Croatia	•	•••					••	•	•	
Cuba	•	•••					••	•		•••
Cyprus	•	•••					•		•	
Czech Republic	•••						••	•••	•	
Denmark								•		

	LANDSCAPE	OCEAN	SNOW	DESERT	WILDLIFE	MARINE LIFE	HISTORIC STRUCTURES	CITIES	MUSEUMS & MONUMENTS	FESTIVALS & TRADITIONS
Dominican Republic	•	•••					•			
Ecuador	•••					•••	•	•		
Egypt		•••		•••			•••	••	••	
Ethiopia	••				•		••		•	
Finland	••		•••							••
France	•••	•••	••				•••	•••	•••	•
French Guiana	••				••		•			
French Polynesia		•••					•		•	
Germany	•		•				•	•	•	•
Greece	••	•••					•••	••	•••	
Guadeloupe	••	•••								
Guatemala	••						••			••
Hong Kong								•••		•
Hungary	•						•	•		
Iceland	•••				•	•				
India	•••	••		•	••		•••	••	•	•••
Indonesia	•••	•••				••	•••	•		••
Ireland	••						•	•	•	•
Israel	•	•					•••		•	
Italy	••	•••	••				•••	•••	•••	••
Jamaica	•	•						•		
Japan	••						••	••		•
Jordan	•	•		•••			•••		•	
Kenya	••	•••			•••					
Laos	••						••			
Madagascar	•••	••			•••					

	LANDSCAPE	OCEAN	SNOW	DESERT	WILDLIFE	MARINE LIFE	HISTORIC STRUCTURES	CITIES	MUSEUMS & MONUMENTS	FESTIVALS & TRADITIONS
Malaysia	•••	•••			•	•				
Maldives		•••								
Mali	••			••						•••
Malta		••					•	•		•
Martinique	•	•••								
Mauritius	•	•••				••				•
Mexico	•••	•••					•••	••	•	
Mongolia	••			••						••
Montenegro	••	••								
Morocco	••	••		••			••	•••	•	•
Myanmar	•••						•••			
Namibia	•••			•••	•••	••				
Nepal	•••				••		••	••		
Netherlands	••							•••	•••	
New Caledonia	••	•••								•
New Zealand	••	••			•	•				••
Niger	•			•••	••					••
Norway	•••		•••					•		
Oman	••	•		••			•			
Peru	•••						•••	••		•
Philippines	••	••						•		
Poland	•				•			••	•	
Portugal	••	••				•	••	••	•	•
Reunion	••	••								
Romania	•	•			•		•	•		
Russia	••						••	••	••	

	LANDSCAPE	OCEAN	SNOW	DESERT	WILDLIFE	MARINE LIFE	HISTORIC STRUCTURES	CITIES	MUSEUMS & MONUMENTS	FESTIVALS & TRADITIONS
Senegal	••	•••			••			•	•	
Seychelles		•••			•	••				
Singapore								•••		•
Slovakia	•						•	•		
Slovenia	••	•	•					•		
South Africa	••	••			•••	•		•		
South Korea	•	•					•	•		
Spain	•	•••					•••	•••	•••	••
Sri Lanka		•••			•		•••			••
Sweden	••		•••					•		
Switzerland	•••		•••							
Syria		•					•••	•		
Taiwan	•	•						•	•	
Tanzania	•••	••			•••		•			
Thailand	•	•••					•••	••		•
Tunisia	••	•••		•••			••	•		
Turkey	••	••					•	•••	••	
United Arab Emirates		•						•		
United Kingdom	••	•			•		•	•••	•••	•
United States	•••	••	•	•••	•	•		•••	••	
Uzbekistan	••						•••	••	••	
Venezuela	•••	•••				•		•		
Vietnam	••	•	•					•••		
Zimbabwe	••				••		•			

The Right Trip for Your Lifestyle

You don't travel the same way when you're 20 as you do when you're 60, with children or as a couple, for two weeks or two days. The chart below lists destinations according to types of travel.

	TRAVEL AS A COUPLE	WITH CHILDREN	SENIOR TRAVEL	A LONG WEEKEND	A WEEK	TWO WEEKS OR MORE	LUXURY TRAVEL	ADVENTURE	ENCOUNTERS WITH LOCALS	ACTIVE PURSUITS
Alaska						•			•	
Antarctica						•				
Argentina						•				
Armenia					•					
Australia						•	•	•	•	•
Austria	•		•	•	•		•			
Azores (Portugal)					•			•		•
Balearic Islands (Spain)		•	•		•		•			•
Baltic Countries	•		•	•						
Belgium	•		•	•			•			
Bolivia						•			•	
Botswana						•		•		
Brazil						•				•
Bulgaria					•					
Cambodia					•	•			•	
Canada		•				•	•			•
Canary Islands (Spain)	•	•	•		•			•		•
Cape Verde					•				•	•
Chile						•		•		
China						•			•	
Costa Rica						•		•		
Croatia	•	•	•	•	•					
Cuba					•					
Cyprus	•	•			•					
Czech Republic	•	•	•	•						

	TRAVEL AS A COUPLE	WITH CHILDREN	SENIOR TRAVEL	A LONG WEEKEND	A WEEK	TWO WEEKS OR MORE	LUXURY TRAVEL	ADVENTURE	ENCOUNTERS WITH LOCALS	ACTIVE PURSUITS
Denmark	•	•		•						
Dominican Republic			•		•	•	•			•
Ecuador						•			•	
Egypt		•	•		•				•	
England	•	•	•	•						
Ethiopia					•	•			•	
Finland		•	•	•	•			•		•
France										
French Guiana						•		•		
French Polynesia	•									•
Germany	•		•	•	•		•			
Greece	•	•	•		•		•		•	
Guadeloupe		•	•		•					•
Guatemala						•			•	
Hong Kong					•		•			
Hungary	•		•	•	•					
India						•			•	
Indonesia	•					•			•	
Ireland	•	•	•	•	•					•
Israel					•				•	
Italy	•	•	•	•	•		•			•
Jamaica										
Japan						•	•		•	
Jordan	•				•				•	
Kenya	•	•				•		•		
Laos						•			•	
Lipari Islands (Italy)	•	•	•	•	•		•			•

	TRAVEL AS A COUPLE	WITH CHILDREN	SENIOR TRAVEL	A LONG WEEKEND	A WEEK	TWO WEEKS OR MORE	LUXURY TRAVEL	ADVENTURE	ENCOUNTERS WITH LOCALS	ACTIVE PURSUITS
Madagascar						•		•		•
Madeira (Portugal)	•	•	•	•			•			•
Malaysia	•					•				
Maldives	•					•	•			•
Mali					•			•	•	
Malta	•	•	•	•						•
Martinique	•	•	•		•					•
Mauritius	•	•				•	•			•
Mexico	•		•			•			•	
Mongolia						•		•	•	
Montenegro		•		•						
Morocco	•	•	•	•	•		•		•	
Myanmar						•			•	
Namibia	•					•		•		
Nepal						•			•	
Netherlands	•	•	•	•			•			
New Caledonia						•				•
New Zealand						•		•		
Niger					•			•	•	
Norway		•	•		•		•			
Oman					•				•	
Peru	•					•			•	
Philippines						•		•	•	
Poland	•		•	•	•					
Portugal	•	•	•	•	•					•
Réunion	•				•					•
Romania			•	•	•					
Russia			•		•					

	TRAVEL AS A COUPLE	WITH CHILDREN	SENIOR TRAVEL	A LONG WEEKEND	A WEEK	TWO WEEKS OR MORE	LUXURY TRAVEL	ADVENTURE	ENCOUNTERS WITH LOCALS	ACTIVE PURSUITS
Sardinia	•	•	•		•		•			
Scotland	•		•	•						
Senegal					•			•	•	
Seychelles	•					•	•			•
Sicily	•	•	•		•		•			
Singapore						•	•			
Slovakia			•		•					
Slovenia			•		•					
South Africa						•			•	
South Korea						•			•	
Spain	•	•	•	•	•		•			•
Sri Lanka	•					•			•	
Sweden	•		•	•	•		•			•
Switzerland		•	•		•		•			•
Syria					•				•	
Taiwan										
Tanzania		•				•				
Thailand	•		•			•	•			
Tibet	•					•		•	•	
Tunisia		•	•	•	•		•			•
Turkey	•	•	•	•	•				•	
United Arab Emirates				•	•		•			
United States	•	•	•			•	•			•
Uzbekistan					•				•	
Venezuela	•					•		•		
Vietnam	•					•			•	
Wales	•		•	•	•					
Zanzibar (Tanzania)					•					
Zimbabwe	•					•		•	•	

The Right Trip for You

Cost and length of stay, quality of hotel and transport, safety—there are many reasons for choosing a trip. The charts below compare many important criteria.

	AVERAGE COST IN DOLLARS	AVERAGE COST IN POUNDS	HEALTH ISSUES	TRAVEL DOCUMENTS REQUIRED: U.S. CITIZENS	TRAVEL DOCUMENTS REQUIRED: U.K. CITIZENS	TRAVEL TIME FROM NEW YORK	TRAVEL TIME FROM LONDON	TIME DIFFERENCE: NOON IN NEW YORK	TIME DIFFERENCE: NOON IN LONDON	INFRA-STRUCTURE	SAFETY	PEAK SEASON
Antarctica	$5,800 for a 10-day cruise	£3,700		Passport	Passport	from Ushuaia, Argentina: 14 hrs connecting	from Ushuaia, Argentina: 19 hrs connecting	all time zones	all time zones			Between November and March
Argentina	$2,200 for 12 days of excursions	£1,800	Malaria warning near the borders of Bolivia and Paraguay	Passport	Passport	10 hr 30 min nonstop	15 hr 40 min connecting	2:00 PM	9:00 AM	Good lodging, car rentals expensive	Vigilance required in the cities	Northern winter
Armenia	$2,000 for 12 days of culture and excursions	£1,000		Passport & visa	Passport & visa	16 hr 35 min connecting	5 hr nonstop	9:00 PM	4:00 PM	Limited lodging and difficult roads	Avoid traveling alone	
Australia	$2,540–$3,175 for 15 days of excursions	£1,640–£2,010		Passport & visa	Passport	22 hr 30 min connecting	21 hr 30 min connecting	4:00 AM next day	11:00 PM	Excellent infrastructure		End of the year in Sydney
Austria	$900	£600		Passport	Passport	8 hr 45 min nonstop	2 hr 15 min nonstop	6:00 PM	1:00 PM	Excellent infrastructure		New Year's Eve and in summer in Vienna
Baltic Countries	$350 for a 4-day weekend in Riga or Tallinn	£225		Passport	Passport	9 hr 45 min connecting	3 hr nonstop flight to Riga	7:00 PM	2:00 PM	Excellent infrastructure		
Belgium	$200–$250 for 3 days/2 nights	£125–£165		Passport	Passport	8 hr 30 min nonstop	1 hr nonstop	6:00 PM	1:00 PM	Excellent infrastructure		
Bolivia	$2,500–$3,000 for 3 weeks of excursions in connection with Peru	£2,000–£2,500	Yellow fever immunization advised, except for the Altiplano	Passport & visa	Passport	12 hr connecting	21 hr 15 min connecting	1:00 PM	8:00 AM	Few paved roads, renting a car with driver is advised	Vigilance required when traveling alone	
Botswana	$3,000 for 12 days on safari	£2,000	Malaria warning in certain regions	Passport	Passport	18 hr 45 min connecting	13 hr 20 min connecting	7:00 PM	2:00 PM	Good road network, lodging expensive		

	AVERAGE COST IN DOLLARS	AVERAGE COST IN POUNDS	HEALTH ISSUES	TRAVEL DOCUMENTS REQUIRED: U.S. CITIZENS	TRAVEL DOCUMENTS REQUIRED: U.K. CITIZENS	TRAVEL TIME FROM NEW YORK	TRAVEL TIME FROM LONDON	TIME DIFFERENCE: NOON IN NEW YORK	TIME DIFFERENCE: NOON IN LONDON	INFRA-STRUCTURE	SAFETY	PEAK SEASON
Brazil	$2,000 for 12 days of excursions	£1,200	Yellow fever immuniza-tion advised for the west, malaria warning for the Amazon	Passport & visa	Passport	10 hr 15 min nonstop	13 hr connecting	1:00 PM	8:00 AM	Lodging plenti-ful, rent a car	Safety some-times a prob-lem in the large cities and favelas	Mid-January to mid-February
Bulgaria	$1,300 for a week of excursions	£800		Passport	Passport	11 hr 25 min connecting	3 hr 5 min nonstop	7:00 PM	2:00 PM	Hotels, pensions, and private lodging		Summer on the Black Sea
Cambodia	$2,540–$3,175 for 15 days in com-bination with Vietnam	£1,640–£2,010	Malaria warning for most of the region, including Angkor Wat	Passport & visa	Passport & visa	20 hr 25 min connecting	14 hr 10 min connecting	12:00 AM the follow-ing day	7:00 PM	Roads difficult, renting a car with driver is advised	Land mines possible in isolated areas	
Canada	$1,905 for a week of mul-tiple snow activities	£1,230		Passport	Passport	Montreal: 1 hr 30 min non-stop; Vancou-ver: 5 hr 50 min nonstop	Montreal: 7 hr nonstop; Vancouver: 9 hr 30 min nonstop	Atlantic: 12:00 PM; Pacific: 9:00 AM	Montreal: 7:00 AM; Vancouver: 4:00 AM	Excellent infrastructure		Summer and winter
Cape Verde	$1,651 for a week of hiking	£1,066	Yellow fever immuniza-tion advised, malaria for São Tiago	Passport & visa	Passport & visa	21 hr 25 min connecting	7 hr 50 min connecting	4:00 PM	11:00 AM	Narrow roads, good lodging		December
Chile	$3,810 for 15 days of excursions	£2,460		Passport		10 hr 50 min nonstop	16 hr 15 min connecting	2:00 PM	9:00 AM	Good infrastruc-ture and good bus connections		
China	$1,900 for 10 days of a classic tour	£1,230	Malaria warning for Hainan and Yunnan	Passport & visa	Passport & visa	13 hr 30 min nonstop	10 hr 10 min nonstop	Beijing: 1:00 AM the following day	Beijing: 8:00 PM	Lodging uneven and expensive, rail service slow		Spring and fall
Costa Rica	$1,900 for 10 days	£1,230	Slight malaria risk	Passport	Passport	5 hr 10 min nonstop	13 hr 40 min connecting	11:00 AM	6:00 AM	Difficult roads, good lodging and camping		December and April
Croatia	$1,300 for a 10-day cruise	£850		Passport	Passport	12 hr 40 min connecting	4 hr 10 min connecting	6:00 PM	1:00 PM	Good lodging and transportation	Don't stray from the itinerary	Summer in Dubrovnik and in the islands
Cuba	$1,300 for a beach week	£850		Check with the State Department	Passport		8 hr 30 min	12:00 PM	7:00 AM	Lodging various to good, roads are deserted		

	AVERAGE COST IN DOLLARS	AVERAGE COST IN POUNDS	HEALTH ISSUES	TRAVEL DOCUMENTS REQUIRED: U.S. CITIZENS	TRAVEL DOCUMENTS REQUIRED: U.K. CITIZENS	TRAVEL TIME FROM NEW YORK	TRAVEL TIME FROM LONDON	TIME DIFFERENCE: NOON IN NEW YORK	TIME DIFFERENCE: NOON IN LONDON	INFRA-STRUCTURE	SAFETY	PEAK SEASON
Cyprus	$775 for a week of excursions	£500		Passport	Passport	12 hr 45 min connecting	4 hr 30 min nonstop	7:00 PM	2:00 PM	Excellent infrastructure		Summer
Czech Republic	$450 for 3 days and 2 nights in Prague	£275		Passport	Passport	8 hr 40 min nonstop		6:00 PM	1:00 PM	Excellent infrastructure		May to August
Denmark	$375 for a weekend in Copenhagen	£250		Passport	Passport	8 hr 5 min nonstop	1 hr 50 min nonstop	6:00 PM	1:00 PM	Excellent infra-structure, but expensive		
Dominican Republic	$1,000–$1,275 for a week's beach vacation	£650–£800	Malaria warning in the west	Passport	Passport	3 hr 45 min nonstop	11 hr 55 min connecting	1:00 PM	8:00 AM	Acceptable roads		End of the year and February
Ecuador	$2,540 for a 15-day tour, more if the Galápagos are included	£1,640	Yellow fever and malaria warning in rural areas	Passport	Passport	8 hr 30 min connecting	14 hr connecting	12:00 PM	7:00 AM	Difficult roads	Problems on the northern border, vigilance required in the cities	
Egypt	$1,000 for a week's cruise on the Nile	£650		Passport & visa	Passport	10 hr 45 min nonstop	4 hr 45 min nonstop	7:00 PM	2:00 PM	Excellent vessels and lodging on the Nile	Police surveillance	On the Nile, October to May; on the Red Sea, March to June and September to December
Ethiopia	$3,175 for 15 days of all-terrain travel	£2,050	Yellow fever immuniza-tion advised, malaria warning below 6,000 feet	Passport & visa	Passport	17 hr 45 min connecting	6 hr 45 min nonstop	8:00 PM	3:00 PM	Roads difficult	Avoid travel-ing alone	
Finland	$1,650 for a week of mul-tiple snow activities in Lapland	£1,050		Passport	Passport	8 hr 5 min nonstop	2 hr 55 min nonstop	7:00 PM	2:00 PM	Excellent infrastructure		Summer and during holidays
France	$380 for a weekend in Paris	£250		Passport	Passport	7 hr nonstop	1 hr 10 min nonstop	6:00 PM	1:00 PM	Excellent infrastructure		April to Sep-tember in Paris

	AVERAGE COST IN DOLLARS	AVERAGE COST IN POUNDS	HEALTH ISSUES	TRAVEL DOCUMENTS REQUIRED: U.S. CITIZENS	TRAVEL DOCUMENTS REQUIRED: U.K. CITIZENS	TRAVEL TIME FROM NEW YORK	TRAVEL TIME FROM LONDON	TIME DIFFERENCE: NOON IN NEW YORK	TIME DIFFERENCE: NOON IN LONDON	INFRA-STRUCTURE	SAFETY	PEAK SEASON
French Guiana	$2,550 for a 15-day forest adventure	£1,650	Yellow fever immuniza-tion advised, malaria warning for interior	Passport	Passport	20 hr 30 min connecting	22 hr 55 min connecting	2:00 PM	9:00 AM	Good outfitters for roads and rivers	Avoid travel-ing alone	
French Polynesia	$3,810 for 12 days of cruising	£2,460		Passport	Passport	16 hr 45 min connecting	22 hr 45 min connecting	6:00 AM previous day	1:00 AM previous day	Excellent infrastructure		Summer and end of the year
Germany	$800 for a week's cruise on the Rhine	£500		Passport	Passport	8 hr 35 min nonstop	1 hr 50 min nonstop	6:00 PM	1:00 PM	Excellent infrastructure		
Greece	$775 for a week on the beach	£500		Passport	Passport	Athens: 10 hr 5 min non-stop; Her-aklion: 13 hr 40 min connecting	Athens:3 hr 35 min non-stop; Her-aklion: 6 hr 5 min connecting	7:00 PM	2:00 PM	Excellent infrastructure		July to August
Guadeloupe	$1,000 for a week's beach vacation	£650		Passport	Passport	8 hr 15 min connecting	15 hr 20 min connecting	1:00 PM	8:00 AM	Excellent infrastructure		Holidays and February
Guatemala	$2,540–$3,175 for 15 days of clas-sic touring	£1,640–£2,010	Malaria warning below 6,000 feet	Passport	Passport	7 hr 21 min connecting	15 hr 5 min connecting	11:00 AM	6:00 AM	Small family hotels, private lodging	Avoid travel-ing and driv-ing alone	December to April
Hong Kong	$900 for 3 days and 2 nights	£575		Passport	Passport	16 hr 5 min nonstop	11 hr 35 min nonstop	1:00 AM the follow-ing day	8:00 PM	Excellent infrastructure		Spring and fall
Hungary	$2,200 for a 10-day cruise on the Danube	£1,400		Passport	Passport	11 hr connecting	2 hr 30 min nonstop	6:00 PM	1:00 PM	Excellent infrastructure		Spring and summer in Budapest
Iceland	$1,200 for a week of hiking	£800		Passport	Passport	5 hr 45 min nonstop	3 hrs nonstop	5:00 PM	12:00 PM	Excellent infrastructure		Summer
India	$2,550 for 15 days of touring	£1,650	Malaria warning below 6,000 feet	Passport & visa	Passport & visa	Mumbai: 14 hr 15 min non-stop; Kolkata: 18 hr 35 min connecting	Mumbai: 8 hr 15 min con-necting; Kol-kata: 12 hrs connecting	New Delhi: 10:30 PM	New Delhi: 5:30 PM	Difficult roads, overcrowded trains, lodging variable		November to April

	AVERAGE COST IN DOLLARS	AVERAGE COST IN POUNDS	HEALTH ISSUES	TRAVEL DOCUMENTS REQUIRED: U.S. CITIZENS	TRAVEL DOCUMENTS REQUIRED: U.K. CITIZENS	TRAVEL TIME FROM NEW YORK	TRAVEL TIME FROM LONDON	TIME DIFFERENCE: NOON IN NEW YORK	TIME DIFFERENCE: NOON IN LONDON	INFRA-STRUCTURE	SAFETY	PEAK SEASON
Indonesia	$2,800 for 15 days in Java and Bali	£1,800	Malaria warning outside of Java, Bali, and Jakarta	Passport & visa	Passport & visa	22 hr 45 min connecting	15 hr 10 min connecting	1:00 AM the following day	8:00 PM	Buses and trains in good order, lodging variable	Occasional conflicts	April to September
Ireland	$1,500 for a 10-day excursion	£1,000		Passport	Passport	6 hr 40 min connecting	1 hr 15 min nonstop	5:00 PM	12:00 PM	Excellent infrastructure		Summer and St. Patrick's Day
Israel	$1,400 for a week of excursions	£900		Passport & visa	Passport	10 hr 40 min nonstop	4 hr 55 min nonstop	7:00 PM	2:00 PM	Excellent infrastructure	Persistent political tensions, vigilance required	
Italy	$1,400 for a week of excursions	£900		Passport	Passport	8 hr 10 min nonstop	2 hr 20 min nonstop	6:00 PM	1:00 PM	Excellent infrastructure		Easter week and summer
Jamaica	$1,275–$2,500 for 7 nights at an all-inclusive resort	£800–£1,600		Passport	Passport	3 hr 45 min nonstop	14 hr 50 min connecting	12:00 PM	7:00 AM	Numerous resorts, paved but poorly kept roads	Avoid inner-city areas of Kingston and Montego Bay	Mid-December to mid-April
Japan	$3,800 for 15 days of touring	£2,450		Passport	Passport	14 hr nonstop	11 hr 35 min nonstop	2:00 AM	9:00 PM	Excellent infrastructure		
Jordan	$1,650 for 9 days at Petra and hiking in Wadi Rum	£1,050		Passport & visa	Passport & visa	11 hr 35 min nonstop	5 hrs nonstop	7:00 PM	2:00 PM	Excellent infrastructure		Spring and fall
Kenya	$1,550 for a week of safari	£1,000	Yellow fever immunization advised, malaria warning below 6,000 feet	Passport & visa	Passport & visa	16 hr 45 min connecting	8 hr 30 min nonstop	8:00 PM	3:00 PM	Good roads, but car rental not advisable	Avoid northern borders, general vigilance required	July to August, reserve entire trip ahead of time
Laos	$2,550 for a 15-day excursion in combination with Cambodia	£1,650	Malaria warning, except in Vientiane	Passport & visa	Passport & visa	22 hr 25 min connecting	15 hr 50 min connecting	12:00 AM the following day	7:00 PM	Few paved roads, no trains		November to February

	AVERAGE COST IN DOLLARS	AVERAGE COST IN POUNDS	HEALTH ISSUES	TRAVEL DOCUMENTS REQUIRED: U.S. CITIZENS	TRAVEL DOCUMENTS REQUIRED: U.K. CITIZENS	TRAVEL TIME FROM NEW YORK	TRAVEL TIME FROM LONDON	TIME DIFFERENCE: NOON IN NEW YORK	TIME DIFFERENCE: NOON IN LONDON	INFRA-STRUCTURE	SAFETY	PEAK SEASON
Madagascar	$2,540–$3,175 for 15 days of touring	£1,640–£2,010	Malaria warning, especially in coastal areas	Passport & visa	Passport & visa	22 hr 45 min connecting	13 hr 25 min connecting	8:00 PM	3:00 PM	Driving difficult, all-terrain vehicle and driver recommended		
Malaysia	$3,800 for 15 days of touring	£2,450	Malaria warning for interior	Passport	Passport	20 hr 45 min connecting	11 hr 25 min nonstop	1:00 AM the following day	8:00 PM	Little comfort in Sarawak and Sabah		
Maldives	$2,200 for 15 days in combination with Sri Lanka	£1,400		Passport	Passport	18 hr 5 min connecting	12 hr 30 min	10:00 PM	5:00 PM	Seaplanes, fishing boats, island resorts		Holidays at the end of the year
Mali	$2,000 for 15 days in the Dogon area and the Niger River	£1,300	Yellow fever immunization required, strong malaria warnings	Passport & visa	Passport & visa	11 hr 35 min connecting	8 hr 5 min connecting	5:00 PM	12:00 PM	Limited comfort, roads difficult	Avoid traveling alone in the north	
Malta	$625 for a week's beach vacation	£400		Passport	Passport	11 hr 55 min connecting	3 hr 10 min nonstop	6:00 PM	1:00 PM	Excellent infrastructure		July to September
Martinique	$775 for a week's beach vacation	£500		Passport	Passport	7 hr 55 min connecting	17 hr 30 min connecting	1:00 PM	6:00 PM	Excellent infrastructure		Holidays and February
Mauritius	$1,275 for a week's beach vacation	£825		Passport	Passport	24 hr 10 min connecting	16 hr 30 min connecting	9:00 PM	4:00 PM	Excellent infrastructure		Holidays and October to March
Mexico	$1,275 for a week's beach vacation at Riviera Maya	£825	Malaria warning in Oaxaca and Chiapas	Passport	Passport	5 hr 5 min nonstop	11 hr 40 min nonstop	11:00 AM	6:00 AM	Good infrastructure		October to April
Mongolia	$3,175 for 15 days of touring	£2,050		Passport	Passport & visa	18 hr 40 min connecting	12 hr 30 min connecting	1:00 AM the following day	8:00 PM	Conditions difficult, but quaint (yurts)	Few individual travelers, important to be well informed	
Montenegro	$900 for a week's beach vacation	£575		Passport	Passport	14 hr 10 min connecting	4 hr 35 min connecting	6:00 PM	1:00 PM	Excellent infrastructure		Summer

	AVERAGE COST IN DOLLARS	AVERAGE COST IN POUNDS	HEALTH ISSUES	TRAVEL DOCUMENTS REQUIRED: U.S. CITIZENS	TRAVEL DOCUMENTS REQUIRED: U.K. CITIZENS	TRAVEL TIME FROM NEW YORK	TRAVEL TIME FROM LONDON	TIME DIFFERENCE: NOON IN NEW YORK	TIME DIFFERENCE: NOON IN LONDON	INFRA-STRUCTURE	SAFETY	PEAK SEASON
Morocco	$900 for a week's beach vacation	£575		Passport	Passport	11 hr 10 min connecting	5 hr 40 min connecting	5:00 PM	12:00 PM	Various lodgings (riads), good bus connections, group taxis		Spring and summer in Marrakech and Agadir
Myanmar	$3,175 for 15 days of touring, driver and guide included	£2,050	Malaria warning below 3,000 feet	Passport & visa	Passport & visa	15 hr 20 min connecting	10 hr 9 min connecting	11:30 PM	6:30 PM	Slow trains, moving around difficult	Forbidden to travel in certain regions, vigilance required	November to March
Namibia	$1,900 for 12 days on safari	£1,230	Malaria warning in the north	Passport & visa	Passport	19 hr 45 min connecting	12 hr 50 min connecting	7:00 PM	2:00 PM	Good roads, lodging varies, but expensive	Avoid the northern region	November to March
Nepal	$1,900 for 15 days of trekking	£1,230	Malaria warning in the south	Passport & visa	Passport & visa	20 hr 8 min connecting	11 hr 10 min connecting	10:45 PM	5:45 PM	Good conditions for trekking and lodging	Vigilance required, depending on the political situation	
Netherlands	$325 for a 4-day weekend in Amsterdam	£200		Passport	Passport	7 hr 10 min nonstop	1 hr 15 min nonstop	6:00 PM	1:00 PM	Excellent infrastructure		Tulip season and in Amsterdam May to September
New Caledonia	$3,810 for 15 days of cruising	£2,460	Malaria warning	Passport	Passport	25 hr 40 min connecting	25 hr 30 min connecting	4:00 AM the following day	11:00 PM	Excellent infrastructure		
New Zealand	$3,810 for 21 days of touring	£2,460		Passport	Passport	21 hr 5 min connecting	23 hr 45 min connecting	6:00 AM the following day	1:00 AM the following day	Bed & breakfasts, camping, farms		
Niger	$1,150 for a week in the desert	£750	Yellow fever immunization required, malaria warning	Passport & visa	Passport & visa	15 hr 30 min connecting	8 hrs connecting	6:00 PM	1:00 PM	Good conditions for the desert	Avoid traveling alone	End of the year and February
Norway	$2,540 for 13 days of cruising	£1,640		Passport	Passport	9 hr 5 min connecting	2 hr 5 min nonstop	6:00 PM	1:00 PM	Excellent infrastructure		Summer
Oman	$2,540 for a 10-day all-terrain excursion	£1,640		Passport & visa	Passport & visa	14 hr 45 min connecting	8 hr 45 min connecting	9:00 PM	4:00 PM	Excellent infrastructure		
Peru	$3,175 for 15 days of hiking on the Inca Trail	£2,050	Malaria warning below 4,500 feet	Passport	Passport	7 hr 55 min nonstop	15 hr 50 min connecting	12:00 PM	5:00 PM	Excellent infrastructure	Avoid traveling alone in certain regions	Summer

	AVERAGE COST IN DOLLARS	AVERAGE COST IN POUNDS	HEALTH ISSUES	TRAVEL DOCUMENTS REQUIRED: U.S. CITIZENS	TRAVEL DOCUMENTS REQUIRED: U.K. CITIZENS	TRAVEL TIME FROM NEW YORK	TRAVEL TIME FROM LONDON	TIME DIFFERENCE: NOON IN NEW YORK	TIME DIFFERENCE: NOON IN LONDON	INFRA-STRUCTURE	SAFETY	PEAK SEASON
Philippines	$3,175 for 15 days of excursions	£2,050	Malaria warning below 1,800 feet, except in the cities	Passport	Passport	20 hr 35 min connecting	14 hr 25 min connecting	1:00 AM	8:00 PM	Excellent infrastructure, but expensive	Vigilance required in the south	
Poland	$500 for a 4-day weekend in Krakow and Warsaw	£325		Passport	Passport	10 hr 45 min connecting	2 hr 25 min nonstop	6:00 PM	1:00 PM	Excellent infrastructure		
Portugal	$1,150 for a week's beach vacation in the Algarve	£750		Passport	Passport	9 hr 50 min connecting	2 hr 30 min nonstop	5:00 PM	12:00 PM	Quaint lodging in *dormidas* or *pousadas*		July to August
Réunion	$1,900 for 10 days of excursions	£1,230		Passport	Passport	22 hr 20 min connecting	17 hr 45 min connecting	9:00 PM	4:00 PM	Rural lodges, bed & breakfasts, good roads		Summer
Romania	$750 for a week's beach vacation on the Black Sea	£500		Passport	Passport	11 hr 35 min connecting	3 hr 15 min nonstop	7:00 PM	2:00 PM	Hotels, hostels, private lodging, camping		July to August on the Black Sea
Russia	$1,650 for 12 days of cruising on the Volga	£1,050		Passport & visa	Passport & visa	Moscow: 9 hr 15 min nonstop; St. Petersburg: 10 hr 5 min connecting	Moscow: 3 hr 45 min nonstop; St. Petersburg: 3 hr 20 min nonstop	8:00 PM	3:00 PM	Excellent infrastructure, hotels expensive	Avoid travel to the autonomous republics in the Caucasus	June in St. Petersburg
Senegal	$1,000 for a week's beach vacation	£650	Yellow fever immunization required, malaria warning	Passport	Passport	11 hr 10 min connecting	7 hr 25 min connecting	5:00 PM	12:00 PM	Good road network, lodging in camps and with families	Avoid traveling near the borders of Gambia and Guinea-Bissau	November to May
Seychelles	$2,800 for a week of beach vacation and diving	£1,800		Passport	Passport	22 hr 45 min connecting	12 hr 20 min connecting	9:00 PM	4:00 PM	Excellent infrastructure		July to August
Singapore	$1,000 for 4 days and 3 nights	£650		Passport	Passport	20 hr 40 min connecting	12 hr 35 min nonstop	1:00 AM the following day	8:00 PM	Excellent infrastructure		Year-round
Slovakia	$1,150 for a week of hiking and cultural sites	£750		Passport	Passport	10 hr 50 min connecting	4 hr connecting	6:00 PM	1:00 PM	Excellent infrastructure		

	AVERAGE COST IN DOLLARS	AVERAGE COST IN POUNDS	HEALTH ISSUES	TRAVEL DOCUMENTS REQUIRED: U.S. CITIZENS	TRAVEL DOCUMENTS REQUIRED: U.K. CITIZENS	TRAVEL TIME FROM NEW YORK	TRAVEL TIME FROM LONDON	TIME DIFFERENCE: NOON IN NEW YORK	TIME DIFFERENCE: NOON IN LONDON	INFRA-STRUCTURE	SAFETY	PEAK SEASON
Slovenia	$1,270 for a week of hiking or touring	£820		Passport	Passport	10 hr connecting	3 hr 20 min connecting	6:00 PM	1:00 PM	Excellent infrastructure		
South Africa	$3,175 for 15 days	£2,050	Malaria warning October to May	Passport	Passport	15 hr 10 min nonstop	10 hr 50 min nonstop	7:00 PM	2:00 PM	Good roads and lodges in the parks	Vigilance required	November to February
South Korea	$3,175 for 12 days	£2,050		Passport	Passport	14 hr nonstop	10 hr 50 min nonstop	2:00 AM the following day	9:00 PM	Excellent infrastructure		
Spain	$2,540 for a classic 15-day stay	£1,650		Passport	Passport	Barcelona: 7 hr 35 min non-stop; Málaga: 9 hr 50 min connecting	Barcelona: 2 hr non-stop; Malaga: 2 hr 45 min nonstop	6:00 PM	1:00 PM	Excellent infrastructure		Summer
Sri Lanka	$1,775 for 15 days of touring by minibus	£1,150	Malaria warning, except for Colombo, Kalutara, and Nuwara Eliya	Passport	Passport	18 hr connecting	9 hr 45 min nonstop	10:30 PM	5:30 PM	Good train net-work, good roads and lodging	Avoid the northern end of the island	January and February
Sweden	$1,775 for 10 days of mul-tiple snow activities in Lapland	£1,150		Passport	Passport	8 hr 10 min nonstop	2 hr 30 min nonstop	6:00 PM	1:00 PM	Excellent infrastructure		
Switzerland	$750 for a week of hik-ing in the Alps	£500		Passport	Passport	7 hr 55 min nonstop	1 hr 35 min nonstop	6:00 PM	1:00 PM	Excellent infrastructure		
Syria	$1,900 for 15 days in com-bination with Jordan	£1,230		Passport & visa	Passport & visa	12 hr 30 min connecting	5 hr 10 min nonstop	7:00 PM	2:00 PM	Good bus and train network		
Taiwan	$80–$250 per night at a 3-star or above hotel	£50–£165		Passport	Passport	18 hr 35 min connecting	13 hr 35 min nonstop	1:00 AM the follow-ing day	8:00 PM	Lots of tour-ist facilities, but congested city streets and poor mountain roads	Avoid politi-cal demon-stration areas and local businesses operating as covers for prostitution	Year-round
Tanzania	$3,175 for 15 days on safari, includ-ing Zanzibar	£2,050	Yellow fever immuni-zation advised, malaria below 4,600 feet	Passport & visa	Passport & visa	19 hr connecting	9 hr 35 min nonstop	8:00 PM	3:00 PM	Various lodges in the reserves, but expensive	Avoid travel-ing near the borders of Rwanda and Burundi	All year except summer

	AVERAGE COST IN DOLLARS	AVERAGE COST IN POUNDS	HEALTH ISSUES	TRAVEL DOCUMENTS REQUIRED: U.S. CITIZENS	TRAVEL DOCUMENTS REQUIRED: U.K. CITIZENS	TRAVEL TIME FROM NEW YORK	TRAVEL TIME FROM LONDON	TIME DIFFERENCE: NOON IN NEW YORK	TIME DIFFERENCE: NOON IN LONDON	INFRA-STRUCTURE	SAFETY	PEAK SEASON
Thailand	$1,270 for a week in Bangkok and Phuket	£820	Malaria warning in rural areas	Passport	Passport	19 hr 55 min connecting	11 hr 5 min nonstop	12:00 AM	7:00 PM	Good road and train network, lodging variable	Avoid traveling in the deep south	End of the year for the beaches
Tunisia	$900 for a week's beach vacation	£575		Passport	Passport	Houmt Souk: 20 hr 6 min connecting; Tunis: 11 hr 20 min connecting	Houmt Souk: 6 hr 35 min connecting; Tunis: 4 hr 35 min connecting	6:00 PM	1:00 PM	Excellent infrastructure		June to September
Turkey	$750 for a week's beach vacation	£500	Malaria warning in the southeast (Cukorova, Amikova)	Passport & visa	Passport & visa	Antalya: 13 hr connecting; Istanbul: 9 hr 40 min nonstop	3 hr 45 min nonstop	7:00 PM	2:00 PM	Excellent infrastructure	Avoid traveling in the southeast	June to September on the Mediterranean coast
United Arab Emirates	$900 for a weekend in Dubai	£575		Passport	Passport	12 hr 30 min nonstop	6 hr 45 min nonstop	9:00 PM	4:00 PM	Excellent infrastructure, rather luxurious		November to April
United States	$500 for a weekend in New York	£325			Passport		7 hr 40 min nonstop		New York: 7:00 AM	Excellent infrastructure		
United Kingdom	$500 for a weekend in London	£320		Passport		6 hr 45 min nonstop		5:00 PM		Excellent infrastructure		Spring and summer in London
Uzbekistan	$1,775 for a week's excursions	£1,150		Passport & visa	Passport & visa	17 hr 45 min connecting	8 hr 10 min connecting	10:00 PM	5:00 PM	Good road network, hotels, bed & breakfasts	Avoid traveling toward the southeast border	
Venezuela	$3,175 for 15 days of excursions	£2,050	Yellow fever immunization advised, malaria warning in rural areas and the Amazon	Passport	Passport	7 hr 55 min connecting	13 hr connecting	12:30 PM	7:30 AM	Posadas, lodges, ranches, camping		
Vietnam	$2,540 for 15 days of touring	£1,640	Malaria warning, especially in the south and below 4,500 feet	Passport & visa	Passport	20 hr 35 min connecting	13 hr 40 min connecting	12:00 AM	7:00 PM	Hotels, lodging with families, interesting trains		
Zimbabwe	$3,175 for 18 days at Victoria Falls and game reserves	£2,050	Malaria warning below 3,600 ft.	Passport & visa	Passport & visa	19 hr 40 min connecting	13 hr 35 min connecting	7:00 PM	2:00 PM	Excellent lodges, but expensive		

The Best Time to Travel in Tropical Climates

Contrary to the popular belief, the skies are not always blue in the tropics. The chart below indicates the best times to travel in these regions. Three different colors mark the travel periods: The months in orange are best avoided, be it for excessive heat or possible hurricanes. The months in yellow are less hot, but the best time to travel is indicated in green.

	JAN	FEB	MAR	APR	MAY	JUN	JUL	AUG	SEP	OCT	NOV	DEC
Australia (Center)												
Australia (North)												
Australia (South)												
Brazil (Amazonia)					rainy season							
Brazil (North)												
Brazil (South)												
Cape Verde												
China (South)								typhoon season				
Costa Rica												
Cuba									hurricane season			
Dominican Republic									hurricane season			
Egypt							very hot					
French Guiana					rainy season							
French Polynesia												
Guadeloupe									hurricane season			
Guatemala									hurricane season			
Hong Kong								typhoon season				
India (South)				rains	typhoon season					typhoons		
Indonesia												
Jamaica									hurricane season			

	JAN	FEB	MAR	APR	MAY	JUN	JUL	AUG	SEP	OCT	NOV	DEC
Kenya												
Madagascar	hurricane season											
Malaysia	typhoons (east)											
Maldives												
Martinique								hurricane season				
Mauritius	typhoon season											
Mexico (South)								hurricane season				
Myanmar												
New Caledonia	typhoon season											
Oman												
Philippines												
Réunion	typhoon season											
Senegal												
Seychelles												
South Africa												
Sri Lanka												
Taiwan						typhoon season						
Tanzania												
Thailand												
United Arab Emirates					very hot							
United States (Gulf Coast)								hurricane season				
Venezuela												
Vietnam												

Index

Boldface indicates main entry
with illustrations.

Illustrations Credits

AGE
Kord.com: 366-367

ASK IMAGES
Frédéric Mouchet: 171

CORBIS
Daniel Boschung/Zefa: 24; Martin Harvey: 36; Theo Allofs: 37, 56; José Fuste Raga: 39, 40, 60, 94-95, 266-267, 306-307, 342; Staffan Widstrand: 57; Bob Krist: 62, 350; First Light: 65; Geray Sweeney: 68; Mike McQueen: 87; Danny Lehman: 92; Robert Harding World Imagery: 96; Richard Bickel: 105; David C. Poole: 114-115; Jorma Jaemsen/Zefa: 116; Tibor Bognar: 133; Sergio Pitamitz: 136-137; Wolfgang Kaehler: 144, 169; Christophe Boisvieux: 158; Free Agents Limited: 165; Charles & Josette Lenars: 170; Richard Cummins: 172-173; Bruno Barbier/Robert Harding World Imagery: 174; Brigitte Bott/Robert Harding World Imagery: 175; Christian Kober/Robert Harding World Imagery: 190; Peter Adams: 196; DLILLC: 197; Hugh Sitton/Zefa: 202; Dallas and John Heaton/Free Agents Limited: 207; Keren Su: 232-233; Gavin Hellier/Robert Harding World Imagery: 248; Darrell Gulin: 252; Michele Falzone/JAI: 256, 356; John Hicks: 282-283, 286-287, 302; Ric Ergenbright: 298; Gideon Mendel: 315; Günter Rossenbach/Zefa: 321; David Muench: 345; William Maning: 355

FOTOLIA
Marc Grandmaison: 187

GETTY IMAGES
Stephen Frink: 16; Bruno Morandi: 21, 32-33, 168, 222-223, 308, 326, 327; Stewart Cohen: 28-29; James P. Blair: 30; Howie Garber: 35; Martin Barraud: 38; Peter Adams: 46-47; Hideo Kurihara: 48; Keren Su: 50, 80, 88-89; Gerald Hinde: 52-53; Ary Diesendruck: 58; Will & Deni McIntyre: 59; Daryl Benson: 67; Doug Hamilton: 69; Yves Marcoux: 70; Steve Bly: 72; Darwin Wiggett: 73; Aaron McCoy: 76; James Strachan: 79; Luciano Lepre: 82-83; Paul Chesley: 83; Nigel Hicks: 84; Yann Layma: 86-87; Jerry Driendl: 90; Angelo Cavalli: 97; John Miller: 98-99; Neil Emmerson: 100; Upperhall Ltd: 109; Michael McQueen: 110; Sylvain Grandadam: 113, 167, 210, 261; Wayne Walton: 124; Ron Whitby: 126-127; Siegfried Layda: 128-129, 130; Guy Thouvenin: 134; John Elk III: 135, 228; Johner: 138-139, 304-305; Ellen Rooney: 139; Frans Lemmens: 142, 238-239, 240, 246-247; Hiroshi Higuchi: 146; Martin Gray: 153; Grant Faint: 157, 333; Anthony Cassidy: 161, 258; Mark Lewis: 166; Photolibrary.com: 179; Oliver Benn: 180; Gary Yeowell: 181; Gavin Hellier: 182, 227; Joe Cornish: 183; Chad Ehlers: 191; Renee Lynn: 194-195; John William Banagan: 198, back cover; Tim Davis: 204; Bill Hatcher: 217; Carolyn Brown: 221; Raphael Van Butsele: 229, 268, spine; Karan Kapoor: 230; Nicholas DeVore: 230-231; Chad Henning: 234-235; Hugh Sitton: 237; Thierry Dosogne: 241; Alejandro Balaguer: 254-255; Joao Paulo: 262; Simeone Huber: 263, 318; David Sutherland: 273; Benelux Press: 275; Ian Cumming: 290-291; Shaun Egan: 295, 296, 341; Robert Everts: 296-297; Vega: 300; Chris Johns: 313; Daryl Balfour: 314; Chris Cheadle: 319; Travel Ink: 323; Amanda Hall: 328; Glenn Beanland: 334; Ben Hall: 337; Walter Bibikow: 343; Mitchell Funk: 346; Cosmo Condina: 348-349; Andy Caulfield: 349; Glen Allison: 351; James Randklev: 353; Christopher Veer: 354; Kevin Schafer: 361; Margaret Gowan: 364; Martin Puddy: 365

HACHETTE PHOTOS
Jacques Brun/Explorer/Hoa Qui/Hachette Ethnie: 19; Sylvain Grandadam/Hoa Qui: 71; Emile Luider/Rapho: 131, 242-243; Jean-Pierre Lescourret/Hoa Qui: 184-185; Ariel Fuchs/Hoa Qui: 212-213; P. Narayan/Hoa Qui: 274; Wojtek Buss/Hoa Qui: 277; Emmanuel Valentin/Hoa Qui: 288-289; Miguel Angel Munoz/Hoa Qui: 332; Mattes R./Explorer/Hoa Qui: 347

HEMIS.FR
Gil Giuglio: 14; Stéphane Frances: 23, 278-279; Bertrand Rieger: 43, 208; Jean-Baptiste Rabouan: 81, 358-359; Pawel Wysocki: 102, 360; Bertrand Gardel: 106, 200, 219, 224-225, 276; Luis Orteo: 112-113; Franck Guiziou: 119, 159, 160, 316-317, 324-325; Bruno Morandi: 122-123; Michel Gotin: 151; Stefano Torrion: 152; Paule Seux: 154, 155, 162-163, 322; John Frumm: 192, 344; Hervé Hugues: 215; Patrick Frilet: 220-221; Christian Heeb: 245, 250; Christian Guy: 270; José Nicolas: 299; Romain Cintract: 362-363

ISTOCKPHOTO
Lorena Molinari: cover (inset, up left); Mlenny Photography-Alexander Hafemann: cover (inset, low left); Karim Hesham: cover (inset, low center); Alija: cover (inset, low right); Domen Colja: 4; Xavi Arnau: 25; Sculpies: 111; Brien Chartier: 311

NATIONAL GEOGRAPHIC STOCK
Jim Richardson: cover (inset, up right)

PHOTONONSTOP
Giovanni Simeone/Sime: 12, 44 (up), 121, 140-141, 331, 335; Reinhard Schmid/Sime: 44 (low), 45; Günter Gräfenhain/Sime: 55; Simeone: 74, 264, 265; Bruce Coleman Inc: 85; Eurasia Press: 120; Jacques Kerebel: 148-149; David Ball: 156; Sime: 176, 218, 266, 284, 300-301, 339; Sato Hitoschi/Sime: 188-189; Valdin: 203; Anne Montfort: 205; Johanna Huber/Sime: 280; Riccardo Spila: 336; Massimo Ripani: 338

REA
Martin Sasse/Laif: 102, 292-293

SHUTTERSTOCK
Carlos Caetano: cover (background); Joseph Calev: 2-3; Galina Barskaya: 6; Plazas I Subiros: 22

STUDIO X
Steinhilber Berthold/Bilderberg: 18

100 COUNTRIES 5000 IDEAS

PUBLISHED BY THE NATIONAL GEOGRAPHIC SOCIETY

John M. Fahey, Jr., *President and Chief Executive Officer*

Gilbert M. Grosvenor, *Chairman of the Board*

Tim T. Kelly, *President, Global Media Group*

John Q. Griffin, *Executive Vice President; President, Publishing*

Nina D. Hoffman, *Executive Vice President;*
 President, Book Publishing Group

PREPARED BY THE BOOK DIVISION

Barbara Brownell Grogan, *Vice President and Editor in Chief*

Marianne R. Koszorus, *Director of Design*

Barbara Noe, *Senior Editor*

Carl Mehler, *Director of Maps*

R. Gary Colbert, *Production Director*

Jennifer A. Thornton, *Managing Editor*

Meredith C. Wilcox, *Administrative Director, Illustrations*

STAFF FOR THIS BOOK

Karin Kinney, *Project Editor*

Thomas Bowie, Karin Kinney, Patricia Skinner, *Translators*

Sanaa Akkach, *Art Director*

Al Morrow, *Designer*

Ashley Mathieu, *Researcher*

Sven M. Dolling, Michael McNey, Richard McNey, David B.
 Miller, and The M Factory, *Map Research and Production*

Judith Klein, *Production Editor*

Lisa Walker, *Production Manager*

Melissa Phillips, *Design Intern*

MANUFACTURING AND QUALITY MANAGEMENT

Christopher A. Liedel, *Chief Financial Officer*

Phillip L. Schlosser, *Senior Vice President*

Chris Brown, *Technical Director*

Nicole Elliott, *Manager*

Rachel Faulise, *Manager*

Robert L. Barr, *Manager*

The National Geographic Society is one of the world's largest nonprofit scientific and educational organizations. Founded in 1888 to "increase and diffuse geographic knowledge," the Society works to inspire people to care about the planet. National Geographic reflects the world through its magazines, television programs, films, music and radio, books, DVDs, maps, exhibitions, live events, school publishing programs, interactive media and merchandise. *National Geographic* magazine, the Society's official journal, published in English and 32 local-language editions, is read by more than 35 million people each month. The National Geographic Channel reaches 320 million households in 34 languages in 166 countries. National Geographic Digital Media receives more than 13 million visitors a month. National Geographic has funded more than 9,200 scientific research, conservation and exploration projects and supports an education program promoting geography literacy. For more information, visit nationalgeographic.com.

For more information, please call 1-800-NGS LINE
(647-5463) or write to the following address:

National Geographic Society
1145 17th Street N.W.
Washington, D.C. 20036-4688 U.S.A.

For information about special discounts for bulk purchases,
please contact National Geographic Books Special Sales:
ngspecsales@ngs.org

For rights or permissions inquiries, please contact National Geographic Books
Subsidiary Rights: ngbookrights@ngs.org

Library of Congress Cataloging-in-Publication Data
100 countries, 5000 ideas : where to go - when to go - what to see - what to do / prepared by the Book Division, National Geographic Society.
    p. cm.
 Includes bibliographical references and index.
 Summary: "100 Countries, 5000 Ideas highlights 100 must visit countries from Antarctica to Zimbabwe. This travel planner features more than 200 color images as well as detailed maps. The guide also contains specific charts and sections, disseminating important travel information such as climate, language, currency, and required travel documents"--Provided by publisher.
 ISBN 978-1-4262-0758-7 (softcover: alk. paper)
 1. Travel--Guidebooks. I. National Geographic Society (U.S.). Book Division. II. Title: One hundred countries, five thousand ideas.
 G153.4.O87 2011
 910.4--dc22

                          2010045077

Printed in U.S.A.

13/QGT-CML/4